THE DOWNFALL OF MONEY

THE DOWNFALL OF MONEY

Germany's Hyperinflation and the Destruction of the Middle Class

FREDERICK TAYLOR

BLOOMSBURY

NEW YORK · LONDON · NEW DELHI · SYDNEY

First published in Great Britain 2013

Copyright © Frederick Taylor 2013

The moral right of the author has been asserted

No part of this book may be used or reproduced in any manner whatsoever
without written permission from the publisher except in the case of brief quotations
embodied in critical articles or reviews

Every reasonable effort has been made to trace copyright holders of material reproduced
in this book, but if any have been inadvertently overlooked the publishers would
be glad to hear from them

Bloomsbury Publishing Plc
50 Bedford Square
London
WC1B 3DP

www.bloomsbury.com

Bloomsbury Publishing, London, New Delhi, New York and Sydney

A CIP catalogue record for this book is available from the British Library

ISBN 978 1 4088 3991 1 (hardback edition)
ISBN 978 1 4088 5026 8 (trade paperback edition)

10 9 8 7 6 5 4 3 2 1

Typeset by Hewer Text UK Ltd, Edinburgh
Printed and bound in Great Britain by CPI Group (UK) Ltd, Croydon CR0 4YY

MIX
Paper from
responsible sources
FSC® C020471

For Alice

'At the outset the masses misinterpreted it as nothing more than a scandalous rise in prices; only later, under the name of inflation, the process was correctly comprehended as the downfall of money.'

– Konrad Heiden, *Der Führer: Hitler's Rise to Power* (1944)

'By a continuing process of inflation, governments can confiscate, secretly and unobserved, an important part of the wealth of their citizens. By this method, they not only confiscate, but they confiscate arbitrarily; and, while the process impoverishes many, it actually enriches some. The sight of this arbitrary rearrangement of riches strikes not only at security, but at confidence in the equity of the existing distribution of wealth.'

– John Maynard Keynes

'Inflation is a crowd phenomenon . . . one can describe it as a witches' Sabbath of devaluation where men and the units of their money have the strongest effects on each other. The one stands for the other, men feeling themselves as "bad" as their money; and this becomes worse and worse. Together they are all at its mercy and all feel equally worthless.'

– Elias Canetti, *Crowds and Power*

'Believe me, our misery will increase. The scoundrel will get by. But the decent, solid businessman who doesn't speculate will be utterly crushed; first the little fellow on the bottom, but in the end the big fellow on top too. But the scoundrel and the swindler will remain, top and bottom. The reason: because the state itself has become the biggest swindler and crook. A robbers' state!'

– Adolf Hitler, 1923

'There is no subtler, no surer means of overturning the existing basis of society than to debauch the currency.'

– Vladimir Ilyich Lenin (attr.)

Contents

Introduction

This book seeks to provide a narrative description of the origins, progression and effects of the German hyperinflation and to place this extraordinary phenomenon in the turbulent, ominous human context of the world in which it occurred. It is not by any means a book about economics in the narrow sense. The ills of the German currency between 1914 and 1924 arose out of, and then fed back into, the ills of the country itself. It contains elements of economic explanation, without which there would be no background to the story. It is, however, also about war, politics, greed, anger, fear, defiance, desire and (a key element, even if usually in short supply at that time) hope, and the way in which all these things affected and reflected the lives of ordinary people. The history caused the economics, the economics brought on more history, and back and forth and so it went, in a dizzying and frightening continuation that, even when it appeared to end, haunted – and arguably still haunts – the German national narrative.

Nine decades ago, the most populous, technologically advanced and industrious country in continental Europe had suffered a terrible reversal of fortune. Germany had fought and lost a great war that cost her 2 million young men dead, large chunks of territory and vast amounts of treasure. Vengeful enemies had declared their intention to make Germany pay, not just for her own expenses of that war, but for theirs too. Meanwhile, the hereditary dynasties that had ruled in

Germany for a thousand years, grand symbols of stability and continuity, were overthrown in a matter of days – remarkably easily, in fact
– by their mutinous subjects, who blamed them, the archetypal
warlords, for not leading Germany to victory.

The familiar, once unshakeable representatives of the monarchical
state had been replaced in November 1918 by parliamentary politicians
who, whatever their virtues, lacked both the glamour of aristocracy
and the authority that it had seemed, however spuriously, to confer.
Those politicians, many from humble backgrounds and experiencing
real power for the first time, knew that the future of the new post-war
Germany depended on producing order from chaos, prosperity from
deprivation, respect from humiliation. They were also determined
that, despite the defeat of the Reich's armies and the harsh demands
of the countries that had vanquished them, the ordinary German
people, who had suffered so much in four bitter years of war, should
be able to look forward to a better, more secure future. The question
was, given the country's problems, the demands of the victorious
enemy and the (literally) murderous divisions in German society,
could these men – on the whole rather ordinary individuals – succeed
in this awesomely difficult task?

The state the politicians coaxed into being after the revolution
came to be known as the 'Weimar Republic'. The constitution-
makers who met in early 1919 had been forced to evacuate themselves
from Berlin to this attractive, modest-sized central German city
(population at the end of the Second World War around 35,000),
because the capital was still too violent and politically unstable for
their safety to be guaranteed. They remained there until the situation in Berlin was somewhat restored.

Weimar had become famous 120 years or so previously as the
home of the great writer Johann Wolfgang von Goethe, Germany's
Shakespeare – and more. In a long life, spanning the eighteenth
and nineteenth centuries, Goethe had also gained renown as a
statesman and scientist. A fitting environment for Germany's new
start, perhaps, despite the circumstances. From now on, though,

to the wider world the first thing the name would bring to mind would no longer be the greatest achievements of the German enlightenment. Instead, it would conjure up the struggles, and eventually the failure, of the first German democracy. Beyond this, we now know, lay the rise of Hitler and the most terrible war in human history.

In some important ways, though, for all its problems the fifteen-year democratic interlude represented a signpost to the future. Our future. It was a consumer society. It had cinemas and shops, a lively and astonishingly free press, and sports events of a scale and popularity unknown just a few years earlier in more untroubled times. And, even while the inflation was laying waste to some parts of the economy, Germany had its first passenger airlines, opening up global opportunities for business and pleasure for its citizens. It also saw the beginnings of radio broadcasting to a public as eager for distraction as its twenty-first-century counterparts.

Nonetheless, because of what followed, 'Weimar' would become an adjective, ruefully affixed to indicate something well-meaning and even brilliant, but fatally divided and doomed. Weimar Republic. Weimar Culture. Weimar Decadence. Weimar Inflation.

This, then, is the core of the story that will be told here. But it would be of academic interest if we couldn't keenly feel the resonances in our own time.

After sixty years of political stability and more or less steady economic growth, the once-solid edifice of post-war Europe finds itself in a state of decay, and facing a crisis of identity that threatens to turn ugly. The European Union, which was supposed to ensure that a third universal war would never happen, is at risk of disintegration. Hard-edged nationalism is back in fashion, and it is at least in part basing itself on economic differentials. Far-right chaos-makers stalk swathes of the continent, from Budapest to Bayonne, Vienna to Vilnius. Racism and intolerance are manifested in virulent forms unseen since the 1930s. Last but not least, during the past few years the global financial tide has gone out, revealing that the apparently sound underpinnings of many European economies were in fact rickety and rotten.

These twenty-first-century countries borrowed too much and spent too much. They have been forced to tell their citizens that the generous welfare provisions and public services they have come to take for granted are unaffordable. The eurozone union was supposed to bring the continent's economies into harmony and balance under a common currency. Just as the political union was designed to avoid new military conflicts, so the rise of the euro would, such was the hope, end for ever the threat of financial anarchy for countries that had suffered so much from it in the past hundred years. Now, the euro's days seem numbered, and the continent's future more uncertain than at any time since 1945.

It is true that, at the time of writing, runaway inflation is not at the root of the problem in Europe. Rather, it is the austerity policies being forced on the troubled members of the eurozone as the price of staying in this stable currency and avoiding just such an inflation. There can be little doubt, though, that if and when Greece, Spain, Ireland or any other of these countries left the euro and returned to having their own currencies – overseen once again by independent finance ministers and central banks –these currencies would rapidly depreciate against the euro and other major currencies. This would bring on a steep decline in the exchange rate, capital flight on the part of foreign (and home-grown) investors, and sky-high interest rates, possibly progressing hence to serious inflation, and perhaps even, if unchecked, to hyperinflation. Countries whose economies are out of whack can be choked by too little money or too much.

There is, moreover, one other major – one might say all-important – difference between the situation in the 1920s and our current plight. Then, it was Germany that was the reprobate of the story. Europe's foremost economy found itself in a state of financial chaos, its currency all but worthless. Furthermore, it was generally agreed that she had only herself to blame. Ninety years ago, Germany was branded the world's miscreant, refusing to accept financial disciplines as other nations did. Germany was spending money she did not have; molly-coddling her people with over-generous welfare schemes; dishonestly devising strategies to defraud bondholders and investors; deliberately – so it was alleged – allowing her economy to get out of control so that she could shirk her financial commitments and avoid payment of debts. It was countries such as Britain, the USA, Italy, Belgium and France that were wagging their collective national fingers at Germany in the early 1920s.

Now, ninety years on, it is the debt-ridden countries surrounding a prosperous, stable Germany that teeter on the brink of bankruptcy and – should the euro be abandoned – the collapse of their monetary systems, with all the horrors that might follow. And now it is Germany that takes the high moral tone. From Berlin these days all the talk is of sound finances, stern austerity measures for the 'bad' countries, of loans granted only under the strictest conditions. It's been suggested that if Greece, Italy, Portugal, Ireland and the rest want to be lent the money (chiefly by Germany, of course) that will save their economies, then they will have to guarantee those loans with their gold reserves. In other words, although, again at time of writing, the euro still exists, Germany wants precious metal backing in case one day it doesn't, and so whatever currencies the debtors reintroduce prove to be more or less worthless. We are back, so many years later, to the central question we had long thought dealt with: what happens when we lose confidence in our money?

Of course, there are differences between the current disorder and the crisis that followed the First World War. The problems of the 1920s originated in the destruction of a hitherto stable global trading system, with Europe at its heart, as the consequence of an appallingly bloody and morally pernicious breakdown of peaceful relations between the great powers. Those of the early twenty-first century can be seen as occurring against the backdrop of something like the oppo-site: the onset of a new global trading system, with the Pacific and Asia at its centre, coinciding with the end of the long, credit-fuelled boom that the West indulged in after the end of the Cold War in

Europe and the outbreak of peace between the great powers. It might
have been wars between the great powers that ruined the twentieth
century, but in the first years of the twenty-first it was arguably the
lack of them.

So much for the 'big picture'. However, what really matters to
the individual or family or community in any war or economic crisis
is not what these events signify for the world order, but what they
mean for them. Whether the victim is the Greek engineer reduced
to poverty by twenty-first-century austerity, the Irish civil servant
sent to the unemployment queue, the American auto worker whose
home has been foreclosed on, or the debt-laden British university
graduate unable to find a job, every economic crisis feels personal.
The same went for the Germany of the 1920s: the university teacher,
once a high-status and prosperous figure in society, whose fees and
salary no longer put food on his family's table or offered a decent
future for his children; the war widow whose pension became worth
less with every passing week – even, towards the end, every passing
day – until it was literally worthless; the small craftsman, his business turnover plunging, ransacking the attic for family possessions,
however humble, to sell at auction and so get through the week.
The big picture, on proper examination, is actually a vast mosaic of
microscopic scenarios, all intense and urgent for those lonely
millions who struggle to inhabit them.

So this is the story of generals and bankers and politicians. And,
equally, of clerks and industrial workers and widows and soldiers and
small business people. Their society is historically distinct from ours,
yet all too easily recognisable.

The downfall of money proved, in the final analysis, to augur
the downfall of all. We can only hope that, decades from now,
when the story of our own anxious times is properly told, it has
a happier ending.

Finding the Money for the End of the World

Not so long ago, a friend sent me a postcard from Berlin. I still have it pinned to my office wall. The card carries a close-up, almost intimate view of the great Berlin thoroughfare Unter den Linden. It is dated 1910.

The photograph reproduced in that postcard captures the zenith of Kaiser Wilhelm II's rule over Germany. The country, united for a mere forty years, but buoyed by sensationally rapid industrial development and possessed, by consensus, of Europe's most effective army, seemed destined for world-power status. Nevertheless, the scene on Unter den Linden is a relaxed one. In the picture it is summer. Dapperly dressed flâneurs and their ladies saunter along the leafy boulevard or disport themselves on benches. To use a classical comparison, this city looks like Athens, not Sparta. The time, according to the public clock, is half past noon.

Across the wide street, for 200 years Berlin's most glamorous thoroughfare, we see Café Bauer, the best known of the Viennese-style coffee houses that had gained in popularity towards the end of the nineteenth century. Perhaps the café is the true target of the photographer, rather than the elegant Berliners who people the foreground. This may even be a publicity shot – the Bauer family had recently sold their establishment to a large catering company – which is why it has been preserved and immortalised in a commercial postcard and why the street, the café, and even the human beings in the image look

their very best. All the same, the air of prosperity, stability and
optimism that permeates the scene is convincing. These are, by the
look of them, enviable human beings living in an enviable city in
an enviable country, at a time when Germany was continental
Europe's most powerful and efficient country, and Europe itself still
ruled the world.

That world was, as we now know, approaching its end. Soon it
would be gone for ever. Astonishingly, considering how favourable
the fundamentals of the country seemed at that juncture, this was
the last time until well into the latter half of the twentieth century
that Germany would be simultaneously fully solvent, fully employed
and fully at peace.

Four years later, in much the same season, the flâneurs had gone. In
their place, crowds thronged to watch young Berliners parade, smartly
dressed this time not in elegant summer suits but in field-grey uniforms
and spiked helmets, off to war. At the end of July 1914, the latest in a
series of diplomatic crises – in this case arising out of the assassination
of the heir to the Austro-Hungarian imperial throne by Serb nationalists
– had finally tipped Europe over the edge. The interlocking mechanism
of alliances and their concomitant military imperatives had turned a
regional problem into a continent-wide conflagration. This was a war
that seemed to promise much for the Kaiser's Germany but would end
instead in military defeat, human catastrophe and economic ruin.

Such a terrible outcome must have seemed inconceivable to the
vast majority of Wilhelm II's subjects. As she entered the war, Germany
appeared to be blessed with great strengths. The Reich boasted rich
iron and coal deposits (much of it in areas annexed from France in
1871), a booming industrial base, a skilled and industrious population
of some 68 million, and, of course, a feared and admired military
machine. Even before general mobilisation, the German army disposed
of half a million men under arms. Millions more trained former
conscripts could be – and were – summoned to the colours within
weeks and distributed to the various fronts by way of an efficient

Germany-wide railway system that had been adapted and extended with precisely such military needs in mind.

Every German knew these things. What most did not realise was that she also suffered from weaknesses, weaknesses that her enemies were either spared, or shared only in part. First, Germany was tied to the moribund Austro-Hungarian Empire, whose gilded façade concealed a snake-pit of warring nationalities, and whose frantic attempts to hold on to its recently acquired Balkan territories had caused the war in the first place. In her alliance with Austria-Hungary, Germany was, as the saying in Berlin went, 'shackled to a corpse'. Second, despite frantic attempts to build a German navy to rival Britain's, the Reich and her allies, known collectively as 'the Central Powers', were essentially land-locked, susceptible to a British sea blockade that would gradually reduce their populations to a state of semi-starvation. And third, for all her confidence and martial excellence, in the final analysis Imperial Germany was short of the money she would need to fight this war, and more lacking still in ways of acquiring it.

Those who controlled the Reich's finances were well aware of the problems that would arise if the country undertook a major war against the 'Triple Entente' of France, Russia and Britain. So far as such a conflict's military side was concerned, the Imperial General Staff had a scheme to deal with this by means of a massive, no-holds-barred attack through neutral Belgium against France, delivering a swift knockout blow that would enable Germany to turn its full strength quickly against the 'Russian steamroller' to the east. The original plan had been developed almost ten years earlier under the late Chief of the Prussian General Staff, Field Marshal Count Alfred von Schlieffen, and though it had been modified since, in the history books it still bears his name. Likewise, the financial mandarins at the Reichsbank in Berlin – founded after German reunification in 1871 to manage the value and volume of the new nation's currency – had reacted to the increasingly unsettled international scene by developing a secret blueprint that would enable the country to rise above its financial limitations for the duration.

Of course, like all the major powers that went to war in the summer of 1914, Germany believed that, if she had to fight, she would win quickly. So, any radical measures taken to secure the financial sinews of war would, it was thought, be pretty short term in nature.

The planners' way of thinking seemed justified by past events. During the hundred years since the twenty-year struggle against Napoleon had been decided at the Battle of Waterloo, Prussia and its German allies had needed to fight no war longer than a few months in duration. Two out of the three wars that Otto von Bismarck, Chancellor of German unification, had won during the forced march to nationhood (against Denmark and against Austria) lasted a matter of weeks. Even the third, the defeat of France, though dragged out to six months, from the outbreak of war on 19 July 1870 to the formal surrender of Paris on 28 January 1871, had been all but decided from a military point of view by the second week of September.

Just as the Schlieffen Plan was put into action by the Imperial General Staff (in an arguably fatally modified form) during the last days of July and first days of August 1914, so the men who ran the Reichsbank set in motion the modifications of the banking and currency system that would make it possible, they hoped, for Germany to survive the breakdown of the hitherto extremely open global economy for long enough to win the war.

The first part of this financial plan of campaign involved abandoning the gold standard.

For decades, the routine convertibility of Germany's paper currency – two-thirds of the money in circulation by July 1914 – into solid gold (or silver) coinage had meant that notes were not money in themselves but, because exchangeable, represented real and constant (precious metal) value. And, indeed, the amount of paper money issued could, by law, never exceed two-thirds of the money in circulation. The remaining one-third had to be backed directly by gold. This was the promise, so the theory went, that for the previous forty years had kept the value of the German currency, like those of other major countries before 1914, concrete and graspable.

Exactly why the Reichsbank's drastic step away from the gold standard was necessary would have been clear to any interested observer who, as Europe teetered on the edge of war, had found themselves at No. 34–38 Jägerstrasse. Here, hard by the historic Gendarmenmarkt in the heart of Berlin, stood the Reichsbank's imposing neo-classical head offices. Concerned citizens, alarmed by the headlines in the newspapers during the first part of July, had begun to form lines at the doors of the country's private banks, and finally at the Reichsbank itself, which was also a retail bank, though a very privileged and special one. The threat of war had revived old anxieties about paper money, inspired a desire for the tangible, the immutable. They wanted to exchange their mark notes for gold and silver coins, those ancient, reliable stores of value.

With war on the near horizon, Hans Peter Hanssen, a member of the German Reichstag, finished a meal in a Berlin restaurant. He offered the waiter a hundred-mark note in payment. The waiter refused it. Everyone, he said, seemed to be paying in notes and wanting coins in return. The next day, in another restaurant, Hanssen tried to pay with a twenty-mark note. The waiter, like his colleague the previous day, was displeased, but went off to look for change. He came back fifteen minutes later, empty-handed. The restaurant had run out of coins. Hanssen was forced to ask for credit.[1]

Despite attempts by the government-guided press to convince them of the solidity of the everyday currency, many Germans suddenly didn't trust paper any more. They wanted the security of the gold that the currency was alleged to represent. In the first weeks of July, around 163 million gold marks* were redeemed from German banks and stuffed under the nation's collective mattress.[2]

On Friday 31 July 1914, the doors of the Reichsbank were closed (private banks had already stopped exchanging currency for gold three days earlier) and they did not reopen until the following Tuesday – by which time there was no point in demanding gold for your paper

* Roughly a billion and a half euros at 2011 values.

money, because the bank would not give you any. On 4 August a raft
of emergency currency and financial laws formally declared the
convertibility on demand of paper money to gold suspended for the
duration of the conflict. It was at this point, actually, that the term
'gold mark' came into usage, referring to the actual gold coin worth,
by metal weight, either five, ten or twenty marks. There were also
one-, two-, three- and five-mark coins struck from 900/1000 silver,
and their convertibility was suspended as well. After all, until then
all notes had been convertible, merely representing a gold value, so
there were only 'marks'.

Paper currency – fiat money, it has often been called – now rapidly
became the only currency in circulation. Gold coins, from now on,
were either hoarded by individuals, therefore being removed from circulation, or became the property of the government, which was from the
start keen to persuade an often reluctant populace to hand over whatever
gold it still had, whether in the form of money or valuables. Gold
represented, to the German government, something they could trade
internationally, for precious militarily important minerals and products
that had to be purchased abroad. Most important of all, under the Loan
Bureau Law (*Darlehenskassengesetz*) that had also been included among
the 4 August measures, the more gold the government had in its vaults,
the more paper money it could issue while still maintaining the all-
important appearance of a gold-backed currency.

The problem was that, although the Reichsbank knew that 5 billion
gold marks were in circulation at the outbreak of war, even by the end
of 1914, after several months of an intensive propaganda campaign to
persuade citizens to exchange gold for paper ('gold for the Fatherland!'),
it held only 2 billion of that total. Although all over the country patriots
had obediently given up their gold and silver coins, many other Germans
– especially in rural areas – proved immune to patriotic blandishments.
They held on to the value they knew they could rely on, whatever the
outcome of the developing European catastrophe. Somewhere, a lot of
gold and silver was being hoarded.

*   *   *

By 1915, the military conflict had settled into a bloody stalemate. German and Allied forces faced each other in the west across no-man's-land, each huddled into networks of trenches running 700 kilometres from the Belgian coast to the Swiss border. Germany had not triumphed, as so many of her people had expected, but she remained well placed. She controlled all but a tiny strip of Belgian territory. The great cities of Brussels, Antwerp (the port captured in October after a costly siege lasting more than three months) and historic Bruges, and the country's rich industrial and coal mining area including Charleroi, Namur and Liège, all lay in German hands. The same went for much of northern France, including the major textile-producing city of Lille with a pre-war population of half a million, which finally fell to the Germans in October after vicious to-and-fro fighting.

Although Paris was saved by the 'Miracle of the Marne', by the end of 1914 ten of the French Republic's eighty-seven *départements* lay entirely or partly under German occupation. The more than 14,000 square miles of territory that for almost four years would remain behind the German lines included more than half of French coal mines, two-thirds of her textile manufacturing and 55 per cent of metallurgical production; altogether 20 per cent of the country's gross domestic product.[3] In short, France's industrial heartland lay for most of the war in enemy hands. Although almost 2 million of the local population fled the German advance, that still left 2.25 million French citizens under an occupation that was to prove bleak, lonely and harsh – sometimes brutally so.[4]

On the Eastern Front, after a brief Russian thrust into East Prussia in August 1914 was repulsed at the Battle of Tannenberg, Germany stabilised the general situation, regrouped, and after the war's first winter began a slow but inexorable advance into the Baltic countries and Russian Poland. Most of the latter, including Warsaw, its capital, was conquered in the course of 1915.

While from a military point of view, at this stage of the war and for a long time to come, Germany still held many advantages, her financial outlook was not nearly so positive. So desperate did the government become to separate its citizens from their hoarded gold that schoolchildren were enlisted into the campaign to cajole adult family members, neighbours and acquaintances to the 'gold exchange bureaux', where helpful officials waited to relieve them of their all-too-solid wealth and swap it for paper. One propaganda pamphlet, 'The Gold Seekers', was aimed at children via their teachers. It told the fictional story of three teenage high-school (*Gymnasium*) students and their campaign to get a well-off local grain merchant, Herr Lehmann, to part with his gold hoard for the country's good, so that paper money could be printed for the war effort on the back of the exchange. It went without saying that they would accuse him of being a 'betrayer of the fatherland' if he refused to do so.

Initially, Herr Lehmann was shown as resisting their pressure, and expressing scepticism that the Reichsbank would adhere to its side of the bargain by only printing paper money that was covered by the acquisition of gold such as his. After all, he craftily reminded them, though the law might prevent this at the moment, the law could be changed. But the imaginary youngsters were also prepared to do battle against Herr Lehmann's financial arguments. One of them finally asked Lehmann if he would lend his own money to someone without the resources to repay him, even at a high interest rate. When the merchant said no, of course not, the young propagandist swooped:

Why does everyone take paper as readily as gold, although, for example, even a thousand mark bill is nothing more than a scrap of paper? Because he knows that the Reichsbank is in a position to give gold for it at any moment, because he knows he can count on the Reich. What would happen if the Reich began to print notes without paying attention to its gold stock? It would immediately suffer a loss of confidence. The notes would no longer be accepted, especially abroad, or if accepted, then it would be like those profiteers who supply 750 marks of goods for the 1000 marks you pay them. A mark would only be worth 75 pfennig abroad or, as one would say, the mark has a low value (exchange rate) . . .[5]

The words put into the precocious boy's mouth were meant to sound convincing and, according to the propaganda playbook, they finally convinced Herr Lehmann, too. The last bit about the Reich's trust-worthiness, the bit about how the Kaiser and his Reichsbank would never do anything that endangered the soundness of the currency and the welfare of ordinary Germans, must have done the trick. Unfortunately, it was precisely this part of the argument that was – let us not mince words – a lie.

The fact was that under the Loan Bureau Law of 4 August 1914, the Reichsbank was no longer, in practical terms, limited in its ability to print paper money by the amount of gold it held in its vaults. The Loan Bureau Law relieved the Reichsbank of the duty to provide credits to the individual German states and communities, as it would normally have done before the war. In place of these credits, the law set up a system of 'loan bureaux' – to be found, as it happened, in local branches or offices of the Reichsbank – which would provide nominally three-month (but in reality infinitely renewable) credits to these states and communities, backed by guarantees of either goods or securities. These acceptable securities included Treasury bills issued by the German states, some of them very small, and also, crucially, war bonds.

So far, so innocuous seeming. But there was a hook concealed within the stipulations of this so-called Loan Bureau Law. The Loan Bureaux were entitled to issue bureau notes. These bills, which, though not fully legal tender, had the status of currency, were almost univer-sally accepted as such, and rapidly passed into general circulation alongside regular paper money issued by the Reichsbank. The notes would also, inevitably, fall into the hands of the Reichsbank. And when they did, unlike the various other quasi-official bills in circula-tion, under the Loan Bureau Law they acquired the status of proper money, or as the technical term goes, specie. They became capable, like gold coins held by the Reichsbank, of being used to generate three times their value in normal paper money. So, for instance, there was nothing to stop a state or community using war bonds as security to acquire loan bureau notes, which could then be used to buy more war bonds from the Reichsbank, which could then be used as security to buy more loan bureau notes . . . and so on. And each time, the Reichsbank would increase its ability to print money that could be funnelled into the war effort.

Admittedly, the law of 4 August limited the issue of loan bureau notes to 1.5 billion, but three months later, in November 1914, the ceiling was doubled to 3 billion to coincide with the first war bond drive. From then on, the ceiling was regularly raised. By the end of 1918, loan bureau notes with face value of a little over 15.5 billion marks were in circulation. More than a third of these were held by the Reichsbank, which could therefore legally print 15.7 billion fully legally valid marks on the base of this 'security', while still keeping up the façade of 'sound' money. Several German economists realised this and tried to protest. At least one had his article suppressed (written for publication in January 1915, it was not published until the war was over in order to 'protect the public'), while another was told by the Reichsbank's grandees that if he did not desist, they would be forced to 'seek the assistance of the military authorities'.[6]

Herr Lehmann was therefore right in his first arguments, and wrong to have let those pesky kids persuade him to change his mind and exchange his gold for paper. Although a fictional character created for propaganda purposes by a writer doing the bidding of a government desperate for the wherewithal to wage war, the irascible old grain merchant represented millions of real Germans. They, too, would succumb to the blandishments of the official pamphleteers, the tub-thumping politicians and the patriotic press, not to mention the sellers of war bonds. They would give away their solid wealth in exchange for a mess of paper, so that Germany might triumph.

Within a few years, they would feel betrayed. Their patriotic pride would turn to anger; a slow-release anger that would fertilise a post-war harvest of intolerance and totalitarianism.

2

Loser Pays All

The civilian populations of all the countries involved in the First World War experienced hardship. There were shortages and anxieties, even for those not occupied by the enemy or living close to the fighting zones. All the millions of men who fought – and in huge numbers died – in the war had friends, families, relatives, many of whose waking (and perhaps also their dreaming) hours were filled with apprehension on their behalf. However, especially in Germany and Austria-Hungary, the physical conditions under which civilians lived on the home front while their menfolk fought and died in the trenches and battlefields far away were not merely difficult or austere; hunger stalked Europe from the Rhine to the Vistula, from the Skagerrak to the Danube.

On 1 August 1914, when Britain's entry into the war was not yet certain, the German shipping journal *Hansa* had predicted that if she did join in on the side of Serbia, France and Russia, 'economic life [would] suffer a collapse unprecedented in history'.[1] The author of that judgement was proved right within a matter of months. Despite the huge sums that Germany had spent on building up its naval strength, the Reich did not have the surface ships to challenge the Royal Navy and thus to make the trading routes safe for German imports and exports during wartime.

During the first months of the war, the British slowly tightened the screws on German trade by a series of restrictive measures, though these stopped short of a total, indiscriminate blockade. When, however, it became clear that the war was not going to be decided on the battlefield any time soon, the cabinet in London decided to step beyond the accepted rules of conflict. Exploiting the Germans' declared intention in February 1915 to wage unrestricted submarine warfare against Entente shipping in the North Sea, the British initiated a total ban on imports and exports of all kinds, to and from the territories of the Central Powers, including food and other goods entering via neutral territories such as Holland and the Scandinavian countries. The measures were to be rigorously enforced by the Entente's navies. On 1 March 1915, a British Order in Council declared 'the British and French governments will hold themselves free to detain and take into port ships carrying goods of presumed enemy destination, ownership or origin'.[2] For the remaining duration of the war, and for the months of armistice that followed, German overseas trade was confined to the Baltic and to occasional forays into the North Sea.

The Reich's enemies knew perfectly well that before the war Germany had needed to import large quantities of food to supply her population. It became clear that the Entente's (and especially Britain's) intention was to bring about Germany's defeat at least in part by a policy of deliberate starvation. The German civilian population was quite specifically targeted. As Britain's most senior defence official, Maurice (later Lord) Hankey, asserted in a confidential memorandum from the summer of 1915, 'Although we cannot hope to starve Germany out this year, the possibility that we may be able to do so next year cannot be dismissed . . .'[3]

That the Entente blockade killed large numbers of Germans directly or indirectly, there can be little doubt. The suffering increased as the years went on. It was estimated that in 1915 some 88,000 German civilians died of causes attributable to the blockade, and in 1916 around 121,000. The months straddling 1916–17 were known as the 'turnip winter', because of the lack of protein and other vital foodstuffs available to the German population – especially in the country's cities.

By the end of the war the total number of victims was thought to have reached more than 760,000.[4]

In the city of Düsseldorf, in the northern Rhineland – its adult population a mix of white-collar officials and industrial workers – staples such as potatoes were often unavailable for months at a time.

In 1916, the shortage of fats began in earnest. Legumes such as lentils, barley and peas were available only rarely or not at all. By 1917, 'war coffee', which contained no real coffee at all, was the only kind for sale. The city officially allotted one egg to each adult every three weeks, but did not always have them to distribute. All kinds of cheese were scarce; dried fruit was not to be found. The only type of food available steadily in Düsseldorf was vegetables, and the kind and quantity depended on the season.[5]

By 1917 the diet of the average industrial worker in Düsseldorf compared very unfavourably, as regards both quantity and diversity, with that provided to an adult male in the pre-war poorhouse in the city of Hamburg.[6]

Germany's inability to trade meaningfully also reflected her inability to participate in what was left of the global financial system. Britain and France could continue, to some extent, to import and export, and to raise money for the war through borrowing on the international markets. In the four years between 1914 and 1918, Britain earned £2.4 billion from shipping and other 'invisible' sources, sold £236 million of its foreign investments, and borrowed almost £1.3 billion abroad.[7] Before August 1914, Germany had held overseas investments of between £980 million and £1,370 million in countries with which she later found herself at war. At least 60 per cent of these were subjected to outright confiscation.[8] Moreover, unlike Germany, Britain and France remained in possession of large overseas empires. This meant that they could also make good any shortfalls in domestic food supplies, as well as calling on vast extra material resources and manpower.

After the failure of early attempts by Germany to raise funds on the New York financial markets, it became clear that by contrast the Reich stood alone. Again, though Britain also had to raise vast sums of money for the war, the capacity (and willingness) of the City of London, the world's greatest financial centre, to absorb far greater quantities of short-term 'floating' debt than the comparatively tiny German money market, gave it a vital advantage, in particular lessening the inflationary effect of such borrowing on the general economy.[9]

True, Germany managed to raise £147 million through sales of foreign securities. All the same, the vast majority of any money required to cover the immense cost of waging war on such a scale, and for the kind of duration now expected, would have to be raised from among Germany's own citizens by various means, including the sales of long-term interest-bearing war bonds, as well as increases in existing taxes and the levying of new ones. This created a burden of debt that would haunt the country for many years to come. There was also, as we shall see, the hidden time bomb of the vast loans taken out by Germany's municipalities to cover their wartime expenses, which, since German law devolved such responsibilities, included vastly increased welfare expenditure for victims of the fighting, their families and dependants.

It was a daunting prospect. But Germany's rulers – and most of the country's citizens – expected that such outlay, however burdensome, would be merely temporary. When the Reich finally won the war, so the nation assumed, these expenses would be recouped from the losers – Britain, France, Russia and their allies. On 20 August 1915, the conservative-nationalist Secretary of State for the Treasury, former chair of the board of the Deutsche Bank and later Reich Vice-Chancellor, Dr Karl Helfferich, openly declared as much to an enthusiastic Reichstag:

Gentlemen, as things stand, our only way through remains to postpone the final regulation of war costs through the means of credit, to a future time when peace is concluded, until we are at peace. And on this subject I should today like once more to emphasise this: If God grants us victory and thus the possibility of shaping the peace according to our needs and the necessities of our national life, we intend and are entitled, along with everything else, not to forget the question of costs.

[Lively agreement]

We owe this to the future of our people.

[Calls of 'very true!']

The entire future maintenance of our life as a nation must, insofar as is at all possible, remain free of, and be relieved of, the enormous burden that the war has caused to accumulate.

[Further calls of 'very true!']

It is the instigators of this war who deserve to bear this lead weight of billions.

[Calls of 'quite right!']

Let them drag it through the decades to come, not us.

[Calls of 'very good!'][10]

Of course, Germany's enemies believed exactly the same. In the case of France and Belgium, they also fully intended to seek compensation for physical damage inflicted on their territory as a result of fighting, and the activities of German occupation forces.

This last imposition, should Germany in fact lose the war, was going to be extremely onerous. Except for a brief though violent Russian incursion into the easternmost part of Germany in the first weeks of the war, and some fighting in the border fringes of Alsace and Lorraine, the Reich's territory remained untouched by war to the end.

In France, by contrast, as a result of the fighting and the occupation, more than half a million private dwellings and 17,600 public buildings were reckoned completely or largely destroyed; 860,400 acres of farmland were laid waste or rendered unsuitable for cultivation; and 20,000 factories and workshops were destroyed or seriously damaged. Some factories, especially those containing modern machinery, were dismantled and shipped to Germany. At least a million head of cattle were also transferred east of the Rhine.

Most appallingly, when the Germans 'rationalised' their front and

fell back to the supposedly impregnable 'Hindenburg Line' early in
1917, at some points retreating up to fifty kilometres, they carried out
a ruthless, systematic policy of destruction. Demolition teams obliter-
ated all industrial plant, farms and infrastructure before abandoning
the territory the Imperial Army had occupied for just over two and
a half years. Coal pits were dynamited and flooded. The local civilian
population of around 125,000 was forcibly evacuated. The area was
sown with mines and public buildings booby-trapped.

It is not so surprising that estimates of the total monetary cost to
France of the fighting and occupation ran to between 35 billion
pre-war gold francs ($7 billion) and 55 billion gold francs ($11 billion).[11]

In Belgium the country's population and its industries suffered
even worse abuse. Factories were subjected to massive requisitions or,
if seen as post-war competition for German industries, closed or
allowed to decay. Many were totally demolished. Machinery was
commandeered and sent to Germany. The country lost 6 per cent of
its housing stock and two-thirds of its railway tracks. One hundred
and twenty thousand Belgian workers, many robbed of their employment by factory and mine closures, were deported to Germany and
used as forced labour.[12]

All this happened with the approval not just of the Kaiser and
his commanders, but of many German politicians and industrialists. As early as September 1914, Chancellor Theobald von
Bethmann-Hollweg had circulated a discussion paper written by
an aide that envisaged outright annexation of extensive areas of
Belgium and north-eastern France, turning the remains of Belgium
into a vassal state and effectively crushing France as a military and
economic threat to Germany once and for all. It was effectively a
'shopping list' of maximum demands rather than a formal policy
document, but nevertheless showed the extent of ambition within
German elite circles.

It is hard to see the paper as anything other than a blueprint for a
German Europe:

The general aim of the war is security for the German Reich in west and east for all imaginable time. For this purpose France must be so weakened as to make her revival as a great power impossible for all time. Russia must be thrust back as far as possible from Germany's eastern frontier and her domination over the non-Russian vassal peoples broken.

France.
The military to decide whether we should demand ceding of Belfort and western slopes of the Vosges, razing of fortresses and ceding of coastal strip from Dunkirk to Boulogne.

The ore-field of Briey, which is necessary for the supply of ore for our industry, to be ceded in any case. Further, a war indemnity, to be paid in instalments; it must be high enough to prevent France from spending any considerable sums on armaments in the next 15–20 years.

Furthermore: a commercial treaty which makes France economically dependent on Germany, secures the French market for our exports and makes it possible to exclude British commerce from France. This treaty must secure for us financial and industrial freedom of movement in France in such fashion that German enterprises can no longer receive different treatment from French.

Belgium.
Liège and Verviers to be attached to Prussia, a frontier strip of the province of Luxemburg to Luxemburg.

Question whether Antwerp, with a corridor to Liège, should also be annexed remains open.

At any rate Belgium, even if allowed to continue to exist as a state, must be reduced to a vassal state, must allow us to occupy any militarily important ports, must place her coast at our disposal in military respects, must become economically a German province. Given such a solution, which offers the advantages of annexation without its inescapable domestic political disadvantages, French Flanders with

Dunkirk, Calais and Boulogne, where most of the population is
Flemish, can without danger be attached to this unaltered Belgium.
The competent quarters will have to judge the military value of this
position against England.

Luxemburg.
Will become a German federal state and will receive a strip of the
present Belgian province of Luxemburg and perhaps the corner of
Longwy.

We must create a central European economic association through
common customs treaties, to include France, Belgium, Holland,
Denmark, Austria-Hungary, Poland, and perhaps Italy, Sweden and
Norway. This association will not have any common constitutional
supreme authority and all its members will be normally equal, but
in practice will be under German leadership and must stabilise
Germany's economic dominance over Mitteleuropa.

The question of colonial acquisitions, where the first aim is the creation of a continuous Central African colonial empire, will be
considered later, as will that of the aims to be realised vis-à-vis Russia.
A short provisional formula suitable for a possible preliminary peace
to be found for a basis for the economic agreements to be concluded
with France and Belgium.

Holland.
It will have to be considered by what means and methods Holland
can be brought into closer relationship with the German Empire.

In view of the Dutch character, this closer relationship must leave
them free of any feeling of compulsion, must alter nothing in the
Dutch way of life, and must also subject them to no new military
obligations. Holland, then, must be left independent in externals,
but be made internally dependent on us. Possibly one might consider
an offensive and defensive alliance, to cover the colonies; in any case
a close customs association, perhaps the cession of Antwerp to

Holland in return for the right to keep a German garrison in the fortress of Antwerp and at the mouth of the Scheldt.[13]

Even as a summary of daydreams experienced during a time of euphoria – the Germany army was still advancing on the Marne, with Paris in its sights – the memorandum is a drastic piece of work. It cannot be asserted that this amounted to a firm policy – historians have been arguing about this issue since the document was discovered in the 1950s in an East German archive – but it seems unquestionable that according to these lights, if she won, Germany planned to exercise dominance in Europe. Ruthlessly so.

Admittedly, on the other side, agreements were also being made as the war went on which, to modern sensibilities, appear monstrously unjust and high-handed. There was the secret treaty between the Entente powers awarding Imperial Russia control over the Dardanelles and Constantinople (now Istanbul) after victory. Another set of secret agreements, under which Italy entered the war on the Entente side, promised Rome substantial chunks of Austria and the Aegean islands as well as German colonies. Finally, there was the breathtaking hypocrisy of the so-called Sykes–Picot Agreement, which, even as the Entente encouraged Arabs to raise the standard of rebellion against their Turkish overlords, proposed to divide up the Arabic-speaking Middle East (Syria, Lebanon, Palestine, Iraq) between Britain and France. Though concealed beneath slogans of peaceful development and democracy, this amounted to a new, even more toxic final bout of opportunistic imperialist expansion, one for which our world is still paying a heavy price.

Bethmann-Hollweg's 'September Programme' was a radical proposal, but by no means the most extreme of the plans being floated around quite respectable mainstream political circles in the Reich during the course of the war. These also included large-scale annexations in western Russia and the Baltic lands as well as even more sweeping losses for France and Belgium.[14] The peculiarity of the discussion within Germany, however, rested in the participants'

blatant assumption of the absolute and permanent dominance in
Europe that would follow victory. Everyone from government figures,
industrialists and extreme nationalists – sometimes all three functions
were combined within individual human beings – discussed such
plans for boundless supremacy of German political, military and
economic interests as if they were natural and right.

The purpose of detailing all this is not to apportion blame – though
that would all too soon become a game everyone would play and
which continues in historical circles to this day – but, rather, to show
that all the countries involved in the war knew that they couldn't
afford to pay for their folly. The losers would have to do that.

On the German side, the chief way of ensuring that the country
recovered quickly after the hoped-for victory was to put the Reich in
a situation of such crushing superiority that it could do, and take,
what it wanted. And then came the question of compensation. As
Helfferich had put it in his famous speech on the 1915 budget, it was
'the instigators of this war who would have to bear this lead weight
of billions'. And he had been right. It just depended who, when the
savage music of mass slaughter stopped, was going to be found sitting
in the chair marked 'instigator'.

A reparations bill of 5 million gold francs – amounting at the time
to 25 per cent of the defeated country's annual gross domestic product
– had been imposed by Bismarck on the French in 1871. This huge
windfall to the Reich's economy was said to have helped fuel the
near-disastrous boom that followed German unification. The 1871
imposition was not to make restitution for damage to Germany. No
fighting had taken place on German soil. Again, in the First World
War, any reparations demanded by Germany would not have been
for devastation of the Reich's territory, resources or infrastructure, for
(apart from a few early and fairly ineffectual aerial bombing raids and
some fighting in German Alsace-Lorraine) there had been none. So
what would Germany have demanded? Enough to compensate her
for the quite enormous cost of the war?

Some indication of how a victorious Germany might have treated the Entente in the war's aftermath came with the Treaty of Brest-Litovsk, signed early in 1918.

Imperial Russia's huge but mediocre and often poorly led army had been slowly pushed back out of Poland and most of the Baltic lands and into what is now Ukraine and Belarus. There had been some temporary Russian successes. The so-called Brusilov Offensive in the summer of 1916, named after the general who planned and launched it, had at great cost forced the Austro-Hungarian forces to abandon their early gains. Nevertheless, the story of Russia's participation in the war became one of ineffectuality at the front and increasing political and social chaos at home.

By February 1917, the British Military Attaché to the Russian army, Colonel Knox, sent his superiors in London a message on the situation there that augured disaster. More than a million Russian soldiers had been counted killed, and a further 2 million missing or taken prisoner. Another million had deserted. 'These men,' Knox wrote, 'were living quietly in their villages, unmolested by the authorities, their presence concealed by the village communes, who profited by their labour.'[15]

In the course of February and March, sections of the Tsar's army began to disobey orders and in Russia's cities there were huge demonstrations against the war and the regime, followed by strikes in key industries. On 12 March, the soldiers of the 17,000-strong garrison in the capital, Petrograd,* joined the demonstrators and the old regime's days were numbered.

The overthrow of the Tsar led to the establishment of a weak provisional government dominated by the moderate left. Committed to a democratic system, it nevertheless did little to change the situation at home or at the front, except perhaps for the worse. The radical 'street' and the newly established soldiers' committees wielded just as much power as the bureaucracy and its new reformist masters. Both the new republican government and the military command were

* Formerly St Petersburg, later Leningrad, now once again St Petersburg.

forced to share power with unofficial, hastily elected 'Soviets' and their appointed commissars. The death penalty for offences against military discipline was abolished.

In July 1917, an attempted assault by this hastily democratised Russian army on the German/Austro-Hungarian defences (named the 'Kerensky Offensive' after the socialist firebrand who had been appointed Defence Minister in March) collapsed within a couple of weeks, turning into a full-scale rout accompanied once more by massive desertions. The catastrophe brought German forces deep into Russia proper, their capacity to advance at will hindered by little except problems of transport and supply.

By early November (October under the old calendar still used in Russia, and hence always celebrated as the 'October Revolution'), a coup in Petrograd brought to power the far-left Bolshevik party. It was led by the brilliant Marxist theorist and agitator Vladimir Ilyich Lenin, whose passage from Swiss exile back to Russia during the summer had been arranged by the German authorities precisely in order to facilitate Russia's exit from the war.

Sure enough, negotiations between the Bolsheviks – committed to ending the war and desperate to consolidate their uncertain grip on power – and the representatives of the triumphant Central Powers led in December to an armistice on the Eastern Front. Further negotiations soon stalled, however. The recently appointed Bolshevik Commissar for Foreign Affairs, Leon Trotsky, defied Lenin's wishes and held out against the tough German and Austro-Hungarian demands – possibly in the hope that, if the war dragged on, discontent in the enemy countries, like that in Russia during the earlier part of the year, might yet bring about revolutions in Berlin, Vienna and Budapest. Finally, in February 1918, talks broke down. The Germans and their allies resumed their all but unopposed advance into Russia, within just a couple of weeks of taking control of further huge areas of Ukraine and Belarus. At one point, they managed to push forward 150 miles in a little over five days.[16]

On 3 March 1918, with the advancing Germans drawing close to

Petrograd, the Bolshevik leadership at last agreed terms. A treaty was signed at a ceremony in the imposing early nineteenth-century tsarist fortress of Brest-Litovsk, on the border between historic Poland and Russia, which had been in German hands since August 1915. Leading the Bolshevik delegation was Trotsky's deputy, Georgi Chicherin, a close ally of Lenin.

So what price was the revolutionary clique in control of Petrograd prepared to pay? The cost of peace was, in fact, a lot worse than the one the Bolsheviks had rejected earlier in the winter. The new Marxist Russia was forced to acknowledge the loss of Poland, the Baltic lands, plus Finland, Ukraine and Belarus. Georgia became independent, and strategic parts of the Caucasus were ceded to Turkish control.

The areas forfeited contained a third of the former Russian Empire's population, a third of its arable land and nine-tenths of its coal mines. At a stroke, the Bolsheviks abandoned virtually all the territory Russia had gained since the eighteenth century, and their domain was reduced almost entirely to the ancestral Russian-speaking lands. Huge swathes of the Tsars' Russia became effectively a German protectorate. Although technically both sides renounced any claim on conventional war reparations, after further negotiations the Bolsheviks also agreed to pay a sum of 6 billion gold marks. This supposedly represented restitution for German property and businesses confiscated as a result of war and revolution, as well as the Bolsheviks' default on pre-war tsarist bonds bought by German investors.

With the Germans so uncomfortably close to Petrograd, a little more than a week after signing the treaty the Bolsheviks moved their capital back to the relative safety of Moscow, which had been the seat of the Tsars until the time of Peter the Great. The centre of gravity of the new revolutionary republic switched therefore almost 400 miles inland and south-eastwards, away from the Baltic and the occidental influences to which Peter the Great, Petrograd's builder, had been so eager to expose his subjects.

As to how the Treaty of Brest-Litovsk was received in Germany itself, there was celebration among the extreme nationalists, who were delighted by the dramatic extension of German occupation and control into territories long seen in such circles as ripe for incorporation into the Reich.[17] Even those who understood the treaty for the brutal thing it was experienced a certain weary relief that, on one front at least, the war had been brought to a victorious conclusion. Almost everyone hoped that triumph in the east might presage the breaking of the bloody stalemate in the west, to Germany's advantage.

There was universal hope that the commitment of the new, independent Ukraine, which had signed a separate treaty with Germany, to supply the Reich with wheat would alleviate the now desperate shortage of bread. The treaty was popularly known as the 'bread peace', even though, as things turned out, disappointingly little of the grain from the fertile Ukrainian steppes ever found its way to the German civilian population before the fortunes of war and revolution made the treaty redundant.[18]

Romania was also brought to its knees that spring. At the Treaty of Bucharest, signed in June 1918, Germany claimed Romania's agricultural output and virtual ownership of the country's crucial oil industry. This, too, was not a treaty to impress the world, and especially Germany's vengeful enemies, with the Reich elite's benign intentions.

3

From Triumph to Disaster

Then, as now, the international financial world respected power. By the time of the Bolshevik Revolution, the mark had depreciated in the currency markets to a rate of 7.29 marks to the US dollar, as opposed to 4.20 on the outbreak of war in 1914. Five months later, in March 1918, with the victorious conclusion of the war on the Eastern Front giving apparent grounds for optimism, it had climbed to 5.11, the strongest level for almost three years.

It may be that the firming up of the mark's official value (to be distinguished from its informal or black market rate, and, more importantly, from its actual domestic purchasing power) was the result of renewed optimism in Germany and elsewhere about the country's prospects in the war. If so, what it did not take into account was the fact that in other, perhaps less obvious, regards Germany's situation had actually become decidedly worse.

A little less than two weeks before the Treaty of Brest-Litovsk was signed, American troops saw their first real action on the Western Front. Two dozen of them joined a French raid on enemy trenches near Chevregny in Picardy. German prisoners were taken.[1] It was an unremarkable event in itself, but the point was that these troops were among the million Americans who would join the Allied forces in France by July 1918. Moreover, even after July they were still arriving at the rate of 10,000 a day.

As Winston Churchill later wrote:

> The impression made . . . by this seemingly inexhaustible flood of gleaming youth in its first maturity of health and vigour was prodigious. None were under twenty, and few over thirty. As crammed in their lorries they clattered along the roads, singing the songs of a new world at the tops of their voices, burning to reach the bloody field, the French Headquarters were thrilled with the impulse of new life . . .[2]

The contrast with the state of Germany's population, soldiers and civilians alike, could not have been more stark.

The spring of 1918 saw a rise in popular hopes that the war would finally turn in Germany's favour. However, the situation for most of the Reich's hard-working and long-suffering population remained in almost all other ways dire.

Although conditions were not quite as appalling as they had been during the 'turnip winter' of 1916–17, food prices were moving ever higher – where food was available. Rationing for basic foodstuffs had begun in 1915 and was extended as the war went on, though even this did not guarantee a decent diet for the population. A ration system could hope to distribute food more fairly; it could not of itself increase the amount available.

The authorities, later acting in tandem with a network of 'price examination agencies' set up under government decree, tried to enforce their own, varying interpretations of fair pricing in their own districts, and to combat profiteering and black marketeering. This led to widespread withholding of supplies by hard-pressed farmers, who resented the restrictions, and in turn to large-scale requisitions by the military authorities. Towards the end of the war, the army even organised searches of farms suspected of hoarding produce.[3] Some military districts were less stringent in their enforcement of price controls, and, like water running downhill, produce tended to find its way to those areas.[4]

It was clear that Germany was turning into two countries: an urban

Germany, dependent on food imported from abroad or the country-side; and a rural Germany, which was self-sufficient and reluctant to release what it grew or reared unless the price was right. The division would continue well into the unhappy peace.

Germany's cities were not just suffering a crisis over food. Amid desperate government attempts to control rents, the housing shortage in the cities worsened steadily as the war went on. The flood of labour into areas containing large numbers of war factories put accommodation there at a particular premium. Ordinary Germans were also suffering from disastrous shortages of shoes, clothing, coal and soap. The last problem affected miners and heavy-industrial workers especially seriously. This led, shamefully for a people that took pride in its cleanliness, to an epidemic of lice.[5]

In fact, arguably it was mostly the renewed hope of military victory that kept the lid, for the moment, on popular discontent. As the liberal German journalist and writer Sebastian Haffner (b. 1907), then a schoolboy in Berlin and keen fan of the war, wrote twenty years later in a memoir of the time:

Bad food – OK. Later also too little food, clacking wooden soles on my shoes, threadbare suits, collecting bones and cherry stones* in school, and, curiously, frequent illness. But I have to admit that all this made no deep impression on me . . . I thought as little about food as the football enthusiast at the cup final thinks of food. The daily Army Reports interested me much more than the dinner menu.[6]

Young Haffner was the son of a senior Prussian civil servant and at that time an enthusiastic, not to say excitable, nationalist. Unlike him, not everyone found patriotic fervour, or the thrill of the daily Army Reports, to be acceptable substitutes for a square meal. Towards the end of January 1918, the pot threatened to boil over. Four hundred

---

* Fruit stones (especially cherry and plum) were collected in an organised way by schools as part of a government campaign. The kernels were pressed for the nutritious oils they contained, to help make up for the shortage of imported oils.

thousand workers in Berlin had downed tools, partly in protest at
reductions in bread rations for heavy work, but more importantly
also in support of a peace without annexations, an end to the milita-
risation of the factories, and democratic political reforms. These
political strikes spread quickly to Kiel, Hamburg, Halle and Magde-
burg before being suppressed with the aid of harsh measures that
included conscription of many strikers into the military, and long
prison sentences for ringleaders.

The major industrial stoppages were over by the second week of
February. Between March and July, after the Treaty of Brest-Litovsk
and while the drama on the Western Front was still being played out
with some prospect of success, there ensued a period of relative political and social calm.

The 'peace bonus' from victory in the east, such as it was, had been
meant to manifest itself in more (and more successful) war in the
west. The formal end of the war against Russia meant that a large
proportion of the German forces hitherto tied up there could be sent
into action in the west. In a matter of weeks, hundreds of thousands
of German troops and their equipment – including many guns
captured from the Russians during the final German advance – were
transferred from one front to the other.

The Army High Command (OHL), and in particular its head,
seventy-year-old Field Marshal Hindenburg, and his deputy,
Quartermaster-General and de facto commander-in-chief, General
Erich Ludendorff, had begun to exercise a virtual dictatorship over
the country from 1916 onwards, albeit one disguised by a veneer of
law and a not entirely compliant Reichstag. With hundreds of thousands of fresh American 'doughboys' pouring into France, and the
USA mobilising its finances and its industries for war, the High
Command knew that Germany would soon face a far stronger enemy
than before. Best to strike the decisive blow now. A great offensive in
France had therefore been in preparation for some months.

On 21 March 1918, the High Command launched a massive attack on the British 5th Army. The German planners had chosen a perceived weak point of the enemy front, the hinge between the British and French forces, near St Quentin on the Somme. Preceded by the most massive artillery bombardment of the war – involving 6,000 heavy guns and 3,000 mortars – and assisted by extremely foggy conditions on the ground, elite German 'storm-troop' units punched holes in the enemy lines and forced the British back.

The German offensive gained four and a half miles in a day and took 21,000 British prisoners. Within two days, they had reached the key barrier of the Somme River, and by dawn on 23 March three giant guns specially manufactured by Krupp were in position and bombarding Paris, which was now only seventy-four miles distant. Two hundred and fifty-six Parisians were killed in a single morning. The Kaiser declared 'the battle won, the English totally defeated'. The next day, the Germans crossed the Somme and began to advance on Paris itself.[7]

There were further gains over the following weeks, here and elsewhere on the long front line, and on a map the bulge created by the German offensive looked impressive. But the 'English' were not defeated. Nor were the French or the Americans. As spring turned to summer, there were no more quick, dramatic advances. The German army found itself short of reserves and having to man a much longer, less easily defensible line than the one they had occupied in March, before the offensive began.[8] In fact, the strength of the German field army fell between March and July from 5.1 million to 4.2 million – many of the casualties its best, most experienced soldiers[9] – just at the same time as the Entente forces were being strengthened by a total of 2 million fresh Americans. Certain categories of light artillery and flame-throwers had their production quotas reduced because there were simply not enough trained fighting men at the front available to use the quantities being shipped from Germany's factories.[10]

The German thrust was eventually held in mid-July 1918, sixty miles or so north-east of Paris. For the first time, American troops, fighting around Château-Thierry, played a decisive role. Within a matter of weeks, the enemy had begun to advance once more, and German troops were forced into a retreat that would end only with the Reich's plea for an armistice little more than a hundred days later.

The collapse of the final, desperate German offensive in the west accentuated the growing social and political polarisation in the Reich. In 1914, almost the entire German political spectrum (with a few exceptions on the far left) had united in a so-called *Burgfrieden* (literally 'fortress peace'), or wartime truce. Something similar occurred in France, where the Prime Minister of the time dubbed it the *union sacrée* ('sacred union').

Immediately following the outbreak of the war, only one Social Democrat Reichstag deputy, Karl Liebknecht, had voted against war credits. By the next year, Liebknecht was no longer alone. Within two years the Social Democratic Party (SPD) had split down the middle, and the anti-war left mushroomed as the bloody struggle continued, seemingly without sense or end. By the third and fourth years of the war, although the large majority of Germans of all classes remained committed to victory, a substantial proportion of the population, including socialist, Catholic and liberal Reichstag deputies, had turned in favour of either a negotiated compromise peace or even peace at any price. In July 1917 a majority of the Reichstag, in a telling act of defiance which showed how far the split within the nation had widened, ignored pleas from the government and the High Command and passed a resolution calling, albeit in ringing patriotic phrases, for just such a negotiated peace without annexations on either side.

In reaction to the Peace Resolution, on 2 September 1917 the nationalist and radical right, supported behind the scenes by the political soldiers within the High Command, created an organisation devoted to uniting all groups and individuals in Germany committed to conquest, annexations and a fight to the bitter end. Called the 'Fatherland Party' (Vaterlandspartei), by July 1918 it could claim a million and a quarter members.[11] This figure, if accurate, gave it a bigger membership than the Social Democratic Party, hitherto the largest political grouping in the country. However, it is questionable whether the Fatherland Party was really a 'party' at all – any more than, under the Obama administration of the present century, America's 'Tea Party' is a political party – but actually a pressure group, albeit a very impressive one during its heyday.[12]

The war had been a disaster for most of the population in Germany, as it had in every country involved except America. The polarisation within the Reich reflected the different situations of different sections of society. Those industrialists involved in supplying arms and equipment for the war effort had done well – in some cases spectacularly so, with some large firms achieving dramatic growth. Others, especially in consumer goods and services, had suffered disastrous declines in production and profits. By 1918, for instance, the number of males employed in the textile industry was only a quarter of what it had been in 1913, with even the female workforce only three-fifths of its pre-war strength. Numbers in the building industry had more than halved.[13]

Overall, taken throughout the war years, industrial production in Germany had declined by between a quarter and a third, more than that of any of the Entente powers.

Indices of industrial production (1914 = 100)[14]

	Germany	Britain	Russia	Italy
1914	100	100	100	100
1915	81	102	115	131
1916	77	97	117	131
1917	75	90	83	117
1918	69	87	83	117

Increases in the production of weapons and other materiel of war contrasted with a related decline in consumer manufacturing and non-war-related services. This became especially pronounced after the 'Hindenburg Programme' was inaugurated in late 1916, a greatly, in fact almost grotesquely, accelerated armaments production programme that threw all consideration of Germany's actual material and human resources to the wind. It resulted in an even more distorted economy by war's end.[15]

The wine and tobacco harvests proved bumper ones, but other food products suffered badly. Production of beer in Germany, for instance, was reduced by two-thirds in the course of the war. Agriculture in general was hit by severe manpower shortages (the army took no account of the crucial nature of food production when scouring the countryside for recruits) and shortages of imported fertilisers due to the British blockade. Production of wheat was halved.[16] The shipping industry, hit by the slump in trade and the Entente blockade, with many of its vessels either marooned in neutral ports or seized by the enemy, virtually collapsed. Forty-four per cent of the pre-war merchant fleet had been either sunk or confiscated.[17]

Like the owners of defence-related companies, many workers in the war industries had done relatively well, and a few splendidly. Between 1914 and 1918, the daily wages of male workers in war-related industries increased by 152 per cent, and those of females – with millions of men at the front, a group whose participation in the labour market increased dramatically during the war years – by 186 per cent, while the figures for the non-war sector were 82 and 102 per cent respectively. Skilled workers in high demand within certain sectors of war production experienced even higher increases. There was discontent among less well-paid workers at the ability of these privileged labour groups – especially if the husband and wife were both employed – to buy scarce goods on the black and grey markets, to invest in war bonds and maintain bank accounts and live a life resembling in some ways that of the pre-war middle class.[18] This type of worker, certain to attract snobbish disapproval, was not, however, typical, any more than was the blatant war-profiteering capitalist. The problem was that both groups existed in sufficient numbers to cause a generalised resentment among their fellow Germans.

Most industrial workers – especially those in the non-essential service and consumer sectors – saw their real earnings eroded by price inflation during the war. Calculations of price inflation are complicated, but, all in all, the cost of living seems to have roughly trebled during the course of the war.[19] So, while the external exchange rate of the German mark might have recovered quite a lot in 1918, its actual internal purchasing power – reflecting the real inflation of prices, on the ground, for ordinary people – had declined much more drastically. In Hanover in the summer of 1918, a woman's weekly wage bought two kilos of butter.[20] By the end of that year, the mark had lost around three-quarters of its 1913 value. 'In other words,' as one historian of the First World War put it, 'most of the deterioration of pre-war money savings had already occurred by the Armistice, well before billions of marks were needed to post a letter or buy an egg.'[21]

All the same, those producing in factories and workshops for the war effort were on the whole better placed to minimise the damage to their living standards. Labour shortages and the essential nature of their work meant that the authorities, eager to maximise war production at all costs, were prepared to indulge their demands for better wages.

The old middle classes found themselves in a very different situation. Widely seen as the pillars of society before 1914, these were the Germans who suffered most from the war and its economic pressures. The differences in earnings between working- and middle-class Germans were reduced during the war, not so much because the industrial workers became dramatically richer – a common myth based on a few exceptional cases – but because their 'betters' became, with few exceptions, altogether poorer.

The lower ranks of officialdom, previously used to relatively modest rates of pay, with their real compensation taking the form of social status and job security, also felt themselves under wartime conditions to be – and they were – underpaid and overworked. There were cost-of-living adjustments in their salaries from time to time, but these never covered the constant, unpredictable real price increases. Their standard of living fell sharply during the war years and their resentment became palpable. In 1914, a civil servant's income in real terms had been on average five times that of a manual worker. By 1918, it was only three times greater, a drastic, not to say traumatic, drop in comparative living standards in a very short time.

The Deputy Commander of the Frankfurt military district painted a gloomy picture of these white-collar workers' plight in a report filed in October 1917:

> . . . all those living on fixed salaries are facing a change of social position; they are slipping from the level upon which they have stood and are approaching the level of those who find it necessary to live from hand to mouth. This social decline of the officialdom contains a not-to-be-underestimated danger to the state and society. Previously the officials could be counted among those who stood for the regulation of working conditions without great economic conflicts. The state and the communities must guard against letting the officials feel that they are being given up to the storms of economic developments without protection.

The same went for white-collar staff in industry, who, unlike their manual co-workers, were unwilling to compromise their hard-won and precious social standing by going on strike for higher wages. As for small businessmen and craftsmen, the backbone of the much-admired German *Mittelstand*, many found their businesses shut down as inessential to the war effort, starved of raw materials diverted to more vital sectors or simply bereft of customers.[22] They represented millions more Germans subjected to dramatically reduced incomes and loss of status – and accordingly ripe to blame those seen as profiteering.

Again, the one thing that could be seen by such victims of the war economy as providing possible recompense for their suffering – and even enabling restoration of their previous way of life – was the promise of victory. For the first half of 1918, with Russia knocked out of the war and the army advancing in France, this seemed to many

Germans to have become inevitable. Annexations or no annexations, with France and Britain defeated, Germany would perforce dominate Europe economically and politically as well as militarily. She would be even more prosperous than before. There would be enough to eat, and the necessities of life would be once more plentiful and afford-able. Normal economic conditions would return, bringing with them a strong German mark based once more on the gold standard. Stable prices would nurture the rebirth of a stable society.

Nurtured by endless, triumphant daily press reports, these happy hopes lasted, for most ordinary Germans, until July 1918, when reality bit with a vengeance. In August, another report from a military commandant admitted the negative effect the renewed German reverses were having on morale at home:

> The joyous – partially exaggerated – hopes which were attached to the renewal of our offensive . . . have been strongly shaken by the enemy counterattack and the withdrawal on our front. While the great mass of the people, because of the successes during the spring, have become accustomed to counting on the ending of the war this year, the prospect of another war winter has created a certain dullness and indifference in many people, and the economic cares and priva-tions have come to the forefront again more than before.[23]

Following the British counter-attack near Amiens on 8 August, spear-headed by tanks, 70 per cent of German losses were in the form of men taken prisoner, rather than wounded or killed, a sure sign that morale among the front-line soldiers was starting to collapse.[24] By late October, the German front line had been pushed back more than fifty miles. A liberating British Army had been welcomed by delirious crowds in Lille on 28 October, and many other major towns were also taken back into French control.

The military fate of Germany was all but decided. Though her armies had still not been put to flight, a sense of hopelessness was spreading both at the front and at home. Clearly, there would be no more advances, and certainly no victory of the all-conquering kind so many had imagined just a month or two previously.

In the final weeks of the war, the prospect of defeat also drastically changed the shape of Germany's political life. Attempts by the Reich's elite, above all the High Command, to stem the swelling tide of discontent led to a drastic change of policy. On his generals' advice, the Kaiser reluctantly assented to a brief, quasi-democratic interlude. A new cabinet was formed under the relatively liberal Prince Max of Baden, and at the end of October the right to name a chancellor was transferred from the monarch to the Reichstag. No one seemed to grasp the irony of offering the German people democracy under yet another prince. It couldn't last. The angry masses began to take to the streets and demand far more radical changes than the Berlin establishment could, or wanted to, concede. Sporadic rioting and fighting began.

Bizarrely, the life of the city, and that of its elite, went on. On 8 November 1918, there was a press reception in Berlin for the director Ernst Lubitsch's new film *Carmen*, featuring the twenty-one-year-old Polish actress Pola Negri, who would later become a huge Hollywood star of the silent era. Everyone was dressed up. There was champagne. An orchestra played selections from Bizet's famous opera. The producers began to show the film, but, as it ran, Negri heard the sound of what, after a while, she recognised as gunfire. It grew louder as the performance went on. Finally, she turned to Lubitsch and quietly asked if he could hear it, too. Yes, he said, then shushed her. 'There's nothing anybody can do. Watch the picture.' Afterwards, Miss Negri scuttled through empty streets to the nearest underground railway station in fear of her life.[25]

Sebastian Haffner remembered those final wartime days in the capital, and also their sudden end:

On November 9 and 10, there were still Army Reports in the old style: 'Enemy breakthrough attempts repulsed', '. . . after a brave defensive battle, our troops fell back to prepared positions . . .' On

November 11, when I arrived at the usual time, there was no Army Report fixed to the blackboard outside our local police station.[26]

It was, in fact, the day of the armistice on the Western Front. By the time the guns fell silent, at eleven on the morning of Monday, 11 November 1918, a revolution had taken place. The elegant expanse of Unter den Linden was thronged, not with the well-dressed ladies and gentlemen of 1910, but with noisy, excited crowds – among them workers and also soldiers of the German army, many wearing red revolutionary armbands and paying no heed to their officers.

Germany was now a republic. Her kings and princes and dukes were no more. Monarchs whose dynasties, in some cases, had lasted a thousand glittering years, disappeared from the scene with astonishingly little fuss. The previous Saturday, the Kaiser had found himself standing on a railway platform at his Grand Headquarters at Spa in Belgium, waiting with a handful of loyal officers for the imperial train to shunt its way to him. Once his transport was ready, he scuttled over the border into neutral Holland, seeking the protection of the Dutch government. It was said that his final comment, before beginning his journey into exile, had been: 'Yes, who would have thought it would come to this. The German people are a swinish bunch [*eine Schweinebande*].'[27]

Contrary to the pronouncements of the politicians in Berlin, the Kaiser had not, at this time, formally abdicated in favour of a regency – he would wait for three weeks in his Dutch hideaway before reluctantly giving up his dual crowns as King of Prussia and Emperor of Germany.[28] All the same, one thing was certain: whatever his technical status, after 9 November 1918 Wilhelm of Hohenzollern was no longer a proud monarch but a refugee from revolution – and from the victors' vengeance.

Now was the time for thinking about what all this horror had cost – not just in lives, but in marks and pfennigs for Germany, and pounds, francs and dollars for the Allies.

Since August 1914, Germany had spent something like 160 billion gold marks on what was now, undeniably, a lost war. Of this, around 60 per cent (98 billion) had been financed by the sale of war bonds (usually bearing 5 per cent interest). These bonds, representing a huge loan by the nation to its own government, had been sold to the German public and business community in nine remarkably successful war bond drives, beginning in November 1914 and ending in October 1918, just weeks before the armistice.[29]

Each war bond drive had been accompanied by massive patriotic campaigns, including early cinema advertising, and of course by government assurances that, not only would the money raised contribute to a German victory, but the bonds themselves would provide a decent investment income for their holders. The interest to the bond holders was supposedly still due, of course, win or lose. Not only that, but it was clear that the nation would also have to find the money to pay an as yet unspecified but predictably huge sum to the victors as reparations. The Reich's financial situation, as the Kaiser fled and the democrats took over, was disastrous.

The fighting on the battlefield was over. However, the economic and financial struggle that had begun in August 1914 would carry through not just to the period of armistice, but to the peace treaty and far beyond.

In fact, there were those who saw everything that happened to the German economy and currency by government action over the next five years as simply the continuation of war by other means. And to some extent, there is reason to believe they might have been right.

4

'I Hate the Social Revolution Like Sin'

On the morning of 9 November 1918, with a general strike called, Berlin full of excited crowds and rumours of an armistice coursing the streets, Prince Max of Baden, last hope of the old regime, decided to lay down the chancellorship he had accepted from the Kaiser barely a month earlier.

The Kaiser, of course, had departed Berlin some days earlier for Spa, whence his next stop would, it turned out, be refuge in neutral Holland. But what now? Prince Max had hoped to save the monarchy by skipping two unpopular royal generations and holding the crown in regency for the Kaiser's infant grandson. Even though the Kaiser had not yet formally abdicated, Max had announced his dethronement two days earlier. In this he was supported by the leader of the party that for so many years had been excluded by the old Prussian-dominated hierarchy but since August 1914 had become part of the war establishment: the Social Democrats.

Since the new Chancellor had taken power, two top-ranking Social Democrats had even been awarded posts in the government. Not yet a minister, but of prime importance to Prince Max's project, was the chairman of the Social Democratic Party, forty-seven-year-old Friedrich Ebert.

A stocky, not especially articulate party bureaucrat, the Heidelberg-born Ebert grew up in modest but reasonably secure circumstances as the seventh of nine children of a master tailor and his wife. He himself learned the trade of a saddler but spent little time plying it before devoting himself to politics. Sebastian Haffner, no enthusiast for a man he saw as one of the prime betrayers of the German revolution, painted an unflattering and somewhat patronising portrait of a bloodless political bureaucrat who presented 'an unprepossessing figure':

> He was a small, fat man with short legs and a short neck, with a pear-shaped head on a pear-shaped body. He wasn't a riveting speaker either. He spoke in a guttural voice, and he read his speeches from a prepared text. He was not an intellectual, or for that matter a real proletarian . . . Ebert was the type of the German master craftsman: solid, conscientious, limited in his horizons but a master precisely within those limitations; modest and respectful in his dealings with genteel clients, taciturn and commanding in his own workshop. Social Democratic officials were a bit afraid of him, in the way that journeymen and apprentices are afraid of a strict master . . .[1]

Becoming a convinced socialist and trade unionist, Ebert first worked as manager of a tavern in the northern port of Bremen (one that functioned as a social centre for political leftists), all the while working his way up the Social Democratic Party apparatus. He showed a strong talent for organisation, a taste for hard work and a firm attachment to the political centre. By the time he was in his thirties, 'Fritz' Ebert was a nationally known figure on the moderate German left, and at the age of thirty-four he became its national organising secretary and a member of the party's central committee.

It was telling that Ebert put a stamp on his new position at party headquarters not by making great speeches or coming up with new political ideas – these were always tasks he tended to leave to others – but by ensuring that telephones and typewriters were installed in the offices, and a proper membership filing system instituted.[2] He was not elected to the Reichstag until the age of forty-one, in the socialists' great victory of 1912, when the SPD became the largest party in the parliament. All the same, clearly the party wanted an organisation man at the top. When the veteran leader August Bebel died the following year, Ebert was elected to take his place as the party's co-chairman.

Between 1878 and 1890 the German Social Democratic Party had been illegal. Bismarck's attempt to crush the socialist left in his new Reich was, however, only very partially successful. Despite some of them being sentenced to terms of imprisonment, the party's leadership and basic apparatus had remained intact. Social Democrat candidates continued to be elected to the Reichstag as supposedly 'non-party' individuals. In the January 1890 elections their vote reached almost 20 per cent, making this (officially non-existent) party the largest in terms of share of the popular vote, although because of the unfair way the seats were distributed it got a mere 35 seats out of 397.

The formal ban was lifted later in 1890, but for almost a quarter of a century thereafter the SPD was still considered 'beyond the pale' by the monarchist German establishment. In August 1914, so concerned were Germany's socialists that war would bring a new political crackdown on their party that Ebert and a fellow committee member were delegated to head for Switzerland – along with a strongbox containing the party's funds – and to wait out the immediate emergency.

In fact, Ebert, having got the party treasury to safety, returned to Berlin on 5 August. He found the Reich at war, and the vast majority of his party's hitherto overwhelmingly internationalist and pacifist parliamentary representatives committed to supporting Germany's cause. Ebert never voted for that near-unanimous acceptance by the Reichstag of the war credits (which turned out to be a virtual blank cheque for the German government), but he lost no time in leading his party in enthusiastic support for the *Burgfrieden* and for the war.

The Kaiser had declared at the onset of hostilities that he 'no longer recognised parties, only Germans'. Ebert and the majority of German Social Democrats took him at his word. For more than four years, they loyally supported all of the government's financial demands. They mediated conscientiously between restive war workers and their demanding employers, and though they nodded when required in favour of a peace more in accordance with their earlier internationalist convictions than with the keen annexationist demands of the right, and kept up the pressure for a full democratisation of the monarchical political system, they were now clearly part of the wartime establishment. As the war went on, and many on the left became disillusioned with Germany's cause, considerable numbers of their political representatives, including fifteen Reichstag deputies, as well as large numbers of the original party's most passionate activists, peeled off to form a breakaway Social Democrat party that called for an immediate peace. Ebert's faction, still considerably the larger, became known as 'Majority Social Democrats', while the anti-war left took the name of 'Independent Social Democrats'. That was how things remained until the autumn of 1918 arrived, and with it the sudden and, to many, surprising collapse in German hopes of victory.

Prince Max was forced to take on the chancellorship because in September the armed forces – more specifically Ludendorff – had looked at the military situation and decided that the army could not go on. On 29 September, Ludendorff marched into a meeting of the High Command and announced as much. The Macedonian and Italian fronts could no longer hold. With Bulgaria, Germany's chief Balkan ally, suing for peace, Turkey on its knees and Austria-Hungary likewise on the brink of surrender, even if by some miracle Germany managed to hold on to what was left of her gains on the Western Front, she could not survive more than a matter of weeks before the enemy came roaring up from the south.

Not only had Ludendorff announced the imminence of defeat, but the general – hitherto a fiercely anti-democratic Pan-German nationalist – had also told the appalled commanders, including Wilhelm II, that they would have to concede real liberal reforms. Only in this way could they keep the support of the masses, and mollify the enemy with whom they would soon have to negotiate.

Had not President Wilson of the United States, in whose rapidly expanding industrial power and limitless reserve of fighting men the Entente was placing its hopes of victory, not proclaimed as part of his 'Fourteen Points' a conviction that the coming peace should be based not on revenge and conquest but on the democratic self-determination of peoples? Then let Germany become the political creature that America desired!

Count Hertling, a Catholic Bavarian nobleman in his mid-seventies who had been a largely figurehead Chancellor for the past year or so, refused to serve a parliamentary regime. On Hertling's recommendation, the Kaiser called on Maximilian Alexander Friedrich Wilhelm von Baden. Nephew and heir presumptive of the Grand Duke of Baden, in south-west Germany, Prince Max was known for his relatively liberal views. He had opposed unrestricted submarine warfare (the step, vigorously promoted by Ludendorff and the ultra-nationalists, which had finally brought America into the war against Germany), was prominent in the Red Cross, and until the end of American neutrality had chaired a German-American prisoner of war aid society set up under the auspices of the Young Men's Christian Association. He immediately invited Social Democrat, Catholic (Centre) Party and Liberal Reichstag deputies to join his government. The day after his appointment, as instructed by the High Command, the Prince formally submitted to the enemy powers his request for talks that would lead to an armistice and ultimately to a peace treaty based on Wilson's Fourteen Points.

Whether it was a matter of the military recovering its nerve, or of there having been a plan all along aimed at shuffling off the blame for a humiliating peace on to democratic politicians, towards the end of October Prince Max and his ministers found that Ludendorff had reverted from peace campaigner back to his old, diehard, victory-or-death self. The military and political realities that had caused Ludendorff's decision a month earlier to push for peace had not changed. However, although Prince Max's government had agreed to abandon the submarine campaign and to withdraw the army from the remaining occupied areas, in a third and increasingly harsh exchange of communications President Wilson also demanded guarantees of changes in the German political system and of military measures that would make a resumption of the war impossible. Ludendorff promptly withdrew support for the peace negotiations upon which he had formerly been so insistent. Now, he demanded in an order to his soldiers, co-signed by Field Marshal Hindenburg, Germany must continue to 'resist to the utmost of her power'.

Such defiance of government and Kaiser could not be permitted. On 26 October 1918 Ludendorff, for more than two years the real ruler of Germany, was dismissed, though to save embarrassment it was claimed that he had resigned of his own volition. He was replaced as Quartermaster-General and Deputy Chief of Staff by fifty-year-old General Wilhelm Groener, a transport and logistics expert who had been the High Command's linkman with the Food Supply Office and, for some months after August 1916, Deputy Prussian Minister of War and head of the Reich War Production Office.

Two days later, a crucial change in the Reich constitution finally made the Chancellor and his ministers no longer responsible only to the Kaiser, as had been the case since 1871, but to the Reichstag. Germany was now formally a constitutional monarchy.[3] Prince Max was from this point on theoretically free to conduct policy as he desired, or at least as events dictated, but in fact power had already begun to slip from his hands. This time, it was not the High Command that presented the threat, but the mood of the common people.

On 24 October, Admiral Scheer, commanding the German North Sea Fleet, issued secret orders for the fleet to prepare to put to sea once more. Senior naval commanders had decided, in defiance of the Berlin government, which was in the middle of delicate armistice negotiations, to take on the British fleet in a 'decisive battle' (*Entscheidungsschlacht*) – a final, suicidal attempt to salvage what they perceived to be the German navy's honour.

Despite the secrecy surrounding Scheer's order, word spread

through the ships waiting at anchor off the North Sea naval port of Wilhelmshaven. The men below decks had been penned up in port in cramped conditions and under harsh discipline for more than two years since the inconclusive Battle of Jutland (known in Germany as the *Skagerrakschlacht*) in June 1916. Unsurprisingly, most were not keen on dying just as peace was about to break out, simply to satisfy the naval elite's desire for a heroic seaborne *Götterdämmerung*. Open mutiny followed. During the night of 29–30 October, several warships in Wilhelmshaven were seized by their crews. One of the sailors would write in his diary attributing the cause: 'Years and years of injustice have been converted into a dangerously explosive force that is now coming to a head.'[4]

The Imperial Navy stood on the brink of disintegration, but the naval command held its nerve. German submarines and torpedo boats took up position among the ships off Wilhelmshaven. The mutineers were given a deadline. If they did not return to their stations, these vessels would torpedo their ships. At the last minute, the crews gave in. The ships were handed back to their commanders. The mutiny was, for the moment, over.

Nonetheless, in a victory of sorts for the men, the plan for the 'decisive battle' was abandoned. The ordinary crew could clearly not be trusted to die 'with honour'. The fleet was split up, with the 3rd Squadron – whose crews had been the most troublesome – ordered to enter the North Sea Canal and sail through to Kiel, the great German naval port on the Baltic. On the way through the canal, forty-seven naval ratings and stokers considered to have been ring-leaders in the rebellion were picked out and placed under arrest. On arrival at Kiel, they were transported to a naval prison.

The uprising at sea might have been stifled, but on shore it was a different story. In Kiel, rumours about the arrested mutineers spread like a virus among the discontented naval personnel. On 1 November, several hundred gathered at the trades union building. They sent a petition to the local naval command, demanding that the prisoners be freed. It was ignored.

The next day, the sailors found the entrance to the trades union building barred by police. In response, an even larger group of protesters met a few streets to the south at the Großer Exerzierplatz, once a parade ground but now a broad public square in the centre of the city. Flyers were printed and circulated. On 3 November, another meeting on the square attracted several thousand protesters, now including both sailors and war workers of both sexes. This time they demanded not just the liberation of the imprisoned mutineers, but also an end to the war and an improvement in the food situation. As the demonstrators attempted to move out of the square towards the military prison to demand their comrades' release, in the process 'liberating' some weapons from nearby military billets, they encountered an army unit. Fire was exchanged. Seven protesters were killed and twenty-nine wounded. The lieutenant commanding the army unit was seriously injured and taken to hospital.

By the next morning, 4 November, armed groups of sailors were roaming the streets. In a final attempt to restore discipline, the commander of the big naval base at Kiel-Wik, two miles or so to the north of the city centre, ordered all sailors and soldiers to form up for a roll call on the main parade ground. The commander's appeal to the men's loyalty failed to prevent spontaneous demonstrations against his authority. Soon the men from the base had joined up with those already active in the city. The soldiers of the city garrison likewise refused orders to resist the rebels. The city's military governor received a delegation of workers and sailors and was forced to grant their demands, including an assurance not to call in military assistance from outside – at one point urged on by a threat by the mutineers to turn their ships' guns on the quarter containing many officers' private villas.[5]

According to a personal account by one of the leaders of the uprising, the military governor had, actually, broken his word:

That evening, we then got the news that despite the governor's declaration four outside infantry units were marching in our direction.

We immediately jumped into our automobile and drove straight towards them. We reached them just by the post office, and spoke with them . . . Then I requested that they either give up their weapons or join the revolutionaries. The infantrymen joined our revolutionary movement. The officers were disarmed.[6]

With that, there was no military unit prepared to support the status quo. At the end of the day, the city of Kiel was in the hands of the mutineers and their supporters. Within hours, 'soldiers' councils' had been formed. 'Workers' councils' would follow. The next morning, disturbances had also broken out in the ports of Wilhelmshaven, Lübeck and Cuxhaven. Workers' groups were also readying themselves for protests in Hamburg, Germany's second largest city.[7]

On 5 November the new masters of Kiel issued a list of demands:

1. Release of all detainees and political prisoners.
2. Absolute freedom of speech and the press.
3. Lifting of censorship of mail.
4. Correct treatment of men by their superiors.
5. Return of all comrades to ships and barracks without punishment.
6. The fleet under no circumstances to leave port.
7. All protective measures involving the shedding of blood to cease.
8. Withdrawal of all forces not belonging to the garrison.
9. All measures for the protection of private property to be established by the soldiers' council with immediate effect.
10. Off duty, no more superior ranks.
11. Each man to be permitted complete personal freedom between one period of duty and the next.
12. Officers who declared themselves in agreement with the measures of the now established soldiers' council to be welcomed into their midst. All the others to quit the service immediately without claim of compensation.
13. Every member of the soldiers' council to be freed of all duties.

14. All measures arrived at in future to be implemented only with
     the agreement of the soldiers' council.

The German revolution had begun.

By 9 November, the Kiel mutiny had spread to most of the country.
    The sailors had set off for other parts of Germany, on the way
successfully calling on local people to set up their own revolutionary
councils. In Munich on 7 November, the revolutionary movement
toppled its first crowned head. Before a crowd of some 60,000
assembled on the Theresienwiese, site of the modern Oktoberfest,
the left socialist leader Kurt Eisner demanded an end to the war, an
eight-hour working day and improved unemployment benefits, the
creation of soldiers' and workers' councils, and the abdication of
Ludwig III of Bavaria. The seventy-two-year-old king quickly disappeared into exile.
    There was scarcely a town or city of any size in Germany, during
these dramatic and, to many, exhilarating few days in November,
where the old authorities had not been pushed aside and the local
government assumed by revolutionary councils. The exception, curiously enough, was Berlin. All the same, on 8 November, the breakaway
Independent Socialists (USPD), who had split from the main party
because of its leadership's continuing support for the war, had declared
a general strike and day of demonstrations for Saturday 9 November.
It was a direct challenge to Max of Baden's government, which had
banned all public gatherings.
    Calls for the abolition of the monarchy were becoming louder by
the hour. Prince Max, nervous that the capital would dissolve into
what he viewed as anarchy, decided to take action. He summoned
from its base south of Leipzig the 4th Rifle Regiment, which had
fought against the Bolsheviks in German-occupied Russia and was
seen as a particularly loyal pillar of the Prussian royal house. These
reinforcements arrived on 8 November. Early on the following
morning, 9 November, the regiment's officers began to distribute

grenades to their men, with the obvious intent of suppressing any demonstrations by force. But the riflemen, or at least the lower ranks, were not quite the obedient tools of the palace the Chancellor had believed them to be. Few, it turned out, were prepared to massacre their fellow Germans for the sake of . . . what?

To the astonishment of their superiors, the men of the 4th Rifles insisted on engaging them in discussion. Not satisfied with the officers' answers, they voted to send a delegation to the Social Democratic Party requesting political clarity. They were duly addressed by the Social Democratic Reichstag Deputy and party central committee member Otto Wels, who in an eloquent speech appealed to them to take the side of the people and of his party. His appeal succeeded. So convinced were the riflemen that they voted to send an armed unit to the offices of *Vorwärts* ('Forward'), the Social Democratic Party's official newspaper, charged with protecting its production.

When it became clear to Prince Max that even such elite troops could not be relied on, he realised that the game was up. Having secured the Kaiser's somewhat ambiguous assent to abdication over the telephone line from Spa, the Chancellor did not wait for a formal written announcement before releasing the news to the press.

Then, at around midday, Friedrich Ebert appeared in the Reich Chancellery with a delegation of Social Democrats. Prince Max admitted that without any loyal troops at his disposal he could no longer control the masses. The government should be in the hands of a man of the people. Would the Social Democratic leader take on the job of Chancellor? But first, could they settle the question of who was to be regent, acting on behalf of the putative child-emperor who would succeed if the Kaiser and Crown Prince gave up their rights?

That same morning, *Vorwärts* had published, apparently approvingly, a declaration announcing the formation of a regency. Now, however, Ebert told Prince Max that the survival of the monarchy could no longer be guaranteed. After some show of reluctance, he agreed to take on the chancellorship.

Ebert remained prepared to keep the monarchy, subject to a

parliamentary decision on the form the post-war state should take. For now, though, the priority was to keep control of events, which meant going with the flow of the popular demonstrations. As Philipp Scheidemann, chair of the Social Democratic parliamentary party and, since October, an appointed State Secretary, effectively a minister in Prince Max's government, had said some days earlier: 'Now it's a matter of putting ourselves at the head of the movement, or there'll be anarchy in the Reich.'[8]

Ebert, and other of the moderate Social Democratic leaders, were not – or were no longer – radical firebrands. Even before the war, the march of the moderates had been a feature of the party's progression, to a point where in the last elections before the war it had been supported by more than a third of the population, far beyond the loyal ranks of the industrial proletariat.

Tellingly, when on 7 November Ebert had pressed Prince Max for the Kaiser's abdication and his replacement by a regency, his reasons had been far from revolutionary. According to Prince Max's later account, as the two men walked around the autumnal setting of the Reich Chancellery's garden, he told Ebert of a plan to travel, if necessary, to the Imperial Headquarters at Spa and persuade the Kaiser to abdicate in favour of regency by the Kaiser's second son, Prince Eitel Friedrich. 'If I succeed in persuading the Kaiser, then do I have you on my side in the fight against social revolution?' the Prince asked Ebert. The Social Democrat leader did not hesitate in his answer: 'If the Kaiser does not abdicate, then the social revolution is unavoidable. But I don't want it, I hate it like sin.'[9]

In the end, Prince Max did not go to Spa. The wildfire of revolution was sweeping the country and threatening Berlin. The Chancellor could not leave the capital. Instead, the not strictly accurate announcement of the Kaiser's abdication two days later followed an untidy sequence of long-distance phone calls.

So, at around noon on 9 November, Germany had no Kaiser, but technically remained a monarchy. For about an hour and a half, that is. For, while on 7 November it had been possible to discuss questions of monarchy or no monarchy as if these were debatable alternatives, events outside the Chancellery were well on their way to changing the country for ever.

While these conversations were going on in Prince Max's office, vast crowds, numbering hundreds of thousands, had assembled in the heart of the city. Demonstrators surrounded the Reichstag and the parkland adjacent to it, pouring over into Unter den Linden and from there to the nearby Berlin Stadtschloss (City Castle), the Kaiser's official residence when he was in the capital. The masses as represented at that moment in the streets were calling with one voice for the end of the monarchy. By the time Friedrich Ebert accepted Prince Max's offer of the chancellorship (with no monarch, no regent and no other kind of head of state to formally appoint Ebert, they had to simply ignore the rules and just do it), rumours were spreading throughout the government quarter that the crowds were to be addressed by various far-left figures. The speakers would include Karl Liebknecht, anti-war firebrand, veteran leftist leader and co-founder of the ultra-radical 'Spartacist' group (named after the slave rebellion in ancient Rome), who was well known for his support of the Bolshevik regime in Russia.

It was not Ebert who personally took control of the crucial moment, however. He had returned from his meeting with Prince Max and was having a meagre wartime lunch of potato soup in the restaurant of the Reichstag. Meanwhile, the crowds took the famous phrase carved two years earlier beneath the main pediment of the building, *Dem Deutschen Volke* (To the German People), seriously, and it was into the building that they swarmed to make their feelings clear.

It was now shortly before 2 p.m. A group of demonstrators entered the deputies' restaurant. Ebert was urged by the intruders, who were Social Democrat party loyalists, to address the crowd. Liebknecht was planning to declare a socialist republic on Bolshevik lines, they said. The moderate left had to assert control of the situation. The newly minted Chancellor, not a natural orator, declined. However, also among the deputies having lunch was Philipp Scheidemann. At

fifty-three, the former printer from Kassel was one of the main leaders
of the party, chair of the parliamentary faction and vice-president of
the Reichstag. An easily recognisable figure with his bald dome and
goatee beard (strangely similar to that affected by the departing
Kaiser), Scheidemann, unlike Ebert, was known as a rousing orator.

According to his memoirs, Scheidemann learned enough in the
minutes that followed to convince him that the talk of a regency was
no longer realistic. Clearly, if Scheidemann did not take immediate
action, then someone else – someone with much more radical plans
– would do so.

Leaving Ebert at the table, Scheidemann and some companions
navigated their way through the Reichstag's labyrinthine corridors
until they reached a big window overlooking the front of the Reichstag, where many thousands of noisy demonstrators were gathered.
Perched on the narrow balcony in front of the open window, Scheidemann addressed the crowd in an improvised oration that ended
with the words:

> The Kaiser has abdicated. He and his friends have disappeared, and
> the people have proved victorious on all fronts. Prince Max of Baden
> has transferred the office of Reich Chancellor to Deputy Ebert. Our
> friend will form a workers' government to which all socialist parties
> will belong. The new government must not be impeded in its work
> for peace and its concern for work and bread. Workers and soldiers,
> be aware of the historic importance of this day: unheard-of things
> have occurred. Great work lies ahead of us, a task that cannot be
> shirked. Everything for the people! Everything through the people!
> Nothing can be permitted to happen that brings the workers' move-
> ment into disrepute. Be united, loyal and aware of your duty. That
> which is old and rotten, the monarchy, has collapsed. Long live the
> new! Long live the German republic![10]

The speech might have sounded radical in tone. Except for Scheidemann's historic, off-the-cuff proclamation of the Republic, however,

it was nothing of the kind. Essentially, the routine socialist rhetorical devices aside, Scheidemann was telling the war-weary masses to knuckle down, stop revolting and get on with the disciplined work of saving Germany under the new, democratic regime.

When Scheidemann got back to the restaurant, a furious Ebert – 'livid with fury' by Scheidemann's description[11] – banged the table in outrage at his colleague's presumption. The future form of the German state was something for a Constituent Assembly to decide! But it was, of course, too late for such niceties. There is little question that Scheidemann's prompt action was, under the circumstances, correct.

It was not, in fact, until around four in the afternoon that the firebrand Karl Liebknecht addressed another crowd from another balcony – this time, in a piece of deliberate stage-setting, on an upper floor of the royal Stadtschloss – and made his call for a far more profoundly revolutionary change.

Liebknecht declared a 'free socialist republic', based on the soldiers' and workers' councils that had been established in the past few days. The new Soviet-style state would reach out to 'our brothers throughout the world . . . and call on them to complete the task of world revolution'.[12] After his speech, according to the American journalist Ben Hecht, the Spartacist leader went and lay down, in his underwear, on the bed in the Kaiser's private chamber, where he caused the bedside table to collapse under the weight of his briefcase full of files.[13]

For all Liebknecht's passion, and for all the enthusiasm of his supporters, his proclamation turned out be something of a damp squib. The overwhelming majority of the crowds that day in Berlin did not want a repeat of the Bolshevik coup of October 1917. There were big crowds around the so-called 'government district', but no truly transformational uprising occurred that day. Scheidemann's unauthorised proclamation, and the news that Ebert, a Social Democrat, had assumed the chancellorship, were sufficient for most of the people thronging the streets, eager for change. Many Berliners recalled only too well that Lenin and his comrades' seizure of power had been followed, in January 1918, by their violent dismissal of the freely

elected parliament – the first in Russia's history – and the rapid establishment of a one-party dictatorship. Certainly the likes of
Scheidemann and Ebert were acutely aware of the danger of the
quasi-tyranny of the old monarchy being replaced, as in Russia, by
an absolute tyranny of the far left.

While all the speech-making was going on, one eyewitness – a
businessman just trying to get to a meeting with his lawyer at his
office on the Wilhelmsplatz – noticed this strange passivity and
contrasted it with the potentially world-changing events taking place.

Young boys of sixteen and eighteen had opened fire at the war ministry with shotguns because no one would open the doors. There was
said to have been answering fire from the windows. Pointless, infantile
behaviour. Serious men are calling for calm, and commanding the
shooting to stop. It is a real revolution, but strange – the great, world-
changing thoughts and events, and these boys, children with red, hot
faces contorted into unpleasant expressions, who look more like they
are players in a game of cops and robbers than bearers of a revolutionary power that will move the world.

There is a complete lack of enthusiasm among the masses on the
street. The public is standing curiously to one side, and being enter-
tained by the commotion as if it were at the theatre. Motor vehicles
roar past, and the well-dressed middle class people in the Leipziger
Strasse humbly edge away to the side of the street.[14]

The day of the German revolution revealed a people tired of war and
the old ways, eager for peace, and eager for the most part, at this
point, to give a new, democratic and, it was hoped, fairer political
system a chance. On 9 November 1918, the men of the imperial
establishment appeared to retreat, as if they, too, understood that
their system had failed. What was the point of an elite of warlords
and monarchs if in the end they led their country to defeat? In a way,
it was surprising that the German people let them off so easily.

However, if they had come to despise the *ancien régime* for its failures, most Germans, especially of the better-off classes, feared the anarchy that might follow the end of the monarchy. And, in some cases, they feared unemployment as a result.

Curt Riess, sixteen years old at the end of the war, was the son of a Berlin tradesman who had prospered more than most under the old monarchical regime. This was so because Riess's father made and sold ceremonial uniforms and liveries for the various German royal courts, from Bavaria, Württemberg, Saxony and the like, up to and including that of the Kaiser himself. His son remembers that in the shop there was a closet neatly filled with hundreds and hundreds of different uniform buttons. And the sign in front of the shop sported the warrants of the various German dynasties to which he was a supplier of court dress 'by royal appointment'.

On the day the revolution broke out in Berlin, fearing that the masses would attack all symbols of the old regime, Riess's father and his staff rushed to the shop, which was situated in the heart of the government district, and prepared to defend the place from the mob. The streets, it transpired, were certainly full of republican demonstrators, but no one paid the slightest heed to Riess's father's establishment, then or later, despite its blatantly monarchical character. Riess recalls, in fact, that, although his father switched into conventional made-to-measure tailoring to suit the republican times, the 'by royal appointment warrants stayed where they had always been, to the end of the first German Republic and beyond'.[15]

So the Republic established itself, and not necessarily as something to fear. There was continuity. Unfortunately, that continuity included a continuity of responsibility for the war that the Kaiser, his ministers and generals had foisted on their nation – and then demanded that it pay for.

The left-liberal and cultural Berlin magazine *Die Weltbühne* ('The World Stage') put it concisely: 'when they were victorious, Ludendorff and his men were on top of the world, stamping on mighty seven-league boots through the land, and heaping up debts – debts that not they, but we others will have to pay'.[16]

5

Salaries Are Still Being Paid

The crowned heads and the generals who had dominated the old Germany were a busted flush. Or so it seemed, at least to the outside world.

In fact, the first action Chancellor Ebert had undertaken, within hours of becoming head of the new government, was to issue an appeal to all officials of the old regime to remain at their posts. 'A failure of organisation at this difficult hour would expose Germany to anarchy and to the most terrible hardship,' he declared.

At the same time, Ebert was also aware that his own party alone could not control events sufficiently reliably to ensure the maintenance of basic order. He therefore decided that he would have to make peace with the radicals as well. That same afternoon, he put out feelers to the leadership of the group of mostly left-wing Social Democrats who had broken away during the course of the war to form the more radical, pacifist 'Independent Social Democratic Party'. The 'Independents', as they were known, had grown strongly in the last year or two of the war, especially in the factories and among serving soldiers. Their influence could reach to places where Ebert's could not. But on that first afternoon, the party's demands were too rigid for Ebert to accept. He was forced, for the moment, to wait and let events on the streets take what course they might.

During the night of 9/10 November, no one was sure who ruled Berlin. Count Harry Kessler, the wealthy aristocratic connoisseur, writer and diplomat, had just returned from an official mission to Warsaw when, at around 10 p.m. on 9 November, he and a colleague gained entrance to the Reichstag building. They pleaded urgent business with Hugo Haase, leader of the Independents, who had himself just returned from a visit to revolutionary Kiel.

In front of the main entrance, and in an arc of illumination provided by the headlights of several army vehicles, stood a crowd waiting for news. People pushed up the steps and through doors. Soldiers with slung rifles and red badges checked everyone's business. The scene inside was animated, with a continual movement up and down the stairs of sailors, armed civilians, women and soldiers. The sailors looked healthy, fresh, neat and, most noticeable of all, very young; the soldiers old and war-worn, in faded uniforms and down-at-heel footwear, unshaven and unkempt, remnants of an army, a tragic picture of defeat.[1]

In fact it would be Haase who played a key role in ensuring that the renewed negotiations with Ebert, which followed on 10 November 1918, met with success. At first, in the absence of their veteran leader, representatives of the Independents had stubbornly refused to allow any non-socialists to join the new government, even as non-executive experts. They had ignored Ebert's protests that such experts were desperately needed to prevent the Reich's food supply systems from breaking down. This stand-off lasted until Haase got back from Kiel and knocked his colleagues' heads together. Unlike his often inexperienced radical comrades, the fifty-six-year-old lawyer was a seasoned politician, having served with Ebert for five years as co-chair of the main Social Democratic Party until decamping to the Independents out of disillusion with the war. Despite the continuing sharp differences with Ebert and co., Haase had a grasp of *Realpolitik* that his more hot-headed fellow Independents found hard to countenance.

By early in the afternoon of 10 November, the negotiators had nevertheless hammered out an agreement of sorts. Some non-socialists would be allowed into the government, though with socialist state secretaries as 'minders'. And ultimate power in the state would lie with a national assembly of workers' and soldiers' councils, which was to be summoned to Berlin at the earliest possible date. A six-member governing council, chosen half from the main Social Democratic Party, half from the Independents, would run the new democratic Republic of Germany until further notice. This council would supersede the office of Chancellor, which Ebert thus held for a mere twenty-four hours. To avoid any whiff of outmoded ministerial privilege, the official title of this inner cabinet would be 'Council of the People's Commissioners' (*Rat der Volksbeauftragten*).

On the surface, over the next days, the revolution rolled on. No Bolshevik-style dictatorship of the proletariat, but lots of revolutionary rhetoric and, for the moment, the workers' and soldiers' councils given their heads. All of this fitted in with the majority socialist leadership's strategy of placing itself at the head of the revolution so as to keep it within bounds.

So the majority socialist leadership decided that it would ride the revolutionary tiger, so to speak. Leaving power with the revolutionary councils might have seemed like a big risk, but the mainstream Social Democratic Party was able to do so with some confidence for two reasons. One, which seemed quite transparent even at the time, was that the majority socialists still held the allegiance of most workers and soldiers (the majority of whom were wartime conscripts, little more than workers in uniform). Ebert and his colleagues could be pretty certain that even when the Bolshevik-sounding directly elected councils met, most delegates would follow the majority socialist line, not that of the Independents, let alone of Liebknecht's proto-Communist Spartacist organisation. And there was a second reason, though it remained secret for years after. Late on 10 November, Friedrich Ebert had spoken on a secure phone line with Ludendorff's successor as Quartermaster-General and thereby *de facto* head of the army, Generalleutnant Wilhelm Groener, and done a deal.

The General and the Party Secretary knew each other quite well. Groener had been a key military functionary on the home front during 1916–17, the High Command's man at the Reich Food Office, then from November 1916 to August 1917 Deputy Prussian War Minister and war production supremo. In these capacities, he had worked together with Ebert and other leading Social Democrats on the crucial tasks of keeping the industrial workforce fed and manageable.

There is a simple way of viewing the conversation between these two men. This says that Ebert, unsure of his longer-term position in the face of the revolutionary process, asked his old acquaintance Groener for the army's support against the far left, in return guaranteeing the position of the army's leadership and the disciplinary powers of its officers in the face of the recent wave of democratisation.

There is, however, another view. The fact was that at that point Groener had virtually no army to lend Ebert. As Prince Max's attempts to use the 4th Rifles against the crowds early on 9 November had shown, there were almost no troops who could be trusted to act as instruments of 'order'. There was plenty of discontent and defeatism at the front, but this was particularly true in the cities of Germany proper, where radical ideas had spread like wildfire among civilians and soldiers alike. Arguably, judging from the evidence of the past few days' events, Ebert had more power over the average soldier than did their nominal commander, Groener. But both men had an interest in an orderly retreat to the armistice lines that had already been agreed with the Entente, and also in an efficient carrying out of the demobilisation process of (more than 8 million) German citizens in uniform that would undoubtedly also be taking place over the following weeks and months. This meant that the Social Democrat was prepared to give the High Command assurances that the essential integrity of the old army and its officer corps would be respected.[2] As for Groener, he would do anything to save what could be saved of the old army, and to buy time for that army to be rebuilt as a post-war factor in the country.

Groener remained a monarchist, of course. However, it is difficult to know what else he could have done other than swear his and the army's fealty to the new regime in Berlin. It had been Groener himself, born in the Grand Duchy of Württemberg in southern

Germany, originally commissioned into the Grand Duke's rather than the Prussian army, who had finally, it could be said, driven the Kaiser into exile on the morning of 9 November. At a headquarters meeting that morning, the Supreme Warlord had conveyed his intention, once the armistice came into force, of marching 'his' army back into the homeland, with his royal self at its head, and suppressing the revolution by force. Few officers were prepared to support his scheme. It would cause civil war and most probably a resumption of hostilities with the victorious Entente as well. The emperor found himself deserted by his paladins. And it was Groener who told Wilhelm II so to his face: 'The army will return to the homeland under its leaders and commanding generals in a quiet and orderly fashion, but not under the orders of Your Majesty; for it no longer stands behind Your Majesty!'[3]

What Groener said was true. There were soldiers' councils springing up everywhere. However, most of the troops – certainly those that, as the end of the war neared, had not informally 'demobilised' themselves – wanted the withdrawal to Germany's borders, as stipulated in the armistice agreement, to occur in an orderly fashion. And almost none of them, except some diehard officers, were prepared to fight for the restoration of Prussian royal power.

It was a strange revolution that overtook Germany in 1918. The parliamentary regime instituted in October had been a creature of Ludendorff and the High Command rather than the result of pressure by parliamentary politicians or, perish the thought, of a popular uprising. The Republic that had been created, in a way by chance and certainly not by Ebert's design, on 9 November, was the most radical transformation of the state in German history. However, it had already been made clear that the old imperial officials would keep their jobs. How else were ordinary Germans to be fed and the order of their day-to-day lives to be assured? Now, it became clear, the old imperial officers would also remain in place, if Ebert and Groener had their way. How else was the army to hold together and its soldiers be got home safely and in good order?

One thing was certain. In the brief vacuum that had followed the announcement of the Kaiser's abdication, the far left had failed to take control. Liebknecht's call for a socialist republic of Germany and for a world revolution had fallen mostly on deaf ears. The masses had stuck overwhelmingly with their familiar democratic socialist leaders, including the relatively moderate leaders of the Independents, with Ebert at the apex of that new power structure.

By the day after the great transformation, Sunday, 10 November, Berlin was surprisingly calm. The theologian and philosopher Professor Ernst Troeltsch described the scene in the leafy Berlin suburb of Grunewald, where he noticed the solid middle-class burghers taking their usual Sunday strolls in the woods, though with one or two concessions to the new era:

> No elegant grooming, a conspicuous 'citizen' look. With many, probably deliberately, simply dressed. Everyone somewhat subdued, as you might expect from people whose fate was being decided somewhere far away, but all the same reassured and comfortable that things had gone so well. The trams and the underground railways were running as usual, a sort of pledge that, so far as the immediate necessities of life were concerned, all was in order. On every face was written: Salaries are still being paid.[4]

The mixture of relief and apprehension that characterised the great majority of Germans' attitudes during this interlude – the armistice followed the next day, on Monday, 11 November – seemed to bode well for change. But most Germans, including the leadership of the Social Democratic Party, typified by Friedrich Ebert, did not want too much of it.

The new governing elite wanted enough to give the country's citizens some more freedom and equality, to brush aside the stuffy authoritarianism of the Empire, and, so far as the outside world was concerned, perhaps to induce a more merciful peace settlement along the lines of President Wilson's Fourteen Points. And perhaps a little socialism, too. Even before 1914, German industry had already developed along lines that diverged consciously from the free-market, individualist 'Manchesterism' of Britain or the USA, and the passions and necessities of war had done much to move the Reich's economy towards a kind of corporate socialism that was even more peculiarly German. But not so much socialism that 'Russian conditions' would be created, for both the prosperous classes and the majority of workers did not want Bolshevism.

The main thing was that the old system seemed both discredited and ruined. The Kaiser, after his apparently panic-stricken flight across the border into Holland, was held in widespread contempt. The generals and the officer class had brought their nation nothing but drawn-out suffering and defeat. Germans had stood together for four years with remarkable fortitude, it was true, but to what end? And what would happen now?

A few months later, Ebert would give a speech in which he spoke of his motives at the time of the November revolution:

> We were in the real meaning of the word the insolvency administrators of the old regime: All the warehouses were empty, all stocks dwindling, all creditworthiness shattered, our morale sunk to the depths. We . . . exercised our best energies to overcome the dangers and the misery of the transitional period. We did not prejudge things that were the business of this National Assembly. But where time and necessity were of the essence, we made every effort to fulfil the most urgent demands of the workers. We did everything we could to restore economic life. If our degree of success did not accord with our wishes, then the circumstances that prevented us from doing so must be properly judged . . .[5]

This speech was many things but it was certainly not the speech of a revolutionary, of someone creating a new world from scratch, with confidence and passion and preparedness to risk all for the chance of a bright future. In fact, there was an air of mild apology about parts of the speech. The phrase 'insolvency administrators' said it all.

Behind Ebert's assurances to the newly elected deputies of the Republic's constituent assembly was an awareness that, for the new Germany to work, it had to offer its citizens a better life than the previous regime. The Social Democratic Party itself had spent the previous half-century promising that, when it won power, it would transform life for the mass of Germans, providing work, social welfare, equality and prosperity within a framework of ideal socialist democracy.

Excluded from power while the German Empire lasted, the Social Democratic Party and its members had come, over more than four decades, to form a parallel society within society. Inside this sheltered environment flourished paradisiacal, even fantastic imaginings of what life would be like when the day of proletarian power finally arrived. The party had never planned on carrying out the transition to this ideal state under the circumstances of a catastrophic lost war. Nor had it foreseen taking power in a nation exhausted by war, heavily loaded with debt, excluded from world markets and threatened with heavy reparations, and half-starved thanks to a ruthless blockade that continued even after the armistice. Worst of all, although the end of the monarchy had been welcome to many Germans at the time of the Kaiser's abdication, the nation was already subject to bitter political and social divisions that promised only to get worse.

A late twentieth-century American political fixer would invent the slogan 'It's the economy, stupid' to express the reality of how elections were decided. There were many other factors responsible for the wild and ultimately tragic ride that would follow the establishment of the First German Republic, but ultimately the economy would indeed dictate how those factors played out.

As for the value of the German currency, it was relatively well placed in the spring of 1918 at a little over five marks to the dollar. By the time Herr Ebert made his less than certain speech to the National Assembly at the beginning of 1919, it was running at 8.20, and the direction of movement was downwards.

6

Fourteen Points

Although the fighting on the Western Front ceased at 11 a.m. on 11 November 1918, the war did not actually end on that day. Technically, it merely paused. The armistice that had been signed early on the same morning, shortly after 5 a.m., was a time-limited agreement, valid for only thirty-six days from that date. The armistice could be – and was – extended by agreement several times until the last belligerent power ratified the peace treaty in January 1920, although the constant threat of resumption of hostilities remained until that final hour.

There was another respect in which the armistice was far from representing a return to 'normality'. Among the Fourteen Points originally proposed by President Wilson as a basis for a fair and lasting peace had been 'freedom of the seas in peace and in war'. During the increasingly ill-tempered exchange of notes preceding the armistice, it had nonetheless been made clear that freedom of the seas would not apply until the conclusion of a peace treaty. This meant that the blockade on all seaborne trade between Germany and the rest of the world, enforced by the British and French navies since 1915, would continue even after the guns fell silent. In other words, Germans would continue to go hungry for an indefinite period to come, and, furthermore, be barred from pursuing the foreign trade through which it could actually pay to feed itself.

Both the insult and the injury were increased by the fact that a sub-clause in the armistice agreement stipulated that 'The Allies and the United States contemplate the provisioning of Germany during the armistice to the extent as shall be found necessary'.[1]

This left the question for the Entente and the Americans (and, indeed, everyone else) to 'contemplate'. What would be considered 'necessary'? The answer was, initially at least, just about nothing. Even though, after German protests, an agreement was reached that allowed food imports, in return for Allied control over 2.5 million tons of German cargo space,[2] the months of nit-picking argument that followed further delayed any progress, stoking (and providing justification for) German resentments. The French in particular refused for the next several months to countenance the idea of the German government importing food for its needy population.[3]

So the end of the fighting would bring no relief. During the period of eight months or so during which the blockade continued after the armistice, Germany would protest repeatedly, and with justice, that the Allied stranglehold not only conflicted with the spirit of the armistice but continued to inflict unnecessary suffering on the country's innocents, especially its poor and its children. It would be well into the new year before some controls were relaxed, and even then the concessions were motivated by anti-Bolshevik political calculation on the part of the victors, rather than pure humanitarianism. And what extra food could be imported by the German government, against payment in gold, turned out, in any case, to be too little, too late.

Of course, not everyone in Germany went hungry. By 1918, few German civilians' lives were not to some extent touched by encounters with the black market. Farmers, manufacturers and retailers had all become adept at circumventing the myriad wartime regulations and restrictions. But those who bought on the black market had to be able to pay the prices that market demanded.

The question of whether Germany was 'really' starving played an important role in the debates on the Entente side about lifting the blockade, or at least supplying the defeated population with foodstuffs. Military missions started conducting visits of inspection, an important part of whose remit was to ascertain how bad (or otherwise) things were in Germany under the continued blockade.

One such military mission, a British one, visited Berlin in February 1919. The three officers involved set off from Cologne, now occupied by the British under the armistice agreement, at the beginning of the month and stayed for nine days at the luxurious Hotel Adlon on Unter den Linden. There they found 'no sign of want of anything'. Dinner in the hotel restaurant consisted of mock turtle soup, boiled turbot and potatoes, followed by a large plate of veal and vegetables and salad, stewed apples and coffee. Price eighteen marks.[4]

The mission found likewise other parts of the city where – for a price – meat, fish and other palatable foods could be had. Other visits, however, to working-class areas and to orphanages and hospitals, did show serious shortages and resultant health problems. And, tellingly, given the currency's escalating inflationary tendencies, even at the Adlon the staff were, according to the officers' report, glad to be rewarded with leftover British military rations as gratuities. These were 'evidently much more acceptable than money would have been'.[5]

Reporters from Allied countries also began to visit Germany again, for the first time since before August 1914, initially tending to stay in the Allied-occupied areas of western Germany, which were not entirely typical of the whole country. All the same, one of their chief tasks seemed to be to judge, on their readers' behalf, the state of the German economy, of the food supply, and of the population's general health.

The tone of their comments veered between the fairly sympathetic and the pitilessly hostile. In fact, even a liberal paper such as the British *Manchester Guardian* could print material that seemed inclined towards an extraordinary callousness in its attitude to the suffering of the defeated Germans.

In the second week of January 1919, one of the *Manchester Guardian*'s correspondents reported on the sorry state of British prisoners of war still in German hands, who, it was claimed, were 'in so feeble and demoralised a condition when brought in that they were like dumb animals, hardly speaking and incapable even of showing joy at their rescue. It was not until they had a meal that a French officer turned on "God Save the King!" on a gramophone . . . it was a moving sight to watch their haggard faces brighten as they heard the familiar tune.' The reporter went on to compare this with what he claimed to be the condition of the Germans. 'Everywhere I have been during the journey of 250 miles on both banks of the Rhine I have seen no sign of food shortage.' He continued:

At Mainz the cafés serve delicious creamy cakes in unlimited quantities. London had not seen such luxuries for a long while until the armistice was signed, and no one needs to remember that here the blockade is still maintained, and that the food one gets now is what the Germans have been having right through the war.

When they complain of shortage, most Germans mean shortage compared with the vast and superfluous quantities they used to eat in peace, and instead of affecting health unfavourably the restrictions, such as they were, that our blockade imposed have probably lengthened many a German life which dyspepsia or fatty degeneration of the heart would have brought to an untimely end.[6]

What the reporter ignored (or, viewed more charitably, perhaps did not know) was that the French authorities, hoping that the inhabitants of the occupied Rhineland could be seduced into a pro-French attitude, possibly even willingness to secede from Germany altogether, had abolished all trade restrictions for their zone. The Allied blockade did not, in fact, apply in the area concerned. As a British official recollected some years later, 'We regarded the occupied territory at that time for trading purposes as if it were part of France or Belgium.'[7]

More balanced reports pointed to the supply problems which had further exacerbated the shortages since the end of the war, especially outside the occupied areas.

Throughout Germany . . . all large manufacturing centres and industrial concentrations of population are suffering for the simple reason
that the hinterlands of supplies have been cut off. The general political
upheaval in Germany and on her borders has thrown a network of
barriers across the complicated transport systems which used to minister to the needs of these thickly populated areas, and the populations
consequently find themselves shut up in narrow little compartments
of territory, which cannot produce nearly enough to supply them,
and where consequently they are in danger of starving . . .[8]

A correspondent who went under the soubriquet of 'An English-
woman in Germany' reported from the spa and casino centre of
Wiesbaden, a haunt of pre-war international high society. Although
her article was headlined 'Wiesbaden Still a Luxury Town', there was
a surprising degree of nuance in her observations, and a recognition
of post-war economic realities.

The people do not look ill-fed; the children perhaps have a somewhat
pinched appearance, but not more than might be the case in our own
East End. Yet the prices tell a tale, and one wonders how the poor
live at all, both as regards food and as regards clothes. Here are a few
prices I noticed in a walk through the streets of Wiesbaden:-
    A plate of ham, 12 marks; brawn, 19 marks a pound; small tin of
paté de foie gras, 16 marks; tea, 37 marks per pound; cotton stockings,
10 marks (children have been allowed four pairs per year); muslin,
40 marks; crêpe de chine, 60 marks; boots (not all leather) 150 marks;
zephyr,* 10.50 per metre; madapollam,† 9.50 per metre; butter, nominally, 30 marks a pound.[9]

'. . . butter, nominally', as the reporter explained, because in fact
butter seemed available only in exchange for commodities such as

* Probably refers to a lightweight worsted cloth popular in the late nineteenth and
early twentieth centuries.
† A type of soft cloth akin to calico.

tobacco, cloth or some such. As for the state of the poor, she noted that 'half the little boys of Wiesbaden are clothed in father's uniform cut down'. And the men disabled by war? 'The German wounded, by the way,' the lady added cheerfully, 'have a most excellent crutch, which can be adjusted very easily to the various heights needed.'

In Berlin, during this harsh twilight of the blockade, fighting between the Spartacist revolutionaries and the authorities increased towards the end of the year, and got worse after the beginning of 1919. Nevertheless, what most observers noticed was the strangely normal feel of the city streets away from the actual places where political violence was occurring.

The trio of British officers noted during their visit in February 1919 that, although in a working-class district of the city they witnessed an armed clash which claimed the lives of five individuals and led to fifty injuries, the 'general public seemed . . . quite content to enjoy themselves on the edge of the precipice'. They then visited a cabaret where they saw 'a huge crowd of middle-class men and women, the majority between the ages of 35 and 50 . . . waltzing and fox-trotting and drinking extremely expensive wines'.[10]

There was no question that the German public's thirst for entertainment and pleasure was, if anything, more pronounced during the peacetime blockade. Nightclubs and dance halls, which had been officially forbidden for most of the war, returned with a vengeance once the ban was relaxed from New Year's Eve 1918. 'The public launched itself like a pack of hungry wolves into the long-forbidden pleasure,' wrote the liberal *Berliner Tageblatt* on 1 January 1919. 'Never have Berliners danced so much, and so frantically.'[11]

Leo Heller, a Berlin journalist, recalled in one of his popular books about the Berlin *demi-monde* visiting a joint called the Magic Flute, one of the nightclubs that opened in the weeks after the armistice. As Heller tells it, at the entrance to the place, waiting to pay his two marks fifty entrance fee, he met a plump Berlin lady of a certain age who seemed to be a regular customer (entrance one mark only for ladies, she told him) and who kindly offered to be his guide.

Although the room was dimly lit, Heller noticed that the woman's red silk dress was stained. 'A little spot of German champagne,' she explained, and blamed the blemish's continued existence on the shortages of cleaning agents due to the blockade. 'You know, cleaning is so expensive, business just doesn't stretch to it. Have to wait until Wilson's Fourteen Points are in the bag.' The mass of perspiring dancers, too, was representative of the time. The owner of a pub from round the corner, dancing with a woman who was not his wife. A young officer and his girlfriend strutting their stuff alongside revolutionary sailors and soldiers taking time off from the struggle: 'See, there's that tall guy, Lulatsch, with the quiff, he's a real crazy. I think he's been a Spartacist from the moment he was born. I'm just sorry for that girl, because she really cares about him.'[12]

After more than four years of war and deprivation, Germans longed for good times, and for a better life. Particularly in Berlin, the tension between political radicalism and the desire for the simple and normal produced bizarre contrasts.

So, for instance, as the first post-war Christmas approached, there were bloody battles in central Berlin between the revolutionary sailors, now organised into the several thousand-strong so-called 'People's Marine Division' and based in the Marstall (royal stables) opposite the Stadtschloss, and the few loyal army units that Groener (with Ebert's secret complicity) had scraped together to provide some alternative pro-government force.

The sailors were restive because they had not been paid – the government insisted that they could only give them their money if they put themselves under the orders of the War Ministry and evacuated the area round the Stadtschloss. This the sailors refused to do, because they suspected – correctly – that counter-revolutionary plans were afoot. As a consequence, on 23 December the sailors stormed the Reich Chancellery, arresting Ebert and his fellow People's Commissioners, cutting the main phone lines, and also holding Otto Wels hostage in the Marstall. They were now promised their pay, but by then several of their number had been killed and the sailors wanted justice, and were not prepared to abandon their gains before they got it.

Things underwent a further escalation the next day. Groener, directing what was left of his army from the High Command's wartime headquarters at Schloss Wilhelmshöhe in Kassel, almost 300 kilometres to the west of Berlin, had managed to talk with the beleaguered Ebert via their secure phone line, which remained unknown to the revolutionaries. The general and the politician agreed that the sailors must be evicted from the Stadtschloss and environs.

Acting on orders from Groener, loyal army units, relatively small in number but equipped with heavy weapons, began to advance against the sailors' rifles and machine guns. Serious fighting broke out, in the course of which the armed sailors, plus a substantial number of Berlin workers who had joined them, beat the regulars soundly. The once all-powerful army was forced into a humiliating retreat. With the government – and arguably the whole of Berlin – now at their mercy, on Christmas Eve the revolutionaries got their pay, and kept their headquarters.[13]

Astonishingly, a few hours later, the victorious revolutionaries put away their weapons, evacuated the occupied buildings, including the Reich Chancellery, and went home for Christmas. It was a Christmas without much in the way of festive food or candles or decorations, but it was the first one for five years unscarred by war, and for these men and their friends and families, to celebrate it together was the most important thing imaginable.

Many of those men, along with ordinary Germans all over the country, hoped that 1919 would see, as the lady in the red dress had put it to Leo Heller, 'Wilson's Fourteen Points in the bag' – a just peace for the new Germany in a just world.

7

Bloodhounds

The blockade was maintained until the very last moment in July 1919. Some food was allowed into Germany from March onwards, but basically her nearly 70 million people were excluded from world markets, from food and raw materials, for almost three-quarters of a year after the armistice had first been signed. This insistence on the Allies' part was no less than a ruthless power-political exercise designed to ensure, whatever the cost in human suffering, that Germany would have no alternative but to accede to the terms of the coming peace treaty.

Meanwhile, the Reich, far from uniting to face the post-war dangers, was riven by continuing political violence.

The Christmas break was used by the government and its allies in the army to regroup and ensure that they were not caught unawares again. The High Command set to work reorganising what forces it could from among the defeated army to act as a bolster for 'order' in post-revolutionary Germany. By the beginning of 1919, a word started to impinge on the public consciousness: 'Freikorps' (Free Corps).

The vast majority of demobilised German soldiers, disillusioned with war and influenced by the revolutionary passions sweeping the country, had either made their own way home from the front, or had disappeared, as soon as humanly possible, back to their communities and families. Nevertheless, not all their comrades felt the same aversion to conflict. With the unofficial approval of the army leadership, anti-revolutionary officers and men loyal to them had begun setting up recruitment and training camps, including in the countryside surrounding Berlin, where those not yet tired of bearing arms, or determined to oppose the revolution, could gather and plan a fight back against the subversives who threatened all they held dear. Many thousands of men were attracted to these ad hoc groups, which rapidly expanded into a force of up to 400,000 fighters. Though individual units gave themselves different names, they became known collectively as the Freikorps.

The name Freikorps had a pedigree going back to the wars of the eighteenth century, and, more importantly for the men of 1918, to the Napoleonic era and the so-called 'war of liberation' fought by German patriots against French occupation. The growth of a resistance movement after 1807 had led to the formation of informal volunteer units, including many students and intellectuals, who fought more out of patriotic idealism than for pay. Initially a guerrilla force, these grew into something resembling conventional army units. In this role they played an important role, in concert with the regular military, in driving the enemy from German soil during the years 1813–15 and bringing about Napoleon's eventual defeat. The tradition continued after Bonaparte's fall, with the uniformed student duelling associations dubbing themselves 'Freikorps' in honour of their fathers' and grandfathers' struggle. However, what had begun in the 1820s as liberal organisations took on a reactionary tone as the nineteenth century progressed and the middle and upper middle classes increasingly came to identify with authoritarian Prussian values.

In October 1918, there had been talk in High Command circles, in response to growing political unrest, of setting up volunteer units, which might prove useful should a revolution threaten. These would be led by young, patriotic officers, and made up of other ranks considered to be politically reliable. It was an idea that particularly appealed to an ambitious thirty-six-year-old major, Kurt von Schleicher, who had advanced to the position of head of the political department of the High Command. Schleicher, soon to rise to prominence as one

of the post-war era's most notorious political soldiers, found it hard
to convince his traditionally minded superiors. However, others, in
the chaos of the Eastern Front (where Germany's eastern borders were
threatened by Bolsheviks and Polish nationalists) and in the disturbed
industrial areas of central and western Germany, where to conservative military eyes the socialist radicals were already running amok,
began to have the same thought.[1]

In fact, it was Major Schleicher who had taken the call when Ebert
had used the secret telephone connection at the Reich Chancellery
to contact Groener in the small hours of 23/24 December 1918. The
two men spoke again after the debacle that followed the attempt to
crush the People's Marine Division. According to Groener's account,
when asked what he planned to do, the defeated Ebert had replied:
'Above all, I'm going to some friends' place to get a good night's sleep,
which I'm in dire need of.' Then he continued, as yet unaware that
the sailors and the other revolutionaries had, in fact, decided to take
a Christmas break: 'Let Liebknecht occupy the Chancellery if he
wants. He'll be landing in an empty nest.' Other eyewitnesses, according to at least one writer, report that Ebert was actually all but
panic-stricken, weighing up whether he should take himself and the
rest of the government out of Berlin, and muttering, 'We simply can't
go on like this. We simply can't govern like this.'[2] A sentiment with
which it is hard not to sympathise.

The Christmas Eve confrontation, and the defeat of the government's few loyal troops by armed sailors and workers, revealed
plainly the impotence of the forces of order in Berlin. In the second
week of December, the Council of People's Commissioners had
agreed to raise a force of volunteers loyal to the new Republic,
organised along 'democratic' lines (with elected officers and so on),
to defend the gains of the revolution. However, two weeks later
little had been done to facilitate this urgent task, despite widespread
support in the big cities and the ready availability of working-class
men who had received military training during the war. Modest
progress was made, but not enough.

And then, a few days after the Christmas Eve confrontation, the Independent Socialist commissioners left the governing Council in disgust at the use (however unsuccessful) of the army against the workers, leaving only the Majority Social Democrat representatives. The rump commission simply co-opted two of their own number to the Council, making it exclusively Majority Social Democrat in complexion. The broad coalition of democratic socialists that had taken charge of the revolution back in November had lasted a mere seven weeks.[3] Ebert and his colleagues, though weakened in one way, could now at least act according to what passed as their convictions.

The new year, 1919, brought more incidents, more fears of chaos. The diarist Count Harry Kessler wrote on New Year's Day of having dinner in a restaurant where the meal was interrupted by the irruption from the street of a delegation of revolutionary waiters, with red tabs in their hats and carrying a red flag, representing restaurant staff on strike in other parts of Berlin. The waiters threatened the proprietor that unless he gave in to their demands (unspecified by Kessler) within ten minutes, they would shut the place down. Five minutes later, the deal was done. 'Blackmail completed,' the Count observed dryly, 'we could return to the matter of food.'

Places where the management refused to capitulate had been attacked and wrecked. Nor was the taste for disorder confined to pseudo-Bolsheviks. 'This afternoon,' Kessler added, 'a party of Roman Catholics together with some Protestants stormed the Religious Affairs Ministry in order to haul out the Minister. We are returning to the days of strong-arm law. The Executive is wholly powerless.'[4]

The latter case of religiously inspired violence had to do with the fact that Adolph Hoffman, the left-wing Independent Socialist and militant free-thinker appointed joint Religious Affairs and Education Minister at the time of the revolution, was threatening to abolish the role of the Church in Prussian schools. Hoffman was forced to resign almost immediately after this incident. But the real danger in Berlin at this point came, not from outraged Christians, who in any case

organised themselves in short order into a respectable political movement and got the proposed law blocked, but from the Spartacist
League – or, as it became on 1 January 1919, absorbing some other
small far-left groups, the German Communist Party.

The Spartacist League had been founded by a breakaway faction
from the Social Democratic Party in protest at its support for the war.
The most prominent Spartacist leaders, Karl Liebknecht and Rosa
Luxemburg, had both been jailed during the war for their anti-
militarist agitation. Liebknecht was freed in October during the liberal
interlude of the Prince Max government, Luxemburg on 9 November.
They immediately set about reviving the organisation, which had
begun to decline during the last months of the war.

Rosa Luxemburg, born to Jewish parents in Russian Poland in 1871,
had gained German nationality through a marriage of convenience
to a political sympathiser in 1897. A brilliant and fearless writer, political thinker and early feminist, Luxemburg became a controversial but
influential figure on the left of the Social Democratic Party after
moving to Berlin. Karl Liebknecht, born in the same year as Luxemburg, was a son of the pioneer Social Democrat and friend of Marx
and Engels, Wilhelm Liebknecht – therefore a born-and-bred member
of the 'socialist aristocracy' – and a fluent writer and propagandist.
His attempt to establish a 'socialist republic' on Bolshevik lines on 9
November had been forestalled by Scheidemann's astute declaration
of a moderate one from the balcony of the Reichstag that same day.
Moreover, even in the elections to the 'Workers' and Soldiers' Councils' in December, the Spartacists had barely managed double figures
in their number of delegates. Nonetheless, they were a powerful force
on the Berlin streets.

A lawyer in a suit, physically unprepossessing, Liebknecht suffered
from a weak voice that, like the ancient Greek orator Demosthenes,
he had to train for years before it became a serviceable, even powerful
political tool. Nevertheless, he commanded fanatical loyalty from his
followers. *Die Weltbühne* captured a snapshot of Liebknecht in mid-
December 1918:

Did you see him speak from the back of a heavy delivery truck to a packed crowd? Did you see machine guns being set up near to him, for his protection? Did you see, amidst the swarthy faces of the audience, the ominous figures keeping watch, their index fingers curled around the triggers of the revolvers they keep in their pockets, ready at any moment to sacrifice their own or another's life for their hero, up there on that makeshift tribune? Did you feel the uncanny suggestiveness radiating out from Liebknecht to that crowd . . . when he spoke? His eyes roll wildly in his head, then protrude, as if endeavouring to bore with the full force of his fanaticism into everyone's brains. He gesticulates constantly. Soon he rips open his jacket, strikes himself on the chest with a passionate gesture, and says – no, cries, shouts, screams, shrieks: 'Here, brothers, comrades, shoot me down on the spot if what I tell you is not true!' Then, the next moment, he runs his hand through his hair, snaps his head forward and tosses out the words: 'To the lamp post*' with the bloodhounds Ebert and Scheidemann!⁵

As for the 'bloodhounds', on the morning of 4 January, realising that the time had come to secure some measure of state force in the face of the likes of Liebknecht and his armed supporters, Ebert travelled to the army base at Zossen, a little less than fifty kilometres' southward drive from the centre of Berlin. Accompanying Ebert was the newly appointed 'People's Commissioner for Defence', Gustav Noske. Noske, originally a basket weaver by trade, who like so many Social Democratic leaders had risen from humble origins through the trade union apparatus and the party press, had been sent to keep control of the revolutionary situation in Kiel at the beginning of November. His success with the revolutionary sailors on the Baltic put him at Ebert's right hand in the struggle against the far left that followed.

The purpose of Ebert and Noske's trip to Zossen was to meet a certain Major General Maercker. Maercker, a veteran of Germany's

* i.e. to the gallows.

pre-war colonial conflicts and a divisional commander during the
latter part of the European war, had started organising and training
a Freikorps on the lines of the units already operating on the eastern
frontiers. In his case, however, it was with the object of taking on the
domestic subversives rather than the Poles and the Baltic Bolsheviks.
The two Social Democrats from Berlin were by all accounts aston-
ished, both at being accorded a full guard of honour – unheard of for
civilian politicians before the revolution – and at the rigorous traditional discipline shown by these hand-picked loyal troops. The regular
soldiers sent against the People's Marine Division on Christmas Eve
had been ineffectual. These ones were much more impressive. Noske
was said to have clapped the much shorter Ebert on the shoulder and
said, 'Take it easy, everything's going to be all right.' He then addressed
the assembled soldiers and told them: 'The orders of your commanders are to be obeyed, even when they order the use of weapons and
hand grenades.'[6]

Meanwhile, armed rebellion had broken out in Berlin itself. The
left-socialist President of Police in the capital, Emil Eichorn, had been
dismissed but refused to leave office. Thousands came out on to the
streets to support him. Fiery speeches from leading radicals, including
Eichorn and Liebknecht, worked the crowd on the Alexanderplatz
into a climax of revolutionary fervour. Within hours, armed far-left
groups had occupied the city's media district (*Zeitungsviertel*), on
either side of the Friedrichstrasse, which for more than half a century
had been home to dozens of publications, printers and press agencies.
They seized the printing works that produced the pro-government
Social Democrat newspaper *Vorwärts* and the liberal *Berliner Tageblatt*,
the offices of several publishers, as well as the Wolff Telegraph Bureau.
The next morning, they also took over the Reich Printing Works,
where official documents – and the capital's supply of paper marks
– were produced.[7]

Despite Ebert and Noske's meetings with the warlords of the
Freikorps, the government seemed to have no physical answer to
the violence. After all, little had been done to create a force loyal

to the Republic. The next day, 5 January, when thousands of Sparta-cists* and their supporters began moving north into the government district, the pro-government forces had summoned the only weapon they had: their thousands of mainstream working-class supporters, many of whom made their way into the heart of Berlin to confront the rebels. In perhaps the last example of ingrained political solidarity among the capital's working class, when the armed Spartacists came up against the cordon of unarmed government supporters, the rebels did not shoot their way through. They were not prepared to harm their fellow workers. The Reichstag and the Chancellery did not fall.

Meanwhile, the revolutionary soldiers and sailors had declared themselves neutral, and most of the Independent leaders who had left the executive the previous week, alarmed at the situation, agreed that they should try to mediate between Ebert and his government and the rebels. Since the government demanded that the rebels evacuate the media district, and the rebels refused, this proved impossible.

It was at this crucial moment that the Council of People's Commis-sioners made the decision to put Noske in charge of bringing order to Berlin. He accepted, with the notorious words, echoing those of Liebknecht on the other side of the political divide, 'Somebody's got to play the bloodhound! I shall not shirk the responsibility!' In short order, Noske decided to bring in the Freikorps to do the job. He managed to make his way out through the Spartacist lines and then established himself in a villa in Dahlem, a leafy suburb in the south-west of Berlin, where he began work organising his Freikorps allies and planning the retaking of the city.

The serious fighting went on for a little over a week. In fact, the actual battle would not be decided by the Freikorps. A combination of pro-Republic loyalists who had managed to organise themselves into a reasonably effective fighting force, supported by loyal regular

* Although the Spartacus League had formally merged into the German Communist Party a few days earlier, the uprising was known at the time and to posterity as the 'Spartacist' uprising, and so the description is used throughout.

army units, reconquered the streets and buildings seized by the Spartacists and their allies. Again, the fighting was bizarrely localised, and
the life of the city went on around it in an eerily normal fashion.
Harry Kessler, who lived not far from the epicentre of the uprising,
made it his business throughout these days to get out and about,
making notes for his diary. Sometimes his accounts read like war
reports, sometimes like travel journalism. He wrote on 8 January:

> At four o'clock I was in the Friedrichstrasse. There was a good deal
> of traffic and a lot of people stood discussing matters in small groups
> when suddenly there was a sound of shooting from the Unter den
> Linden end. Yet the Leipziger Strasse, except for its closed shops,
> looked perfectly normal and the big cafés on Potsdamer Platz were
> open, brightly lit and doing business as usual.
>   . . . At half past seven I had a meal in the Fürstenhof. The iron
> gates were just being shut because a Spartacus attack was expected
> on the Potsdamer Railway Station opposite. Single shots were drop-
> ping all the time. As I left, about nine, street vendors with cigarettes,
> malt goodies, and soap were still crying their wares. I looked for a
> moment into the boldly lit Café Vaterland. Despite the fact that any
> moment bullets might whistle through the windows, the band was
> playing, the tables were full, and the lady in the cigarette-booth smiled
> as winsomely at her customers as in the sunniest days of peace.[8]

Four days later, the last of the rebel fighters had been cleared from
the area or taken into captivity, and the far-left bid to control Berlin
had been defeated. The so-called 'Spartacist Uprising' seems, in fact,
to have been a strange and rather disorganised combination of
Bolshevik-style *coup d'état* on the part of a militant minority and an
extended protest – arguably justified – on the part of many Berliners,
especially in the working-class areas, against the way that the timidity
and conservatism of Ebert and his fellow moderate socialist leaders
was already allowing the old system to make a comeback.[9]

The Freikorps did eventually enter the city but not until the fighting had all but died down, making its actions all but superfluous. On 11 January, Noske marched at the head of Maercker's troops as they advanced through the suburbs into the heart of Berlin. Over the next days, further units, many newly formed, made their way into Berlin. The southern suburbs and the centre were occupied. The working-class districts, where resistance might have been expected, were left alone for now.

One large Freikorps unit, which called itself 'The Guard-Cavalry-Rifle Division', took up quarters at the splendid Eden Hotel, on the Tiergarten opposite the Berlin Zoo, and put signs up outside the building that declared: 'The Guard-Cavalry-Rifle Division has marched into Berlin. Berliners! The Division promises you that it will not leave the capital until order has been completely restored.'[10]

On 15 January, Karl Liebknecht and Rosa Luxemburg were arrested at the flat of a sympathiser and taken to the Eden Hotel. Luxemburg, who had warned against a premature 'adventure' such as the Spartacist uprising became, was questioned and brutally beaten, as was Liebknecht. Then, on the orders of a certain Captain Waldemar Pabst, they were hurried out of the hotel by a side entrance, where waiting soldiers struck theirs skulls violently with rifle butts. The dazed, even half-unconscious revolutionaries were then bundled into separate cars and driven away into the Tiergarten.

The car bearing Rosa Luxemburg had travelled only a few metres when she was shot in the head. The car stopped on a bridge, from which she was thrown into the Landwehr Canal. Her body would not be found until the end of May. In Liebknecht's case, he was ordered out of the car and immediately shot in the back of the head. His body was then returned to the vehicle and driven to a mortuary, where it was labelled 'corpse of an unknown man'. Eventually the body was retrieved, and Liebknecht was buried along with thirty or so other Spartacist dead in a mass ceremony on 25 January 1919.

The statement that went out to the press was that Liebknecht had been 'shot while trying to escape', while Luxemburg was said to have been abducted from the vehicle by a mob and spirited away to some place unknown. Both stories were lies. They had been murdered by anti-revolutionary Freikorps officers, probably with the connivance of Noske. Neither, it seems, had been directly involved in the violence – certainly not Rosa Luxemburg – but their symbolic importance was such that their liquidation became a priority.[11]

The crushing of the uprising was an important event in itself, but the fact and manner of the Spartacist leaders' deaths was more ominously significant still. With the summary murder of Liebknecht and Luxemburg, a line had been crossed. When arrested, Rosa Luxemburg had packed a small suitcase with her belongings, believing herself to be facing yet another spell of imprisonment, something to which she, like Liebknecht, had become hardened. The fate to which she and her co-conspirator were so brutally consigned by Pabst's killers showed what the new, angry post-war right wing was capable of and presaged a quarter of a century of savagery to come. Their deaths also created two martyrs for the German far left, the potency of whose legends remains extraordinarily strong well into our own century.

The January uprising was not the last radical leftist rebellion in Germany. There would be more. In fact, throughout most of the late winter and spring of 1919, Germany underwent a sporadic but bloody civil war that would leave a terrible legacy of bitterness and ensure that what had previously been a united socialist movement could never be put back together again. But what the cruel ends suffered by Liebknecht and Luxemburg showed was that, two months after the November revolution, the reactionary militaristic powers in the land were on their way back, albeit in alliance, for the moment, with Germany's new ostensibly socialist masters.

Like the respectable townsfolk in a western film who hire a gunslinger to protect them, only to find that he turns against them once the job is done, the rulers of the new Republic had created a monster that they would soon find they could not control.

8

Diktat

Between the suppression of the Spartacist uprising in mid-January 1919 and the signing of the armistice in July, the German revolution was stopped in its tracks. Morgan Philips Price of the *Manchester Guardian*, who had been won over to a pro-Bolshevik position while reporting from Russia in 1917–18, wrote gloomily on 17 January 1919:

> A deathly quiet prevails in the city. The quiet of the grave. Military patrols on streets, artillery posted everywhere. Armed White Guards being organised by a certain Reinhardt go about arresting and terrorising at pleasure. Several of my friends disappeared. A fine condition for eve of election for the National Assembly.[1]

Nonetheless, on 19 January, the nation voted freely for the first time since 1912. Eighty-three per cent of a much-enlarged electorate of 36,700,000 took part in elections for the Constituent National Assembly that would frame and pass a constitution for the new Republic.

The reason why the electorate now comprised more than half the population was that women had been enfranchised in November 1918 by decree of the Council of People's Commissioners. Not that this was necessarily a total victory for feminism. One young woman made an early discovery, knocking on doors for one of the non-socialist parties in one of the less prosperous parts of the city, that men often still ruled the family when it came to politics, a fact that would remain true well into the twentieth century all over the democratic world. In a block of modest flats, one housewife opened the door to her and, when asked how she planned to vote, called out over her shoulder, 'What are we voting?' A male voice answered, 'Scheidemann' (Social Democrat). The middle-class young woman pressed a leaflet for her party into the woman's hands, assuring her: 'Read this. Even if the gentleman votes for Scheidemann, you can choose another party.'[2]

Male or female, to the republican government's satisfaction, Germans voted overwhelmingly against further radical change. Ebert and Scheidemann's Majority Social Democrats were favoured by 37.9 per cent of the electorate. The Independent Socialists, tainted in the eyes of some voters by the association of their more radical elements with continued street violence, got only 7.6 per cent. The rest of the vote was divided between the Catholic Centre Party and its Bavarian ally (19.7 per cent), the left liberal German Democratic Party (18.5 per cent), the conservative-nationalist German National People's Party (10.3 per cent) and the right liberal German People's Party (only 4.4 per cent). The Communist Party had decided at its founding congress three weeks earlier to boycott the Assembly elections. Ironically, the delegates had gone against the recommendation of both Karl Liebknecht and Rosa Luxemburg, who paid with their lives for the party's decision to take the revolutionary road to the exclusion of all others.

The elections to the Constituent Assembly, scheduled to come together in Weimar at the beginning of February, were an impressive early expression of support for democracy. Only around a fifth of the vote went to expressly anti-republican or monarchist parties. But it was not a vote for socialism. Between them, the Majority and the Independent Social Democrats had received just over 45 per cent of the total vote. Even had they been able to go into coalition together (unlikely after their recent bitter differences), there would still have been no majority to push socialist measures through parliament.

The National Assembly met in early February at the old Court

Theatre (later National Theatre) in Weimar. Ebert was elected President of the Reich, and Scheidemann its first Chancellor (though, since the country still had no formal constitution, actually he was originally given the title of *Reichsministerpräsident*, or Reich Prime Minister, and only his successor took the title of Chancellor).[3] The ministers were drawn from the Social Democratic Party, the German Democratic Party and the Catholic Centre Party.

For now, apart from Scheidemann, the most important members of the cabinet so far as the outside world was concerned were Matthias Erzberger (Centre), Minister Without Portfolio (but responsible for overseeing treaty negotiations with the Allies), and as Foreign Minister Ulrich Count von Brockdorff-Rantzau, an aristocratic career diplomat reckoned close to, though not a member of, the Democratic Party. Otherwise, Social Democrats, mainly former trade unionists, dominated the ministries involved in the economy, industry and food supply. The ever more controversial Gustav Noske's position was formalised. He was appointed Minister for the Armed Forces, soon to be known as the Reichswehr.

As winter turned to spring, the inter-Allied discussions in Paris about the terms to be presented to Germany seemed to go on for ever. Meanwhile, the German economy groaned under the weight of attempting to reintegrate millions of men into an economy still excluded by the Allied blockade from post-war international markets. Men were returning after years of suffering and danger, and they were demanding their old jobs back, at new and better wages and under improved conditions.

At the same time, there were further far-left uprisings all over the Reich – another, even bloodier revolt in Berlin in March, this time including the People's Marine Division and blamed on the resurgent Spartacists, which cost the lives of 500 government soldiers and more than 1,000 civilians; further uprisings in the Ruhr industrial area, where militants had formed a 'Red Army'; in the ancient port of Bremen (where an attempt to set up a 'Soviet Republic' was suppressed with particular brutality by Freikorps units); in the industrial conurbations of Saxony and Thuringia. The chaos was most extreme in Munich, where the Social Democrat Prime Minister was assassinated by a monarchist fanatic and the far left and the anarchists took charge for a heady few weeks of Bolshevik-style 'dictatorship of the proletariat'.

The so-called 'Munich Soviet' led in short order to a savage counter-terror of the far right, during which the left and its supporters, perceived or real, were massacred wholesale. Six hundred and six alleged 'revolutionaries' were executed within a matter of days – including twenty-one young men who lived in a Catholic Apprentices' Hostel, who, because they were young workers, were presumed to be 'Spartacists'.[4] Many of the executions were officially classified as 'fatal accidents'.[5] If captured, members of the far-left 'Soviet' government were brutally treated. The Bavarian writer and teacher Josef Hofmiller described the fate of the deposed Defence Minister, Wilhelm Reichart:

> Reichart . . . was recognised . . . by a soldier whose sweetheart had lost her life during one of the uprisings. This government soldier immediately gave him a terrible blow to the face. To which the man replied: 'I am Reichart, Minister of War of the Soviet Republic.' Another blow to the face. The soldiers made a sport of forcing him again and again to cry out: 'I am Reichart, Minister of War of the Soviet Republic', after which they repeatedly hit him in the face, so that by the end he had a terribly swollen head. Then they put him on a train, and at each station he was made to shout out of the window: 'I am Reichart, Minister of War of the Soviet Republic', upon which he was again repeatedly beaten about the head.[6]

Whether the far left could ever have taken control of the entire Reich is doubtful. Even in Berlin, in March 1919 – a much better planned and executed attempt at a coup than the poorly organised affair that cost Liebknecht and Luxemburg their lives two months earlier – the revolutionaries never seriously threatened the centre of power. Their main achievement was to divide the German capital into two bitterly hostile camps – the middle and upper class 'West' of Berlin and the proletarian 'East', where the Spartacists had their strongholds – and to push the new government into a ruthless frame of mind.

Noske, the socialist who had accepted the role of 'bloodhound' and now seemed to be playing it with a little too much relish, issued an order during the second Berlin uprising that any civilians found 'in the act of armed conflict against the Government forces' should be shot on the spot. Once passed through the chain of command of the Freikorps, this order turned out to be open to, shall we say, free interpretation. Like their comrades in Munich, reactionary Freikorps commanders such as Captain Pabst of the Guard-Cavalry-Rifle Division clearly saw this as carte blanche to rid the country of dangerous subversives and Communist riff-raff, and the instruction was conveyed to the ordinary Freikorps members in that spirit.

Harry Kessler, appalled at the violence of the government's response, wrote that Noske was 'ensconced in the Ministry of War behind barbed wire. With seven officers, twelve non-commissioned officers, and fifty rankers as his personal guard, just like Nicholas II* or the tyrant Dionysus.'[7]

For the next four or more years, all the same, the danger of armed rebellion from the left or right persisted in Germany. One problem was the ready availability of arms and ammunition, a consequence in part of widespread desertion from the army in November 1918, followed, under circumstances of less than perfect discipline, by mass demobilisation and the disbandment of most regular units. The radical artist George Grosz, at that time a strong Spartacist sympathiser, recalled the near-anarchic situation in 1919:

Guns and ammunition were freely on sale. My cousin, who was released from the army a short time after me, brought me a complete machine-gun one day. I could pay for it in easy instalments, he said. And did I perhaps know anyone who might be interested in buying

* i.e. the last Tsar of Russia.

two more machine-guns and a small field-piece? (He was, of course, thinking of my links with certain political organisations, which had started to arm themselves against their rivals.)[8]

Certainly, while lacking true mass support, the Spartacists and their Communist successors could never complain about being short of weaponry.

Meanwhile, the world looked on. Most Germans were not involved in the fighting. Most wanted peace, employment and the rule of law, and supported measures necessary to achieve those things. This was even true of many who joined the Freikorps, often remaining with the colours for quite short periods of time. In some cases, these relatively brief spells in uniform resemble those experienced by armed volunteer police units at many historical junctures and in many places, from the early nineteenth-century English Yeomanry and Special Constables, to the *Garde nationale* in France, or the National Guard in America.

Hermann Zander, for instance, still in his early twenties, joined a Freikorps unit, 'Bahrenfeld', in the Hamburg suburb of Altona in June 1919, along with several of his colleagues from the bank where he worked as a clerk. Hamburg had recently been subjected to fierce rioting, during which Communist-led groups had seized a number of the city's public buildings, including the prison and the city hall. The Freikorps unit, composed of four companies, totalled around 120 men. Zander's company was assigned to guard the docks, while the other three companies took part in an attempt to drive the 'Reds' out of the city hall. 'The other companies stormed the city hall, but then lost it again to the Reds. We couldn't make headway against the Reds.' The Mayor of Hamburg, a Majority Social Democrat, then called in the Reichswehr. Regular troops under General von Lettow-Vorbeck, a war hero who had waged a successful guerrilla campaign against the British in the former German East Africa, finally cleared the city hall. There were mass arrests and some deaths. 'This military episode ended for me with a parade on the Spielbudenplatz on Saint Pauli,' Zander concluded breezily and with a minimum of fanaticism.[9]

Many, perhaps the majority, including those who, like Zander, took to arms on a purely temporary basis, hoped that beyond the chaos and the violence lay not just an orderly, prosperous Germany but a fair and reasonable new world organised along the lines proposed under President Wilson's Fourteen Points. 'Germans,' as one distinguished historian of the Versailles Treaty wrote, 'clutched at the Fourteen Points like a life-raft.'[10] An American diplomat in Paris, Ellis Dresel, wrote:

> The people had been led to believe that Germany had been unluckily beaten after a fine and clean fight, owing to the ruinous effect of the blockade on the home morale, and perhaps some too far-reaching plans of her leaders, but that happily President Wilson could be appealed to, and would arrange a compromise peace satisfactory to Germany.

This was a delusion. What faced them was the very opposite of a 'compromise peace'. The truth was that the President Wilson of the Fourteen Points had by the spring of 1919 largely given way to an altogether more vengeful American leader, one rarely mentioned in many history books. It was this version of Wilson, appalled by the crushing treaties inflicted by Germany on Russia at Brest-Litovsk and Romania at Bucharest in early 1918, who told his colleagues that the treaty must rightly be 'very severe indeed':

> I must say that though in many respects harsh, I do not think that it is on the whole unjust in the circumstances . . . inevitably my thought goes back to the very great offence against civilisation which the German state committed and the necessity for making it evident once and for all that such things can only lead to the most severe punishment.[11]

The German delegates, led by Erzberger and Brockdorff-Rantzau, travelled to Paris at the end of April 1919, ready to be told, after months of discussion by the bickering victors, of the conditions to be imposed on the defeated Reich. They were kept waiting for more than a week before the fateful day finally arrived.

The date was 7 May 1919, a little less than two months after the suppression of the March uprising in Berlin, and only four days after so-called 'white' forces had entered Munich and bloodily extinguished the remnants of the 'red' republic of Bavaria.

The German delegates to the peace conference had been summoned by the Allies to a large meeting room at the Trianon Palace Hotel in Versailles. Here the venerable French Prime Minister, Georges Clemenceau – at the beginning of his political career, mayor of the Paris district of Montmartre during the German siege of the city in 1870–71 – would publicly inform them of the peace terms being demanded by the victors. There would, it was clear, be no discussion or negotiation, which was why Versailles would become known to the German public as the *Diktat*, or dictated peace.

The space had, it seemed, been arranged so that the delegates of the defeated Reich would be seated at a table facing the Allied representatives and surrounded by those from many nations, military men, journalists, all hanging on the Germans' reaction. Brockdorff-Rantzau had apparently seen the Germans' pre-ordained table described in a French newspaper as 'the prisoners' dock'. He led his delegation into the building, determined to avoid humiliation: 'All eyes turned to the door as they entered, "stiff, awkward-looking figures",' writes Margaret MacMillan. 'Brockdorff-Rantzau, said a witness, "looked ill, drawn and nervous", and was sweating.' There was a brief hesitation and the crowd, observing a courtesy from the vanished world of 1914, rose to its feet. Brockdorff-Rantzau and Clemenceau bowed to each other.

Clemenceau opened the proceedings. Without the slightest sign of nerves, he spoke coldly, outlining the main headings of the treaty. 'The hour has struck for the weighty settlement of our account,' he told the Germans. 'You asked us for peace. We are disposed to grant it to you.' He threw out his words, said one of the German delegates, 'as if in concentrated anger and disdain, and . . . from the very outset, for the Germans, made any reply quite futile.'[12]

The terms were crushing. Germany would lose 13 per cent of her territory and 10 per cent of her population. Moreover, contrary to the 'self-determination' clauses in President Wilson's Fourteen Points, the German-speaking territories of the now defunct Austrian Empire – the rump of Austria proper, including Vienna, and the German-speaking parts of Bohemia – were forbidden to unite with the German Republic. This, despite their inhabitants' express desire to do so, given that their lands were not properly politically or economically viable without the non-German areas they had long dominated, now granted to the new post-war states of Czechoslovakia, Poland and Yugoslavia. It was probably unrealistic for Germans to expect that their country would actually be allowed to *gain* territory as a result of defeat, but then the fine American talk of a just peace had, in its way, encouraged an element of wishful thinking in the vanquished.

And that was not all. Germany must also demilitarise. Reparations to the victors, while not yet definitively fixed, would amount to a sum in the hundreds of billions of gold marks, with Germany paying not just for damage to French and Belgian territory, and not just the cost of the war itself, but also the pensions of the Allied war disabled and of the war widows and orphans (this last was the British Prime Minister Lloyd George's special contribution).

Brockdorff-Rantzau, the picture (to foreign eyes) of the arrogant, stiff Prussian aristocrat, delivered a speech of protest in his (to foreign ears) unattractive, guttural German, laying great emphasis on his refusal to accept his country's responsibility for the war. This last point he clearly saw not just as a moral axiom but also as the legal basis for the coming fight against the treaty's punitive clauses. Although actually Brockdorff-Rantzau was one of the few Prussian aristocrats to welcome the new German democracy, neither his 'Junker' manner nor the substance of his speech went down well with the Allied representatives, or with Allied public opinion. As Philip Kerr, one of Lloyd George's aides, commented drily, 'At the start everybody felt a little sympathy with the Hun, but by the time Brockdorff-Rantzau had finished, most people were almost anxious to recommence the war.'[13]

There was much in the draft terms that, rightly or wrongly, disturbed and angered the German delegates and, as soon as the text of the treaty could be translated and published at home, affected their government and the overwhelming majority of their fellow Germans likewise. The so-called 'war guilt' clause (Article 231) caused especial outrage. It read:

> The Allied and Associated Governments affirm and Germany accepts the responsibility of Germany and her allies for causing all the loss and damage to which the Allied and Associated Governments and their nationals have been subjected as a consequence of the war imposed upon them by the aggression of Germany and her allies.

From a purely practical point of view, it was quite rational that the German government took issue with this clause. It was also quite logical from the Allied point of view that they included it in the first place. If Germany and her allies were not responsible for the war, then there was no moral or legal justification for the imposition of reparations, at least those going beyond actual damage to Allied territory occupied by the German army, which (see Chapter 3) was already quite considerable. Brockdorff-Rantzau realised this, and so, quite specifically, did Lloyd George, who later wrote somewhat sheepishly in his memoirs: 'I could not accept the German point of view without giving away our entire case for entering into the war.'[14]

What was less logical was the passion with which both the German elite and the general public took against the notion of 'war guilt'. It would be true to say that the clause can be interpreted as broadly 'blaming' Germany and her allies for the outbreak of the war. After all, the Allied governments had to answer to electorates that had spent more than four years suffering hardship, deprivation, and often terrible personal loss.

Oskar Münsterberg, a Jewish factory owner in Berlin, nevertheless typified the reaction of most ordinary Germans when he wrote in his diary on 8 May, after the Allied terms had been revealed, that 'all joy in living fails, one's heart falters' on this 'blackest day of the war':

Where are the fine speeches about humanity and rectitude? Where are Wilson's points, whose acceptance by the enemy and by us was followed by the armistice agreement? Has this all been a deception? Must all justice and all belief be as nothing?

It cannot be the end. For the moment it exists only on paper and life goes peacefully on, but slowly, increasing year on year, as the old reserves are used up, worry and want will make their entrance, and the entire people will face impoverishment and despair.

No, this cannot be how a state that remained undefeated in the field will meet its end! The bowstring has been stretched to breaking point, but from where will come our salvation? What would be the effect of a rejection of the treaty? A new revolution either here or abroad. There is nowhere a chink of light, only black clouds! What purpose is there left to life?[15]

Most on the Allied side saw things quite differently. Few voters, especially in France and Britain, were in the mood to accept some wishy-washy 'no-fault' formula after such a hard-won victory. 'Squeeze Germany Till the Pips Squeak' was a popular slogan in the winter of 1918–19. All the same, there is evidence that at the time the American framers of the clause – who included a young lawyer by the name of John Foster Dulles, forty years later to serve as Eisenhower's Secretary of State – were intent on simply doing the lawyerly thing and making sure their 'clients' (in this case the Allied governments) got the 'other guys' (Germany and her allies) to admit liability, as is normal in a civil case involving damages. The next article of the treaty, §232, goes on specifically to state that, notwithstanding the enemy's admission of liability in §231, 'The Allied and Associated Governments recognise that the resources of Germany are not adequate, after taking into account permanent diminutions of such resources which will result from other provisions of the present Treaty, to make complete reparation for all such loss and damage.'[16]

There was a strange contrast, too, in the fact that the Austrians (in the Peace of Saint-Germain) and the Hungarians (in the Peace of Trianon) were presented with the same so-called 'war guilt' article, the only difference being that instead of 'Germany and her allies', their drafts read 'Austria and . . .' and 'Hungary and . . .' respectively. Vienna and Budapest complained bitterly about some aspects of the terms imposed on them, especially the crushing territorial adjustments – much more serious than any of Germany's losses – but they chose essentially to ignore the references to responsibility.

Nonetheless, the terms imposed on Germany, if not ruinous, presaged a great amount of added economic suffering and consequent political instability in a country that had already run up vast internal, and considerable external, debts in order to pay for the war.

The shock at the fact that there would be no 'democratic peace' based on 'solidarity of peoples', or at least not for Germany and the other losers, was traumatic in the extreme, and all the more so because Germans had clung to that hope. In the weeks that followed Brockdorff-Rantzau's agonising appearance before the Allies at Trianon, the German delegation fired note after indignant note at the victors, demanding and pleading changes to the proposed treaty, protesting to the point of exhaustion against its penal clauses, economic, territorial and moral. They argued Germany's case well. Some of the victors' leaders were impressed. General Sir Henry 'Jumbo' Wilson, Chief of the Imperial British General Staff and military adviser to Lloyd George at the conference, wrote in his diary: 'The Boches have done exactly what I forecast – they have driven a coach and four through our Terms, and then they have submitted a complete set of their own, based on the 14 points, which are much more coherent than ours.'[17]

General Smuts of South Africa went further, describing the treaty as 'an impossible peace', the territorial changes 'full of menace for the future of Europe' and the reparations clauses 'unworkable'.[18] As an Afrikaner, a former Boer commander who had thrown in his lot with the British Empire as a consequence of the remarkably conciliatory peace terms granted by the British after their victory in the Boer War, Smuts had some right to express an opinion on such matters.

Many British and American delegates agreed broadly with Smuts. The diplomat and writer Harold Nicolson, who had been in Paris throughout the negotiations, wrote gloomily, 'if I were the Germans, I shouldn't sign for a moment'. The brilliant economist, John Maynard Keynes, resigned from the Allied delegation and threw himself into writing his famous denunciation of the treaty, *The Economic Consequences of the Peace*.[19] Even the Archbishop of Canterbury expressed serious qualms.

In fact, the Germans did get some minor concessions. The most important was a plebiscite in Upper Silesia, where there was a mixed German-Polish population.

More than a month passed. Finally, on 16 June 1919, the Germans were told that they had three days to agree to the Allied terms. The senior members of the German delegation departed by train for Weimar, where the National Assembly was still in session, to report on the final treaty.

Brockdorff-Rantzau had already made it clear that he would recommend refusal of the terms, and back home in Germany other senior politicians – not just the nationalists – were equally vehement. Scheidemann dismissed the Allied draft as a 'murder plan'. 'The treaty,' said the Chancellor at a protest rally in the auditorium of Berlin University, 'is insufferable and incapable of fulfilment. What hand would not wither that bind itself and us in these fetters?'[20] The President of the National Assembly, the Centre Party's Konstantin Fehrenbach, told the parliament's deputies, first in Latin and then in German:

Memores estote, inimici, ex ossibus ultor: Be mindful, you enemies, that from the bones of the fallen an avenger will arise. German women will still continue to bear children, and these children will break the chains of slavery and wash away the ignominy that has been made to disfigure the face of Germany.[21]

It quickly became apparent that the three-day time limit was impractical. Berlin was thus granted another four days, until 23 June. Meanwhile, the German cabinet, initially committed to acceptance, fell apart. Scheidemann resigned as Chancellor on 20 June, arguing that after what he had said he could not possibly accede to the Allied terms. The Foreign Minister left office – and German politics – along with his Chancellor.

President Ebert was faced with a grim deadline. If the treaty was not signed by 7 p.m. on 23 June, the Allies had threatened to invade Germany and impose a final settlement by force. Although Lloyd George in particular, along with his ministers, was far from eager to send his rapidly demobilising army back into conflict,[22] he, too, could see no other option. Then, on 21 June, the German naval commander, Admiral Reuter, ordered the scuttling of what was left of the German fleet, which had been interned at Scapa Flow, in the Orkneys. The fleet had been due, under the terms of the treaty, to be delivered up to the victors. The news added powerfully to existing Allied resolve. This was an act of brazen defiance that confirmed, at this crucial juncture, the worst of Allied prejudices regarding German duplicity and fanaticism.

In the end, a Reich cabinet was formed of ministers prepared to accept the treaty, this time under another Social Democrat, the innocuous and frankly dull Gustav Bauer. The new Deputy Chancellor and Minister of Finance was Matthias Erzberger, the Centre Party politician and Minister without Portfolio who had acted as Chairman of the Armistice Commission, and who had been the most prominent German signatory of the armistice agreement at Compiègne on 11 November 1918.

Erzberger, the son of a tailor and part-time postman from Württemberg, had quickly made a name as a journalist and activist in the Catholic trade union movement before being elected to the Reichstag in 1903 at the early age of twenty-eight. Brilliant and phenomenally hardworking, but considered uncouth by his social superiors, and rather inclined to let his version of any given event run away with him, Erzberger was a classic example of the new professional political class, often originating from humble backgrounds, which came into being in Germany in the years before 1914.

During the war, evolving from a fanatical supporter of a war of conquest to a more moderate stance, he had pushed hard, though unsuccessfully, for a compromise peace. As a result, Erzberger had become a bugbear of the nationalist, annexationist right. During the months that preceded the Allied presentation of the draft treaty, he had been engaged in a constant struggle with Brockdorff-Rantzau, whose high-minded rejectionism he considered a romantic indulgence. Now, because of his reluctant endorsement of the treaty and his advance to a position of prominence in the new government, Erzberger became a target for the growing number of right-wingers who, as the post-war horizon darkened and they sought scapegoats for Germany's unconscionable defeat, saw the Republic and its leaders as evils to be fought at all costs and by any means.

Erzberger saw clearly that a German refusal to sign the treaty, though tempting, would bring disaster. He predicted Allied occupation of the country and the probable disintegration of the German state into petty statelets, the crippling of German industry and an even greater risk of civil war than already existed. Not to mention the fact that, according to the Minister for Food, the Reich was on the brink of even more disastrous shortages.[23]

Germany would lose territory as a result of the treaty, it was true, but the country itself, and its infrastructure, remained intact. After all, no fighting had actually occurred on German soil. Even General Groener recognised this fact, sending a telegram to Ebert during those fateful June days in which he recommended compliance. A resumption of military operations held no prospect of success, Groener conceded, and the only chance of avoiding civil tumult at home and chaos on the borders was for the government to firmly state the necessity of signing the treaty. Recovery and, potentially, resurgence were still possible as long as the Reich remained whole and more or less in control of its own destiny.[24]

On 22 June, the National Assembly voted by 237 to 138, with five abstentions, to accept the treaty, though with the proviso that Germany did not accept the 'war guilt' clause, or the section demanding the surrender to the Allies of alleged German war criminals.

The answer from Paris was unyielding. Germany must accept the entire package, without reservations or modifications. After lengthy cabinet discussions and a new debate in the National Assembly, Germany's unconditional acceptance was finally conveyed to the Allied governments at Versailles late on the afternoon of 23 June. The time was 5.40, one hour and twenty minutes before the expiry of the ultimatum.[25]

The actual signing of the peace treaty took place in the Hall of Mirrors at Versailles on 28 June – the fifth anniversary of the assassination of the Archduke Franz Ferdinand at Sarajevo, the spark that had lit the conflagration of the First World War. Date and location alike were thick with historical symbolism. The Hall of Mirrors had been the place where, on 18 January 1871, the Prussian king had been acclaimed as Emperor Wilhelm I of Germany by his peers, in the presence of the genius of German unification, Otto von Bismarck. Forty-eight years later, the signature ceremony took place at 3 p.m., amidst crowds of Allied delegates and also the press, whose photographers crowded around as the two German delegates – the new Foreign Minister, Social Democrat Hermann Müller, and the Transport Minister, the Centre Party's Johannes Bell – entered the enormous room.

Everything about the ritual seemed designed to inflict maximum humiliation on the representatives of the defeated. Pale-faced and dressed in formal dark suits, hands trembling, Müller and Bell wrote their names on the document, using fountain pens they had brought specially from Germany so as not to have to use anything provided by the victors. They were then required to remain seated, and largely ignored, until the representatives of all the Allied countries (and there were many) had also signed. This took three-quarters of an hour. Both the Germans managed a studied calm. Müller wrote afterwards that he 'wanted our former enemies to see nothing of the deep pain of the German people, whose representative I was at this tragic moment'. Once back at his hotel, however, he broke down in a cold sweat. The entire German party left for home that same night.

The atmosphere back in the Reich resembled one of a nation in mourning. Professor Ernst Troeltsch wrote in his regular 'Spektator' column:

> Among the people, the effect was of a visible unity in pain, fury and offended honour . . . One heard once again accusations against a government that had allowed itself to be fooled by Wilson's phrases about peace, and because of that had abandoned a victory almost won. The whole legend was once more spreading abroad that only the defeatists at home, the Jews and the Social Democrats, had broken the backbone of our proud army and that if we had not been so sentimental the most glorious victory could have been ours.[26]

This wave of irrational hatred would cause the nationalist right, including much of the German educated middle class, to damn the entire republican establishment as traitors. It would not matter that Friedrich Ebert had given his political all to the war effort until the very final phase, or, indeed, that he had lost two sons killed in action at the front. He, and all the others, were 'the November criminals'. Although it was Ebert who could be seen as overthrowing the Kaiser, and it was Müller and Bell who had signed the treaty, Erzberger seemed nonetheless to have become uniquely identified with the so-called 'betrayal' that it represented. 'I am very sure,' Harry Kessler had written shortly before the event, 'that Erzberger will share Lieb-knecht's fate.'[27]

This level of loathing was particularly ominous given the fact that the postman's son from Württemberg had just been charged with the crucial task of bringing Germany's broken finances back from the brink. He was determined to do this from the point of view of a socially aware Catholic. Erzberger's first aim as Finance Minister was to make sure that Germans paid the fair taxes the Reich needed to fuel its recovery. Although some reforms had taken place during the war, most taxes were still raised by the individual German states, which jealously protected their ancient fiscal rights under the monarchy. That would have to change in the new republican Germany. Erzberger had already informed the states as much. And the rich had to pay more: 'The State will try through radical laws and radical implementation of laws to make good the injustices of the war. The broad masses of the people have been waiting since the revolution for the great sacrifices on the part of the propertied classes.'[28]

Erzberger also found time to warn Germans against another danger, that of inflation, though he did not call it that. 'Whether rich or poor,' he said, 'we all have too much paper money in our pockets. When the paying of taxes starts, our wallets will become thinner.'

Ah, easier said than done.

9

Social Peace at Any Price?

The German Republic established on 9 November 1918 could not call on divine right to justify its existence, as its imperial and monarchical predecessors had done. It presented itself as democratic, egalitarian, and above all as a state whose whole reason for existence was to improve the welfare of its citizens, and to make Germany a fairer society.

Despite the sometimes devious behind-the-scenes manoeuvring to prevent a Bolshevik-style transformation of society, the first days after the revolution saw the representatives of the new Germany establish the basis for a status quo that they trusted would earn the loyalty of the vast majority of Germans – and, above all, of the industrial working class, which formed the bedrock of the Social Democratic Party's support and therefore of the republic.

The fact that the government of the new Germany felt constrained to do this, though arguably virtuous in itself, underpinned the whole social and political tendency of the post-war years. It also, virtue apart, played an important part in ensuring that, whenever a choice needed to be made by Weimar's politicians, socialist or not, they showed a tendency to make decisions in terms of perceived political and social benefit. Economic considerations, even apparently urgent ones, came a poor second. In other words, a major part of the reason why the Weimar Republic – perhaps the first of many modern states to find itself in this situation – let its economy drift into an inflationary state was because for some years social and political priorities took more or less absolute precedence over economics. This would remain the case until the government had no choice in the matter but to change it. However that lay a long way down the line.

On 10 November, Friedrich Ebert made his famous (or notorious) phone call to General Groener, and began the process of making an accommodation with the status quo, so that his version of the 'revolution', which was a very modest one, might win out.

A major reason why the government found itself in this situation was, of course, that it had decided to keep the capitalist economy and therefore, perforce, allow the country's capitalists to survive. A Bolshevik-style reorganisation of the economy might have allowed the kind of central control that would permit the government to dictate terms (though admittedly the Bolsheviks themselves had to cope with a vicious, if temporary, inflation during their own civil war). This, however, was not what Ebert and his colleagues wanted, and probably rightly so.

Of course, in public Ebert and his Majority Social Democrats preached the end of capitalism. This would theoretically enable the peaceful transition to a new, more efficient and equal socialised economy that would function alongside a democratised, egalitarian society. But we know that in fact Ebert 'hated the social revolution like sin'. That is why he did the deal with Groener.

The alternative to the social revolution was a social agreement. Accordingly, on 15 November 1918, another meeting took place in Berlin that would, in its way, be just as significant in ensuring that, whatever the revolution of 9 November might come to mean, it would not be the end of German capitalism. Again, men who considered themselves leaders of the working class offered a hand to the beleaguered establishment, and again the aim was not the furtherance but the prevention of radical change.

Carl Legien was the most powerful man in the Social Democrat-controlled trade union movement. Its membership had dipped from 2.5 million before the war to less than 1 million, before entering a steep upward curve during the last months of the war, rising on a steeper trajectory during the first weeks and months of peace as working-class men returned from the front to take up employment once more. In November 1918, Legien was a few weeks short of his fifty-seventh birthday, not only one of the Social Democrats' leading lights but also one of the handful of men who really mattered in post-war Germany.

Born to a working-class family in Thorn, a Prussian city that in 1918 passed to Poland, after the early death of his parents Legien grew up in an orphanage and was then apprenticed as a turner. His rise through the ranks of the trade union movement, from such a heavily disadvantaged background, was astonishingly swift. In 1890, though not yet thirty, Legien became Chair of the (socialist) General Commission of German Trade Unions. He served as a member of the Reichstag between 1893 and 1918 as a Social Democrat. During the war, Legien's status as a practical dealmaker of some genius enabled him to mediate between the employers, government and trade unions. He was a pivotal figure in the fight to keep production going, even in the war's darkest moments.

On the other side of table from Legien on 15 November 1918 was the most prominent – and in his way most mysterious – industrialist in post-war Germany, forty-eight-year-old Hugo Stinnes. Offspring of a middling prosperous Rhenish-Westphalian merchant family, the young Hugo did not go to university, instead dabbling briefly in retail and at one time working for some months as a coal miner before spending a year at the School of Mines in Berlin. After a brief spell in the family firm, while still only twenty-two he branched out on his own, founding a trading company, Hugo Stinnes Ltd.

Dealing initially in coal, but then in just about anything else as well, was an activity for which Hugo Stinnes showed a near-preternatural talent. He gained control of several pits, began manufacturing briquettes, and then went into iron and steel. Within a few years, he owned thirteen steamers, trading in coal, wood, iron ore and grain, through the Mediterranean, the Black Sea, the North Sea and the Baltic. His imports included British coal as well, imported from his depot in Newcastle to Hamburg and Rotterdam. He played a major role over a period of more than twenty years in the growth of the future electricity and energy giant, RWE* (*Rheinisch-Westfälisches Elektrizitätswerk*).

Above all, Stinnes proved himself a master of the leveraged merger and the synergistic amalgamation. By 1914 he was not just an industrial magnate and shipowner; he also sat on the boards of many industrial companies and was involved in all the great German coal and iron syndicates, which wielded enormous economic and political power in the Kaiser's Germany. He was influential, respected for his brilliant organising skills and feared for his ambition. Stinnes, still in early middle age, was reckoned to be worth 40 million gold marks. His operating capital in 1914, however, was said to be still the same 50,000 marks with which he had started out in 1893. 'That was before the war,' wrote a shrewd contemporary observer some years later. 'The lion held an important section of the German business world under his soft paws but had not yet thrust out his claws.'

Do not get a false impression of him. He remained in appearance, in demeanour, in assuming manners, the simple superintendent of his original mine. Thickset but not tall; erect but not military, a heavy featured man with close-cropped hair, a school-teacher's well-trimmed beard, an unimpressive countenance of yellowish complexion. His eyes are somewhat oblique, sly, shifting, not deep, but fixing attention. At the same time, a hail fellow well met. Not much of a talker, but a keen observer. When he does speak, no superfluous words. Nothing but facts. A calculating machine. When he speaks he is calm, cool, has command of data, imposes, though he expresses himself in a sort of weary whisper, a mere murmur.[1]

Although many of his foreign interests and some of his ships were sequestered by the enemy during the war, Stinnes just kept on

---

* RWE is now an international company whose customers include 6.5 million energy users in the United Kingdom alone.

expanding inside Germany itself, buying up or buying into ever more iron and steel and coal businesses, riding the runaway beast of ever-increasing war production. He became a fixture as adviser and secret string-puller at High Command Headquarters in Spa. He acquired shipping businesses in anticipation of a post-war resurgence in trade, at a time when the maritime sector languished. He ordered more ships from the Kiel yards, planning a fleet so big that it would make him entirely independent of fluctuating international charter rates. He bought up vast East Prussian forested estates to ensure he had security of supply for the pine pit props needed for his coal mines. By the end of the war, he and his associates controlled large numbers of lignite (brown coal) mines, enabling the cheap generation of electricity in the huge modern power stations that they had built. He had also started to buy newspapers, hinting at post-war political ambitions.

Stinnes was already well on his way to becoming the richest businessman in Germany. 'How much money did he have deposited in neutral banks?' asked the contemporary biographer. 'How much did he have seeking new investments? The time came when he could not place all his funds through ordinary banking channels. His capital kept madly multiplying.'

This was the man who sat down opposite Legien on 15 November 1918 in Berlin, heading a delegation of employers primed to meet a delegation of trade union leaders. These latter included officials representing the much smaller Christian and liberal workers' organisations as well as Legien's left-affiliated General Commission of Trade Unions, but essentially this was a socialist–capitalist agreement. The revolution of 9 November had brought to power two parties – the Majority and Independent Social Democrats – which were both committed to the socialisation of the German economy, whether immediate (in the case of the far left) or eventual (in the case of the moderates). Non-socialists had, essentially, no executive function in Germany in mid-November 1919. Legien's political comrades were, for now, the power in the land.

Regular meetings between capital and labour had, in fact, taken place throughout the war under the auspices of the government and the military, as part of the drive for wartime industrial peace and continuity of production. Throughout that last wartime autumn, with the country clearly entering a new, more unstable phase, there had been more pointed bilateral talks between the unions and employers, with the unions probing for the settlement of longstanding demands and the employers seeing how much they would have to give in order to maintain what they perceived as 'order in the house'.

The revolution pushed the employers into seeking a deal with the new powers that be. In effect, any deal.[2] As a leading representative of the steel industry's employers had said on 14 November: 'It is not a question of money now . . . right now we must see that we survive the chaos.'[3] Thus it was that some of Germany's most diehard captains of industry affixed their names to the historic treaty between organised labour and capital in Germany that became known as the 'Stinnes–Legien Agreement'.

The agreement gave workers an eight-hour working day with no reduction in pay – a long-standing demand of organised labour – compulsory union recognition, mandatory collective bargaining and wage contracts, and the right to be represented in companies with more than fifty employees through 'workers' committees'. It also guaranteed that industry would re-employ every one of the millions of German men who would soon be demobilised. To ensure that these improvements would work in practice, trade union and employer representatives set up a 'Central Working Group of Industrial and Commercial Employer and Employee Organisations of Germany'. Any agreements arrived at by this Central Working Group would be enforced by both sides.[4]

Clearly, though some more enlightened employers found such an agreement more or less acceptable, this amounted to a U-turn for some of Germany's toughest, hitherto most anti-union employers. These last were represented particularly strongly in the heavy industrial sector and tended to be closely connected with the conservative, nationalist political camp. However, as a group the country's industrialists had evidently decided that it was better to make concessions, however painful in some cases, than to risk losing everything to the wave of socialistic fervour that was sweeping the Reich during November 1918. The more optimistic of them even hoped, by involving the workers in decision-making, to induce more realistic attitudes (from the employers' point of view), in particular to 'give them the opportunity to have the insight into the economic situation, the economic perspectives, the economic interconnections, which are the foundation of all social and wage demands . . . in order . . . to convince them that there is a limit to where social and economic policy are compatible'.[5]

Legien and the unions appeared, like Ebert in his dealings with General Groener, to be giving away a lot in return for relatively little. The agreement was basically a recognition on the unions' part that the existing economic and social system would not be abolished in the near future, but simply subjected to improvement.

Many workers expected the revolution to lead to a socialist state in Germany, in which the capitalists would be expropriated and become irrelevant. That was still, officially at least, the policy even of the moderate Social Democrats. But Legien was a dealmaker, not a utopian radical. This, he could tell his union members, was what Social Democrats had always wanted. Workers and their union representatives were now on the inside instead of, as for so long, the outside of the decision-making process in industry. This was a crucial step-up for the working class, part of the process of learning how to run things and thereby building a new future for a democratic Germany under difficult post-war circumstances. The capitalists had been tamed, and their undoubted managerial skills could now be pushed in socially useful directions. Total and immediate socialisation would risk throwing the babies of efficiency and full employment out with the capitalist bathwater. Or so the story went.[6]

The Stinnes–Legien deal certainly contributed, alongside Ebert's bargain with the military, to stemming the tide of extreme radicalism, of turning the movement of 9 November 1918 into the 'reined-in revolution' (*gebremste Revolution*). The employers got to save their

businesses, and the trade unionists got better hours, better pay and
the employers' promise to give returning soldiers their jobs back.

Business decided to forget about the money, as the man from the
steel industry had put it, and therefore, so employers hoped, to
'survive the chaos'. And, broadly speaking, it did survive and even
prosper. There was, however, a price to be paid for all this sweetness
and compromise, and in the long term not just for the capitalists.

There had been more than four years of hard work and sacrifice,
on the home front and in the trenches. It soon became clear, in the
aftermath of peace, that many Germans felt disinclined to take just
any job that came up, or, if they did, to devote themselves to it in the
conspicuously committed fashion that had become almost a stereo-
typical national trait in pre-war times. Employers and officials
bemoaned this work-shy attitude (*Arbeitsunlust*).

Workers were also liable to be choosy about which industries they
wanted to work in. No one, it seemed, wanted a job on the land, or
in forestry, or in mining – all areas of the economy that were physically demanding and required a high tolerance threshold for
discomfort, but were nevertheless vital to any post-war recovery. This
applied especially to returning soldiers. Those demobilised in time
for Christmas 1918 preferred, it seemed, to use up any savings they
had, and sometimes to claim unemployment benefit, which under
pressure from local workers' and soldiers' councils had now become
more generous, and to wait for a decently paid, more comfortable
job to present itself.[7]

Welfare fraud became a serious problem especially in Berlin, where
one trade union observer estimated that 25 per cent of all claims were
illegitimate. Members of the Republican Guard, for instance – one
of the relatively small number of government-organised militias –
apparently made a regular practice of claiming unemployment benefit
as well as collecting their pay. Extra family members were invented.
Another trick was to claim for welfare in two different areas of Berlin,
knowing that district offices rarely cross-checked with others.[8] The
war had seen a great growth in the black market, and the threshold

for general dishonesty had also clearly been lowered over the past four years. In any case, there was a widespread sense of entitlement, given the sacrifices that these men and their families had made during the war years. This was understandable, but unhealthy from the point of view of the challenges facing the wider German economy.

The situation was further complicated by the fact that unemployment pay, which during the immediate post-war period was the responsibility of municipal authorities, varied fairly radically from one area of Germany to another. In conservative rural districts it might be three marks per day, while in socialistic Berlin in early 1919 it was four marks, and in Dresden as high as six – rates which increased rapidly over the next few months under pressure from the unemployed and the revolutionary councils.[9] Proposals were made to set a national minimum and maximum for unemployment pay, but without success. After all, three or four marks a day might be completely inadequate to keep body and soul together in a big city, while in the remoter parts of the countryside it was probably more than the average labourer could expect for a hard day's work. One thing was for certain: these were arrangements not calculated to discourage returned soldiers from flocking to the cities. They were also not calculated to bring down the price of labour and therefore the price of what labour produced.

As 1919 wore on, the authorities, concerned at the numbers of returned soldiers still unemployed, tried to put pressure on the unemployed to accept available work, however unsatisfactory the pay. Success in that direction was limited. These were turbulent times, where the writ of the bureaucrat did not run as strong as it had once done and the power of the crowd was hard to challenge. The white-collar staff at the labour exchanges faced, as one official observation put it, 'the mistrust of the worker for the academically trained and better clothed person'. In Leipzig, officials who tried to enforce the rules were 'cursed in the crudest manner, insulted, and even threatened'. There were cases of officials being assaulted by groups of the unemployed.[10]

Wages and prices kept drifting upwards, despite the huge

numbers of returned servicemen that the labour market was being forced to absorb.

One of the features of the Weimar Constitution, finally approved in August 1919, was a paragraph (§163) not only granting 'the right to work' but also a dole in case of involuntary unemployment:

> Every German has the moral duty, without prejudice to his personal freedom, so to exercise his mental and physical strength as the welfare of all requires. Every German should be given the opportunity to earn his living through economic work. To the extent that appropriate job opportunities cannot be demonstrated, means will be provided for his necessary upkeep.[11]

Unemployment rose sharply between October 1918, the final month of full-scale war production, and January 1919. War contracts were cancelled or not renewed, and there were widespread shortages of coal and raw materials owing to chaotic circumstances in some of the industrial areas (Alsace-Lorraine and the Saar were occupied by the French, and there was fighting with the Poles in the important industrial region of Upper Silesia). The inevitable switch from turning out armaments and materiel of war back to making goods for civilian consumption, the production of which had diminished dramatically during the war years, had not yet begun.

However, in the period of slightly less than five months that passed between the opening of the National Assembly in Weimar at the beginning of February 1919 and the signing of the Versailles Treaty at the end of June 1919, the percentage of male unemployed (or, at least, the number of unemployed who were trade union members) fell from 6.2 to 2.8 per cent.[12] These figures, though somewhat rosy due to under-reporting, showed a trend that was both undeniable and surprising.

Some of this reduction was achieved by a policy of dismissing female workers wherever possible and replacing them with men. As the war went on, and more male workers were conscripted to the front, women had, in fact, taken on industrial tasks that before 1914 few would have thought them capable of successfully performing. These included strenuous labouring jobs in the mines and steel smelters, and it is clear that they were reliable and hard-working (and generally accepted lower pay than men). This did not stop the authorities from insisting on their dismissal.

At Krupp in Essen, for instance, 52,000 workers were dismissed within weeks of the end of the fighting. Of those made unemployed, almost 30,000 were women, leaving just 500 still employed at the company. They were clearly, in many cases, reluctant to return to the old domestic life. A somewhat sheepish bureaucratic report admitted that the women were 'diligent and skilful' while 'the men were more choosy': 'They [the men] refused to accept heavy or dirty work or left it after a short time. Thus it required especially vigorous measures to remove women from the coking plants, where they were employed at jobs completely unsuitable for them.'[13]

The apparently positive male employment picture was also due to widespread underemployment, whether this meant full-time workers doing relatively little or actual short-time working. A twenty-four-hour week was encouraged in the Demobilisation Decree as an alternative to dismissals of surplus workers.[14] And the employers, many of whom had done very well out of the war, and whose sense of vulnerability in the new post-revolutionary state inclined them to a temporary generosity, could be persuaded to help. One report on army demobilisation stated that 'the chief burden of the readjustment losses was borne by commerce and industry', and went on:

The relatively good position of the labour market was only upheld by the fiction that industry could employ the larger portion of the workers. In actuality, this was impossible given the halved coal supply, the raw-materials shortage, the continuation of the blockade, the uncertainty of the situation. The cost of the transition, therefore, had to be covered by the reserves of industry. These were probably not small in the case of a large number of plants because of the wartime boom.[15]

It was also assumed, by most manufacturers, that they could pay the increased wages required to keep the industrial peace in these politically unstable times, and compensate by putting up the prices of the goods they sold – in other words, by feeding inflation.[16]

The government, while recognising the problems that rising prices brought, was so concerned with the simple demands of keeping order and feeding the population that it openly espoused a similar 'pay-what-it-takes' strategy. Once some food imports were permitted in the spring of 1919, it was clearly vital that the railways needed to be kept running in order to transport these essential supplies into the country. Without them, the labour force threatened to become too physically weak to keep the country's mines working and her factories producing. However, in May, Germany's railway workers – their numbers vastly inflated during the war years – went on strike for more pay.

During a crisis meeting at the Reich Food Ministry in Berlin on 5 May – two days before the shock announcement of the peace treaty terms at Versailles – the moderate Social Democratic Prussian Finance Minister, Albert Südekum, was brutally, and not especially elegantly, frank:

> Every price and every kind of concession is justified to prevent the shutdown of railroad traffic in Prussia. What is not feasible through the ending of the inflation is feasible, and can be carried out, if work becomes possible as a result of improved provisioning with food. In this regard, there is no reason to consider the exchange rate, since every foreign merchant is really only influenced by his mistrust of the general conditions in Germany.[17]

In other words, inflation came a long way second to social peace. Social peace at, literally, any price.

But where was the Reich to get the money, when it was already almost 160 billion marks in debt as a direct result of war spending?

Erzberger's revolutionary tax reforms constituted at least part of the answer. With the presentation of his programme in July 1919, he proposed to decisively assert the supremacy of the central Reich government in taxation matters and thus make possible, for the first time in German history, some kind of clear coincidence between the central government's policies and the raising of the money required to carry them out.

The new Republic was still a federation, with large powers still reserved to the individual states – be they the enormous Prussia, with, at more than 40 million, two-thirds of the country's population, or tiny Schaumburg-Lippe, with a mere 50,000 or so – but clearly no coherent management of the country's finances was possible if the normal means of taxation were the preserve mainly, or even to a significant extent, of these historic (and stubbornly independent) entities.

The Reich took control of income tax, sales taxes, inheritance tax and land purchase taxes among others, and also empowered itself to enforce one-off emergency and windfall taxes on those perceived to be capable of paying them.

Compared with other countries, post-revolutionary Germany became a very highly taxed nation. Erzberger quite specifically targeted war profiteers and speculators, the kind of smartly dressed people that visitors to Berlin and other major cities saw stuffing themselves with black-market food in upmarket restaurants while the majority of Germans struggled to feed and clothe themselves. He provided the legal and administrative basis for the modern German tax system. However, he did not solve the government's problems with debt and deficit.

Only inflation, as it turned out, could do that.

Erzberger set out his tax reforms before the National Assembly on 8 July 1919. The next day, 9 July, the Versailles treaty was ratified by 209 votes to 116. The tax reforms would be passed piecemeal in different legislative packages between September and the following March.

The bespectacled, overweight but infuriatingly cheerful and self-confident Finance Minister had presented his proposals with remarkable energy, clarity and determination. He immediately found himself (argu-ably, put himself) in the eye of a storm that saw a rising tide of rage on the nationalist right against the Versailles treaty and at the same time against the fiscal reforms. The new taxes would particularly affect the old landowning, industrialist and property-owning classes, from which the nationalist right drew a great deal of its support.

Erzberger was the man who had proposed the 'Peace Without Annexations' resolution in 1917, who in November 1918 had signed the scandalous armistice, who had, moreover, then openly preached acceptance of the *Schmachfrieden* (literally 'shame peace') of Versailles. Many held him responsible for weakening the Reich's morale and its bargaining position in its hour of greatest need. Now he was also the man who demanded that the burden of tax on the less wealthy be moderated, while the classes that formed the backbone of Germany (certainly in their own view) should be hit harder in their tax liabili-ties. 'Income from capital,' Erzberger declared, 'must bear a much greater share of the burden than income from labour.'[18]

But for what? To pay unjust reparations to the vengeful Allies! Thus, despite Erzberger's protests that such sums would be ring-fenced, argued the resurgent nationalist right. And it was hard to deny their claim. Whatever the technicalities of what was collected and where it was supposedly spent, it was true that reparations amounted to 'a tax collected from German citizens by the German government acting as the Allies' fiscal agent'.[19] The propaganda connection between the Republic, its new, more egalitarian tax system, and the national humiliation of Versailles was personified by Erzberger. He was a gift for the enemies of the treaty and of the Republic. Now that Liebknecht and Luxemburg had been killed, he in many ways became an even greater hate figure for the reactionary extremists than any other Weimar politician.

Especially unpopular among the anti-republican middle and upper classes was Erzberger's so-called *Reichsnotopfer* (literally 'Reich Emergency Sacrifice' but perhaps better translated as 'Emergency Capital Levy'), a one-off property tax levied on all individual citizens (it began at 10 per cent but rates from upwards of 7 million marks in taxable assets reached 65 per cent) or corporate entities of various kinds (levied at a flat 10 per cent), which became law in December 1919. The levy unleashed outrage even though it could be paid off in instalments (admittedly subject to interest) over a period of up to thirty years.

Erzberger's reforms were courageous and necessary, they were passed by the National Assembly even in the face of the right's vigorous opposition and they were implemented. However, they did not solve the country's problems, though they may have prevented them from getting even worse.

Erzberger was nonetheless full of ideas to bring stability and what he considered fairness to Germany's finances. Apart from the new taxes, and the rise in tax rates for the better off, he was also concerned to plug the widening hole in the national wealth created by capital flight. This was a process that increased in 1919 as wealthy German individuals and corporations, disturbed by the revolution, by the threat of high taxation and by the continuing slide in the value of the mark, began to place more and more of their money and assets abroad. Apart from tightening up the requirements for banks to report and explain foreign currency transactions, Erzberger had another part-answer to this: high-value banknotes and securities would be called in by the banks and overstamped or replaced with new paper; the old or unstamped ones would become invalid. This would inhibit capital flight, as well as forcing the peasant with the proverbial concealed stocking full of money to bring his hoard out into the light for inspection.[20]

The stubborn opposition of the Reichsbank, which viewed such a process as technically impracticable, would eventually result in Erzberger's banknote-recall plan being reluctantly dropped, but in the meantime the idea was out in the public sphere and contributed to a further deterioration of the currency. The problem was that, while conversion of marks by Germans into foreign currency was a bad thing, because it meant that German wealth was leaving the country, the proposed remedy would also affect the existence of large and small holdings of marks by foreigners in other countries, which were actually a good thing – these holdings by foreigners served to buttress the external value of the currency and thereby contributed to keeping domestic inflation at bay. When, as a consequence of measures such as that proposed by Erzberger, foreigners started selling marks, because they were frightened that their holdings might suddenly become worthless, it undermined confidence in the German currency.

A respected Lübeck merchant, L. Possehl & Co., described this knotty problem to the Minister of Commerce in September 1919:

> Foreign speculation in mark notes is our only salvation today given stagnating exports. It was our good fortune that every peasant in Denmark bought mark notes and securities in the hope that the value of the mark would go up again after peace was restored . . . The situation is similar in Sweden, where many large and small speculators took advantage of the low value of the mark to purchase it. All these people place their hopes in the arrival of normal conditions in Germany and then consider an increase in the exchange value of the mark to be self-understood . . . The rumours reaching Sweden that the mark notes would be stamped called forth a real panic . . . Even many northern banks had the idea that the bank notes in their possession could become worthless if they overlooked some formality. In any case, countless persons decided to free themselves from holdings which were threatened with confiscation and enormous holdings of marks were thrown onto the market.[21]

Numerous double binds of this kind apart – few fiscal reforms in any time or place are without unintended consequences – Germany's finances had to be repaired, of that there could be no doubt. The Reich's debts in 1913 had totalled 5 billion marks. By 1919 they had risen more than thirtyfold to 153 billion – of which almost half were not long-term debt but 'floating', meaning that they had either to be paid back or refinanced on a short-term basis. The amount of paper money in circulation in 1913 had been 2 billion marks; in 1919 it was 45 billion.[22] Something had to be done to reintroduce discipline to Germany's finances. In the fifth century AD, the pleasure-loving St Augustine had pleaded with God, 'make me chaste, but not yet!' Likewise, the German government's agonising dilemma from 1918 onwards was not just how to apply the bitter prescription required to restore the country's finances but when. The time never seemed to be right, the consequences of the reimposition of financial chastity potentially too painful. So, although the tax reforms went some way to mending the broken German economy, they were the only real medicine that the government dared administer during these early months. In the absence of genuine retrenchment, they made only a marginal impact on the country's huge problems.

There was, after all, a price to be paid for bold, tough action. In fact, there were several prices – economic, political and social. All of these were costs that a still weak, newly established Republic with vengeful enemies abroad, a restless, newly assertive population at home that expected swift, concrete improvement in its welfare and standard of living, and increasingly numerous and aggressive far-right critics in the political arena, could ill afford to risk taking on.

As for Matthias Erzberger himself, a flawed individual but, with hindsight, perhaps post-war Germany's most courageous political figure, he would in the fullness of time be made to pay the ultimate personal price.

Consequences

As the keen-eyed Professor Troeltsch had observed in November 1918, seeing the upper middle class of Berlin out, as usual, on their Sunday strolls in the Grunewald, 'salaries continued to be paid'. One of the peculiarities of Germany's financial situation after the armistice was that, regardless of revolution and counter-revolution, victory and defeat, monarchy and republic – or, for that matter, the collapse of the gold standard and the pre-war global trading system – the same two salaried officials remained at the helm of the German Reichsbank who had been in charge, under very different conditions, since well before the war.

Rudolf Havenstein had been fifty-seven years old when war broke out in 1914, so by 1919 he was well into his sixties. He had entered the Prussian civil service when in his early thirties, and risen rapidly through the ranks at the Finance Ministry to become President of the Prussian State Bank (*Königlich-Preußische Seehandlung*) in 1900 and a much-admired President of the Reichsbank from 1907. This industrious and conscientious Prussian civil servant was joined at the helm of the bank by his deputy and trusted adviser, Otto Georg von Glasenapp. Four years older than Havenstein, his speciality was government debt, money and coinage. The currency changes embodied in the August 1914 decoupling of the mark from gold had been largely Glasenapp's work.

These, then, were the distinguished, patriotic and apparently reliable officials who unwittingly set Germany and its currency on the road to ruin. Both were lawyers by education and training rather than economists or financiers. Both were very much men of the pre-war era. Glasenapp, in particular, was a man of broad culture, with a deep interest in the works of Germany's and perhaps Europe's greatest polymath, Johann Wolfgang von Goethe (for many years he served on the committee of the Weimar-based Goethe Society). In fact, Glasenapp did a bit of writing himself, reportedly setting his son's translations of Indian poetry into polished German verse in his head while walking to work in the morning.[1]

Having played such a leading role in the growth of Germany's indebtedness during the previous four or more years, the Reichsbank's response to the armistice and the threat of a normalisation of the country's economy was to demand austerity from the revolutionary government, while, paradoxically, at the same time the dubious underpinnings of the money supply, which implicitly encouraged the debauchment of the currency, remained in place. The 'old gentlemen' in the Jägerstrasse could, in any case, advise and remonstrate, but they could not force the new democratic ministers to espouse economic and financial policies they didn't want or feel politically able to pursue.

Erzberger's reforms and his new taxes helped a little in the austerity direction, but not enough. Though the rate of inflation had slowed, coaxing taxes out of the non-salaried sections of the population – landowners, business people, traders – was not easy, and even when a decent tax haul was achieved, the fact that it was inevitably collected in arrears undermined its usefulness. The capacity of shrewd operators to further delay payment until the real value of the assessment had diminished, often drastically, would prove an almost insuperable problem throughout this period.

The most hopeful aspect for Germany's real economy, rather than a decisive rise in tax revenues, was the fact that, in the second half of 1919, the labour situation began to improve, especially in the crucial coal industry. General productivity compared with pre-war standards remained relatively low, a fact that the employers in particular blamed on the newly introduced eight-hour day, widespread part-time working and a general lack of discipline in the labour force. However, miners agreed to work extra shifts. Sources of foreign credit started to open up once more in the USA and also in the former neutral countries such as Holland for German companies and municipalities, which were considered a better risk than the national government.[2]

It was true that the German mark nevertheless continued to fall against other currencies, especially after the more onerous foreign exchange restrictions (which during the war had helped keep it at an artificially high level) were lifted, and the mark began to be legally traded again throughout the world.

Beginning 1919 at 8.9 marks to the dollar, the mark rate deteriorated to 13.5 in May, consequent to the announcement of the harsh terms at Versailles; then 16.5 to the dollar in July, just after the Allied blockade was formally lifted; and then down some more to 21 to the dollar at the beginning of September, where it stuck for a while.[3] In the early winter, however, as expectations of Germany's willingness or ability to meet the Allied demands declined, so did the currency. On the last day of 1919, the rate had more than halved from that of September to 49 marks per dollar.[4] The mark was now worth less than one-tenth of its pre-war value.

The Versailles peace treaty between Germany and the Allies finally came into force on Saturday, 10 January 1920, despite the USA having not yet ratified the document (which it never would, the treaty finally failing to pass the Senate in March 1920). Harry Kessler wrote gloomily, but with his usual astuteness, in his diary:

> Today the Peace Treaty was ratified in Paris. The War is over. A terrible era begins for Europe, like the gathering of clouds before a storm, and it will end in an explosion probably still more terrible than that of World War. In Germany there are all the signs of a continuing growth of nationalism.[5]

Despite his support for the Republic, his internationalism and his cosmopolitan background – Kessler's mother was Irish and he had been brought up partly in England – like most Germans, whether conservative, liberal or of the moderate left, he considered Versailles an outrage. The so-called 'war guilt' clause was therefore an ugly victors' fiction, and the treaty itself an unjust imposition to be circumvented, if not openly defied.

The German far left, on the other hand, took what seemed to be a radically different view. All the participants in the world war, up to the time the Bolsheviks took over in Russia, were merely capitalist hyenas, fighting over the spoils of imperialism. Imperial Germany had been just like the rest of the gang, no better or worse. This might have seemed to put the Communists and the far-left socialists poles apart from their compatriots, but so far as the war guilt question was concerned, it was not so simple. After all, since the war was the creation not of the German masses but of their pre-war, undemocratic government and of the international capitalist system in general, there could be no 'guilt' on the people's part and therefore no penalty. So, in short, even the far left, though attacking the old elite for its warmongering and the military for its bad behaviour in the occupied countries, not to mention its ruthless sacrificing of millions of proletarian lives, could not stomach the notion of exclusive German war guilt.

Whatever the complications around the war guilt issue, there were a few figures in German political life who believed that the problem of responsibility, even if confined to a small elite, had to be faced for the country's sake. In the winter of 1918–19, the ill-fated Bavarian socialist Premier, Kurt Eisner, had sponsored the publication of secret Bavarian diplomatic reports, sent from Berlin during the July 1914 crisis, that seemed to support the notion of strong German (or, rather, since this was Bavaria, Prussian) responsibility for the outbreak of war. It was a bold and idealistic move that Eisner hoped might encourage the Allies to take a kindlier view of the new forces now ruling in Germany. In fact, the result was to mobilise the right and the military

against him and lead to accusations of 'treachery' that certainly played
a role in his assassination in April 1919. It was a strong indicator of
the violence to come.

In Berlin, meanwhile, a government committee meeting under the
supervision of the Social Democratic elder statesman Karl Kautsky
was also trawling through German Foreign Office documents covering the events of July and August 1914. From the documentary
evidence its members found, they were convinced, as were their counterparts in Munich, that the Kaiser and his advisers had encouraged
the 'hawks' of Austria-Hungary in their aggressive response to Serbia,
following the assassination of Archduke Franz Ferdinand at Sarajevo
by Serb nationalists. It followed that the German elite (not the same
thing as the German people), seemingly obsessed with the idea of a
preventive war against Russia, must bear a major share of responsibility for the outbreak of the First World War. Kautsky's initial report
in April 1919 was, however, held back, partly because most of the
Republic's ministers, including the Social Democrats, found the
version of events that emerged to be intolerable, but also partly for
fear that it would influence the still continuing treaty negotiations in
a negative way for Germany.

What difference it would have made to German domestic opinion,
had these documents – undifferentiated, it is true, and lacking
comparable evidence from the records of the other powers involved
– been published in the spring following the armistice, we shall
never know. Kautsky himself believed, like Eisner, that the evidence
contained would both encourage the Allies to view the new, honest
revolutionary Germany more favourably, and would also cement
the Republic's status in the minds of the German public, by making
it aware of the full depth of the old regime's irresponsibility. Others
disagreed, most decisively Chancellor Scheidemann, and publication
was not permitted.

What we do know is that the nationalist right had no such inhi-
bitions when it came to setting out its position. Appearing before
an investigative committee of the National Assembly in November

1919, Field Marshal von Hindenburg put his powerful stamp of approval on the 'stab in the back' myth, blaming Germany's collapse not on military defeat but on a domestic political conspiracy by Marxists, pacifists and Jews. The nationalist right seized on his remarks and used them to establish a radically false narrative among many Germans as to both the causes and the end of the war, one which suited their own disruptive political purposes and would dictate the tenor of the debate for years to come.[6] A reasonable denial of Germany's sole responsibility for the war was turned into a denial of any guilt whatsoever, a mass fantasy of Germany as totally innocent victim.

The so-called 'Weimar parties' (Social Democrats, Centre, German Democratic Party), which had supported the Republic from the outset, overwhelmingly denied sole German war guilt, and also therefore the liability to pay reparations (although compensation for damage done to the occupied areas of France and Belgium was another matter, which most Germans outside the extreme right acknowledged to be reasonable). All the same, it was deputies belonging to these republican parties that passed the treaty through the National Assembly in July 1919, 'war guilt' clause and all, having tried to include a protest against §231 but failed to prevail.

The 'Weimar parties', and the governments chosen from their members, whose composition would change with alarming frequency – seven governments came and went in the first five years of the Republic's existence – became, to the nationalist right, the 'Versailles traitors'. The country split down the middle, in other words, but not about the acceptability of the treaty. Almost everyone agreed that it was unjust and immoral.

The question had been, in the summer of 1919, whether to reject the treaty and dare the Allies to do their worst, or to formally accede to it and then somehow find ways to nullify the worst of its provisions. The division was not so clear cut as it would come to appear in retrospect. During that fateful week following the formation of a new government on 21 June 1919, it had often seemed that, even under the new circumstances, a majority would not be found in the Assembly for acceptance. It was only when General Groener advised the politicians of the impossibility of a resumption of hostilities that the Catholic Centre Party's deputies – united by their religion but ranging in other respects from right-wing nationalists to near-socialist radicals – swung behind the dictated treaty.[7]

In a last faint echo of the 1914–18 *Burgfrieden*, during the negotiations the nationalist right in the Assembly, while still opposing peace on the Allies' terms, conceded that those who voted for acceptance, though wrong, might have honourable *vaterländisch* (patriotic) motives. Tragically, this outbreak of reasonableness (or perhaps hypocrisy, for the last thing the nationalist right wanted at this point was to take charge of the country's fate) would prove short-lived.

So, Foreign Minister Müller and Labour Minister Bell took the train to Versailles – carefully routed by their French hosts to trundle slowly through the devastated regions of what had been German-occupied France[8] – and they signed the treaty that they, like the vast majority of their fellow countrymen, hated with a passion.

The government's policy now became known as 'fulfilment': that is, the German government formally accepted the treaty, even though doing so under duress, and would not show itself openly in breach of its provisions. But in its apparent compliance with the agreement, while attempting to 'fulfil' its terms, the German government would consistently aim to show the impossibility of any such thing. To do so, it would use every weapon in its political, propaganda and economic armoury.

Including manipulation of the currency.

One of the things that had given the deputies of the Weimar National Assembly pause during their final deliberations on the Versailles Treaty had been an announcement by General Maercker of Freikorps fame. The general had been put in charge of security arrangements for the Assembly. In case of acceptance of the peace terms, Maercker declared, his forces would no longer stand behind the government. Fortunately, his warning had been trumped by the telegram from General Groener that followed. Though couched in Groener's usual somewhat ambiguous style, this had seemed to confirm the army's support for the Army Minister, Noske, and thereby the government.

All the same, the outrage in the armed forces and on the nationalist right against the signing of the Versailles Treaty was widespread and passionate. The treaty stipulated that the army would have to be reduced to a force of no more than 100,000 enlisted men and officers, to be known, along with a 15,000-strong navy, as the Reichswehr (Reich Defence). Germany would have no air force. Under the terms of the treaty, the High Command and the General Staff were declared abolished. On 25 June 1919, Field Marshal von Hindenburg therefore resigned as Commander-in-Chief, and Groener as his deputy.

Gustav Noske became officially Reichswehr Minister. Immediately beneath him, as head of the so-called *Truppenamt* (Troop Office) stood Major General Hans von Seeckt, and, beneath Seeckt, the commander of Reichswehr forces in Prussia, Colonel (soon promoted to General) Walther Reinhardt. As it turned out, the *Truppenamt* would embody the restoration of the High Command in all but name. As in so many other aspects of apparent 'fulfilment' of the Versailles Treaty, the reorganisation of the German army barely obeyed the letter, and certainly not the spirit, of the agreement.

Kessler had predicted, when he wrote his morose lines about the ratification of the Versailles Treaty on 10 January, that it would fuel the fires of nationalism in Germany. He was right, but the situation was complex and became more so during the early months of 1920.

One crucial event of the post-ratification era was the publication of John Maynard Keynes's *The Economic Consequences of the Peace*, which appeared at the end of 1919 in Britain, in early 1920 in the USA and very shortly after in German translation.[9]

Keynes had resigned in despair from the British negotiating team at Versailles shortly before the draft treaty was presented in June 1919, retreating to Charleston, the country house in Sussex that he shared with his bohemian Bloomsbury friends. It was there, mostly during July and August 1919, that he wrote with some haste what turned out to be a passionate, concise but stingingly comprehensive, root-and-branch attack on the peace settlement. *The Economic Consequences* quickly became a sensation, a highly influential international bestseller that brought Keynes world fame.

From the German point of view, the beauty of Keynes's book was that it confirmed most of the Berlin government's objections to Versailles. Keynes, the brilliant economist and British government insider, also considered the terms of the treaty impossible! Delighted to find support from such a quarter, a committee including leading German bankers (some of whom were personally close to Keynes) began drawing up new proposals to modify the treaty, specifically encouraged by the success of his polemic.[10]

During the first part of that new year, there were also more hopeful signs for Germany's economy, and, committees of bankers apart, for her fight to chip away at the restrictions and penalties contained in the treaty. Agreements with France began to close the so-called 'hole in the west', the areas under French occupation where the writ of German customs did not run. As a consequence, illegal importation and smuggling were rife, as well as illegal capital flight on a massive scale (although Switzerland and Holland remained notorious safe havens for dubious German money, despite Erzberger's attempts to limit such losses to the national wealth). The Allies had dropped their demand for German 'war criminals' to be surrendered to them for trial, permitting these individuals to be tried at home in Germany, which they eventually would be, with predictably farcical results. Though no direct international loans to the German government were as yet available, a group of smaller American finance houses had started to lend money to German companies and municipalities. Americans were, furthermore, buying in expectation of a rise in the value of the mark, when they would be able to sell bonds and securities back to the Germans at a tidy profit.[11]

After another stomach-churning tumble in the new year, to 75 marks per dollar at the end of January 1920, to 93.5 on 22 February, by the end of the first week of March the mark had started to firm at a level of around 90 to the dollar, with a strong pull towards an improved value.[12] On 11 March 1920, there was a meeting in Berlin of experts, including the Independent Socialist theoretician and future Finance Minister, Rudolf Hilferding. During these discussions, serious thought was given to curtailing the Reichsbank's printing of money, introducing some correlations between domestic and international pricing, and in the longer term preparing a return to a gold-backed currency.[13]

Then came the realisation of Harry Kessler's fears regarding the nationalist right. On 26 January 1920, Matthias Erzberger had been shot at twice by a young army ensign, Oltwig von Hirschfeld, recently subjected to compulsory demobilisation and determined to 'deal with' the most prominent of the 'Versailles traitors'. The young would-be assassin's first bullet inflicted a shoulder wound, while the second was deflected by the minister's watch chain. It was a warning of things to come. Hirschfeld was convicted not of attempted murder but of 'dangerous bodily harm' (*gefährliche Körperverletzung*) and sentenced to a mere eighteen months in prison, then paroled after four months on 'health grounds'.[14]

Following the ratification of the treaty, it had become clear that most of the personnel of the new Reichswehr and the still-existent Freikorps, between which there were naturally enough many personal connections, were hardening in their hostility against the German Republic. After all, with the treaty in force, dramatic reductions in Germany's armed forces had become imminent. And, despite the fact that the Allies had 'conceded' that the 900 or so alleged 'war criminals' could be tried in Germany, the very notion that a German government could agree to such a thing outraged the vast majority of the officer corps and thereby brought the legitimacy of the republican government even more drastically into question.

Though technically an official of the Reichswehr Ministry, directly responsible to Noske, the Social Democratic Defence Minister, General Seeckt, kept a cool distance in his political relations. General Reinhardt, the next in line, was one of a minority of pro-Republic senior officers, a fact with which the government could console itself. However, the commander of the Reichswehr forces in Berlin itself, General Freiherr von Lüttwitz, was an arch-reactionary. Lüttwitz had long been in contact with right-wing extremists in parliament and elsewhere, as well as with ultra-nationalist Freikorps leaders, discussing plans to force new Reichstag elections and impose a more authoritarian constitution on Germany.

The crisis began to come to a head towards the end of February. Noske, acceding in part to the demands of the Allies that the German armed forces be reduced, decreed the dissolution of one of perhaps the most effective (and fiercely political) of the Freikorps units, the 5,000-strong so-called 'Marine Brigade Erhardt', named after its leader, naval captain Hermann Erhardt.

Erhardt, a torpedo boat commander in the war, had organised a group of anti-revolutionary sailors and soldiers to defeat a Communist coup in his home port of Wilhelmshaven in January 1919. He had then proceeded to build up a private army that took part in the suppression of various far-left uprisings in northern and central Germany, before playing a prominent role in the brutal extinction of the short-lived 'Soviet Republic' in Bavaria. Later in the year, the brigade had intervened to crush a Polish uprising in the disputed territory of Upper Silesia.

By the winter of 1919–20, the Erhardt Brigade, battle-hardened and armed to the teeth, was stationed at Döberitz, near Berlin, in close contact with Lüttwitz's regular forces. Its commander, now thirty-eight, fizzing with ambition and afire with loathing for the post-war government, had begun planning to use his force to over-throw the young German democracy in favour of a radical-nationalist dictatorship which would, the fantasy ran, restore Germany to its pre-war position of power.

Barely more than a year after the revolution had seemed to vanquish the old system, Germany now faced a new, violent threat. From the right.

II

Putsch

When Minister Noske finally issued his order for Erhardt's Brigade to be disbanded, it was the signal for a showdown.

On 10 March 1920, General Lüttwitz was granted an audience with Minister Noske and President Ebert, in which the General demanded an end to reductions in the armed forces and the abandonment of any of the Allied-imposed 'war crimes' trials. He also called for the immediate dissolution of the National Assembly, direct elections for the presidency (Ebert had been chosen by a simple majority of the National Assembly), the appointment of 'expert' (i.e. conservative) ministers at Foreign Affairs and the Economics and Finance Ministries, and the sacking of the pro-republican commander, General Reinhardt. Last but not least, he, Lüttwitz, would be promoted to the post of Commander-in-Chief of the Reichswehr. Oh, and Noske would have to withdraw the order disbanding the 'naval brigades' commanded by Captain Erhardt.[1]

This extraordinary shopping list from a would-be military dictator could hardly be approved by a Social Democratic president and a Social Democratic (if pro-military) minister, and, sure enough, it wasn't. The next day, Noske announced Lüttwitz's dismissal. During the night of Friday 12 to Saturday 13 March 1920, Erhardt's Freikorps left its barracks on the western outskirts of Berlin in full combat array and began its advance into the heart of the capital, aiming for the government district. The men's helmets bore a white-painted symbol that was rapidly becoming the badge of the post-war far right: the Swastika.

Meanwhile, the putative civilian leader of the coup had been in hiding. Wolfgang Kapp, a senior Prussian civil servant who had co-founded the rabidly nationalist and imperialist Fatherland Party in 1917, was lying low in a fashionable part of Berlin, at the apartment of an admirer, the wife of a former German ambassador to the Ottoman Empire.[2] After the Freikorps forces occupied the Reich Chancellery, at around 7 a.m. on 13 March, the sixty-one-year-old Kapp was proclaimed Chancellor, and Lüttwitz, the would-be regime's military strongman, his Defence Minister.

It all seemed remarkably easy. One major reason for this was that the government had fled Berlin. As had been the case at the beginning of the left-wing Spartacist uprising a little over a year earlier, ministers were forced to face the uncomfortable truth that they had no military force they could rely on to protect them. The reasons for this were, however, very different from what they had been back in January 1919 when the Spartacists had tried to march on the Reichstag.

A senior Social Democrat, Otto Braun, described a visit to the Reich Chancellery, where Ebert, Noske and the rest of the cabinet held an emergency meeting in the small hours of 12/13 March:

> As I hurried through the grand library, there was a group of officers standing there, including Seeckt and others. I can still see the self-satisfied smile on their faces. It was as if to say: Go back, you can't save your friends now. In the ante-room I encountered the Prussian Minister of War, General Reinhardt, who gave me a brief account of what had happened. The mutinous troops were marching from Döberitz to Berlin under the command of Erhardt and Lüttwitz. He had declared himself ready to take up arms against them, but the commanders of the troops stationed in Berlin had told him: Reichswehr does not fight against Reichswehr.[3]

Braun asked Reinhardt whether their attitude would be different if the troops they were being asked to fire upon were marching in support of communism. Reinhardt merely smiled wryly in reply. It was shortly after this that the majority of the Reich cabinet made the decision to leave Berlin. Decamping in the middle of the night to Dresden, they suffered a further humiliation when the commander there, the same General Maercker who had declined to protect them during the National Assembly's deliberations at Weimar, also indicated that he was not willing to take up arms on the legitimate government's behalf. Finally, the cabinet's caravan headed south-westward, to Stuttgart, where the ministers managed to establish a temporary seat of government.

One of the things that the Social Democratic members of the cabinet found time to do on their unexpectedly lengthy tour of central and then south-western Germany was to contact the leaders of the trade unions in Berlin. They might not have the active support of the Reichswehr, but they had the support of organised labour's big battalions, and they decided to use it. Carl Legien and the other leaders, including those considerably to the left of him, agreed to a general strike in the capital.

Even before the general strike was declared, it had become clear that the coup's chances of success were modest, and they became yet more modest as the hours and then days went on. Politically astute Reichswehr officers, including Seeckt, were unwilling to use violence to suppress the uprising. They nonetheless realised that if, as seemed probable, it failed, then the chief beneficiaries would be the far left – the very 'Bolsheviks' from whom they were supposed to be protecting the German people – whose leaders would now argue, more convincingly than before, that the only alternative to a military dictatorship was a dictatorship of the proletariat.

Nor did most civil servants carry out the new regime's orders. In the Berlin ministries now supposedly under the control of the Kapp supporters, the great majority of officials obeyed their departmental heads, who, although not necessarily sympathetic to the Republic, stuck almost to a man with the legitimate government. Only in the ultra-conservative, monarchist backwoods of eastern Prussia was there widespread support among senior officials and military men for Kapp – who was, after all, one of their own.

The strike started on Saturday, 13 March, and though it took until Monday, 15 March, the first proper working day of the week, to reach its fullest extent, the paralysis of the transport, power and communications systems and the shutdown of the shops and factories, allied to the refusal of civil servants to carry out the would-be government's instructions, caused, as one historian has described it, 'the appeals of the "Reich Chancellor" Kapp to fizzle out into thin air, and nullified the attempts of the rebels to undertake any real governmental activity'.[4]

Sebastian Haffner, the civil servant's son, was at that time, aged thirteen, still, like his school fellows, nationalistically inclined. He had heard awestruck comments that 'the Kaiser was coming back' when the rebels first marched into Berlin on the Saturday morning. More news trickled in as they completed their morning lessons, for a half-day's school at the beginning of the weekend was still the rule then. But soon the strike began to take effect:

> We had no more news, because even by that first evening there were no more newspapers, and in any case, as it turned out, no electric light to read anything by. The next morning there was no water either. No mail. There was no public transport running. And the shops were shut. In short, there was nothing.[5]

The locals in Haffner's respectable area of Berlin were forced, since mains power and water had been shut down, to fill buckets from ancient municipal springs that still existed on a few street corners and to haul them gingerly home, careful not to spill the precious liquid. Otherwise there were no demonstrations, he recalled, no real discussions, unlike during the revolution eighteen months earlier. And those few supporters of the putsch in the neighbourhood rather made fools of themselves:

It's true that our PE teacher, who was very 'national' (all the teachers were 'national', but no one more so than the PE teacher) explained many times with great conviction that 'You can feel immediately that there's a quite different hand on the tiller'. But to tell the truth, we noticed nothing at all, and even he was probably only saying that to console himself for the fact that he noticed nothing at all either.

From school we made our way to Unter den Linden, roused by a deep sense that this was where you had to be when 'patriotic events' were afoot, and also in the hope of seeing or experiencing something there. But there was nothing to see and nothing to experience. A few soldiers were standing in a bored fashion around pointlessly high-mounted machine guns. No one came to attack them. In fact everything had a kind of Sunday feeling, contemplative and peaceful. That was down to the general strike . . .

On 18 March, Morgan Philips Price of the *Manchester Guardian* wrote succinctly: 'We are living now in Berlin without light, gas or water. The new Government is caught like a rat in a trap.'[6]

It was not an entirely peaceful struggle. There were some armed clashes between supporters of the Republic and the Kapp rebels. Walter Koch, the Saxon state government's representative in Berlin, reported frequent flare-ups in the government quarter, where he had his offices and his home.

There was shooting pretty much day and night around our building, so that we quickly moved our furniture out of the line of fire. It was a frequent occurrence during the day that the call sounded from the Potsdamer Platz: 'Clear the street!' It was amusing to see how the numerous passers-by would crowd into the building entrances like mice. Wicked automatic fire raked the Budapester Strasse. Once the rattle of the machine guns ceased, the people would gradually risk emerging from the buildings, and ten minutes later the traffic would be flowing as if nothing had happened.[7]

All the same, by 15 March the rebels had already begun covert talks with the handful of cabinet members who had stayed behind after the rest of the government left town. There was already talk of 'compromise'. The ministers in Berlin, worried that the general strike, peaceful or not, might get out of hand, and eager to restore peace and normality to the capital, understandably gave more ground than the ministers observing from the safety of the provinces were, equally understandably, prepared to countenance. It was obvious that the putsch had failed in its main object. Moreover, with the unions and the (in many cases armed) supporters of the far left now mobilised in defence of the Republic, any concessions to the anti-democratic right – which had, after all, committed an indisputable act of high treason – could only count as the crassest provocation.

On 17 March, Kapp fled Berlin and, using a false passport, found his way to Sweden. Lüttwitz took refuge in Hungary, where a right-wing monarchist government had replaced the Soviet-style regime of the immediate post-war period. Other leaders of the putsch also made themselves scarce, like Kapp, often using false passports.

As for the Erhardt Brigade, its men may have seemed peaceful to Sebastian Haffner that afternoon on Unter den Linden at the height of the general strike, but when they left Berlin once more, on 18 March, there was nothing mild about them. As they passed in full order back through the Brandenburg Gate, the brigade band playing 'Deutschland über Alles', insulting comments were shouted from among the onlookers thronging the adjacent Pariser Platz. The Freikorps promptly opened fire directly into the crowd, killing twelve civilians and wounding thirty more. The fatal division within German society – expressed in the tendency of many Germans to treat as less than human fellow countrymen of whose politics they disapproved – was widening alarmingly.[8]

Even worse were the events that followed. This time it was not the right but the left that rose up. The call to a general strike in Berlin had been raised elsewhere in Germany, including in the industrial areas of Saxony and the Ruhr. But when the putsch was over, the strikers – and in some areas the armed worker militias that had been formed to support them – refused to return to what passed for normality. The far left, criticising the weakness of the Social Democratic–Liberal–Centre Party coalition government in allowing the Freikorps and the military to get so far out of control, and using the crisis as an opportunity to put forward revolutionary demands, escalated the situation into one of near-insurrection. Especially in the Saxon city of Leipzig, and in the Ruhr industrial area, the clashes between Reichswehr and Freikorps forces supporting the government, were willingly – some would say eagerly – turned into full-scale battles that would last days and in some cases weeks.

The fighting between the leftist militants of the so-called 'Red Army of the Ruhr' and the Freikorps/Reichswehr forces in the first half of April 1920 was ferocious. It cost the lives of more than 1,000 workers (mostly, it is thought, shot after being taken prisoner) and of 208 members of the Reichswehr, with another 123 posted missing. Major military operations continued through April and into the month of May and resulted in the complete defeat of the workers' insurrection.[9]

The problem was that, technically speaking, the area in which the fighting was taking place was supposed to be a 'demilitarised zone', where the Reichswehr was not supposed to operate. In response to the Berlin government's use of Reichswehr troops against the Ruhr uprising, the French ordered their army to occupy the city of Frankfurt on Main and several other important neighbouring towns, including Offenbach and Darmstadt. The force included French colonial troops, which caused special outrage. On the first day of the occupation in Frankfurt there was an incident where Moroccan troops, surrounded by a crowd of protesters, lost sight of their officer and fired into the crowd, killing and injuring several civilians.[10] The acting Chancellor, Hermann Müller, told an outraged National Assembly: 'In Frankfurt on Main, French militarism has advanced as if into an enemy country. There are Senegalese at Frankfurt University and at the house where Goethe was born . . .'[11]

If the Kapp–Lüttwitz putsch, though a failure, had achieved one thing, it had been to reveal the extremes which German nationalists were capable of less than a year and a half after the revolution. It was also, as the subsequent fighting in the Ruhr showed, the spark that fired a civil war within the union and working-class movement, sealing the divisions that would make a government by a unified left in Germany impossible and thereby condemn the country to weak, divided governments for the rest of the Weimar era.

Strangest of all, it was as if these multiple terrible things were happening in compartments, separated from each other. The Reich was big, and traditionally localised in its interests and loyalties. Even while epoch-making, often bloody events were occurring in the country's cities and industrial centres, provincial Germany on the whole went its near-oblivious way. A chronicler of the 'German Civil War' wrote :

> . . . it was precisely this diversity that stood in the way of any conscious unified effort on the part of either revolution or counter-revolutionary groups. A revolution in Berlin did not necessarily give rise to similarly directed consequences all over Germany, and a success for the counter-revolution in another part of Germany did not inevitably mean that it would find similar success elsewhere. This diversity in the cultural and social structure of the German state goes some of the way to explaining why the most explosive consequence of the Kapp putsch, the workers' uprising on the Ruhr in March and April 1920, not only ended in failure, but also why it impinged on the consciousness of most Germans outside the area immediately affected little more than a host of other everyday events.[12]

All this was true, but there were some things in Germany that still held together, no matter which part of the country one was in, or which political tendency held sway there. The most important of these was, despite everything, the German military, rapidly developing, in these hazardous post-war conditions, into a self-reliant state within a state. In early 1920, no two cities could have been further apart politically than socialist-liberal-ruled Berlin and reactionary Munich, where, since the violent suppression of the Soviet Bavarian Republic in the late spring of 1919, the nationalist right dominated. But Reichswehr in Berlin spoke to Reichswehr in Munich, and vice versa.

So it was that on 16 March 1920, when the coup was still in progress, a military aircraft from Munich landed at Tempelhof in Berlin, a landing strip attached to what had been the Prussian army's old training area and parade ground. Two men, one in his fifties and one just thirty years old, climbed out and demanded to be led to the headquarters of the Kapp–Lüttwitz rebels. Carrying an introduction from a Reichswehr intelligence officer in Munich by the name of Captain Karl Mayr, they were to inform the insurrectionist 'government' of events in Bavaria and while doing so sound out the Berlin situation. Unfortunately, their mission proved in vain. The Kapp rebellion was, it turned out, teetering on the brink of failure. They never met the 'Chancellor', who was already preparing to make himself scarce. The men flew back to Munich with little to show for their trouble, except perhaps a lesson in how not to carry out a successful *coup d'état*.

The elder visitor went by the name of Dietrich Eckart, a nationalist writer, poet and gadfly on the Munich literary scene. The younger was a protégé of Mayr and, according to the officer's account to his Berlin co-conspirators, 'a good German man, if also something of a wanton anti-Semite'.[13]

Captain Mayr's favourite was not yet quite thirty-one years old and, though already very active in far-right politics, until his formal demobilisation on 1 April 1920 would still hold the rank of corporal in the army. His name was Adolf Hitler.

Captain Mayr kept in touch with Wolfgang Kapp, despite the abject failure of the first fully-fledged nationalist attempt to overthrow the Republic. He wrote six months later to his political friend, now exiled in Sweden:

The national workers' party must provide the basis for the strong assault-force (*Stoßtrupp*) that we are hoping for. The programme is still somewhat clumsy and also, perhaps, incomplete. We'll have to supplement it. Only one thing is certain: that under this banner we've already won a good number of supporters. Since July of last year I've been looking . . . to strengthen the movement . . . I've set up very capable young people. A Herr Hitler, for instance, has become a motive force, a popular speaker of the first rank. In the Munich branch we have over 2,000 members, compared with under 100 in summer 1919.[14]

12

The Rally

For now, despite the far-left uprisings in the Ruhr and elsewhere that followed the Kapp–Lüttwitz fiasco, the return of the legitimate government to Berlin restored something of the feeling of progress that had been cautiously present before 13 March.

The trade unions, having saved the government, now demanded political changes as their price. They kept the strike going for a day or two just to make their point absolutely clear, and the changes came.

Bauer, the colourless trade unionist, who had proved a weak chancellor, resigned after 219 days in office, continuing a pattern of short-lived administrations that would prove the rule in the first German democracy. Gustav Noske lost his post as Reichswehr Minister, having clearly not lived up to his promise of keeping the army on the government's side. The rangy former basket weaver from the Prussian heartland of Brandenburg had trusted the generals and his trust had been betrayed.

Noske would tell Harry Kessler, when they met by chance three months later on a train journey, that 'Lüttwitz had been represented to him as a deeply religious man who, having sworn an oath of loyalty, would keep it. His dismissal would moreover have upset the officer corps.' Kessler continued, with his characteristic mix of humanitarian concern and crashing snobbery:

Noske is manifestly a perfectly sincere and dyed-in-the-wool militarist, whom the officer corps, with the help of his prejudices and their catchwords, has led by the nose . . . Though unemployed, he looks prosperous enough, travels first class, wears brand new yellow boots, and consumed during the journey large quantities of ham rolls and beer. Were there not so much innocent blood on his hands, he would be a slightly comic, almost likeable figure.[1]

The replacement for Bauer as Chancellor was the Foreign Minister, Hermann Müller, another Social Democrat, but of an altogether tougher and smarter sort. There was little for Müller to do, however, other than to hold the government together until new elections could be organised. It was certainly high time the German people were consulted afresh. The government's critics on the right and left were correct in declaring that the National Assembly, elected to give Germany a constitution, had outlived its function and needed to be replaced by a proper parliament. Elections were eventually fixed for June 1920. The omens for the governing parties' popularity with the voters were not good.

During the Kapp putsch, with a general strike paralysing Berlin, the exchanges and telegraph offices were closed and no official rates had been quoted for the mark. Not so in London and New York and the other world financial centres. Before the coup there had been signs of improvement in the mark/dollar rate. The German currency had firmed dramatically from 91.40 marks to the dollar on 7 March to 68.90 on 11 March.[2] 'Exchange Rallying' read the headline in *The Times* of London, reporting on the New York markets' performance on 11 March. *The Times* especially noted the German mark's strong showing, 50 per cent up on the week, citing eager purchasing by American investors of German municipal debt at a million dollars-worth a day, improvements in the Reich's balance of trade and rumours that the Allies might ease restrictions on Germany's overseas borrowing.[3] Then, on the same day as this enthusiastic report, came the Kapp putsch.

Three days into the crisis, *The Times* reported that the mark had suffered a precipitous fall from 267.5 marks per pound sterling the previous Wednesday (10 March) to a low of 370 on Tuesday, 16 March, before recovering slightly to close at 337.5. With the dollar running at approximately $3.65 to the pound, this gives a rough rate of 92.50 on the dollar reckoning, in other words a loss of around a third on its value of a few days earlier.[4] The day before the Berlin exchanges were due to open again on Thursday, 25 March, after the putsch had been defeated and the general strike called off, the mark was reported to be trading at around 75 marks to the dollar. There it remained for the rest of the week. By the following Wednesday, preceding the Easter break, it was at 71. It then opened on 6 April at 66.90, before on 9 April reaching 57.60 – the sort of exchange rate not seen since early January. It remained at around 60 for the rest of the month.[5]

The mark seemed to be holding at a manageable value. Violent challenges from the reactionary right and the revolutionary left had been beaten off. There would soon be new elections and a new government. Employment and trade numbers alike were looking more positive.

None of this was happening before time. During the rapid inflation of the previous winter, Morgan Philips Price of the *Manchester Guardian* had written of the distress even of the employed German working class:

I have just received the following figures of the monthly budget of a Berlin tram driver who has a wife and a daughter of twelve. His monthly wage is 400 marks, which is equivalent in English money at present rates to £4. The weekly wage of a Berlin tram driver, in English money, is therefore £1 a week. Against this there are the following expenses monthly.

	Marks
Rent	55
Taxes	20
School money	16
Fire and lighting	38
Washing	12

Travelling expenses	17
Clothing	25
Footwear	12
Pocket money, newspapers, odd repairs	25
Food	180
TOTAL	400

The 180 marks (36 shillings) for food has to last three persons for one month. The other day I went into the restaurant of the Adlon Hotel and found that a luncheon there costs 30 marks without wine. It is impossible to get through the day there without paying 60 marks for food alone. In other words, in a day in a fashionable Berlin restaurant one person spends on food as much as a member of a working-class family spends in a month . . . The food of the family whose budget I quote above consists on most days of black bread, potatoes and vegetables. Occasionally a pound of butter is bought at speculative prices [i.e. on the black market] for 28 marks a pound. That has to last for six weeks or two months.[6]

In April 1920, after the Kapp putsch, a further report in the London Sunday newspaper the *Observer* described how the German lower middle classes were becoming 'compulsory vegetarians':

> They taste no meat from the beginning of the year to the end. An egg is a rare luxury . . . To the Englishman travelling in Rhineland it does not seem particularly extravagant to pay 350 marks for a lunch for two people. But this amount represents a German workman's wages for three weeks' toil.[7]

Nor was such misery – it is hard not see these British reporters, however well intentioned, as what a later, more cynical age would call 'misery tourists' – confined to the working and lower middle classes. Quite grand members of Germany's intellectual elite, if they were on a fixed salary, could find themselves subjected to a humiliating drop in their standard of living. The same correspondent added:

An English businessman, who found it imperatively necessary to travel from Berlin to Cologne during the recent general strike, had to pay 40,000 marks for the single journey, in addition to a guarantee to indemnify the garage proprietor in case of anything happening to the car. 40,000 marks! – and the yearly salary of the Director of one of the greatest museums in Germany is 30,000 marks, not allowing for heavy taxation. This Director, notwithstanding his keen desire to entertain an English visitor, who could in many ways be helpful to him, was unable to offer him a sandwich or a biscuit in his almost palatial home. There was practically no food in the house.

All the same, it seemed in the early summer of 1920, though much in Germany was still confusion and deprivation, that an era of stability might at last be beginning.

Inflation had been held, and perhaps now it could be defeated.

Inflation afflicted every nation involved in the First World War, not just the losers. In Britain, prices more than doubled between 1913 and 1919; in France they were multiplied by around 3.5 per cent, directly comparable with Germany. Even America suffered a doubling of pre-war prices. As was the case in Germany, this trend continued into the early post-war era. In Great Britain, between May 1919 and May 1920, prices jumped further by 40 per cent from 246 to 325 (1913 = 100); in America, in 1919–20 prices rose by another quarter. In France, the victor country with the most serious economic and financial problems, the rise between April 1919 and 1920 was a spectacular 77 per cent.[8]

Every one of the belligerent nations had spent vast amounts on things that didn't count as items of human consumption, and borrowed or printed money to do so. Then came peace, and, accompanying the relief at the end of violence, the gnawing anxiety of how to pay the bill for it.

A latecomer to the war and by 1918 the only major power with a surplus to invest rather than a deficit to finance, only America came through the conflict without serious damage to its economy, or to its financial and fiscal structures. Even Britain, which at the beginning of the war was in spectacularly good financial shape, with the lowest debt-to-income ratio of any European country,[9] had by the third spring of the war drained its once-burgeoning imperial economy near enough dry.

America's entry into the war on the Allied side in April 1917 was the *deus ex machina* that saved a financially exhausted Britain from running out of the cash it needed to pay for the American goods – food, raw materials and munitions – that were by now vital to the Allied war effort. In a splendid irony, Germany's high-stakes switch to unlimited submarine warfare, pushed through by Ludendorff and the ultra-nationalists against the advice of cooler heads among the Reich's elite, served as the *casus belli*. It was thus arguably the British Empire's bitterest enemies in Berlin whose blunder, by tipping the USA into the Allied camp, managed to arrange Britain's (and the Entente's) salvation. As the German banker Max Warburg, a consistent opponent of unrestricted submarine warfare, had remarked in 1916: 'If America is cut off from Germany, this means a fifty percent reduction in Germany's financial strength for the war and an increase of a hundred percent for England and France's.'[10]

Germany had financed her campaign mainly by domestic war loans, with some foreign borrowing from neutrals – she owed 1.5 billion gold marks to Holland by the end of the war and as much again to other neutrals – but she relied on foreign money far less than the Entente. This placed Germany in a different position to the Entente post-war, as well.

True, the German government owed its own people vast sums, but who was going to enforce the repayment of that? In any case, by the end of the war 5 per cent annual interest on the face value of a war bond was already worth a lot less in real terms than in 1914, and the value took a further dramatic dive between 1918 and 1920. Already, even though the inflation was not yet at the hyper stage – indeed, in the late spring of 1920 it had apparently reached a kind of plateau – a lot of Germany's domestic war debt had effectively been liquidated. No one expressed it more clearly than Keynes, who knew full well from the outset what was going on in Germany, in his *Economic Consequences of the Peace*: 'By a continuing process of inflation, governments can confiscate, secretly and unobserved, an important part of the wealth of their citizens.'[11]

No, the biggest debt Germany was going to have to deal with in the post-war era was that pertaining to reparations. While, following the Kapp putsch, the mark continued its recovery, the Allies were still haggling over the exact sum, nature and distribution of the reparations they planned to demand. The negotiations, mainly at Spa in Belgium, would go on throughout 1920 and into the early part of 1921. The wait for a decision, from the point of view of Germany and the other defeated powers, was agonising, and destabilising.

Part of the problem arose from the web of inter-Allied debt that had come into being during the war. The United States had lent the European Allies around $10 billion altogether, with Britain often acting as intermediary. By the end of the war, France owed $4 billion to the United States directly, and $3 billion to Britain. Britain in turn owed $4.7 billion to America, while being owed $11.1 in total by the other Allied powers, including the minor ones. Britain was therefore relying on getting paid by France and other Allies in order to pay back its debt to America; while France was counting on getting reparations from Germany.[12]

This gives some idea of the war debt versus reparations merry-go-round that followed the end of the war. Whatever the rights or wrongs of the financial penalties forced upon Germany, it helps to explain why the French in particular – but also, try as they might to hide the fact, the British as well – were so insistent on their billions of pounds of flesh. If we take the pre-war gold mark/dollar rate as 4.2, then it comes out that the Allies owed America 42 billion gold marks.

The notional transfer into gold marks is useful because it helps look at the reparations totals that were up for discussion between the Allies in a meaningful way. So, if we add an estimate for damage caused by the German occupation of northern France and the fighting that went on there of between $7 billion and $11 billion (see Chapter 2) and take a median of $9 billion, we must add another bill of around 38 billion gold marks. So that is already a running total of 80 billion gold marks. Belgium's economy was paralysed at the end of the war. In the spring of 1919, the country still suffered from 75 per cent unemployment, and meanwhile was looking for at least $3 billion (12.6 billion gold marks) for civilian damage, war debts and pensions. This was before she embarked on trying to get compensation for the financial shenanigans that the Germans had indulged in during their four-year occupation. These had included flooding the Belgian economy with paper marks which depreciated rapidly during the course of the war but were still redeemed at the ludicrously high compulsory rate of 1.25 Belgian francs to the mark. The cost of this forced conversion, the Belgian government claimed, amounted to 7.5 billion francs.[13] Our running total now reaches somewhere between 95 and 100 billion gold marks. And these were by no means the only financial losses the Allied powers had suffered and for which they might feel inclined to seek recompense.

Understandably, none of the victorious Allied governments wanted to have to tell their taxpayers that this money, which they had been told for more than four years was being spent on a just war against a brutal German tyranny, was going to be levied on them rather than on the defeated enemy. This nervousness on the part of the Allied rulers when explaining the post-war settlement to their populations affected not just the substance of the penalties inflicted on Germany but, perhaps even more significantly, the appearance of these penalties. Reparations were bound to be complicated, and the governments of the victor nations were not at all above exploiting this complexity, using it to hide milder terms within tough-sounding rhetoric, smaller net figures within impressively punitive-sounding gross numbers.

So, reparations were a way for the victorious Allies – all except America, the lender – to repay their own war loans without additional pain. Had the American loans to their co-belligerents been forgiven, as some had believed and many hoped they would be, then it seemed logical that the pressure for imposing crippling reparations on the Germans would have been correspondingly lessened.

However, America gave not an inch in that regard. Both in Congress and in government, there was pretty much universal agreement that the loans made to the Allies during the war were commercial loans, to be repaid in full. As early as November 1918, when, just after the armistice, the British first made a suggestion that debts might be cancelled, they got a dusty answer from Treasury Secretary William McAdoo.[14] This insistence on every cent being repaid by America's struggling former allies turned 'Uncle Sam' in popular parlance into 'Uncle Shylock'.

Germany therefore found itself not just the loser in a major war but also, initially at least, a powerless spectator in a post-war economic game of some complexity and danger. The debtor nations among the victors – in practice, everyone except the USA – needed to run consistent export surpluses for some years in order to earn the gold necessary to pay back America. Looked at through this lens, Germany was no different. She also owed a lot of money, much of it indirectly to America via future reparations payments to America's debtors – Britain, France, Belgium and the rest. Germany therefore also needed, in the post-war period, to vastly increase her taxes to put money in her government's coffers. Since the Allies would accept reparations only in hard, gold-backed currency, not in paper marks, Germany also needed to achieve a spectacular increase in her exports, in order to earn the foreign exchange required to meet her obligations.

In effect, it followed that every European nation had to create a large export surplus during the post-war years. But if that was so, under widespread conditions of slump everywhere except Germany, who was going to actually buy these exports? For Britain, France, Belgium and so on – or for that matter, Germany – to run surpluses, they needed someone to run a deficit. And who was that going to be? The country they owed all the money to, i.e. America? In Europe's dreams, perhaps, but in reality, never.

America was pretty self-sufficient, and, especially in commodities such as foodstuffs, a strong net exporter. Not, therefore, a great candidate for the role of sucker-in of imports from the desperate Europeans. The American economy was also a highly protected one. It would become even more so when the Republican candidate, Warren G. Harding, won the presidency in late 1920 on an 'America First' platform, based on the lower taxes and even higher tariff walls which were an article of faith for the GOP's industrial and agricultural supporters. Harding's Secretary of Commerce, Herbert Hoover, would argue, one must suppose disingenuously, that American purchase of European services, especially through the growth of transatlantic tourist visits to Europe, would help get round this problem.

In fact, the only realistic way of squaring the circle was for American banks, which were awash with potential credit, to lend the Europeans the money needed to set off the recovery that would enable those same Europeans to pay the debts they owed from the war.[15] The similarity of this strategy to the modern one of running up debt on one credit card in order to pay off another hardly needs to be mentioned.

The international debt problem was made even worse by the domestic-economic decisions that were made by Western governments in the aftermath of victory. In both America and Great Britain, the powers that be decided to prioritise financial stability over production, private over social welfare, and capital over labour, thus reversing the trends that had been followed during the war.

In Britain, the release of pent-up demand for goods, normal in a post-war period, had led to a spectacular boom that was brought to an abrupt halt in April 1920 when the Bank of England raised interest rates sharply. In America, the Federal Reserve followed a similar strategy. The consequence of this espousal of a balanced budget, spending cuts and tight money by the two major English-speaking powers, was a slump known in its time, though not for long, as the 'Great Depression'.[16] In mid-1921, between a fifth and a quarter of the insured working population of Britain was out of work: 2.4 million people.[17]

Even in Britain, the harsh new economic policies led to strikes and riots, and were justified by a government rhetoric that exploited the fears of the middle classes. In America, the political atmosphere was thick with the 'Red Scare'. Attorney General Alexander Mitchell Palmer pushed through arrests and deportations of foreign activists and agitators (the so-called 'Palmer Raids'), and there was a rise in violent strike-breaking activity.

So, again, in the light of the slump in two of its biggest foreign markets, to whom was Germany supposed to export in order to earn the gold that would soon be demanded by the Allies under the terms of the Versailles Treaty? In any case, the country remained in very poor shape politically. It was all very well for the two most well-established democracies, Britain and the USA, to subject their populations to ruthless post-war economic health cures, but could newly democratised Germany, in which the electorate was sharply – not to say violently – divided, risk such a daring strategy?

The consensus among the supporters of the Weimar Republic was that it could not, and if the international value of the mark had to be sacrificed to save democracy, so be it.

13

Goldilocks and the Mark

The purpose of the new German elections that took place in June 1920 was to replace the National Assembly with the first post-war Reichstag, in other words to follow a predominantly constituent body with a law-making and governing one. It was surely right that this should be so, but if the government's object in sending the people back to the polls was to further the process of post-war stabilisation, it could not have made a worse miscalculation.

The vote showed, if the chaos of the year's early months had not already done so, that whatever degree of consensus had carried the country through the revolution and the painful path to the peace treaty, any such unity of purpose belonged to the past.

The losses for the moderate parties were devastating. The Majority Social Democrats, who had won almost 38 per cent of the vote in January 1919 and 165 seats, had their vote almost halved, to 21.7 per cent, giving them 102 seats. All the other government parties suffered losses, most seriously the democratically minded liberal German Democratic Party, which saw its support, mostly among the educated middle class, reduced even more markedly, from 18.6 to 8.3 per cent.

The Majority Social Democrats had lost most votes to the Independent Social Democrats, whose share soared from 7.6 per cent and 22 seats to 17.9 per cent and 84 seats. The fledgling German Communist Party received 2.1 per cent. The next biggest gainer was the 'German People's Party', the right-of-centre liberals, led by Gustav Stresemann, whose attacks on the Versailles Treaty and on Erzberger's swingeing new taxes had found a response among the beleaguered middle classes. The right-liberals enjoyed a tripling of their vote (from 4.4 to 13.6 per cent) and an increase in Reichstag seats from 19 to 65. The nationalist-conservative, stridently anti-Republic German National People's Party also benefited from popular disillusionment, winning 71 seats.

With a total of 459 seats to be distributed in the new Reichstag, the previous governing coalition could only win 205. Never again would there be a majority in the German parliament that gave the Republic its unconditional support. For the rest of the decade, the country would suffer from weak, unstable governments, subjected to an insistent and well-funded barrage of criticism from the radical nationalist camp that could not help but exercise a long-term negative effect on the German public's conception of democracy.

For now, however, to become viable, the new post-election government would have to follow public opinion and political mathematics, and shift to the right. The new Chancellor would have to come, for the first time since the revolution, from a non-socialist party.

The Majority Social Democrat Chancellor, Hermann Müller, resigned. Sixty-eight-year-old Konstantin Fehrenbach, of the Catholic Centre Party, formed a minority administration composed of Centre, German Democratic Party, and, for the first time, the German People's Party. It could command the loyalty of only around 170 deputies, and therefore was dependent on Majority Social Democratic support on most major issues.

The new coalition was in any case not a strong combination. The German People's Party was opposed both to the Republic – in theory at least – and to the Versailles Treaty. It was also reliant on the financial support of many powerful industrialists, including Hugo Stinnes, adding to the party's strongly pro-business and anti-socialist tone. The dream of a democratic Germany was not yet a thing of the past, but the 1920 Reichstag election certainly spelled the end for a social-democratic one.

If the period after the defeat of the Kapp conspiracy represented

Germany's window of opportunity to turn back the tide of inflation – and if there was one, this was probably it – Fehrenbach and his ministers were, sadly, not equipped with the instruments to turn that chance into a reality. Fehrenbach himself was a decent man who had previously been President of the National Assembly and was therefore experienced in crafting compromises. However, for the period of almost a year that followed the June 1920 election, he and his ministers were doomed to spend most of their energy and ingenuity, not getting the country out of its financial hole, but haggling over the interpretation of the Versailles Treaty and the final sum that would soon become due as reparations.

Precisely at the end of June 1920, as fate would have it, the mark reached its most favourable rate against the dollar in more than a year: 37.95. Good news! Except that the improvement caused problems elsewhere in the economy.

That spring, State Secretary Hirsch of the Finance Ministry had been waylaid at a railway station by a Communist agitator carrying a placard that read: 'See what this "comrade" Hirsch has given you. First, he promised to make the mark strong again. Now it is stronger, but we cannot export any more. Instead of inflation, he has brought us unemployment and hunger.'[1] It was certainly true that, although the strengthening mark was in principle a positive development, it did make German goods less competitive on world markets and thereby brought a rise in unemployment. The stronger the mark, the more Germans out of work.

A table comparing unemployment with the exchange rates for 1920–21 shows a pretty precise correlation:

Month	Marks to Dollar Rate	Unemployment (per cent)
April (1920)	72	1.9
May	57.5	2.7
June	39.3	4.0

July	37.95	6.0
August	42.25	5.9
September	49.75	4.5
October	61.55	4.2
November	77.87	3.9
December	62.18	4.1
January (1921)	74.72	4.5
February	65.48	4.7
March	60.93	3.7
April	62.55	3.9
May	65.65	3.7
June	63.30	3.0
July	74.92	2.6
August	74.92	2.2
September	84.41	1.4
October	124.37	1.2
November	181.31	1.4
December	217.00	1.6

There is evidence that during the late spring/early summer of 1920, foreign customers began to baulk at the international price of German goods; domestic consumers, meanwhile, went on a 'buyers' strike', perhaps in anticipation of even lower prices, but perhaps, because of the hefty price rises that had been imposed during the previous bout of rapid inflation, they really couldn't afford the goods.[2]

As a consequence of the uncomfortable situation that the now-unaccustomed health of the mark caused during the period of May to August 1920, it seems that, in fact, the Finance Ministry and the Reichsbank covertly combined their efforts, not to strengthen the currency but to keep the value of the mark from rising any further.

The authorities seem to have seen their job as maintaining the exchange rate at what might be dubbed a 'Goldilocks' level – not so high as to inhibit exports, not so low as to increase the economic and financial chaos within the Reich itself. More especially, a reasonable exchange rate against foreign currencies was necessary to keep essential imports of food for the working population affordable. The value during most of this time of 60–70 marks to the dollar apparently represented this 'not too hot, not too cold' value that the financial elite in Germany favoured.[3] In other words, there was no incentive, even at this relatively favourable point, to actively promote the strength of the national currency and thus start to halt and even reverse the unstoppable march of inflation.

Walther Rathenau, head of the AEG electricals conglomerate founded by his father, heroic co-architect of Germany's wartime economic effort, bestselling author, and latterly democratic politician, was minuted as having told a meeting at the German Foreign Office in January 1921 that the Anglo-American slump must be prevented from infecting Germany, whatever the cost. The meeting secretary's note read:

> He was not afraid of inflation, if he might make an aside not strictly relevant to the agenda: should the depression that has attacked England with full force spread across to us, we ought to print money a bit faster and start construction works, using the employment these create as a dam against the depression. It was incorrect when people said that printing money was bringing us to ruin.[4]

Fatal words. For the meantime, however, the fragile stability of the mark was maintained. There were two more changes of government in this time. No new elections, but reshufflings of the political pack.

Fehrenbach's government collapsed at the beginning of May 1921, when the Allies, meeting in London for the last of seemingly count-less post-Versailles conferences, finally presented the big reparations bill that Germany had been kept waiting for since November 1918. It amounted to 132 billion gold marks (around $31.5 billion at pre-war rates). The figure had actually been drastically reduced from an original 269 billion gold marks (around $64 billion) put forward in January 1921. Mind-boggling (and astonishingly variable) as these sums were, everyone took them extremely seriously. Or so it seemed. Certainly, the demand was coupled with an Allied threat to occupy the Ruhr industrial area, should Germany not accept the demand and the payment schedule attached to it.

Despite the Chancellor's efforts to persuade the German People's Party to accept the so-called 'London Ultimatum', the Fehrenbach government fell apart as soon as a decision was required. The right-liberals of the German People's Party could accept the Republic as a reality, they could even serve in one of its governments, but they could not – yet – stomach the reality of accepting the Versailles settlement.

The curious thing was that, though the language of the Ultimatum was tough – even two and a half years after the end of the war, there were still those angry French and British voters to think about – its substance, when properly examined, was much less so.

The reparations payment schedule, for instance, divided the payment of German liabilities between three sets of bonds: A, B and C bonds. The A bonds represented the unpaid balance of the 20 billion marks that Germany was supposed to have paid since 1919, but hadn't. The B bonds were to cover war damages. Both bore interest of 6 per cent and totalled 50 billion gold marks. The other 82 billion gold marks were payable via issuing of so-called C bonds, whose role was left a little vague but was thought to have to do with cancellation of inter-Allied debt. The C bonds, however, would be issued only when Germany had proved itself capable of meeting the other obligations (the A and B bonds). These first-priority obligations would be calculated via a formula involving a fixed annual payment (reckoned at 2 billion gold marks) and a variable payment (a British-created imposition called an 'export levy') corresponding to 26 per cent of the value of German exports in any given year (at current 1921 levels around 1 billion gold marks). This made, for 1921, an annual German liability of 3 billion or so.

The almost entirely theoretical nature of the C bonds becomes clear when the actual level of German exports in the straitened, protectionist post-war world economy is taken into account. The average annual level of German exports during 1920–22 was 4.8 billion gold marks. A quarter of that (roughly the amount claimed by the export levy) amounted to around a billion. By one expert calculation, for the issue of C bonds by Germany to be triggered, German exports would have needed to more than quadruple to a total of 22 billion gold marks a year, representing five times current exports and twice what the country had managed to sell abroad even in the highly favourable, liberal peace-time trading conditions of 1913.[5] The likelihood of such a number ever being reached was further lessened by the fact that official German government statistics on imports and exports, dependent on figures supplied by businesses, were notoriously unreliable. According to a leading German financial journalist, no less a person than State Secretary Hirsch had admitted this at a meeting:

> . . . imports and exports were being falsified for the purposes of capital flight. Imports are exaggerated with the purpose of more easily permitting the actually unused portion to be kept abroad, and at the same time the exports are set at a lower level for the same purpose: to leave the surplus profit abroad.[6]

The trick with the C bonds meant that the Allies had, in fact, reduced the practical German liability to 50 billion gold marks, or even 41 billion gold marks if sums already paid in cash or in kind by Germany since 1919 are taken into account.[7] Of the C bonds, the Belgian Prime Minister of the time reputedly jested that the Reparations Commission 'could stick [the C bonds] in a drawer without bothering to lock it, for no thief would be tempted to steal them'.[8]

There were those politicians in Germany who realised immediately that the burden, though still unpleasant and to their minds unjust, was nowhere as bad as most of their fellow countrymen and country-women had expected. One Centre Party politician remarked at a party meeting just the day after the London Ultimatum that 'the Entente will only demand the 50 billion marks, not the rest. They have only called for the rest for domestic political reasons.'[9]

'Domestic political reasons' cut both ways. The public in the Allied countries saw the 132 billion marks in notional reparations and rejoiced. The public in Germany saw the 132 billions, ignored the technical sleight of hand that drastically reduced their country's actual liability, at least for the foreseeable future, and was enraged. Neither the Allied governments, who wished to conceal their relative moderation from their voters, nor the German government, keen to exaggerate the impossible economic burden of the demand as part of its long-term campaign to avoid payment, felt it in their interests to tell the truth.

All the same, however you reckoned the schedule, 50 billion marks was a great deal of money to come up with. Not only that, but the German government had to hand over a billion in an approved foreign currency (dollars, as it turned out, which were still convertible into gold) or acceptable Treasury bills, by the end of August. This demand was met, but only after a hair-raisingly complicated and difficult set of financial manoeuvres that included putting 560 cases of the Reichsbank's gold on four steamers just before the deadline, hurriedly selling paper marks in huge quantities on the foreign exchange markets, shaming several large corporations into lending the government money from their own extensive foreign exchange holdings, and, through the offices of the Mendelssohn Bank's representative in the Netherlands, raising more than a quarter of a billion in hard currency loans from a Dutch-British banking consortium.[10]

So the government got the money to the Allies in time to avoid default and a possible occupation of the Ruhr, but the procedures it had needed to go through to get the money did not bode well for future cash payments. Moreover, the German government's sale of so many paper marks within such a short period had spooked the foreign exchange markets, hence ending the period of relative stabilisation in the value of the mark abroad. Germany's currency declined from around 65 to the dollar in May to 85 in September, with a falling tendency that would further accelerate as autumn came on.

The horrified, and in many cases violent, reaction of the German public to the Allies' reparations ultimatum brought enormous political problems for the government that succeeded Fehrenbach's. The right-liberal German People's Party had walked out in protest at the settlement, after which Josef Wirth, a younger Centre politician, had put together a coalition with the Social Democrats, who were prepared go through the motions of complying with the Allied ultimatum.

The psychological effect on the German nation, and on its confidence in the future – not to mention its currency – was severe and lasting. After almost two years of living in a 'fools' paradise', they finally knew (or thought they knew) the sum they would have to pay, and for which they had signed up in June 1919, in effect issuing a blank and post-dated cheque to the Allies.

In 1806, as almost any German schoolboy – and absolutely any German nationalist – would remind everyone, Prussia had paid a huge indemnity to Napoleon Bonaparte in cash, territory and men. In 1815, with the roles reversed, defeated France had paid hefty reparations to the Allies who beat Napoleon. In 1871, under the Treaty of Frankfurt, France had been forced to pay the new German nation its notorious reparations bill of 5 billion gold francs, a sum precisely calculated on the basis of the 1806 penalty extracted by Napoleon from the defeated Prussians. All these treaties, with their heavy financial penalties for the losers in the wars to which they provided the legal conclusion, stated clearly at the time of signature what indemnities were due. And paid those indemnities were.

Versailles was the first treaty where reparations were left open-ended, and remained so for a matter of years. Unsurprisingly, under these circumstances, when the Allies' bill was finally issued, the mark tumbled. It would never again, in its current form, reach a level comparable to that in the spring of 1921. The only way now was down.

Although Matthias Erzberger had been elected as a member of the Reichstag in June 1920, he was, meanwhile, no longer Finance Minister. He had been forced to resign his post shortly before the Kapp putsch, under circumstances that caused most observers to consider him politically finished.

Karl Helfferich, the former banker and establishment economic wizard who had blithely told the Reichstag in 1915 that the Allies would have to pay for the war, had moved radically to the right under the influence of defeat and Versailles. He was now a passionate and vocal leader of the anti-republican nationalist opposition. Helfferich had made it his business to bring about the downfall of Erzberger. In his budget speech in July 1919, Erzberger had publicly blamed Helfferich's allegedly lax behaviour in office as Imperial Treasury Secretary during the war for both the size of Germany's post-war deficit and the large-scale, unhindered profiteering by arms and munitions contractors. Helfferich responded to these accusations by publishing a broadside, *Fort mit Erzberger!* (Away with Erzberger!) in which he in return accused the reforming Finance Minister of corrupt relations with big business.

Erzberger felt compelled to sue Helfferich for libel – it was while emerging from a Berlin court building after one day's legal proceedings that he was wounded by the would-be assassin, Hirschfeld – but although his persecutor was convicted of a 'defamatory statement (*üble Nachrede*), Helfferich was fined only 300 marks. Much of the evidence presented had cast Erzberger in a very unflattering light. Substantial parts of Helfferich's accusations were considered justified by the court, and in any case he had acted, so the judge said in a remark typical of the judiciary at that time, 'from patriotic motives'. Meanwhile, the right-wing *Hamburger Nachrichten* had published leaked copies of Erzberger's tax returns which also led to suspicions of tax evasion. Erzberger resigned that same day.[11]

Since the spring of 1920, Erzberger had assumed a low profile. However, perhaps inevitably for a man of his talent and energy, he was clearly planning a political comeback at some point, an ambition in which he was encouraged by further court rulings that cleared him of tax evasion and various other financial chicanery. With the Reichsbank's attempts to scrape together the tranche of a billion gold marks demanded by the Allies spread all over the newspapers, and feelings running high on the right against the politicians who had acceded to the London Ultimatum, towards the end of the summer Erzberger left Berlin to take a health cure at Bad Griesbach, a spa in the Black Forest in his native south-west Germany.

Erzberger was fully aware of the degree of hatred he aroused among German nationalists. He reportedly announced in the spring of 1921 to his daughter, Maria: 'The bullet that will kill me has already been cast.'[12] On 26 August 1921, he set off for his regular morning walk in the woods with a friend and fellow Centre Party politician, Karl Diez. At around eleven o'clock, they came under fire from two armed young men, who had been lying in wait among the trees. Erzberger, seriously wounded, scrambled down a slope in the hope of evading his attackers. Eighteen months earlier, Hirschfeld's second bullet had been deflected by Erzberger's watch chain. This time, he was not so lucky. The assassins pursued him relentlessly, raining fire on him until he fell still. They then stood over his body and shot him twice more in the head. It was a brutal, professional 'hit'.[13]

A police hunt was set in motion, and the assassins were rapidly identified, but to no avail. The two young men, both in their late twenties, were named as Heinrich Schulz and Heinrich Tillesen. The first was a former army lieutenant, the second the son of an artillery general and former torpedo boat officer. Both were Freikorps volunteers who had fought with the Erhardt Brigade and taken part in the Kapp putsch the previous year. Both were fanatical nationalists and enemies of the post-war German state.

Captain Erhardt was directly responsible for the murder of Erzberger. After the failure of the March 1920 coup, aware of being a marked man so far as the democratic government in Berlin was concerned, he had dissolved his Freikorps and headed south to the reactionary stronghold of Munich. There he had the protection of powerful friends within the authorities. Once established in Munich, over the next few months he gathered loyal followers around him and set up a conspiratorial group, codenamed Organisation Consul. The group, whose purpose was to murder politicians and public figures considered to have 'betrayed' Germany during the war and its aftermath, soon commanded a loose network of branches throughout the country, though Munich remained its nerve centre and place of refuge.

Schulz and Tillesen were duly selected from among Organisation Consul's members to kill Erzberger. After the murder, they fled back to Munich. They were quickly supplied with fake passports and spirited away to Hungary, where a 'white' terror had replaced the red. Like many other fugitive members of the German far right, they were afforded shelter by sympathetic authorities.[14]

The murder of Erzberger showed firstly that the nationalist right was prepared to kill anyone judged to be responsible for the country's post-war condition (a judgement which was, of course, arrived at entirely according to their political prejudices), but, more shockingly, it also showed that the more mainstream anti-republican elements were prepared, if not to actively participate in such violence, to tolerate, even half condone, it. The venerable *Kreuz-Zeitung*, mouthpiece of landed Prussian conservatism, compared the killers of Erzberger with Brutus, William Tell, and Charlotte Corday, who in 1793, as France's revolutionary terror reached its climax, had stabbed the Jacobin demagogue Marat in his bath. The like-minded *Berliner Lokalanzeiger* wrote, 'any other country would extend boundless understanding to such conspirators', and in East Prussia – heartland of the Kapp putsch – another local newspaper proclaimed that 'we must sow hatred':

A man who, like Erzberger, probably bears the main responsibility for our country's misfortune, must, so long as he remained alive, have presented a constant danger to Germany. It may seem coarse and heartless to write such an epitaph for a dead man, but sentimentality will get us nowhere . . . only through extremes can Germany once more become what she was before the war.[15]

Ernst Troeltsch, one of an always small and now dwindling band of liberal academics, wrote two weeks later that he expected more political murders:

The current Reich ministers and others are receiving masses of anony-
mous death threats, and they know that this is no joke. Some months
ago one of these gentlemen said to me that being a minister today
was an uneasy business; he knew that it was a matter of riding for a
fall, but he felt it his duty to persist.[16]

Erzberger's long-term legacy would be recognised. He created the
modern German tax system and might have done much more for his
country had he not been cut down at the age of not quite forty-six,
but that was for posterity to realise. At the time it was more the
symbolism that mattered, to both right and left, authoritarians and
democrats. The government responded with an ordinance forbidding
anti-republican propaganda and the glorification of anti-constitu-
tional and disorderly acts. Bavaria, where Organisation Consul and
its killers were being sheltered by the authorities, refused to obey, and
there was nothing the central government could do about it.

The perilous raising of the billion gold marks for reparations; the
murder of one of the republic's founding fathers; the renewed decline
in the value of the mark and the continued rise in the prices of life's
necessities: Germany in the late summer of 1921 seemed economically
and politically doomed.

Except that the coming months would seem to witness not doom
but boom.

14

Boom

Nearing the third anniversary of the end of the world war, Germany was not the only country in Europe in which violence and political chaos were rife.

If 1920 had been a turbulent year for the world, 1921 was scarcely less so. There were race riots in Tulsa, Oklahoma, in which twenty-one whites and sixty blacks died. There was a coup in Portugal, during which the Prime Minister and several of his cabinet were murdered. The Prime Minister of Japan was assassinated, the Prime Minister of Spain likewise. Russia remained convulsed by civil war and racked by famine. Greek and Turkish forces were engaged in a bloody war in Anatolia. Karl I, deposed King-Emperor of Austria-Hungary, undertook two separate and equally unsuccessful attempts at restoring himself to the throne of Hungary. An upstart demagogic leader by the name of Benito Mussolini was elected to the Italian parliament along with twenty-nine deputies, representatives of a thuggish new political movement known as the *Fascisti*, which made no bones about its determination to seize power when the opportunity arose. Until a truce was declared in July, Britain continued to be involved in a vicious and costly war against Irish Nationalists demanding independence for the whole island of Ireland; in the course of the struggle, the London government had recruited a force of officially approved irregulars not dissimilar to the Freikorps in Germany, made up of unemployed war veterans and known dismissively by most Irish people, because of colour of their ad hoc uniforms, as the 'Black and Tans'.

Post-war political disturbances were in almost all Western countries poisonously combined with post-war economic depression. In Britain, after the 1918–19 boom, there had been no growth in 1920, while in 1921 industrial production fell by a massive 31 per cent. In America the figures were 3 per cent growth followed by a shrinkage of 22 per cent, leading to around 12 per cent unemployment in 1921.[1] France experienced 8 per cent growth in 1920 followed by a fall of 12 per cent. Unemployment among trade union members in Britain in 1921 was 17 per cent. By comparison, in Germany industrial production during 1920–21 grew by 45 per cent, in the next year by 20 per cent. Unemployment among trade union members in Germany (more than 9 million at that time) was 4.5 per cent in January 1921, and fell to a record low of 0.9 per cent in April 1922.[2]

Germany was apparently, so far as the figures went, booming. And yet almost all the talk was still of hardship and shortages. The cheap mark – getting cheaper all the time once the fall in its value resumed in the summer of 1921 – was fuelling increased exports even in a generally depressed industrial world, but outside of a minority of industrialists, speculators and black marketeers, it was not actually feeding through into the general standard of living. Already, voices were asking how this could be. It was a situation unknown in a modern industrial country.

'German Trade Boom and the Sinking mark: How Long Will It Last?' ran the headline in the *Manchester Guardian* in October 1921. Sub-headlines referred to 'Wild Stock Exchange Gambling' and the 'Soaring Cost of Living'. The crisis over the 1 billion gold mark reparations payment and the consequent fall in the value of the mark had, the paper's correspondent in Berlin wrote, led to:

. . . wild gambling on the German stock exchange – gambling wilder than has ever been known before. The public does not seem to care what it buys so long as it can get rid of marks.

The results of the depreciation are threefold. In the first place German industry is flourishing in an unprecedented manner. Profits are enormous, big dividends are being paid, export trade has been stimulated, production has increased, and unemployment has almost vanished. In the second place the cost of living is going up and the standard of living down. In the third place foreign countries are being hit harder than ever by German competition.[3]

But the paradox was blatantly apparent:

The cost of living in Germany has risen by about 40 per cent during the last three months, and will probably continue to rise at an accelerated pace. The buying power even of full-time wages is steadily decreasing. The price of cereals has reached its highest point since the abolition of *Zwangswirtschaft.*[*]

The price of wheat has risen about 300 marks per ton and of rye about 250 marks per ton during the last fortnight. Railway tariffs are to be raised by 30 per cent . . . Potatoes cost 1 mark a kilo on February 5, 9 marks on June 4, and 10 marks now.

German children are again showing symptoms of under-feeding and malnutrition. People with fixed salaries are feeling the pinch more and more severely . . .

Many Germans suffered, and continued to suffer, even three years after the end of the war. So, who benefited from the way that Germany boomed during this 'take-off' phase of the inflation, while all around the world seemed in a phase of 'bust'?

In September 1917, after America's entry into the war, the German-Jewish shipping magnate and friend of the Kaiser Albert Ballin had expressed what he hoped was a basic truth about Germany's likely post-war position:

* Literally, 'compulsory economy', the word used to describe the centralised, state-directed German war economy, especially as applying to food distribution and pricing.

[I regard] our gravely ailing currency as an admirable means of dispelling the hatred felt abroad against Germany, and of overcoming the reluctance to trade with us [likely to be felt by] our enemies. The American who no longer gets for his dollar 4.21 marks' worth of goods from us, but 6.20 marks' worth, will rediscover his fondness for Germany.[4]

By 1920, the currency was seriously ailing, and a great deal more still by 1921–22. Ballin himself was long dead. Seemingly unable to bear the prospect of German defeat, the loss of much of his fleet and the confiscation by the Allies of his remaining ships, the Director of the famous Hamburg-Amerika Line had taken an overdose of sleeping pills on 9 November 1918.

All the same, at least some of what Ballin had said proved true. The advantages of inflation to Germany's export industries were obvious. As the exchange rate tumbled, German goods became progressively cheaper in foreign markets. The pricing strategies of German manufacturers were further aided by the fact that, although workers, especially union members, were constantly demanding inflation-adjusted wage increases, those same wages were starting from a low real base. The need for inflation-adjusted increases was also mitigated by continuing government support for food prices and by the continuance of wartime rent controls (what that meant for the government's control of the deficit – or lack of it – was another matter).

The patriotic British, French or American (or Danish, or Dutch) businessman might prefer to buy from his own countrymen, but German quality was high and German prices, at that time, were hard to resist. In any case, it was common for large German companies and conglomerates to trade through wholly or partly owned foreign subsidiaries, especially those based in Holland. It was a quite deliberate strategy in the early post-war period when goods labelled 'Made in Germany' still encountered plenty of hostility in former enemy countries.[5] Germany's net national product grew by 10 per cent in 1920 and by 7 per cent in 1921.[6]

Meanwhile, German industrialists could ship out their wares and get foreign exchange for them, which they could either hoard abroad as an insurance against further deterioration of the mark (and as a way of avoiding Herr Erzberger's irritating taxes) or repatriate at a more favourable exchange rate than had existed at the original time of production of the exported goods. Since domestic price rises lagged behind falls in the exchange rate, anything which industrialists then purchased inside Germany – whether other businesses, plant and machinery, land or property – was extraordinarily cheap.

In 1920 a British journalist reported that, although the exchange value of the mark to the pound was substantially less than one penny, its purchasing power inside Germany itself was 2½ to 3 pence. So the German businessman could change back the proceeds of his exports at a certain rate and immediately find himself able to buy three or four times what an ordinary German could buy with his or her hard-earned paper marks.

Once the international rate of the mark started to tumble again in the late summer of 1921, and exchange rate changes became so swift and frequent that the domestic market prices found it harder and harder to keep up with them, the opportunity for any savvy business-man with access to foreign currency became, if anything, even greater. There was, in any case, absolutely no point in leaving rapidly depre-ciating paper money in a bank account and watching it waste away, as the less fortunately placed, or less worldly, members of the old middle class were forced to do.

The rich industrialist bought and bought and got richer and richer, not so much in paper marks but in physical things. The flight into 'material assets' (*Sachwerte*) became, for a minority of the German nation, a way to solid riches among the growing financial chaos. As the prominent German industrialist Emil Guggenheimer, a director of the MAN mining and engineering company, remarked ruefully and with only slight exaggeration, 'we are all actually no longer manu-facturers, but have become speculators'.[7]

Even Curt Riess's father, who had once plied his trade as a maker

of ceremonial uniforms for the courtiers of Germany's pre-war king-
doms and principalities but was now a plain, though highly skilled,
tailor to the gentry, entered into the practical spirit of the time.
Finding that, having contracted to make a suit at a specific price, by
the time he got to work the three metres or more of cloth he needed
cost more than the customer was due to pay him, Herr Riess swiftly
changed his policy so that he accepted payment only in hard currency
– dollars, pounds, Swiss francs. This was how he stayed in business
when many colleagues were bankrupted.[8]

The fact that there were laws against what Herr Riess was doing
made little difference to him or to millions of others who were protecting their fortunes in this way. After all, even if the business owner
was prosecuted, the penalty was usually a fine – payable in rapidly
depreciating paper marks.[9] So individuals salvaged their livelihoods
and continued to enjoy the standard of living to which they felt
entitled.

On a quite different scale of reckoning, these were also the circumstances under which Hugo Stinnes, the human 'calculating machine',
became Germany's most powerful businessman, seen by conspiracy
theorists as the secret ruler of the country. As he wrote to the tax
authorities with 'a mixture of contempt and pride' in 1920:

> The Reich, which today has 236 billion in debts and whose burden
> of debt grows from month to month, whose credit-worthiness is
> well shown by the value of its currency, that prints notes upon notes
> without any coverage and that has long been bankrupt . . . This
> poor Reich cannot give any guarantees or present a prospect of their
> realization upon which a businessman can base his balances. The
> basis for my business is my personal credit at home and abroad,
> this credit is until now unshaken; I can get any credit I need today
> at home and abroad.[10]

Access to domestic credit at low rates, especially from the Reichsbank,
and to foreign currency, was everything. In an inflationary situation,

someone like Stinnes could borrow almost unlimited amounts at favourable rates, courtesy of the Reichsbank's policy of automatic loans to German industry, and, moreover, by the time he began to pay back the loan it would be worth less in real terms – as time went by, a very, very great deal less.

Hated by millions as a personification of capitalism's ugly excesses, the curious thing was that Stinnes bore little resemblance to the stereotype of the plutocrat. Photographs of him at the height of his wealth and power show him as a slight, undistinguished figure. Often, when photographed in the street or some other public place, he would seem to be glancing at the camera with wary unease. Even in family photographs, he seems tense. When out and about – and he travelled a great deal – he wore a slightly shabby, old-fashioned dark suit and a bowler hat. In appearance, then, Stinnes more resembled a Charlie Chaplin everyman character than an economic super-villain.

Germany's most powerful businessman lived in a surprisingly modest villa in his native Mülheim on the Ruhr with his wife and seven children. It was a happy marriage by all accounts, and he was an affectionate, if demanding, father. His daughter, Clärenore (b.1901), acted as his secretary and his 'eyes and ears'. Personally rather shy, with a somewhat high-pitched voice and strong traces in his accent of his native Westphalia, Stinnes was nevertheless a stubborn optimist. When in difficult situations, according to his son Edmund, he would say: 'I never give up hope. If they want to hang me and the noose is already round my neck, I simply think how often ropes have broken.'[11]

Tellingly, on his business card Stinnes called himself not an industrialist or a company director but simply a 'Merchant' (*Kaufmann*). Stinnes is so strongly identified with Germany's great inflation that it can be forgotten that he made a very large fortune before the war, when prices were more or less stable. However, his was a cool, calculating and unflappable psychological make-up perfectly attuned to the roller-coaster ride that was inflationary Germany after the First World War.

Hugo Stinnes and the men (they were all men) of his ilk became ever more wealthy as the Germany economy lurched onward, and even as the country's political and social systems creaked with the strain. The new democratic Germany, paradoxically, was feeling more like the plaything of a small elite than the pre-war Empire ever had. Whatever the true statistics, two or three years after the revolution the country felt like an early example of the '1 per cent' ruling the '99 per cent'.

Any German, whether industrialist or private individual, who had access to foreign currency as the inflation gathered pace was in a highly advantageous position. Naturally enough, however, the main institutions and individuals holding valuta (foreign currency) were the foreigners themselves. This applied especially to the Americans. Every nation, in the aftermath of war, was a debtor nation, with the exception of the United States. During the period after the First World War, its citizens had money burning a hole in their collective national pocket – in dollars, suddenly the hardest currency in the world – and were looking for places to invest or lend it.

In 1920, after the initial fall in the mark's international value had temporarily subsided – when it was hovering around sixty to the dollar for months on end – many in America started to think that the only way the mark could go was up. After all, Germany had, in one sense, been artificially reduced to a state of near-penury. Post-war Germany was, by this estimation, the same country as pre-war Germany – one of the main engines of the global economy – but with, admittedly, a few bruises to show from the four-year fight that had brought it low. Why should these 70 million industrious and skilled people not soon be back at the top of the European industrial league, with full order books for their industries, their political scene calmed down and their currency once more as solid as before? Anyone who held on to marks until they got back to something like pre-war parity would, so this narrative would have it, make a huge killing.

An American loan – or, as the deceptively cheerful twenty-first-century phrase goes, a 'bail-out' – was the holy grail for most Germans in the post-First World War era. A share of the money waiting to be invested by the rich cousins across the Atlantic – and it should not be forgotten that many millions of Americans were of German descent – would give Germany a breathing space and help her to cope with the reparations demands being heaped upon her by the Belgians, the French and the British. And not just that. American loans and investments to Germany would also give America a stake in the country's future, thus potentially garnering Washington's support in the Reich government's struggle against the other victorious nations' demands on her. A post-'bail-out' Germany bankrupted by reparations would no longer just suffer alone. It would be a Germany where American bankers and investors had lost a very great deal of their own money.

It would, however, take some years, and some radically changed circumstances, before any official loans from the United States would become available. In the meantime, however, starting from the spring of 1919, Germany faced a growing tide of foreign speculators eager to make money out of the falling mark, precisely in anticipation that at some point it would stop falling and rise again. In the period 1919–20, at least 36 per cent of all deposits in the seven major Berlin banks were thought to originate from such sources.[12] In October 1920, 100 million dollars (at that time a little over 6 billion paper marks) in German industrial securities and 30 million (1.8 billion marks) of municipal bonds were bought on the American market. There were also plenty of American institutions and individuals simply speculating in marks or mark options, betting on a rise. Such options were advertised for sale by brokering companies, who dangled juicy profits before the bold investor.[13]

The German government and the country's financial sector had no objection to this wave of speculation. It is true that the Reich became unhealthily dependent upon these unreliable sources of hard currency – this was speculative money that could be withdrawn at any time, not long-term, productive investment in Germany – but the fact remained that at this stage it was just about the only way the Reich and its institutions were going to get any funding from the victorious nations, and particularly the United States.

The foreign craze for buying marks did, for a while, help bolster its value. As John Maynard Keynes put it at the time, for Germany the speculative inflow took the place of 'her much discussed international loan': '. . . and on the easiest terms imaginable – as for interest, most of it bears none; and as for capital, only such proportion is repayable as Germany may herself decide to when she comes to fix the value of the paper mark'.[14]

The American government stopped short of formal control of private investment abroad, though it was understandably concerned at the way its citizens, corporate and individual, were putting their money into Europe, and especially Germany, without necessarily considering the risks involved. And in the summer of 1921 the value of the mark did start to slip once more. Sure enough, by the following spring, the Republican Treasury Secretary Herbert Hoover would estimate that Americans had lost nearly $500 million (over 2 billion pre-war gold marks) in bad foreign investments, including in Germany.[15] This was even before German inflation got seriously out of control. Recent expert estimates have put the total speculative transfer to Germany during the years immediately following the First World War at in excess of 15 billion gold marks ($3.5 billion).[16]

Let it be said, all the same, that it was not only naive investors who lost their money betting on the German mark and on German industry during this period. John Maynard Keynes, brilliant economist and lifelong (on the whole extremely successful) speculator in the financial markets, had also looked at the fundamentals of the German economy. Despite his gloomy prognostications about the effect that the Versailles Treaty would have on Germany, he put his money into marks in 1919. The great man ended up losing £20,000, mostly his own money, a sum that today would equal at least half a million pounds sterling. Obliquely admitting that he was no better than all the other common speculators, he would write two years later:

Everyone in Europe and America bought mark notes. They have been hawked by itinerant Jews in the streets of the capitals, and handled by barber's assistants in the remotest townships of Spain and South America . . . the argument has been the same . . . Germany is a great and strong country; some day she will recover; when that happens the mark will recover also, which will bring a very large profit. So little do bankers and servant girls know of history and economics. [17]

Keynes also knew by then the full extent to which there would be no winners in the game that Germany and her erstwhile enemies had embarked upon:

Yet it must not be supposed that Germany, too, has not paid a penalty. In the modern world, organisation is worth more in the long run than material resources. By the sale of paper marks, Germany has somewhat replenished the stocks of materials of which the war and blockade had denuded her; but she has done it at the cost of a ruinous disorganisation, present and still to come. She has confiscated most of the means of livelihood of her educated middle class, the source of her intellectual strength; and the industrial chaos and unemployment, which the end of the present inflationary boom seems likely to bring, may disorder the minds of her working class, the source of her political stability. The money of the bankers and servant girls, which would have been nearly enough to restore Europe if applied with prudence and wisdom, has been wasted and thrown away. [18]

The mark began to fall again after the London Ultimatum of May 1921 forced the German government into a scramble to pay the first big tranche of cash reparations. The murder of Erzberger at the end of August, coinciding almost exactly with the deadline for the reparations transfer, showed that the frenetic economic activity was doing less than nothing to curb post-war Germany's endemic political violence, leading to another fall. The mark to dollar rate moved even more drastically downwards after the rich industrial and mining region of Upper Silesia was declared forfeit to Poland in October 1921, despite plebiscites that saw most of its population voting to stay within the Reich, thus robbing Germany of another substantial slice of its pre-war economic potential. This also represented yet another injustice for the nationalist right to brood over, in this case justifiably.

At the end of trading on the first working day of January 1922, the mark languished at 186 to the dollar, as opposed to just under 75 four months earlier. All the same, Germany's factories kept busy. Unemployment in the December just past remained at a mere 1.6 per cent.

The New Year's editorial in the liberal Berlin newspaper the *Vossische Zeitung* took a generally optimistic tone. 'Germany's path of suffering is beginning to lead up out of the valley,' wrote editor Georg Bernhard, himself a prominent figure in the German Democratic Party and a member of the Reich Economic Council, a government-sponsored forum for discussion of economic problems. 'In the past year we have put a substantial part of our journey through the darkness behind us.' However, regarding the inflation, he added less cosily:

That the inflation in Germany must be reduced has now, gradually, become a commonplace. But until now no one has had the confidence. Everyone who has some knowledge of economic matters and connections also knows why. Inflation is a gigantic fraud, which causes pleasing images to dance before our senses. The lively state of business, the rise in all prices and wages, does, it is true, mean everything sells at below the real price, but it also means that as consumers the masses are the victims of profiteering and as producers the working population is underpaid. But because there is a constant rise in the numbers, to which our old concepts of price still adhere, we notice only slowly, or not at all, and because everyone who wants to work finds employment and payment, the favourable labour market statistics only serve to thicken the mist and fog that surround us. Against this, deflation means a cruel awakening, as if after an opium trance . . .[19]

15

No More Heroes

On 17 April 1922, the *Manchester Guardian* printed an admiring piece about Herr Walther Rathenau, now the German Republic's Foreign Minister. The context was a speech he had delivered the previous day at a gathering in the Italian port city of Genoa, where yet another international conference was under way. Like the others, its aim, three and a half years after the fighting had stopped, was to try to sort out the continuing post-war mess.

There were many, many conferences in those early years following the First World War, but the remarkable thing about Genoa was, firstly, that thirty-four nations took part. Secondly, for the first time since the war, these included Europe's so-called 'pariahs'. This was at the insistence of Lloyd George, the main organiser of the talks. Germany, the loser and alleged culprit of the First World War, was finally there on an equal footing with other countries, and so was revolutionary Russia, only just emerging from civil war and famine, still not officially recognised by the major powers and until now excluded from international forums. Everyone distrusted the Communist government in Moscow, but everyone wanted access to their huge country's natural resources – timber, oil, minerals.

The theme of Genoa was supposedly economic reconstruction. Among other things, Lloyd George, politically and economically beleaguered at home and in desperate need of an international success, had plans for a reorganisation of economic relations so as to draw

Russia and Germany back in as partners. The Russians would provide the raw materials and Germany the finished products and capital goods (and some of the profits Germany made would be siphoned off to pay those still problematic reparations). This would not benefit only Russia and Germany. The ripple effect would supposedly help revive the entire European economy.[1]

Change was in the air, and although reparations were not officially on the agenda, here Rathenau made his mark. Having served since May 1921 in Wirth's government as Minister for Reconstruction, he had been appointed Foreign Minister in January 1922. The fact that he spoke, according to contemporaries, perfect, accent-free English, French and Italian was not without significance. Exploiting his favourable international reputation and contacts, he had begun what could only be described as a 'charm offensive' on his country's part, of which this speech, delivered in the garden of a villa rented by the German delegation to an international audience that included J. M. Keynes, was clearly an important component.

Standing in the spring sunshine surrounded by Europe's great and good, Rathenau argued that the only problems the world faced were essentially 'mental and moral'. In practical terms, there was nothing Europe possessed that she had not possessed ten years earlier. But 'huge errors and deviations of the way in which humanity thinks' were stopping the world from finding its way through the post-war maze. 'The first error,' the *Manchester Guardian*'s man reported him as saying, 'is that of peace. Everyone is talking of peace as if it exists in Europe'; 'The cannon are in their bastions. You may walk from the Rhine to the Vistula and not hear a shot fired nowadays. Yet peace does not exist. Peace means something positive, not merely negative . . .'[2]

The other two 'errors' were disarmament – a nonsense, since only Germany had disarmed so far – and debt. The whole of Europe was being strangled by an 'infernal circle' of debt. Rathenau reached out both to France and Russia, whom he saw as the other serious victims of this evil. All needed temporary loans to get them through the crisis.

My illustrious friend Keynes will not, I know, agree with me wholly here. We must enlarge the circle temporarily in order to breathe. For three nations cannot wait. These are France, Germany, Russia. Only we understand the awful financial difficulties of France.

Germany's difficulties are less understood. We are living on our own fat. Our prosperity is a bubble. Our companies pay dividends – but in fairy gold. We are eating our own accumulated resources, the result of generations of work of our ancestors. That will end.

The barometer of our position is the value of the dollar at the Berlin bourse. At present it hovers around 300 marks to the dollar. Let the needle start to move in the direction of 400, 500, 1,000 to the dollar and we are gone the way of Austria. It will be too late to talk of reparations then; we shall have to speak of charity.

It was a different point of view from the one he had expressed to the government, when he was still no more than an adviser back in January 1921. Then, with the mark at around 60 to the dollar, the possibility of inflation had been seen as a necessary evil. Now, at 300 to the dollar, it was just an evil.

Rathenau was on to something of a hiding to nothing when it came to pleading Germany's case, especially to the French. Having made one cash payment at the end of August 1921, the German government had promptly begun once more to plead poverty and to agitate for a moratorium and/or a loan to help the country while it got its affairs properly in order.

At a meeting in Wiesbaden in October 1921, the French under the moderate leftist Prime Minister Aristide Briand had shown signs of willingness to compromise. Rathenau, then Reconstruction Minister, and his French counterpart had signed an agreement to that effect. There had also been a possibility of a loan from the Bank of England, although that had finally fallen through in December 1921. At a bilateral meeting with the French in Cannes in January 1922, Lloyd George persuaded – some said bullied – Briand into agreeing to German attendance at the Genoa conference, though on condition that reparations and Versailles were not on the agenda.

Unfortunately there were plenty of French politicians who nevertheless thought that Briand had sold out French interests. Among them was the French President, M. Millerand, and the leader of the patriotic right in the Chamber of Deputies, Raymond Poincaré. On 12 January, Briand was forced out of office and replaced by Poincaré, who stood for a tough, in fact unrelenting, line on reparations.

The Genoa conference, nice speeches by the new and generally popular German Foreign Minister apart, went on for six weeks, from 10 April to 19 May 1922. A major problem was that the Americans had refused to participate, dismissing the conference as another futile 'Lloyd George conjuring trick', no substitute for the real political progress in Europe that was the only long-term solution to the continent's problems. Since the Americans controlled the world's purse strings at that time, the possibilities of meaningful success as a result of the Genoa discussions were therefore practically zero.[3]

Moreover, there was another problem. On Easter Sunday 1922, 16 April (not long after Rathenau's garden lecture), Russian and German representatives met secretly at the nearby resort of Rapallo, just thirty kilometres along the coast from Genoa. There they signed a treaty allowing for mutual recognition, cancellation of all financial claims – including reparations – favoured trade status, and an extensive programme of economic cooperation (which, in fact, continued until the end phase of the Weimar Republic in 1932–3).

The Rapallo Treaty was certainly a big surprise, and, for Lloyd George especially, a very unwelcome one. Though Genoa limped on to its inglorious conclusion, nothing was decided there that made any real difference to the direction Europe in general was heading. If Lloyd George was disappointed – his coalition government, already in serious difficulties, finally fell in October – the French were furious, interpreting the separate agreement between Germany and Russia both as a cause of Genoa's failure and as a typical act of bad faith. As for Rathenau himself, he had fought against the Rapallo Treaty, believing that Germany risked returning relations with the Western powers to the dark days of 1919. Only when it became clear that the Russians might otherwise make a deal with Britain and France and the rest which would leave Germany out in the cold again, did the Foreign Minister relent.

The final decision to sign the Russian treaty came during what was described as a 'pyjama party' in Rathenau's hotel suite during the night of 15/16 April. Even then, to retain some shred of good faith, Rathenau wanted to inform Lloyd George of their intention before the event. It was only when the architect of the treaty, 'Ago' (an acronym for Adolf Georg Otto) von Maltzan, State Secretary and powerful head of the Foreign Ministry's Eastern Section, threatened to resign, that Rathenau agreed not to tell the British. Thus it was ensured that the German–Russian deal would become one of the twentieth century's most notorious diplomatic bombshells.[4]

Particularly in the German Finance Ministry, there remained serious doubts about the wisdom of the Russian alliance. Finance Minister Hermes, who had attended Genoa, still thought that preparing the ground for changes to the reparations settlement was more important than a treaty with Russia whose benefits were impossible to predict. 'It's not enough to have a treaty with Russia in our pockets,' he wrote. 'We should also be taking home a fund of trust with the Allies with regard to the reparations question.' State Secretary Hirsch was snappier and more to the point, expressing his worry that 'for the Russian bird in the bush' Germany had sacrificed 'the plump reparations bird in the hand'.[5]

A response to Rapallo was not long in coming. On 24 April, the French Prime Minister Poincaré gave a speech in which he openly declared the treaty a hostile act, and emphasised the possibility of French military action if Germany did not keep to her agreements. The French military and the Paris government discussed the possibility of forcing Berlin's hand by occupying the Ruhr.

That the international exchange rate depended as much on political as on purely economic events, was witnessed by the mark's gyrations in the spring and early summer of 1922. It had slipped to 326 to the dollar at the beginning of April, recovered a little as hopes of an agreement at Genoa rose, then surged back to 252 amidst the generally positive domestic reception to the Rapallo Treaty. By mid-May, however, with Genoa clearly a damp squib and the hostile French reaction to Rapallo clear for all to see, the mark's value tumbled once more to 314. Then came a conference of bankers in Paris set for early June, and high hopes of an international loan for Germany that would break the reparations deadlock. These factors took the mark back up to 272 on 2 June. Then the bankers' conference also turned out to be a disappointment – no one wanted to lend Germany money until it had sorted out its finances, for one thing – which meant postponing the matter of the loan indefinitely and depressing the markets. So, 318 to the dollar on 11 June . . . [6] And then came a slightly weary comment from a financial journalist the next working day, Monday 12 June, concentrating on the strength of the dollar against the mark rather than vice versa:

> On the foreign currency market today the effects of the loan postponement were sharply expressed. The dollar, which on Saturday had closed at 297, leapt up, and during the morning for a while touched a rate of 322. Later the tendency relaxed a little, because some speculators took in their gains. The dollar rate dipped as a result to 315, soon firmed once more, however, and then oscillated between 316 and 318.[7]

Although Germany's politicians might have private reservations about Rapallo – even President Ebert had his doubts – the public's reaction had been by and large positive. Germany had acquired a friend to the east and had shown that she would not be bullied by the Allies. The treaty was accepted by the Reichstag against only a few dissenting votes from the nationalist-conservative and virulently anti-Bolshevik German National People's Party. The still small but increasingly vocal German Communist Party was, naturally enough, noisy in its approval.

Count Harry Kessler thought the whole thing a success, at least from Germany's point of view:

> Germany . . . had regained her status as a great power. Besides this, she was bringing home, in the teeth of French opposition, her treaty with Russia; and Rathenau had prepared the ground for a further advance on the path of negotiation and understanding by establishing relations of mutual confidence with some at least of the Allied statesmen.[8]

The strange economic 'boom', which still seemed, during the first months of 1922, to be carrying Germany through this difficult period, had done nothing to prevent both the far left and the far right from ceaseless agitation – in the case of the far left, against the capitalist, 'national' world of Stinnes and Rathenau, and of the far right against the socialistic, 'anti-national' world of Ebert, Chancellor Wirth – and Rathenau.

As a patriot and as heir to a major business empire, it was clear that Walther Rathenau, for all his evident intelligence and desperately needed political imagination, would always be a figure of suspicion for socialists and Communists. But for those at the other political extreme, the antipathy functioned on an altogether more violent level. As a Jew and supporter of the German Republic, the new Foreign Minister would never be able to avoid the sheer, toxic and ultimately irrational hatred of the nationalist right.

In the aftermath of Rapallo, a German National People's Party deputy, Wilhelm Henning, published an article in which he poured pure poison over the reputation of his country's Foreign Minister. Henning dredged up the assassination of the German ambassador, Count Mirbach, in Moscow in July 1918, exploiting that murky episode (which actually was carried out not by the Bolsheviks but by disaffected members of the rival Social Revolutionary Party) as a vehicle for abuse and anti-Semitic myth-peddling. The 'honour' of Germany had been trampled in the dust by a minister who would make pacts with the murderers of Mirbach, so Henning claimed:

Scarcely does the international Jew Rathenau have Germany's honour
in his hands than it is no longer spoken of . . . German honour is
not some object for international Jewry to haggle over! . . . German
honour will be avenged. You, however, Herr Rathenau, and those
who stand behind you, will be brought to account by the German
people . . .[9]

A nationalist drinking song of the time lumped Foreign Minister
Rathenau, the Jew, and Chancellor Wirth, the Catholic, together as
outcasts in language of sickening violence:

> If just the Kaiser would come back,
> Wirth to a cripple we would hack.
> The guns would rattle, tack-tack-tack
> Against the black* and the red pack.
> Whack that Wirth like no tomorrow,
> Whack his skull until it's hollow!
> Shoot down that Walther Rathenau,
> The God-accursed Jewish sow . . .[10]

The Spartacist Rosa Luxemburg, the Bavarian Prime Minister Kurt
Eisner, the Independent Socialist Hugo Haase, had all been Jewish,
and all been murdered. On the other hand, so had Erzberger, a
Catholic Swabian, and the Bavarian Socialist Karl Gareis, who came
from middle-class local stock, both of whom had fallen to the assassin's pistol in the summer of 1921. On Whit Sunday, 4 June 1922,
another 'Aryan' politician, the first Chancellor of the Republic,
Philipp Scheidemann, had been the victim of an attempted assassination by a group of right-wing plotters. Like Erzberger's murderers,
they were young fanatics associated with the shadowy 'Organisation
Consul' terror gang.

Scheidemann, now in political semi-retirement as High

* Black was the colour of the Catholic Centre Party.

Burgomaster of his native Kassel, had been out for a Sunday stroll in
the city's Wilhelmshöhe park with his daughter and small grandson.
One of the conspirators approached him, carrying a syringe device
used in enemas, whose rubber balloon was filled with liquid cyanide.
The would-be killer lunged towards Scheidemann, attempting to hold
the syringe close to his victim and to squirt the poison into his mouth
and nose at close range.

As it happened, Scheidemann had been subjected to numerous
death threats, especially since Erzberger's assassination, and so
carried a pistol with him whenever he left the house. He staggered
but managed to fire off two shots, forcing his assailant to flee,
before collapsing to the ground. He was unconscious for some
minutes before a passing doctor, correctly diagnosing the substance
that had been used in the attack, managed to revive him. The
ostensibly bizarre attack could, it seemed, have been fatal if a jet
of the poison had been inhaled. Scheidemann, it seems, had not
breathed in at the key moment.[11] Fortunately he made a complete
recovery.

As a Jew, an intellectual, a supporter of the Republic and yet once
as close to the old imperial regime as his racial heritage allowed,
Rathenau was the perfect target for nationalist extremists. He knew
the personal risks involved in serving the German Republic. Even
before he joined Chancellor Wirth's administration in May 1921, as
Reconstruction Minister, he had been subject to a steady undertow
of anti-Semitic abuse and innuendo. The story goes that when the
bachelor Rathenau accepted that ministerial post, he couldn't bring
himself to break the news to his formidable mother, who lived with
him at his villa in Grunewald. Lunching with her as usual the next
day, the atmosphere between them was uncomfortable. Finally, she
broke the silence.

'Walther,' the matriarch said, 'why have you done this to me?'

She had clearly read the newspaper.

The newly appointed minister could only reply, 'I really had to,
Mama, because they couldn't find anyone else.'[12]

After he entered the cabinet, the tidal pull of anti-Semitism burgeoned into a wave.

Although everyone had been impressed with Rathenau's performance there, the Genoa conference ended in almost total failure.

Hopes nevertheless persisted on the German side that the Bankers' Committee appointed by the Allied Reparations Commission would come up with a scheme for the longed-for loan. This would give Germany the 'breathing space' that would enable the country to stabilise her finances while at the same time (supposedly) meeting her reparations commitments. On 2 June 1922 that hope, too, was disappointed, largely because of French opposition. Poincaré had been prepared to consider a loan for Germany, which according to the Bankers' Committee should go along with a reduced reparations bill, only if America agreed to an equivalent reduction in France's share of inter-Allied debt. This, as was affirmed by the mighty New York banker J. P. Morgan, she would not.[13]

There had been some progress, all the same. Although the Reichstag had still not levied the 60 billion marks' worth of new taxes the Allies had demanded and was showing few signs of doing so, Germany had agreed to the Allies' demand to release the Reichsbank from its control by the government. The deputies duly passed a Reichsbank Autonomy Law on 26 May, making the bank no longer directly answerable to the Reich Chancellor and absolving it from its automatic obligation to discount Reich Treasury bills issued to cover the government's budget.*

To the Allies, this was a useful step towards Germany's 'getting her house in order'. It was considered a sufficient indication of progress for a 31 May deadline to pass without the penalties for Germany that had been threatened by the reparations commission, urged on by the ever-suspicious Poincaré. As it turned out, the Reichsbank's President Havenstein would carry on printing money merrily of his own accord

* Essentially this meant that the government could no longer force the Reichsbank to print money.

for a long time to come, but no one knew this yet (in any case, the law did not come into force until July 1922).

Meanwhile, from across the Atlantic came some slightly more hopeful news. The idea of a loan was still 'in play'. Americans had taken a big hit from the continued depreciation of the mark. However, with their own economy now beginning to recover from the brief but savage post-war depression, they were looking to sell to and invest in Europe. But first they needed Europe to recover properly. For that to happen, it was now generally agreed on Wall Street and in Washington, the problems with Germany needed to be dealt with on a level-headed, businesslike basis.

J. P. Morgan, Jr, one of America's most famous (or infamous) bankers, had been sent over as Washington's representative on the Bankers' Committee. It was in this capacity that he had delivered the bad news to the French about the loan forgiveness, or lack of it. Even after the announcement that the loan for Germany had been indefinitely postponed, he and other American financiers were concerned that something be done.

Morgan's views were interesting. Well-known as an Anglophile and an enthusiastic organiser of transatlantic loans for Britain and France during the war, Morgan harboured strong anti-German sentiments, asserting that his firm would never do business with the Reich and even refusing to buy paintings for his collection from German sources.[14] Nevertheless, he was nothing if not a hard-headed operator. At a high-level meeting in London on 19 June 1922, with the French Prime Minister Poincaré present as well as the British Chancellor of the Exchequer, Sir Robert Horne, Morgan put his views forward frankly, as the account of the meeting recorded:

Broadly speaking, Mr Morgan appeared to think that the Allies must make up their minds as to whether they wanted a weak Germany who could not pay, or a strong Germany who could pay. If they wanted a weak Germany, they must keep her economically weak; but if they wanted her to pay they must allow Germany to exist in a condition of cheerfulness, which would lead to successful business. This meant, however, that you would get a strong Germany, and a Germany that was strong economically would, in a sense, be strong from a military point of view also.[15]

On the British side, Horne largely agreed:

> The difficulty was that they were in a vicious circle. Germany said she could not stop the emission of paper money and repay her obligations unless she was able to raise a foreign loan, and she could not raise a foreign loan until she could pay her obligations. This was the vicious circle they were in.[16]

So both the Americans and the British were convinced that Germany must be given some leeway. Poincaré, on the other hand, remained of the opinion that the Germans were deliberately using inflation to avoid their commitments under the Treaty of Versailles. There was truth in this. Stinnes had told the Reichstag Foreign Affairs Committee in May 1922 with his usual startling, even brutal, frankness:

> Insofar as the presently demanded shutting down of our note printing presses is concerned, we must not overlook the fact that in our printing of notes lies a kind of emergency weapon against the exaggerated demands of the Versailles Treaty. The French have the threat of further occupation as their sole means of pressure to push through these demands. But such an occupation will hardly bring them any advantage.

All the same, the obvious divisions among the Allies, and the stalemate that resulted, did nothing to help the German economy. So far as the immediate situation was concerned, Stinnes thought the French were bluffing. M. Poincaré thought the German government was lying.[17] This mutual distrust, fuelled by mutual incomprehension, did not bode well.

It was with these ominous aspects of the situation in mind that Foreign Minister Rathenau agreed to have dinner with the American ambassador, Alanson B. Houghton, on the evening of 23 June 1922. Also invited was Colonel James A. Logan, an American observer to the Allied Reparations Commission.

Over dinner, the subject came up of the coal supply crisis, which had grown painfully complicated in the last weeks. Germany was bound to deliver high-quality coal to the French and Belgians as part of the Versailles reparations in kind. This left Germany short of fuel for the urgent requirements of her own booming industries. In fact, she had lately found herself, even after being forced to import coal from Britain at world market prices, close to a partial shutdown of her steel and smelting plants.

Rathenau wanted to ensure that the Americans understood the full extent of the crisis. He also knew that Stinnes was in Berlin as part of a delegation of industrialists lobbying the government for concessions on the coal problem. So, at around 10.30, Rathenau suggested that the 'King of the Ruhr' be called over from his hotel to explain the problem from his expert point of view. This was done.

With this powerful additional guest present, the subject of their talk soon broadened out from that of the coal question alone. Thus, late in the evening, the high-minded Rathenau and the hard-headed Stinnes found themselves ensconced with their American hosts in easy chairs, talking reparations and inflation. This went on for three more hours. The two Germans found themselves defending their country's policies. Both, interestingly, defended inflation, for all its economic and social disruption, as a 'political necessity'. Stinnes explained it as a matter of 'your money or your life', adding that 'when compelled to choose between the two, he always gave up his money'. They both insisted that inflation could only be tackled once Germany had a stabilising loan and a more reasonable reparations deal.[18]

Characteristically, Rathenau was less brusquely definite in his approach than Stinnes. The Foreign Minister thought the inflation had gone too far, and especially regretted the damage it had done to the educated middle class, in which as an intellectual he – unlike Stinnes – had many friends and acquaintances. But he also admitted that inflation was a 'necessary transfer of capital from one class to another', as befitted Germany's impoverished post-war position. After all, 'a people that had become as poor as the German people could no longer sustain broad classes of the population living off wealth and pensions'. In effect, Germany could no longer afford Ernst Troeltsch and his privileged academic ilk.

As Logan would later report, Rathenau was also depressed by the incessant political violence in Germany, which was not only bad in itself but was undermining national morale. For the Americans' benefit, he compared Germany's situation to that 'of a sane man taken and confined against his will in an insane asylum during a long period with the result that he gradually assimilates the mental traits of his associates'.

At half past one in the morning, Rathenau accompanied Stinnes back to his hotel, the very grand Esplanade on the Potsdamer Platz. They continued talking, just the two of them, until 4 a.m.

Stinnes would claim later that by this time the old differences between himself and Rathenau, so generally unalike in temperament and in their views of the world, and often strongly opposed on key issues, no longer existed. This, he maintained, their discussion that evening had proved. The truth of his claim could not be verified by his guest because this was, in fact, the last night of Walther Rathenau's life.

The Foreign Minister understandably slept late on the morning of Saturday 24 June, not emerging from his villa in suburban Grunewald – No. 65 Königsallee – until after 10.30. His car, a relatively modest NAG cabriolet, was waiting to take him the ten or so kilometres into the Foreign Office, where he was due for a routine meeting with consular staff.

Rathenau sat in the back seat of the open-topped car, completely exposed to the public view. Despite a constant stream of threats to his life, he travelled with neither bodyguard nor security detail. His chauffeur eased the car out of the drive and set off at a leisurely pace down the wide expanse of the Königsallee. After a few hundred metres they began to slow down, ready to negotiate the sharp double curve that the Königsallee took shortly before joining the famous Kurfürstendamm at Halensee and continuing on into the city.

Opposite this turn in the road, a gang of builders were working on a building site. One of them described to a journalist what happened next:

Coming up to 10.45 two automobiles came down the Königsallee from the direction of Hundekehle.* In the front car, which was travelling more slowly and was sticking around the middle of the road, sat a gentleman on the left side rear seat, you could recognise him exactly, since the car was absolutely open, without even a sun awning. In the car behind, also quite open, a big, six-seater dark-field-grey powerful touring car, sat two gentlemen in long, brand-new grey leather coats with the kind of leather caps that just left the oval of the face visible. You could see they were quite clean-shaven, and they didn't wear driving goggles.

The Königsallee in Grunewald is a very busy highway, so that you don't pay attention to every car that comes along. But we all looked at this big automobile, though, because the fine leather clothing of the passengers caught our eye. The big car moved out on to the right-hand side of the road and overtook the smaller car, which was travelling more slowly almost on the tram lines, probably because it was getting ready to move out on to the big S-curve of the Königsallee, forcing it strongly to the left, almost on to our side of the street. When the big car was maybe half a vehicle's length in front, and the solitary passenger of the other car looked over to his right, probably worrying there was going to be a collision, one of the gentlemen in the fine leather coats leaned forward and picked up a long pistol,

* Literally, 'dog's throat'. At the time a forested area near the south of the Königsallee with a famous hunting lodge of the same name.

cradled it in his armpit, and pointed it at the gentleman in the other car. He didn't really need to aim, he was so close, I looked so to speak right in his eyes, and he had this healthy, open face, as people like us say, sort of an officer's face. I took cover, because the shots could have hit us. And then the shots went crack-crack, quick as a machine gun.

When the one man was finished shooting, the other stood up, pulled the pin on an oval hand-grenade and threw it into the other car, which they were travelling very close to. Before this the gentle-man had already collapsed back into his seat, really all slumped together, and was lying on his side. Now the chauffeur stopped, right on the Erdener Strasse, where there was a pile of rubble, and was shouting, 'Help – Help'. The strange big car suddenly took off at full speed and roared off through the Wallotstrasse, which goes in a big curve past several new buildings which have got piles of stones right by the road and then gives out back on to the Königsallee. None of us could see a number plate on the big car, and there was no rear light to it either.

The car carrying the man who had been shot was meanwhile on the kerb, the chauffeur had bent down, and in that very same moment there was a bang and the grenade exploded. The gentleman in the back seat was absolutely lifted up by the air pressure, even the automobile made a little hop. We all ran over to the scene and found nine cartridge cases on the road and the pin of the hand grenade. Parts of the car's wood panelling had been blown off. The chauffeur started his car again, a young girl got in and supported the gentleman, who was already unconscious and probably dead, and the car set off at a good lick back along the same way it had come, back along the Königsallee to the police station, which lies about 30 buildings further on at the end of Königsallee in the direction of Hundekehle. There he must have roused the police, because after 10 minutes two officers arrived on bikes and asked about the car. One headed off along the Wallotstrasse, the other along the Königsallee, looking for the car. But the car must already have had a quarter of an hour's lead on them.[19]

Such was the fate – the bitter reward – of the man who less than twelve hours earlier had been fighting Germany's corner, along with the country's leading industrialist, at the residence of the American ambassador: to die at the hands of a young man armed with a machine pistol and dressed in luxury grey leather, with 'an officer's face', on the public highway on his way to the office to carry out a mundane, even tedious, official task.

Following the assassination of Rathenau, the government drafted laws for the 'Protection of the Republic'. This set up a special State Court to try future cases and subjected conspiracy against, instigation of, or complicity in acts of violence against the Weimar state and its representatives to severe new penalties, which would be administered by the new court.

No particular enemies of the Republic were named, but shortly after the murder, Chancellor Wirth declared, perhaps in the heat of the moment: 'The enemy is on the right!' He expressed the horror and disgust felt by all the Republic's supporters and by most Germans except those belonging to the still relatively small but growing ultra-nationalist minority. Hundreds of thousands, including huge columns of workers, spontaneously demonstrated on 28 June, the day of Rathenau's funeral in Berlin. All work had stopped at noon. It was a mighty, united recognition of what Germany had lost in this man. The unseasonal weather – rainstorms alternating with sunshine – did nothing to deter the crowds.

Harry Kessler, a friend of Rathenau, described the scene in the Chamber of the Reichstag, where the funeral ceremony was held:

The coffin lay in state, mounted behind the speaker's rostrum and under a huge black canopy suspended from the ceiling. The Chamber was hung with black and transformed into a sea of flowers and plants. Enormous palms flanked the coffin at its four corners. The speaker's rostrum was shrouded in black and buried, as was the Government Bench, beneath magnificent wreaths with ribbons in the Republican colours, black-red-gold . . . The galleries, like the Chamber itself, were packed. There was not one empty seat, not even among the Nationalists. The focal point was the coffin, draped with a huge flag in the national colours. At its foot there lay two immense wreaths, of red and white flowers, to right and left of the colours.

At noon the Chancellor led Rathenau's mother into the Imperial box. She sat down in the seat whose back was still embellished with a crowned W. The old lady was evidently in full control of herself, but her complexion was as pale as wax and the face behind the veil might have been carved from stone. These features, all colour drained from them through grief, touched me most. She stared motionlessly at the coffin.[20]

The *Manchester Guardian*'s man in Berlin reported that monarchist flags had completely disappeared from the city's streets.[21] Enormous crowds turned out to protest at the murder in other major cities: reportedly 300,000 in Hamburg, 200,000 in Leipzig, and 150,000 each in Munich and Cologne.[22]

Rudolf Pörtner, then eleven years old, remembered many years later how a neighbour brought the news to their home in Bad Oeynhausen, a spa town of some six thousand souls on the River Weser in north-western Germany:

His name was Metzger, he was a foreman at the cigar factory, in which my father also worked. He was a Social Democrat and as such had been elected to the Oeynhausen town council. Corresponding to his position as a 'city father', he habitually assumed a distinct tone of gravitas in his relations with others.

. . . But now I saw him, from our kitchen window, rush out of his house, and with no regard whatsoever for etiquette, in his slippers, shirtsleeves, and his waistcoat unbuttoned, head for our front door. Soon the doorbell was ringing a storm, and when my father opened up, [Metzger] was fighting for breath.

'Have you heard?' he asked, clearly bewildered. 'Rathenau has been

murdered.' My father was equally stunned, in fact it was as if he had
been struck by lightning. He declared it a terrible crime. The two
neighbours discussed the event for another half an hour, and agreed
that 'this man' was the only one who could have been trusted to 'get
the cart out of the mud'.[23]

There was no doubt that the vast majority of Germans, except for the
extreme right, experienced Rathenau's assassination as an unequalled
atrocity. Unlike the murdered Finance Minister Erzberger, who for
all his talents had indulged in dubious dealings in both business and
politics, Rathenau was obviously a paragon of competence and integrity and his death was a cruel blow to the young Republic.

Sebastian Haffner wrote, passionately but perhaps overenthusiasti-
cally, that 'If we had called on those same masses on that day to put
an end to those people – who at that time were called "reactionaries"
but in truth were already Nazis – they would have done it without
further ado, quickly, drastically, and thoroughly.'[24]

The reactionary government in Bavaria immediately and predictably objected to the new laws, claiming they undermined its sovereign
jurisdiction. The legislation, which finally completed its passage
through the Reichstag a month after Rathenau's death, fed a continuing crisis between the Reich government in Berlin and the increasingly
separatist (and militantly right-wing) Bavarian government, which
would drag on into the middle of the decade. In response, the defiant
government in Munich actually passed a set of its own laws which,
while reflecting the basic stipulations of the Reich government's legislation, crucially undermined its effectiveness by transferring the power
to prosecute and sentence from the Reich 'State Court for the Protection of the Constitution' to higher Bavarian courts (which were
notoriously lacking in rigour when dealing with far-right criminals).
The central government complained, but other than invade Bavaria
there was little Berlin could do about it.

As for the killers of Rathenau, they were young former Freikorps
volunteers, as were so many of the assassins involved in Organisation

Consul. Twenty-three-year-old Erwin Kern, son of a Prussian civil servant and former wartime naval officer, at the time registered as a law student, had wielded the machine pistol. Hermann Fischer, son of a Professor of Fine Art from Dresden, aged twenty-six and a graduate in engineering, had also served at the front during the war. He tossed the grenade into Rathenau's car.

The assassins had been forced to escape on foot after their car broke down, not far from the scene. After a failed attempt to catch a steamer to Sweden, they went on the run through northern and central Germany, sometimes sleeping rough, sometimes staying with sympathisers, staying one step ahead of the biggest manhunt Germany had ever seen and with a price of a million marks on their heads. They were run to ground on 17 July 1922, more than three weeks after the murder, at Burg Saaleck, a castle in Saxony-Anhalt about 230 kilometres south-east of Berlin, where they had been granted refuge by an Organisation Consul supporter. Betrayed by local peasants – the reward for their capture had meanwhile risen, through public subscription, to 4 million marks – they were besieged by local police. Kern was killed in the ensuing shoot-out, while Fischer, having first arranged his comrade's body in what he perceived to be a more dignified position, took his own life to avoid arrest.

In the end some thirteen young men, from impeccably respectable backgrounds, were tried for their involvement in Rathenau's murder. Their number included Ernst von Salomon, son of a senior police official, who would much later become a well-known writer and pacifist, and the driver of the car used in the murder, twenty-year-old Ernst Werner Techow, who came from a well-connected Berlin legal family and whose father held a high position in the capital's administration. They were tried by the 'Court for the Protection of the Republic', and given relatively severe sentences compared with those usually inflicted on nationalist conspirators by the Weimar courts, who were notoriously 'blind in the right eye'.[25] Techow narrowly escaped the death sentence by making a last-minute confession, and was possibly helped by the publication of an extraordinarily forgiving letter of sympathy written by Rathenau's mother to his. The two women were apparently mutually acquainted from the pre-war Berlin social scene.[26]

Chancellor Wirth, who had served as his own Foreign Minister until Rathenau was appointed in January, took the helm of foreign affairs once more. His government limped on.

16

Fear

On the front page of the *Vossische Zeitung* ('Evening Edition') of 24 June 1922, beneath the banner headline, the first, slightly garbled reports of Rathenau's murder, and early details of arrangements for a service of mourning at the Reichstag, a final sub-headline inevitably read: 'Effect on the Exchange – Dollar reaches 355'.

The rate moved to 402 on 1 July. By the end of July it was 670. There was worse – much worse – to come. Economic fundamentals apart, a country whose finest political minds are regularly murdered does not find it easy to inspire confidence in the rest of the world.

Ominously, with no indication of a recovery in the mark's value for the foreseeable future, the 'inflation mentality' had now finally begun to take a grip on the German population.

Expectations of price rises were becoming built into the system. Until this year, domestic prices had lagged behind the exchange rate, meaning that foreign money, changed into marks and quickly put to work, bought goods, assets and services inside Germany at bargain prices.

Now, with merchants, workers and officials alike all moving quickly to adjust wages and prices, many prices in Germany rose more or less instantly. In the civil service, at national, state and municipal levels, and in the state-owned railways and post office, unions were demanding regular supplements in wages and salaries to compensate for price increases. In tune with the principle of social peace at any price, the government, the states and the cities were, moreover, granting them.

All this meant a further steep increase in the printing of money. In the private sector, businesses had become accustomed to frequent wage rises, paid for by price hikes to consumers. In dealings between businesses, pricing had become subject to sliding scales, causing much bitterness among customers who, given the time elapsing between contract and delivery, ended up paying much more than the original agreed cost for goods and services.

The external mark advantage had diminished, and with it a lot of Germany's recent competitive edge in world markets. The inflation was losing what benefits it had hitherto conferred on Germany, but the government was terrified of the economic and social (which meant ultimately political) price to be paid for stabilising the currency.

'Germans,' as one leading economic historian has put it,

> were now living in fear of both the depreciation and appreciation of the mark. The former was causing prices to skyrocket so that . . . the workers themselves did not know what kind of wage increases to ask for, and the employers, who were fleeing from the marks into goods and engaging in hectic activity, had no choice but to give in. The public appeared totally surprised by the suddenness and rapidity of the latest depreciation. At the same time, everyone was fearful that domestic prices were beginning to reach world-market levels and that the entire inflation boom would collapse.[1]

Foreigners understood the changed situation only too well. Attempts to support the mark through action by the German authorities on the currency exchange markets had enjoyed only very limited success before 24 June.[2] With Rathenau, at this time the one German political figure of real international status, cruelly removed from the scene, there was little to stop panic taking over. Ludwig Bendix, an American-based German-born financial expert close to the German government, reported from New York on 3 July: 'While the standing

German offer of marks, relatively speaking, found willing acceptance until the middle of last month, there has been a complete absence of any demand for German currency since that time. With this has been lost an important support which the mark had previously enjoyed.'[3]

Shreds of foreign confidence had survived into 1922. Now, with the formerly proud, orderly Germany increasingly beginning to resemble a Banana Republic – a term that at the time had existed for around twenty years, used to describe violent, unstable Latin American states, often with unsound currencies – it was not surprising that the mark was finding fewer and fewer takers.

The hitherto ever-refreshing financial spigot of foreign speculative inflow had finally been turned off. As Georg Bernhard, a leading economic commentator and, as editor of the *Vossische Zeitung*, reputed to be one of the highest paid journalists in the world, said on 14 July 1922, 'We face a situation in which there is only one source of money in Germany left, and that is the Reichsbank.'[4]

The Reichsbank duly continued accepting the vast flow of government Treasury notes, although now no longer constrained to do so, and despite the fact that they were becoming ever harder to place with investors. It also went on extending credit to industry, all the time printing money in order to do these things. The amount of domestic bills and cheques held by the Reichsbank had increased sevenfold between the end of December 1921 and the end of July 1922, from 922 million to 6.58 billion.[5]

The British and the Americans seem to have begun to accept, by this point, the German argument that she desperately needed further moderation of the reparations terms in order to avoid national bankruptcy.[6] Not so the French. Combined with a renewed surge in capital flight from Germany into safer jurisdictions abroad, nothing about the increasingly chaotic financial situation seemed calculated to convince the ever-suspicious Poincaré that the German government was not cheating. He believed that Germany was not really unable to meet her reparations bill but was deliberately simulating ruin in order to avoid paying France the money she still owed her. So was this a question of can't pay, or won't pay? The French preferred to assume the latter.

Perhaps it didn't matter now. In any case, the process had acquired its own momentum. With the mark losing value by the week, Germans now wanted foreign currency not so much to pay reparations or to buy goods from abroad but as a way to secure a safe store of value and a steady means of exchange. State Secretary Hirsch, as usual, had spotted the trend at the beginning of July 1922.

Hirsch attributed the decisive role to 'pessimism' and came to the conclusion, especially after reports from New York showing very little speculative activity against the mark there, that the depreciation's 'single truly permanent source' lay in Germany itself. The huge demand for foreign currency in Germany was no longer a result of what it needed to pay abroad but, rather, of the demand for foreign currency in internal transactions. Like the increasingly unmarketable Reich Treasury notes which were backing up on the Reichsbank, so the entire inflation was backing up on the German people themselves.[7]

All the fatal symptoms were starting to show. In the course of July 1922, prices inside Germany rose 50 per cent, month on month – the generally accepted definition of hyperinflation.

17

Losers

The Germany of the inflation was paradise for anyone who owed money. Times were good for highly leveraged businessmen like Hugo Stinnes, for mortgage holders whose contracted payments were shrinking by the month and even the week, and for anyone agile enough to move between money and goods – those magic 'material assets' – and back as required, especially if they also had access to foreign currencies.

By the same token, this was a very bad time for creditors of all kinds, for savers, and for investors depending on a fixed return. That meant large numbers of the old German middle and upper middle classes suffered a drastic, even catastrophic, fall in their standard of living. If the inflation in Weimar Germany brought about a social revolution in the country, it was these people who came off worse in the great re-arrangement.

Looking at the situation of the manual workers, to use a shorthand term for those paid weekly, although wages remained on average lower than before the war, they had benefited from the shorter working hours and more job security after the revolution. During the early post-war years it seems that for the most part, despite the odd wobble, they survived and in some cases even (relatively speaking) prospered. This was especially true if they were unionised. A section of the poorest, however, found themselves in a far worse situation than before the war.

Pensioners, theoretically quite generously provided for in Weimar Germany compared with elsewhere in Europe, also suffered badly from the inflation, though the state tried to make regular compensation for price increases.

In terms of who was winning and who was losing from the economic situation in Germany during these years, however, one thing seemed clear: the situation there was the opposite of what was happening in other large, advanced Western countries. German government policies differed drastically from those prevalent in Britain, America and, though she was still struggling with a strong and continuing element of war-induced inflation, France.

Keen to reduce debt and somehow support the huge sums necessary to pay interest on war bonds, which in the victor countries (as also in Germany) had been bought largely by better-off citizens and wealthy institutions, France and Britain raised interest rates, tightened belts and tried to stabilise and, if possible, reduce the high wages that had been a feature of the war economy. In other words, whereas in wartime, with uninterrupted production an absolute priority, the industrial workforce had been favoured above all other social groups, things changed when peace came. Once the post-war boom had served to move these countries' economies more or less promptly from a war to a peacetime footing, the governments of the victorious powers changed their economic and fiscal policies. These now swung around to favour not the worker and the debtor but the saver, the bond holder and the business owner.

This sudden lunge towards post-war austerity was particularly pronounced in the case of Britain. Here the government, heavily indebted, and also conscious that the nineteenth century's most powerful country was ceding national and economic prestige to the newly ascendant America, aimed to smother inflation, and to do so quickly. London's ultimate ambition was to return to the gold standard as soon as possible, and to regain the pre-war exchange rate against the US dollar (which had remained backed by gold). This involved stringent fiscal and interest rate policies and also cutting government waste and excess of all kinds. Classic austerity politics.

The accusation of chronic waste was one to which, as the government was aware, it had become more vulnerable due to a vastly increased wartime bureaucracy. The large swathes of the British press owned by the Harmsworth brothers, Lords Northcliffe and Rothermere, including *The Times* and the *Daily Mail*, soon began a vigorous and highly effective campaign on this issue, to the extent that a kind of 'waste panic' became widespread. The Harmsworths even sponsored 'anti-waste' candidates, who actually won three by-election victories.[1] The name of the political game was therefore, from 1921 onwards, nothing but cuts – some of the most drastic in British history up to that time, especially affecting social spending, housing, education and defence.

In November 1918, at the general election that had followed the armistice, Lloyd George's government had promised a 'land fit for heroes'. Instead, Britain soon succumbed to a programme of systematic cuts in public expenditure, many affecting the fortunes of returning soldiers. Most notoriously, these savings included those suggested by a committee under the chairmanship of a businessman-turned-politician, Sir Eric Campbell Geddes.

Geddes had made a fortune in the Canadian railroad business. With the firmness of purpose of a man whose considerable wealth resided largely abroad, he recommended slicing £87 million (a huge amount at the time, representing around 10 per cent of British gross domestic product) from public expenditure.

Although less than two-thirds of the recommended cuts were actually carried out, the social and economic effects – combined with tax changes and higher interest rates – were drastic. The new policies smelled to many of renewed class war, with the working class on the receiving end. They encouraged a strike wave that lasted through the mid-1920s, and helped fuel the rapid rise of the British Labour Party. In strictly practical terms, however, the result of the cuts, including the 'Geddes Axe', was indeed a fall in the cost of living. Just as intended, inflation was brought under control.

In France, the post-war interest on domestic debt (including war bonds bought by French individuals and institutions) claimed up to 50 per cent of the ordinary government budget. The country was, as one historian put it, 'held hostage to interest payments on the public debt', which amounted to a 'political time bomb'.[2] The French government, eager to assure foreign bankers and holders of French currency that it paid its debts, and struggling to make the Germans pay, introduced measures to ensure that holders of government and war bonds – mostly banks, insurance companies and so on, plus wealthy individuals – were paid their interest at all costs. 'To meet the interest obligation, the government had to raise immense sums from one group and give them to the other.' The group that suffered was, as in Britain, the ordinary working population, while the beneficiaries were mostly the *haute bourgeoisie* and the powerful financial institutions. This indeed amounted to 'a socialism of the rich'.

Anti-inflationary austerity such as imposed in Britain and, in a different way, in France, was precisely the opposite of what happened in Germany.

In Berlin, the new republican government made no attempt to protect the prudent bond holder and the saver, as occurred in France and Britain. It continued, motivated both by inclination and perceived necessity, to favour the earning-and-spending industrial workforce, and to support employment at all costs, including jobs in the bloated state sector. After all, the welfare of the masses was both the German Republic's *raison d'être* and its existential insurance policy.

Even after large-scale socialisation plans had been abandoned in 1920, the government continued to use wartime legislation to subsidise employment, especially in the state sector, and to regulate food prices and rents broadly in favour of the workers. And, of course, it continued to print money in order to do so. So inflation crept up, slowly at first and then gathering speed. The effect of this was to let the bond holder, the *rentier* (who lived from the proceeds of investments) and the saver survive as he or she might – or, in fact, might not.

The individuals and institutions who benefited from post-war deflation and austerity in France and Britain had their counterparts in
Germany, the old educated class dominated by academics, lawyers
and civil servants, the *Bildungsbürgertum*. However, their German
relations in social status were placed in a very different situation. This
group had always relied on supposedly 'safe' investments such as
German government bonds, savings certificates and fixed annuities
of various sorts to supplement, or in many cases enable, their style of
life. The decline in the mark and the consequent shrinkage of returns
from fixed-rate investments, especially holdings of German domestic
war debt – in which this supremely patriotically inclined class had
invested to a disproportionate extent – exerted a wholly ruinous and
politically toxic effect. Unlike their British and French equivalents,
who were protected from some of the ravages of inflation, German
war bond holders had been completely let down by their government,
and apparently wilfully so.

The question of whether Germany could in fact have managed to
steer some kind of benign middle course, keeping the mass of the
working class in employment but at the same time leaving the middle
classes with some semblance of solvency, exercised many minds at the
time, and has exercised more since.

Britain after the Second World War, for instance, had to deal with
a vast accumulation of debt, mainly owed to America. However, under
the strong and on the whole efficient Labour government that
succeeded Churchill's wartime coalition, she nonetheless managed to
keep up payments on her debt, while at the same time creating a
welfare state and a free national healthcare system, and maintaining
full employment. At the same time the British middle classes, though
generally feeling somewhat shabby and impoverished during the post-
war era, were not wholly ruined by the process. In fact, they survived
sufficiently well to flourish again in the 1950s, once the phase of
socialist austerity was over.

Something similar to the British solution following the Second

World War might, theoretically, have worked for Germany after 1918, if there had been a similar sense of national solidarity as was found among all classes in Britain in 1945; if, as in post-war Britain, the government had enjoyed a clear mandate for its policies; if the increasingly weak governments that ruled Germany after 1920 had not been hampered by their disunity and by an extreme, not to say violent, right-wing opposition. And, perhaps above all, if the debts that Germany owed after 1918 – mostly the costs and reparations it agreed to pay under the Versailles Treaty – had been debts that the country truly acknowledged its duty to fulfil, as Britain had, however reluctantly, in the case of its borrowings from America after the Second World War.

In fact, of course, even German politicians who followed a policy of 'fulfilment' of the treaty terms, including reparations, did so only in order to show their impossibility. Almost no one in Germany, across the entire political spectrum, considered the debts owed to the victors under the Versailles Treaty as legitimate ones.

To structure Germany's economic and financial policies in order to make the country capable of paying reparations – again, theoretically possible, as most historians agree – would have been regarded by many, if not most, Germans, as treachery. Moreover, it would in all probability have imposed a political and social cost feasible only under conditions of strong government, popular moral commitment and unshakeable social solidarity. None of those circumstances characterised Germany after 1918.

The post-war boom that was engineered in Germany, and permitted to continue even after other countries deflated their economies, was by its nature an inflationary one. And the tacit consensus was that an inflationary boom was better than no boom at all.

Sebastian Haffner described the developing division in German society, not just between republicans and anti-republicans but between those who could find ways of living and even flourishing within this strange hollow boom, and those who were shut out of it. The stock exchange had become one way of investing wealth before it slipped away. There was, as ever with share trading, a risk involved. All the same, so long as companies kept selling and growing, as they did for the most part between 1919 and 1922, the market quickly adjusted the value of investors' shares to correspond to inflationary movements. Thus the stock market automatically maintained the value of investments and, if the investor was lucky and a company was doing well, even increased it.

Among his young middle-class friends in the Berlin of the developing hyperinflation, Sebastian Haffner could see who had managed to adapt to the times and who had not.

> Life was good for the young and the nimble. Overnight, they became free, rich and independent. It was a situation where slow thinking and a reliance on previous experience were punished with hunger and death, but impulsive action and swift comprehension of a new situation were rewarded with sudden, huge wealth. The twenty-one-year-old bank manager became a phenomenon, as did the High School senior who took heed of his somewhat older friends' stock market tips. He wore a tie in the fashion of Oscar Wilde, organised champagne parties, and provided for his embarrassed father.[3]

Elsewhere in the country, young bank workers, like the 'high-rollers' of Wall Street and the City of London in the early 2000s, were able to use their access to foreign currency to live the high life. In Hamburg, the bank clerk Hermann Zander, after completing his brief post-war service with the anti-Communist Freikorps, settled into a career as a foreign exchange dealer with the Commerzbank. He described his privileged situation during the hyperinflation in jaunty terms:

> This is the time when we had the ever quicker developing inflation, during which I had the opportunity to make diversions into *Valuta* (foreign currency).
> Any paper marks that were still left over at close of business would

be spent on fun or used to buy goods. We were a merry band of colleagues, to which now and then my father would attach himself.[4]

Some days were jollier than others, and required parental guidance:

One day it happened that, after our last drink at the 'Mampes Stuben' bar on the Jungfernstieg, we decided to go on somewhere. We piled into an electric taxi . . . and, without planning to, ended up on the Herbertsrasse (a red light area). My father noticed this and uttered the memorable words:

'Hermann, my son, this is not the place for us!'

Sebastian Haffner's own father, a senior civil servant, naturally refused to become involved in the black market. However, neither would he engage in any other kind of trading, even of a legitimate sort.

Yes, my father was one of those who did not understand the times, or did not want to understand them, just as he had refused to understand the war. He dug himself in behind the assertion that 'A Prussian official does not speculate', and did not buy stocks.[5]

What Sebastian Haffner's father represented was the old pride of Germany: the cream of the so-called *Bildungsbürgertum*, the classically educated elite. These were the men who since the eighteenth century had filled the roles of higher civil servants, law officers, Protestant pastors, writers and academics in the various monarchical states, large and small, that made up the old Reich.

Until 1914 the *Bildungsbürgertum* had managed to maintain its standard of life and its social status, despite the inroads being made by the new, aggressive class of industrialists and business managers on the one side and the increasingly aspirational junior white-collar and skilled working classes on the other. This small but dispro-portionately influential elite group – calculated, even if their families are included, at less than 1 per cent of the population at this time, or between a half and three-quarters of a million people altogether[6] – had always depended on inherited money and privilege to perpetuate itself. It was in good part due to this fact that in 1913, 15 per cent of Germany's wealth had its origins in investment income rather than wages and salaries. During the course of the inflation, this would be subject to a drastic reduction, falling to a mere 3 per cent.[7]

The money of the educated middle class, be it from academic or legal fees, or from a civil servant's salary, was not the flashy wealth of the big businessman or the great landed aristocrat. All the same, it was steady, and comfortable enough in more stable times, if prudently invested, to house this caste's members in a decent apartment or villa. Above all, until the war and the inflation intervened, it was sufficient to ensure that the males of each generation could afford to take the essential step of studying a traditional subject at a traditional German university. In this way they would acquire the qualifications and connections (the latter often through student duelling clubs) that enabled them to gain footholds on the civil service, judicial or academic career ladders, like their fathers and grandfathers before them.

The old, smooth pre-war career path was now a thing of the past. In the summer of 1921, 92 per cent of students at the technical university in Dresden filled in a questionnaire about their financial circumstances. At that time (when the mark had temporarily stabilised at around 60–70 marks to the dollar) it was reckoned a student needed 450 to 500 marks a month to sustain a minimal standard of living. Of 865 responders, 217 had 450 or more marks a month to live on, and the rest – 648 – less. Often a lot less. Almost a quarter of the students had around 300 marks, and another quarter less than that, in nine cases as little as 100. The situation was similar at other universities.[8]

The post-war period saw the unprecedented rise of the *Werkstudenten* (working students), usually from a newly impoverished middle-class background, who worked their way through university where their fathers would have been treated to a more or less

Pre-war idyll: Unter den Linden, Berlin 1910

War! German soldiers leave for the front, 1914

Paying for the apocalypse: advertisement for
German War Bonds, 1917

Reichsbank President Rudolf Havenstein, chief
enabler of the wartime inflation

Revolutionary soldiers at the Brandenburg Gate, November 1918

Foreign Minister Walther Rathenau in the open-topped car in which he was assassinated hours after a midnight meeting with Stinnes

Hugo Stinnes, richest man in post-war Germany and 'King of the Inflation'

Crime scene photograph of the site of Rathenau's murder, June 1922

© TopFoto

Chancellor Cuno (*left*), November 1922 to August 1923, with President Ebert

Reichswehr troops arrest a Communist paramilitary in Saxony, October 1923

The Ruhr invasion: a French soldier guards a coal shipment in Germany's occupied industrial heartland, 1923

A disabled war veteran begs in post-war Berlin

Destitute middle-class Germans selling their possessions at public auction

A food queue outside a high-class grocer's shop in Berlin during the hyperinflation

The Munich Putsch. Heinrich Himmler, later architect of the Holocaust and Reichsführer-SS (*centre with flag*) mans a barricade. To his left is Max Scheubner-Richter, killed at Hitler's side just hours later

Young Hitler, early 1920s

Collection of the day's wages from the Reichsbank for a small business (15 employees), late 1923

Worthless money finds use, as wallpaper and as a children's amusement

Old paper marks destroyed after the currency reform, early 1924

comfortable parental allowance to do so. The idea of the *Werkstudent* may seem normal to modern readers – and, indeed, 'working your way through college' was already an everyday phenomenon in America in the 1920s – but in the social and political context of Germany after the First World War it was perceived as shocking, a sign of class and therefore (from this hitherto privileged group's point of view) national decline.

It was typical of the inflationary era, however, that the individual who was prepared to improvise and 'think outside the box' – not to mention to go against social conventions – could end up not just surviving but thriving. One such *Werkstudent* from a formerly comfortable middle-class home recalled later in life how his family got by after his father died, and how he financed his university education:

My father had left a fortune of 800,000 marks, but by the summer of 1922 the value of the mark had dropped to 400 per dollar. Every month, it got worse. My mother finally used her last 65,000 marks to buy a typewriter, and she began typing students' theses to support the youngest children. I went to Holland that spring, looking for anything that would earn hard currency, and I found a job at the Queen Anna coal mines in the province of Limburg. We worked far down, at the bottom of the mine, hacking away with pickaxes. It was tremendously hot, usually one hundred degrees or so, and full of dust, but by the end of the spring vacation I'd saved fifty guilders, which was about twenty-five dollars. Then I figured out how to beat the inflation. I used the guilders as security for a short-term bank loan, and then I'd repay the bank loan with the deflated marks and take out another loan. I paid for a whole semester at Heidelberg that way, and at the end I still had the same fifty guilders.[9]

His case was not typical. Perhaps, in a sad way, it helped that his father was dead, that a woman had been forced to take over as head of the family, and that they therefore knew it was a matter of *sauve qui peut.*

During the war, the educated middle class had already suffered a fall in its relative standard of living. Now it found itself both economically and psychologically besieged. The higher civil servants, such as Sebastian Haffner's father, and the museum director who had found himself an object of a British journalist's pity back in the spring of 1920, were especially hard hit. By 1920, the real value of their salaries was reckoned at only 20 per cent of what it had been in 1913.[10] And still the insistence held among such men that 'a Prussian civil servant does not speculate'.

A Prussian civil servant's wife, however – the mother of his children – was in no position to take refuge in a government office, as her husband did, and pretend that nothing had changed. When inflation began to rise again, from the summer of 1921 onwards – good news as this might seem to be for business – a woman such as Haffner's mother finally ceased being a privileged Frau Senior Government Councillor and became a survivor like any other.

On the 31st or the first of the month, my father received his monthly salary, which represented all we had to live on – bank deposits and savings certificates had long since become worthless. How much the salary was worth, it was hard to say; its value fluctuated from month to month . . . In any case, my father would try to acquire a monthly season ticket for the underground railway as fast as he could, so that during the next month he could at least travel to work and back, although this means of transport involved considerable detours and expenditure of time. Then cheques were written for the rent and school fees, and in the afternoon the whole family would go to the hairdresser. What money remained was handed over to my mother – and the next day the entire family, even the housemaid, though not my father, got up at four or five a.m., and took a taxi to the central market. There a big shopping session was organised, and in the course of an hour the monthly salary of a Senior Government Councillor was spent on non-perishable food. Huge cheeses, whole hams, hundredweights of potatoes, were all loaded into the taxi. If there

wasn't enough room, the housemaid and one of us children would
get hold of a hand cart. At around eight o'clock, just before school
time, we would return home, more or less supplied with enough to
see us through a month's siege. And that was the end. For another
month there was no more money.[11]

The middle class had seen its standard of living and status take a severe
tumble since the euphoric days of August 1914. As for senior civil
servants, their continued conservative-monarchist loyalties also began
to affect their traditional command of the corridors of bureaucratic
power. Especially in Prussia and other Social Democrat-controlled
states, democratic politicians started co-opting sympathetic 'political
officials' into their departments to ensure that reforms and changes
were not blocked by the pre-1914 old guard. More insult. More injury.[12]

All the same, the educated class still had advantages. As Haffner's
description shows, the fact that a civil servant's or academic's salary
was paid monthly made bulk buying possible. This became increasingly important as the rate of inflation began to rise still further, so
that prices changed by the week, or even the day. For the manual
worker living close to the existence minimum, especially if he or she
was on piece work or in irregular employment, the day's price had to
paid. It was literally a matter of hand to mouth.

Even if family savings had become more or less worthless, the
middle classes generally had reserves of, for instance, more and better
quality clothing than a working-class household. They possessed superior, more durable household implements, and often still a maidservant
to keep the kitchen, to sew and mend. An extra pair of hands in the
house also allowed more time to search and queue for affordable,
decent food as inflation led to shortages and shopping queues lengthened.[13] And generally the middle class had more spacious houses or
apartments. Rooms could be let for extra income.

None of the above prevented this class from developing a sharp
sense of both deprivation and collective humiliation. Heinz Flügel,
then in his mid-teens, was forced to watch as his father, a former

career diplomat, though still only in his fifties, was gradually shunted into retirement. Now they travelled on wooden seats in fourth class for their increasingly rare summer holidays. They still had the family villa in Zehlendorf, a pleasant Berlin suburb, but life had become noticeably harder. Flügel wrote many years later:

> I can see in my memory how my father, who had been used to being waited upon, had to maintain the stoves at home. While we were busy with our school homework, he would haul the heavy coal buckets, without complaint, up from the cellar into the first floor. Today we may not be so surprised by such a thing; at that time the change felt abrupt.[14]

Ernst Troeltsch, despite being a scholar of international standing and having a civil service job at the Prussian Ministry of Culture and Religion, told of the tight budgets and the 'make do and mend' measures that even such a household as his was forced to adopt. For working people, these were bad times, where *die Teuerung* (rising prices), as most ordinary people referred to the inflation, made already poor living standards even worse. For the educated middle classes, the fall in social as well as economic expectations was dizzyingly steep. Things once taken for granted were now beyond reach.

Writing in March 1922, Troeltsch was acutely aware that, like most German academics and even educational institutions, because of the exchange rate he could no longer afford foreign books and publications. To travel abroad was, of course, impossible. 'All luxury in art and science, all travelling, is at an end in these circles,' he wrote. These were particular humiliations that those who still had money, and foreigners in particular, could not grasp.

> This leads to the main question, which is how Germans are actually faring. The French generally see only the luxury hotels and places of entertainment, which they pay for with German money or with better foreign currency. They see the shops in the cities and the whirlwind

of pleasure seeking. It would be very important to find out from trustworthy people how things really are. But that is a very hard question to answer in definite terms. Few statistics are available to the private citizen, and the official figures no one believes. At base, however, in this area of things we only get our knowledge from chance individual observations and can hardly even make an estimation of our own situation. What is clear is the downright desperate misery of those who live off small investments and pensions. The first group, in many cases, are simply consuming their capital, with the hope – or intention – when it is all used up, of dying. Conditions for workers with children are also very hard. The necessity of returning to a free economy and stopping state subsidies means, with the prices rising as they are, rising poverty. The situation for artists, writers and all sorts of Bohemians is almost as desperate as that of the small investor. The downward pressure on the way of living for the entire middle and official class is also a matter of great sensitivity. These are the new poor, who face the new rich. All their income is swallowed up by housing expenses, heating and food; so far as everything else goes, one lives from old things and uses one's old clothes absolutely to the limit . . . But the old things will wear out, and then the hardship will be bitter, without even taking account of the difficult accommodation situation.[15]

The men of the educated middle class began referring to themselves as 'the intellectual proletariat'. The gap between them and the lower middle class of clerks and self-employed craftsmen no longer looked so wide, or their self-identification as superior to such people so automatic. A mixture of angry nostalgia for what had been lost, and a resentment at what continued to be taken from them, made even those who had initially accepted the revolution and Republic inclined to move further and further towards the anti-democratic right.

Further down the social scale were others disastrously affected by the inflation even during these early years. They may have been accustomed to lower standards of living than the educated classes were used to, but they were equally dependent on schemes with a fixed return. Most seriously affected were those who depended on basic government pensions and benefits of all sorts.

The lost war had created 525,000 widows, 1.3 million orphans and 1.5 million disabled war veterans, all of whom had to be supported by the state and the municipalities from a much diminished national product. Their pensions amounted to a large proportion of public expenditure. Figures for the early 1920s are hard to pin down, but by the middle of the decade, these costs certainly totalled 20 per cent of the government's budget as opposed to 7 per cent in the United Kingdom.[16] This was in addition to those Germans who had reached retirement age and routinely qualified for pensions under the pioneering social insurance system established in the 1880s. Bismarck's famous scheme had based itself on low-risk investment vehicles that had provided a stable income for the pension schemes in times of currency stability. Now, as the mark slid further following the year of stabilisation, they brought (vanishingly) low returns.[17]

The war widows, orphans and war-disabled veterans, meanwhile, were paid out of municipal funds, which from 1920 were mostly provided on a percentage basis by the central government under the tax-centralising stipulations of the late Herr Erzberger's tax law. Even by 1919, the municipalities were hugely in debt, in good part because of their welfare commitments to war casualties and their families – and habituated to going beyond these basic tax revenues and touting bond issues on the financial markets. Come the end of 1921, German cities were finding it even harder to raise the money to care for their needy. Foreign bonds markets, since 1919 a happy hunting ground for the high-spending municipalities, had dried up as in New York, Amsterdam, London, Buenos Aires and elsewhere investors began to avoid anything giving a return in German marks. And so the Reich government was forced to take on at least part of the huge cost of war pensions, yet another reason to print more money – and even then, providing far from adequate support for the war wounded, and for the war dead's wives and families.

Government agencies began introducing strict, complicated and sometimes arbitrary seeming eligibility tests, and insisting that, for instance, war widows should if possible find work. A proportion of state jobs were set aside for the male war disabled, but there was no such provision for women. Once the inflation really began to take off, the dependent poor fell further behind. The 'natural' solution was remarriage, but with two million German males killed in the war, creating an exaggerated gender imbalance, this was not an option for many widows.

What must always be kept in mind, however, is that these bizarre arrangements were still being made in the context of an economy operating at a very hectic pace and suffering from very minimal unemployment. While an underclass of pensioners, widows, orphans and disabled persons was being kept more or less alive through inadequate welfare and varieties of poor relief, these people did not share the company of any substantial number of unemployed.[18]

The contrast between the salaries of the civil servants empowered to grant or withhold these benefits and the standard of living of the recipients caused special bitterness. In January 1922, to take a snapshot, with the so-called 'minimum income index' standing at 1,600 marks, a fully disabled veteran (i.e. completely unable to work) received 1,034 marks and a war widow 716 marks. The average civil servant's salary was 1,965 marks.

The Weimar state's best intentions, its founders' declared aim of building the world's most progressive welfare system as well as its most complete democracy, were falling ever further short, the more the inflation, while seeming to keep the country working and prospering, tore at the government's budgetary plans.

As for prices, they began to rocket. The cost of living, including clothing, increased by 71.5 per cent between August and September 1922 alone.[19] 'The unprecedented fall of the mark in the last few days differs from the previous falls,' wrote Morgan Philips Price of the *Manchester Guardian* from Berlin on 4 August 1922. 'This time it is a general psychological panic wave . . .'[20]

The panic was well founded. In May 1922, the government had been able to announce that the previous financial year's tax income was around 30 per cent above the projected take, but since this was expressed in paper marks that had been dramatically devalued since the projection was made, the figure was worse than meaningless. The real tax take had continued to slump and the deficit, therefore, to grow. Meanwhile, in that same month only 20.87 per cent of the government's income came from taxes, the rest – bar a few fractions of a per cent representing mail and rail charges – from borrowing via Treasury bills discounted by the Reichsbank. And as expectations that the government would manage to run a surplus and thereby cut the deficit any time soon diminished to near-nothingness after June 1922, institutions and individuals both in Germany and abroad became less and less willing to acquire government debt through Treasury bills and other bonds.[21]

The government tightened its welfare policies quite ruthlessly as its own financial crisis became more acute. The living standards of those disadvantaged Germans who should have been taken care of continued to lag drastically behind the ever-steeper increases in the cost of living. This condemned them – even disabled soldiers, and their fallen comrades' widows and orphans, who had sacrificed all for their country and should have been granted a modest sufficiency by the state – to struggle, to beg, or worse.

The good news – what there was of it – for German families during and immediately after the First World War was that private rents were strictly controlled by the government. So long as a tenant held an existing rental agreement, and stayed where he or she was, the proportion of a family's outgoings required to keep a roof over its head constantly decreased as the inflation continued, gradually tending towards zero. A sample of working-class families' living costs, for instance, reveals that rent made up 19.7 per cent of expenditure in 1907, 8 per cent in 1917, 7.3 per cent in 1919, and, at the climax of the inflation, a mere 0.3 per cent![22]

This was, of course, bad news for landlords. While it might be that they were able to pay off mortgages quickly because of the inflation, the financial return on their properties was miserable. Landlords, often not wealthy people but simply once-prosperous members of the *Mittelstand* – skilled artisans, shopkeepers, small tradesmen – who had invested in rental property as a form of saving and supplementary income, made up yet another aggrieved class in Weimar Germany.

Given the virtual cessation of residential construction during the war, and the lack of incentive to build for rent after peace came, the housing shortages, particularly in the big cities, became even more chronic. This caused serious overcrowding, with all the consequent damage to physical and mental health. Louis Lochner, later Associated Press's bureau chief in Berlin, arrived in the German capital during this time. He got the usual foreign visitor's impression of 'cafés crowded with stylishly garbed ladies', but then began to explore the side streets and alleys away from the haunts of the well-to-do:

I visited a typical Youth Welfare Station. Children who looked as though they were eight or nine years old proved to be thirteen. I learned that there were then 15,000 tubercular children in Berlin; that 23 per cent of the children examined by the city health authorities were badly undernourished.[23]

The problems were not confined to Berlin. A survey of large working-class families in Düsseldorf published in 1923 reported an average of 3.7 persons per bedroom, and 1.9 per bed. In a low-income area of Mannheim, where the social services were especially active, of 220 families inspected, 96 failed to have what was thought to be a basic provision of beds – one bed per adult and one per two children. In a few cases, they had beds (presumably of the folding type) but not enough space to open them out. Drunkenness, incest and violence were endemic.[24]

In the big tenement blocks that housed ordinary families in the industrial cities, most notoriously Berlin, the courtyards and inner tenements (the infamous *Hinterhöfe*) were arranged like Chinese boxes, with the most expensive flats on the outside, where there was light and air, and the cheapest, darkest and dampest making up the gloomy heart of the building. Combined with post-war shortages of affordable good quality food, and real wages that rarely rose up near the pre-war level and were usually much less, deteriorating living conditions also meant that diseases associated with deprivation and poverty rose sharply in the post-war inflation even during conditions of apparently full employment.

The incidence in infants of rickets, caused by lack of vitamin D, a result of dietary insufficiencies but also of simple lack of access to sunlight, was estimated in 1921 for those under six months at 27.8 per cent, between six months and a year at 41.1 per cent, between a year and eighteen months at 40.2 per cent, for those between eighteen months and two at 32.4 per cent, and for those infants over two years old at 59 per cent. The two-year-olds counted had been born immediately after the war, when the continuing blockade was causing shortages of basic foods. In the port city of Lübeck on the Baltic coast, evidence of tuberculosis in two-year-olds had doubled from 12 per cent before the war to 23 per cent, and in five- to six-year-olds from 33 to 50 per cent. In Stuttgart in 1922, 40 per cent of female students at a vocational school had thyroid problems, attributable to a lack of iodine in their diets.[25]

Nor was the problem confined to children. One working-class boy from Hanover, born in 1913, lost two adult older brothers to tuberculosis at this time. Both had been conscripted towards the end of the war, and had caught TB while at the front.

It was only later that I realised the almost inhuman mental and physical burdens my mother was forced to endure during the time that both her eldest sons were dying. Even today I can scarcely grasp that she visited my brothers, who lay sick in the Nordstadt Hospital, every other day, and on the day in between would take me to the Polyclinic in the same hospital – on foot, of course, more than an hour's walk,

LOSERS   225

because there was not enough money for the tram. I still think with
gratitude of the solidarity from friends and comrades, who took turns
inviting us boys to eat with them, although their material situation
was no better than ours.[26]

The significant and surprising thing to keep in mind is that while
some of these people were unemployed, or on pensions of one sort
or the other, many, perhaps most, were in work. One unhappy couple,
both factory workers (city not identified), crammed into a small flat
with children from various relationships, provide an example. Since
the case, along with others, was published in 1924, we can reasonably
assume the details are from 1922–3.

The extended family's residence was a two-room flat with a kitchen.
There were six of them in it: a man, a woman, two boys aged eight
and six, a little girl aged five, and a twelve-year-old girl from the
woman's previous attachment. The couple had been legally separated
for some time. The man had been convicted and sentenced to ten
months in prison for molesting the stepdaughter. When he came out
of jail, he returned to the flat. He had nowhere to live and wanted,
so he said, to see his biological children. The woman gained an injunction against him to leave, but he refused. The next step, hiring a bailiff
to evict him, would cost more than she had at her disposal. So the
man stayed. The social worker's report continued:

The cohabitation of the separated parents in one flat seems to amount
to an endless mutual torment.

At the moment the step-daughter, who earlier had been subjected
to the sex crime, is still on holiday with the grandmother for ten days.
The little girl is for this reason alone for the entire night with the
father.

Neither of the couple makes a good impression. The man was and
probably remains today a heavy drinker. Neither of them will vacate
the flat of their own free will. The mother, who for a while looked
after the children well, has now become totally indifferent. The

226 THE DOWNFALL OF MONEY

separation, the injunction for him to leave, nothing changes anything
about the actual situation, and the long-term placement of these
children, who can look forward only to neglect, in homes run by the
city authorities will in the end fail because these are so crowded.[27]

It seems that this was not an exceptional case. The odd detail apart,
the example was just one plucked from many on the social workers'
books.

The government, realising that there was no incentive for anyone
to become a landlord, or for anyone to build new accommodation
that might help alleviate the shortage, passed a law early in 1922 to
allow a tripling of rent levels over the rates frozen since the outbreak
of war in 1914. By the end of the year, of course, the cost of living had
more than trebled, and the advantage was once more lost.

The idea of investing in bricks and mortar, if such could be afforded,
was tempting all the same. For those who, unlike the pensioners and
the impoverished middle class, and the hand-to-mouth working class,
had spare money over and above what was needed for subsistence,
acquiring 'things', material assets, was the key to surviving and even
prospering in these uncertain times. More important than anything
was to get rid of your cash, which might tomorrow be worthless. The
relaxation of the rent control laws was a signal for a new wave of
investment, as the *Manchester Guardian* reported:

The boom that has just set in in the building trade is responsible for
the reduction in the figures of the unemployed, sunk this week to
50,000. This sudden activity is due to two reasons. The older one is
that the fortunate or unfortunate possessor of too many paper marks
is desirous of exchanging them for something tangible in bricks and
mortar even at the incredible cost of construction. The newer follows
upon the heels of the law just passed allowing landlords to raise rents
at fixed percentages of pre-war prices. This benefits the middle classes
to the same extent as it injures them, for house property was the safest
method of investing savings before the war, and, owing to the drastic

regulations controlling profiteering on the part of landlords, many retired couples, owners of considerable property containing residential flats, are today on the brink of starvation. The new statutes provide for an increase in rents all over the country of 300 per cent on pre-war figures. Building a house containing twelve to twenty such flats has thus become the latest form of profitable investment.[28]

The other fashionable speculative object was furniture. That was being hoarded, too, on the basis of the same hopes that the housing crisis would ease in a year or two, as would the inflation, and suddenly people would need to furnish new homes.

The trend had been clear for years. Now, for those who could manage it, the headlong flight into 'things' had begun.

18

Kicking Germany When She's Down

On 22 November 1922, four years and eleven days after the armistice that ended the First World War, President Ebert undertook what appeared to be a desperate throw of the dice for the Republic to which he had been midwife in those dark days of defeat. After the failure of attempts to create a broad coalition to deal with the increasingly grave financial crisis, the former Social Democrat leader showed how far he had travelled since the revolution. He passed over the usual politicians and appointed Wilhelm Cuno, an 'expert' conservative businessman, supposedly without party affinity, to be Chancellor of Germany.

The new Chancellor was not even a member of the Reichstag. The President had a wide range of reserve powers under the constitution, conferred upon him in order to protect the Republic against political chaos-making. Ebert used them now, in what historians have seen as the first, furtive example of what would become an unhealthy habit in the Weimar Republic: Rule by Presidential Decree.

The President's choice was described in the *Manchester Guardian* as a 'new and perhaps dangerous experiment'. As for *The Times* of London, which had initially seen Cuno as a man of 'tact' who could rally left and right alike to defend Germany, as early as the day after his formal appointment it was already describing his cabinet as a 'patchwork' whose 'colour comes from the right' and about which 'nobody has a good word to say . . . and nobody expects . . . to last long'. The *Vossische Zeitung* also felt that, far from being an 'unpolitical' cabinet of experts and businessmen, the new government actually represented a resurgence of the old conservative elite. The *New York Times* was also not sure about the new Chancellor. Its headline, likewise something of a patchwork, read:

CUNO CABINET FACES REICHSTAG FRIDAY;
Baron Von Rosenberg, Chosen Foreign Minister,
Is Yet to Be Heard From.
NO POLITICS IN MINISTRY.
New Chancellor Said to Plan to Handle Economic Situation on
   Non-Partisan Lines.

Since July, the German economy was technically, according to the most commonly accepted definition, in a state of 'hyperinflation', which meant prices were increasing at a rate in excess of 50 per cent per month. The mark on the morning of 22 November had stood at 6,300 marks to the dollar – and that was after something of a positive 'bounce' due to the new, supposedly business-friendly administration. In other words, the mark was now worth around 1/20 of its rate at the beginning of 1922, and 1/1,500 of its pre-war value.[1] And so President Ebert put his faith in a 'cabinet of business' under a man with a reputation as an organisational miracle worker.

Dr Wilhelm Carl Josef Cuno, born in 1876 in what was then Prussian Saxony but is now Thuringia, was tall, distinguished looking and very successful in business. His background was solid, civil-servant middle class. In time-honoured fashion, he had got his doctorate in law and gone, like his father, into the Prussian government service. He rose quickly in the Finance Ministry to the high rank of *Geheimer Rat* (Privy Councillor, and entitled to be addressed as 'excellency'), before transferring in wartime to head the Reich Grain Board, then being appointed a chief adviser to the Reich Treasury on economic affairs. In 1917, Cuno left government service and joined the board of the once mighty but now much diminished Hamburg-Amerika Line (HAPAG) as the protégé of Albert Ballin, friend of the Kaiser and the great German shipping magnate of the age.

Ballin, who had been forced to watch his beloved shipping line's wartime decline and the death of his hopes for Germany, committed suicide in November 1918, and Cuno was appointed to run the company. His success in reviving the fortunes of the HAPAG with extraordinary speed propelled Cuno to international note. As *The Times* reported, 'the remarkable revival of the company's activities since the war shows how very judicious this selection was. It has quickly re-established services to North and South America, to Africa, and the Far East, in the Baltic, and in the Levant, by associating itself with British and American shipping lines, and fresh vessels are constantly being added to its fleet.'[2]

Crucially, given the importance of Wall Street and Washington in the matter of reparations and loans, Cuno was reputed to be good at dealing with the Anglo-Saxon nations in general, but especially with the Americans, as his recent success in getting from them what he wanted for HAPAG seemed to show.

The appointee had been lurking in the background of German politics for some time, seen by many as a potential saviour – he had come into the picture as a possible finance minister the year before but had been vetoed by the Social Democrats – and now this was his chance at the great office his admirers had long wished to see him occupy. His appointment would not have surprised (or for that matter impressed) the late Walther Rathenau, who at the Genoa conference, where the HAPAG Director had been an adviser, remarked wryly that Cuno was 'a fat cigar which will have to be smoked some day for the sake of its lovely band'.[3]

Cuno had been a member of the German People's Party until 1920, when he resigned in protest against the party leadership's ambivalent attitude towards the Kapp putsch. He had been reckoned a moderate compared with the heavy industrialists who dominated the party's authoritarian, fiercely anti-labour right wing and supplied most of its funding. The Social Democrats nevertheless declared themselves unwilling to join his new government, but undertook to support it on a case-by-case basis. So this was, despite all its pretensions to creating a 'new beginning', yet another minority government. A lot was being expected of a man who, for all his evident business talent, had little or no political experience.

What seemed unquestionable was that Germany needed a stronger direction, under a Chancellor who knew what he was doing. In June, Josef Wirth's government had suspended cash payments of reparations, sending the currency into a further tailspin. In July, Wirth had requested full relief on cash reparations payments for the rest of the year and for two years after that, citing the decline of the mark and the sharp increase in inflation inside Germany. The policy of 'fulfilment' was crumbling and being replaced by something more confrontational.

Meanwhile, as summer turned to autumn, the French continued to demand their money and, if not, then a whole range of direct controls over the German economy, as the price of a full-scale reparations moratorium.

The Americans and British, having again failed at an emergency conference in London in August to persuade the French to consider reduction of reparations to a more manageable level, pulled out of the unified reparations policy. This was bad news for Germany in the sense that the two Anglo-Saxon powers would no longer act as a powerful moderating force. French Premier Poincaré vowed to go on alone in demanding 'productive pledges', physical guarantees that reparations for France and Belgium would actually be paid and not somehow constantly postponed to some indefinite future. The new German government was also continuing the dangerous game of delaying the delivery of reparations in kind, or under-delivering, all the time complaining about how much the deliveries were hurting their economy.

By November 1922, a French incursion into the Ruhr to seize control of Germany's richest industrial assets was widely expected.

The expectation did not inspire confidence in Germany, nor in her currency.

Even in late 1922, hyperinflationary Germany remained the world's second largest economy.[4] All the same, the country was beginning to resemble a runaway train filled with unhappy passengers, gradually picking up speed as it hurtled towards an unknown destination.

In first class, the leaders of the new Republic's elite were watching the increasingly neglected landscape whizz past ever faster with a sense of growing panic, but little idea what to do except to keep denying it was their fault. And blaming the Allies for demanding all those reparations.

Back in second class, those resentful souls who had until recently occupied first class were plotting how to get back there, if necessary by murderous means.

In the cramped and ill-supplied aisles of third, a battle royal was shaping up between the growing Communist Party and the new, ultra-rightist mass organisations – most prominently Adolf Hitler's National Socialists – who were competing for the loyalty of Germany's lower middle and working class.

Everyone was shouting instructions. Everyone was insulting everybody else, even when they were supposed to be allies. Fights were constantly breaking out. No one was putting on the brakes. To do so would be to admit that the German train was running out of track.

Rathenau's assassination certainly plunged the German body politic into horrified confusion. All the same, it seems unlikely that the situation in the late autumn of 1922 would have been much better had he not fallen to the assassin's bullets. The German mark might have held up somewhat better, and foreigners might have had a foreign minister they felt more able to trust, but the basic facts would have remained the same: no success in passing the truly effective new taxes that the country desperately needed in order to close the deficit and therefore meet its reparations commitments. No reduction in the bloated bureaucracy. No cuts in the never-ending subsidies to the vastly overmanned state-owned railways and post office (which were such great engines of employment). No curtailment of low-interest loans from the Reichsbank to industry and business. And, of course, no currency stabilisation plan.

The French and the Belgians believed that the German government had not done any of the things that needed doing, not because it could not but because it had no desire to. They would say that the runaway train of inflation was continuing its wild ride because the Germans had deliberately disabled the brakes. The British and the Americans had mostly come to the conclusion that the Germans' difficulties were genuine, but this realisation seemed to make little practical difference. The Americans, in particular, still wanted their wartime inter-Allied loans repaid, especially by their single largest debtor, France. While this remained the case, the French were not going to take the pressure off Germany.

So, when Chancellor Cuno started a number of apparently energetic and bold initiatives to break the reparations deadlock, as was his brief in the role of Germany's dynamic new leader, it was not, with hindsight, surprising that he met with a blank wall of refusal from Poincaré and his chief negotiator, Jacques Seydoux. An immediate reparation payment of 20 billion gold marks, financeable by an international loan? After that, a three- to four-year moratorium with only payments in kind to continue? Thirty-year 'Rhineland Security Pact'? No, no, and no.

At an Allied conference in London in December and then another in January 1923 in Paris, all Cuno's suggestions were shot down. True, Britain's new Conservative Prime Minister, Bonar Law (Lloyd George had finally lost power in October 1922), came up with a hugely complex and not especially generous offer to the French at the Paris conference which involved, among other things, Britain's forgiving at least some of the money the French owed from wartime. Meanwhile, however, it also meant that France would have to abandon a swathe of German reparations liabilities and also give up the more than a billion gold marks' worth of gold she had deposited at the Bank of England as a security for wartime loans. There would, furthermore, be no cash to fix the hole in the French national budget, or to pay for reconstruction of the former occupied areas.

'We having together knocked Germany down, one of us is going to kick her while she is on the ground, and the others will let her,' complained Law regarding the aggressive French demands.

Finally, things started coming to a head. On 26 December, Germany had been declared in default for timber and telegraph pole deliveries due under the reparations clauses. Then, after the Paris conference had brought no financial agreement between the Allies that might have persuaded the French to hold off, on 9 January Germany was also declared, by a vote of three to one in the Reparations Committee (France, Belgium and Italy against Britain), in deliberate default on coal deliveries, too. Germany was accused of delivering only 11.7 million tons of coal during 1922 instead of the agreed 13.8 million (a much more serious, or at least less ridiculous, business, than that with the timber). This triggered a possible use of force which two days later became actual. On 11 January, French and Belgian troops crossed the boundary from their post-war areas of occupation, held since 1919 under the terms of the Versailles Treaty, and advanced into hitherto German-ruled territory.

That same day, sullen Germans stood in the streets of Essen, capital of the Ruhr, watching France's finest taking possession of their proud city, the heart of the Reich's heavy industry. The occupation force stationed in Essen alone would soon total 6,000. By 16 January, the Franco-Belgian force was in control of the entire Ruhr area as far east as Dortmund, an area with a population of 4.25 million and containing (now that Upper Silesia had been given to Poland) 72 per cent of Germany's coal resources, 54 per cent of its pig iron and 53 per cent of its steel production.[5]

According to the Franco-Belgian proclamation that accompanied the Ruhr occupation, the troops were sent there to provide protection for a seventy-strong commission of French and Belgian engineers (plus two Italians), whose job was to take control of the mines and workshops intended to act as 'productive guarantees' for German reparations payments. The engineers, known collectively as the *Mission Interallié de Contrôle des Usines et des Mines* (Inter-Allied Mission for Control of Factories and Mines = MICUM) would ensure that the coal dug by German miners would be collected and shipped to the beneficiary countries.

A note to the German government on the eve of the occupation proclaimed blithely that France had 'no intention thereby of engaging in a military operation or an occupation of a political nature'. 'The French government,' it added, ' . . . is simply sending a mission of engineers and officials into the Ruhr District, whose purpose is strictly limited to ensuring that Germany observes its obligations contained in the Treaty of Versailles.' The innocent sounding 'escort' force would in fact consist of 70,000–100,000 French and Belgian troops, whose equipment would include, on the contrary, an extremely military sounding array of tanks, light artillery and machine guns.[6]

The German government was surprisingly poorly prepared for the crisis. Everyone had suspected during the preceding weeks that the French and the Belgians were becoming increasingly likely to invade. The currency markets certainly reflected this. The value of the mark fell from 7,260 to the dollar on 2 January, to 8,700 on 5 January following the failure of the Paris conference. On Wednesday, 10 January, the day before the occupation, with a Franco-Belgian military operation considered inevitable, it dipped further, to 10,250.

The authorities in Berlin, however, had made little special provision for the occupation. No coal or raw materials had been stockpiled to keep the rest of the country going in case of Germany's main coal-producing area falling into foreign hands. The same went in the financial sphere. A ninth supplementary appropriation to the 1922 budget was about to come into force, and a tenth was in preparation. Neither of these measures, which had become common in the hyper-inflationary age, had anything to do with the Ruhr. The tenth supplementary was all about covering inflation-related pay increases for civil servants. No broad organisational plan was in place. A supplementary finance bill providing for what were clearly going to be

massive costs relating to the Ruhr occupation was not ready for presentation to the Reichstag until 29 January, and would not pass into
law until 16 February.[7]

Kirdorf, Thyssen, Stinnes and co., meanwhile, were not caught so
flat-footed. The shrewd gentlemen of the Rhenish-Westphalian Coal
Syndicate had on 9 January moved the administrative headquarters
of their powerful cartel, including its technical records and key technical staff, 600 personnel in all, several hundred kilometres north
from Essen to the safety of Hamburg.[8] The individual mines were to
make their own policy when dealing with the French and the Belgians.
This was intended to make the occupiers' task of exploiting the mines
a lot harder, and it did.

The only explanation for the government's lack of preparation
seems to be that neither Chancellor Wirth, responsible for planning
until his government fell on 14 November 1922, nor Chancellor Cuno,
properly installed in power since 22 November, expected the French
actually to go through with the Ruhr invasion.

Curiously, the apparent complacency in government circles may
have been in part a result of the reparations guru J. M. Keynes's close
relationship with leading figures in Germany. At the end of August
1922, the great man, who, since publishing *The Economic Consequences
of the Peace*, could do no wrong in German eyes, had visited Hamburg
as guest of honour for its Overseas Week, an event attended by President Ebert, General Groener (now Transport Minister) and numerous
other worthies. The event was generally agreed to have been part of
the continuing German pitch for an international loan. On 26 August,
Keynes delivered an address. First he was introduced by no less a
figure than Dr Cuno, then still Director of the HAPAG, as 'the man
most responsible for the changed attitude in the English-speaking
world towards Germany'. Keynes's speech was equally favourably
received by a cheering audience.

'I do not believe,' Keynes told them, '. . . France may actually carry
into effect her threat of renewing war,' and he continued:

One or two years ago France might have acted thus with the necessary inner conviction. But not now. The confidence of the Frenchmen in the official reparations policy is utterly undermined . . . They know in their hearts that it has no reality in it. For many reasons they are reluctant to admit the facts. But they are bluffing. They know perfectly well that illegal acts of violence on their part will isolate them morally and sentimentally, ruin their finances and bring them no advantage whatever. M. Poincaré . . . may make harsh speeches and inflict futile minor outrages . . . but he will not act on a big scale. Indeed his speeches are an alternative not a prelude to action. The bigger he talks the less he will do . . .

'The Germans,' he added, 'will do well to keep cool and not be much alarmed.'[9]

The lack of foresight on the part of the government was nonetheless remarkable, not just because of the sheer likelihood of the Ruhr occupation, but, whatever the actual odds, because of the immensity of the consequences if and when it happened. The Franco-Belgian seizure of Germany's (and Europe's) most important single industrial area was, in effect – and despite the fact that there was no military resistance – an act of war.

Although it would have been suicide for the Reichswehr to try to resist the French army, at this point in history the largest military force on the European continent, in many other respects the situation resembled that of 1914. Certainly the fierce reaction of the vast majority of Germans, inside and outside the occupation area, was comparable to that which had greeted the outbreak of the last war. Except for the Communists, who, before Moscow decreed otherwise, followed the usual policy of 'a plague on both your houses', every other major political party and national institution in Germany united to condemn the French act and to support any measures necessary to oppose it. The country experienced a temporary revival of the wartime *Burgfrieden*.

The consequence of the national determination to resist the French seizure of such vital national assets was the so-called 'passive resistance' policy. On 11 January, Coal Commissar Stutz, the state's representative and main authority in the Ruhr now that the Coal Syndicate had removed itself from the firing line, instructed the mines to cease supplying coal to the occupying powers.[10] But what if the French and Belgian military authorities forced them to deliver? On 19 January, Cuno's government ordered the railways to refuse to transport coal to Belgium and France. Railway workers and officials were to obey only the German authorities, not the foreign occupiers. This included railway employees in the 'old', i.e. legitimately occupied, areas.[11] The Berlin government also enjoined the population of the Ruhr to keep resistance strictly on a peaceful basis. This would prove hard to enforce in the face both of German patriotic fervour and the French army's increasingly harsh enforcement of its own government's will.

The response of the French and Belgian occupiers to the official non-collaboration policy was severe and often disturbingly inhumane. Martial law was declared in the Ruhr. German customs and tax receipts were declared forfeit. German mine owners were arrested and fined for refusing to obey French orders. German government officials who refused to cooperate with the occupying authorities were arrested and expelled with their families over the new 'border' into unoccupied Germany by French troops, often at short notice and with considerable brutality. During the occupation, close to 150,000 German civilians of all kinds, including civil servants, railway employees, police officials and mine and factory employees, were expelled across the internal border by the French authorities. An unknown number left voluntarily to escape hardship or the threat of persecution.[12]

By February 1923, a customs barrier had been set up between the Ruhr and unoccupied Germany. Initially, this was to enable the occupiers to confiscate German customs revenues in order to pay for the costs of the occupation, but it quickly developed into an economic instrument. Trade between the Rhine–Ruhr area and Germany proper required licences. Exports of coal and raw materials into the Reich were banned and an export duty of 10 per cent on other goods imposed. It was in many ways a second blockade of Germany.

Mine owners and managers, initially at least, worked with the unions and labour force in carrying out the non-collaboration policy. Trade union leaders and their members – Catholics, socialists, even Communists – resisted enemy provocation and for many weeks held out against relentless and increasing intimidation by the occupiers. Although in later decades it was the violent sabotage by the far right which tended to be remembered, the less dramatic, more workaday courage of the labour force, mostly determined supporters of the post-war Republic and its welfare policies, in fact made up the backbone of the resistance.[13] The *Manchester Guardian*'s man in the Ruhr, Morgan Philips Price, a decent reporter though something of a Bolshevik fellow-traveller, believed that the early violent resistance against the French was being carried out by 'thugs imported from Munich'. He wrote in mid-February 1923:

The latter are terrorising shopkeepers to make them refuse to sell anything to the French. The wretched tradesmen are in grave difficulties, threatened with ruin from both sides. At night these German Nationalist bands smash windows and wreck the shop of anyone who displeases them. Against these bands the workmen in a number of mines and metal factories have formed themselves into guards, armed with rubber batons and wire coils, to defend themselves from their own Nationalists, as they have no confidence in the police . . .[14]

It was certainly true that the core of the active, violent resistance movement consisted largely of former and serving Freikorps members, many of whom had been involved just over a year earlier in the armed resistance to the Poles in Upper Silesia. Since, by 1923, Bavaria, and more especially Munich, served as the 'safe' centre of the Freikorps movement, Philips Price's reference to 'thugs . . . from Munich' bore an element of truth; but the fact was that the nationalist underground had been organising in the French-occupied areas since 1920 and that the Ruhr operation was in many ways merely an extension of their previous activities.[15]

The flip side of 'passive resistance' was that the Berlin government compensated employers and workers alike for various forms of economic sabotage of the French efforts at exploiting the Ruhr, including deliberate inactivity, strikes and shutting down of plants and mines. Industrialists were compensated for the 'unproductive wages' paid to their inactive workers by the central government, first at a rate of 60 per cent, then 100 per cent. They were also granted financial credits for lost production and profits owing to inaction or seizure of their production by the occupiers. The ever-vigilant Morgan Philips Price would comment sardonically on this development, which, as the year went on, became an open scandal:

> Seventy per cent of the heavy industry is lying still, large part of the coking ovens and smelting furnaces have gone cold and most of them are not worth rebuilding. There is reason to believe that the German trusts are not shedding tears at this development. The coking and smelting plants in the Ruhr are more than are needed to cover any possible consumption in the German and world markets, which have been reduced since the war. The trusts are getting paid for the furnaces cooled down by the Reich in gold values, which they immediately invest abroad, thus further assisting the collapse of the mark.[16]

The state also paid the wages of railway employees and civil servants who had either been expelled from the occupied zone and were often homeless over the border in the Reich proper. It also compensated men who were left unemployed by their refusal to cooperate with the French and Belgian railway administration, the so-called *Régie des Chemins de Fer des Territoires Occupés*.

Many who lost their homes and were displaced experienced grave suffering as a result, while to others the state aid was a generous dole, affectionately known to its sometimes slightly abashed recipients as the 'Cuno Pension'.[17] 'Cuno pensioners' were, in fact, considered so well off by the (admittedly miserable) standards of the times that there were widespread rumours of fraudulent claims.[18]

Germany put itself into a do-or-die situation, where the end justified the means, just as it had during the war, when it had run up huge debts in anticipation of victory. Except . . . this time, what would 'victory' against the French in the Ruhr actually mean?

Right or wrong, the government's unconditional support for the Ruhr was a vastly expensive business, and the only way to pay for it was to print more marks. The presses ran round the clock. Unsurprisingly, by 5 February 1923, the mark stood at 42,250, a quarter of its 15 January level of a little under 12,000 – which in turn had represented a disastrous decline from the levels maintained until Rathenau's assassination. As fast as it could print them, the government kept sending the ever-increasing quantities of paper marks needed to keep the resistance going.

In an effort to nullify Berlin's crucial financial support for the Ruhr struggle, the French and Belgian occupation authorities confiscated consignments of paper marks at the newly erected customs posts as best they could, though they never succeeded in seizing more than a small fraction.[19] The currency importers showed great ingenuity and bravery. Money was packed into false floors built into vehicles – often driven by women, in the hope that the French would never suspect them – or brought in through the dense woodland that covered the fringe areas of the Ruhr district. It was even imported via labyrinthine mine workings, which in some cases stretched for kilometres beneath the 'border', allowing currency couriers to enter from unoccupied Germany disguised as miners and emerge some time later inside the occupation zone.[20]

The 'passive resistance' was a trial of strength. Initially, surprised by the determined reaction of the Germans, and unprepared for the near-total shutdown of the mines and their inability to transport what little coal they could find at the pit heads, the occupiers seemed to have made a mistake. France, whose own currency was now rapidly depreciating, found herself obliged to buy expensive British coking

coal to fuel her iron and steel industry, negating the entire reason for
the Ruhr invasion. More than a third of French blast furnaces were
forced to cease operation during February and March 1922. It seemed
as if the predictions that the French would hurt themselves more than
the Germans by seizing the Ruhr might turn out to be accurate.

By the beginning of March 1923, 11,000 French and Belgian railway
workers had been imported to run the railways in the absence of their
German counterparts. Foreign labour was also recruited, including
miners from Poland, to dig the coal. Slowly it became clear that,
despite the high moral and financial cost, the French were determined
to make the occupation work for them.

As conditions worsened in the occupied area, so did relations
between the Franco-Belgian forces and the people of the Ruhr. There
were clashes between workers and French troops, including one
confrontation on 31 March at the Krupp casting works in Essen, where
a French army unit had gone to commandeer a large number of motor
vehicles. After resistance to the French escalated, thirteen Krupp
workers ended up being shot dead and another forty-one injured.
Instead of the French soldiers concerned facing an investigation, the
company's management was held responsible by the occupation
authorities. Gustav Krupp von Bohlen und Halbach, head of the Krupp
concern, was sentenced to fifteen years' imprisonment and fined 100
million marks. Several other senior Krupp executives were sentenced
to prison terms.[21] In May there was a major strike and a near-uprising
by workers in the city of Dortmund, on the eastern edge of the Ruhr,
in which a further twenty workers were shot by French troops.[22]

There was also a small but significant amount of armed resistance
against the French. Ignoring the Berlin government's pleas to keep
the opposition peaceful, during March and April an experienced
group of former Freikorps members known as 'Organisation Heinz',
led by a fanatical ultra-nationalist named Hauenstein, carried out acts
of violent sabotage in the Ruhr. These included the dynamiting of
railway tracks to stop coal being shipped to France and Belgium. The
saboteurs used explosives charges made out of lumps of coal hollowed

out, packed with dynamite and furnished with fuses. In this they were almost certainly acting with the agreement of the Defence Ministry – money and instructions came from Colonel von Stülpnagel of the General Staff in Berlin and were channelled through the Sixth District Military Command in Münster, just outside the occupied area – and also enjoyed connections with senior executives at Krupp and the Essen Chamber of Commerce.[23] Nor were they satisfied with acts of sabotage alone. The group also kept watch outside the French headquarters in Essen, the former offices of the Coal Syndicate (now exiled in Hamburg), and made notes on Germans who went in and out. Eight of such subjects were adjudged traitors and 'executed'.[24]

During the night of 7–8 April 1923, a young man by the name of Albert Leo Schlageter was arrested by the French at his hotel. Twenty-eight years old, a Catholic farmer's son from the Black Forest, he had served with distinction in the army during the war and later as a lieutenant with the Freikorps in the post-war campaigns in the Baltic and in Upper Silesia. There he had also served as a member of 'Organisation Heinz' under Hauenstein, helping to carry out anti-Polish acts which quite possibly also included the murders of so-called 'collaborators'. Convicted of espionage and sabotage, crimes of which he was undoubtedly guilty but which to most patriotic Germans were both understandable and praiseworthy, Schlageter was sentenced to death a month after his arrest and executed on a stretch of heathland outside Düsseldorf by a French firing squad on 26 May.

The newly created hero was praised by a wide spectrum of German opinion, from Communists (Comintern member Karl Radek tried to claim him as a brave but politically misguided anti-capitalist) to, more understandably, conservative nationalists. Schlageter was also, like his commander, Hauenstein, a member of an organisation by the name of the National Socialist German Workers' Party (NSDAP). In him the NSDAP had its first martyr, and in the twin curses of Ruhr occupation and hyperinflation its first great opportunity.

19

Führer

The young rabble-rouser who had flown up to Berlin from Munich at the time of the Kapp putsch in March 1920 was now, three years later, a powerful figure in Bavaria with political tentacles reaching out into other parts of Germany. His rise had been astonishing. The NSDAP (or, as it was known for short, affectionately or otherwise, the Nazi Party) had expanded rapidly since Adolf Hitler took charge.

In January 1919, the Spartacists had attempted a coup on the Bolshevik model in Berlin. A hundred insurgents died in fighting for the capital. Disturbances followed throughout Germany, culminating in the short-lived 'Soviet Republic' of Bavaria. A group of idealists and adventurers ruled chaotically and violently in Munich for some weeks before their regime was suppressed in May 1919 by a mix of army troops, Freikorps and armed local volunteers known as the *Einwohnerwehr* (a citizens' militia, literally translatable as 'inhabitants' defence').

The 'white terror' that ensued was, if anything, worse than the red. The battle for Munich is thought to have cost more than 600 lives, only 38 of them on the counter-revolutionary side and 335 of them civilians.[1] With ruthless, unapologetic reactionaries in power in Munich, Bavaria, which had always possessed a keen sense of its own identity even within the unified Reich, now began to drift away from democratic Berlin. During the following years, this would give Bavaria a 'semi-detached' status.

Among those soldiers who had remained with the colours after the war was an infantry corporal of decidedly anti-democratic and anti-Semitic views. He had heard of the November armistice in a military hospital on the Baltic coast while immobilised by the effects of a mustard gas attack on the Western Front. Little except his extreme opinions seemed, at that point, to distinguish Adolf Hitler from the great mass of defeated soldiery. However, unlike millions of others he had no home or family awaiting him when he recovered. Although he had chosen to serve with the German army, he was an Austrian citizen, son of a customs official. Both his parents were now dead, and Austria was, moreover, in any case in an even worse condition than Germany. Neither did he have a career to return to, having eked out a semi-vagrant existence before answering the call to the colours in August 1914. He had only fifteen already somewhat devalued marks in the bank. So, in mid-November 1918, Hitler travelled back to Munich, where he had lived before enlisting, to rejoin his army unit.

Hitler does not seem to have played a role in physically restoring 'order' during the spring of 1919. A great talker, evolving into a nationalist firebrand, he was earmarked for a different role. Hitler attended an army-sponsored political education course, 'graduating' at the end of August.

After the imposition of a conservative-nationalist Bavarian government, the Munich Reichswehr command undertook an operation to shore up grass-roots support for the new regime. Corporal Hitler was ordered to check out promising local organisations. This assignment brought him, on the evening of 12 September 1919, to a meeting of the tiny right-wing, anti-Semitic National Workers' Party (DAP) in a function room at the Sterneckerbräu brewer in the street named Tal, in central Munich.

Hitler remained quiet until an academic gentleman made some remarks that displeased him. This unleashed a crushing torrent of oratory from the newcomer, forcing the Herr Professor to withdraw, defeated. The DAP's founder and leader, a self-educated tool maker named Anton Drexler, remarked admiringly, after hearing Hitler's tirade: 'God, that one's got a mouth on him. We could use him.'

Hitler became an active member of the party. Drexler, by all accounts a shy and indecisive man, was quickly overshadowed by him. Demobilised in spring 1920, Hitler became the party's propaganda chief. His rabble-rousing eloquence was clearly responsible for the rapid improvement in the party's fortunes. A year later, he became Führer of the NSDAP (the words 'National Socialist' had by now been added), armed at his insistence with dictatorial powers that would endure to his and the party's end.

Hitler's challenge to what he referred to as the 'Jew-Republic' was totally uncompromising. Unlike other nationalist parties, the Nazis preached non-involvement in the democratic process and made open preparations for a coup that would install a dictatorship in Bavaria and throughout Germany. This quickly led to the party being made illegal in Prussia, which contained two-thirds of the Reich's population, and in several other of the larger northern states.

The far right (and far left) continued to prosper as reparations started to bite, social and economic unrest grew and the currency's value began its dizzying slide. When Hitler joined, the membership of the DAP amounted to less than a hundred. By the end of 1921 that of the relaunched NSDAP had reached 6,000. Despite being officially banned throughout most of the country, during 1922 the party passed the five-figure mark until, in January 1923, its membership exceeded 20,000 and it was able to stage its first national party congress.

Even Germans living abroad had taken a fancy to young Hitler. It was 1,000 precious dollars, donated by a German-American in February 1923 – with the mark at around 28,000 to the dollar – that allowed Hitler to turn the party organ, the *Völkischer Beobachter* (literally, 'Folkish Observer') from a twice-weekly into a daily paper.

Schlageter was one of the 'underground Nazis' in the north when he was arrested and executed by the French.[2] His allegiances were, it was true, a little more complicated than that. This passionate young nationalist has been said to have joined a number of right-wing organisations, and before his arrest to have strongly criticised Hitler for lack of enthusiasm in support of the struggle against the French in the Ruhr.[3]

Hitler's reaction to the Ruhr occupation had indeed differed radically from that of most German nationalist leaders. Addressing a large rally at the Zirkus Krone in Munich on 11 January 1923, the day of the invasion, he refused to join in the united chorus of opposition, the so-called new *Burgfrieden*, claiming instead that it was the 'Jews' and the 'November criminals' (i.e. the leaders of the 9 November revolution) who were really to blame. It was they, he proclaimed, who had brought Germany so low that the old enemy, France, could humiliate her in this way. Hitler even ordered that Nazi Party members taking part in resistance activities in the Ruhr should be expelled from the organisation.[4]

Hitler's line on the Ruhr was not necessarily popular among the rank and file, though he breathed more than sufficient fire on other matters to send the supporters he referred to as 'an army of revenge' home happy. *The Times*, reporting on the meeting, wrote:

Herr Hitler asked his supporters to return home quietly and to avoid any demonstrations in the streets. In spite of this advice, however, bands of 'storm troops' paraded the streets, singing the Fascist war songs, and a serious attack was made on the Hotel Vier Jahreszeiten, where members of the Allied Control Commission are quartered. The police were prepared, and in a hand-to-hand struggle the attackers were beaten off. Towards midnight, crowds assembled in front of the Rathaus, where, after singing the 'The Watch on the Rhine,' the meeting dispersed, but first of all a solemn oath was sworn 'to be revenged on France for the invasion of the Ruhr'.[5]

It was clear that Hitler saw the Ruhr struggle as a distraction from the main task of building up a Fascist-style formation ready for a 'march on Berlin', on the model of Mussolini's seizure of power in October 1922. In line with this, the Führer's party continued to grow,

and its actions to become more menacing. On 1 May, the Nazis, some
1,200-strong, fought pitched battles in Munich with leftists. By some
accounts, Hitler's followers were armed with light machine guns. 'The
number of men wearing Swastika badges to be seen during a walk
through the streets of Munich is amazing,' *The Times*, organ of the
British Establishment, noted three weeks later. The *Völkischer
Beobachter* was 'sold in most cafés and restaurants every evening by
youths in full fascist uniform. It seems to have a considerable
circulation.'[6]

By the early summer, the Nazis had nevertheless clearly decided to
hedge their bets on the Ruhr issue. Two weeks after Schlageter's execu-
tion, on 10 June, a memorial ceremony was staged on the Königsplatz
in Munich through the initiative of the NSDAP. Forty thousand
members of various nationalist organisations attended, and Hitler
gave 'an aggressive speech' according to *The Times*, advocating 'active
resistance' and declaring that 'a storm would soon break forth'.[7]

Schlageter was on his way towards a position atop the Pantheon
of Nazi heroes. There would be many more. Not that Hitler, though
he had clearly tacked to suit the political wind, fundamentally changed
his policy on the Ruhr. The French actions there were an outrage, but
then the French were . . . simply being French. The real guilty parties
in this affair remained, as ever, the democratic parties of Weimar and
their politicians. Not forgetting their alleged Jewish backers, who
were, of course, also behind the French plutocrats who had engineered
the Ruhr occupation.

The notion of the Jews being to blame for everything fitted even
better into the framework of the post-war inflation. Jews represented,
for the German far right, internationalism, mobile finance capital,
the rendering to mere unreliable (and stealable) paper of the honest,
tangible wealth that came from making and growing things. Therefore
the destruction of real value that the inflation had brought with it
was seen as an essentially Jewish phenomenon.

Interviewed in November 1922 by the American diplomat-cum-
spy Colonel Truman Smith at the NSDAP's still relatively modest

headquarters in Munich, Hitler thundered that 'the printing of paper money must be stopped. This is the worst crime of the present government.'[8] It was a theme the Führer hammered away at even more enthusiastically in the early part of 1923, referring constantly to the 'Jewification' (*Judaisierung*) of the economy. 'The government calmly goes on printing these scraps of paper because, if it stopped, that would be the end of the government,' Hitler declared:

> Because once the printing presses stopped – and that is prerequisite for the stabilisation of the mark – the swindle would at once be brought to light . . . Believe me, our misery will increase. The scoundrel will get by. But the decent, solid businessman who doesn't speculate will be utterly crushed; first the little fellow on the bottom, but in the end the big fellow on top too. But the scoundrel and the swindler will remain, top and bottom. The reason: because the state itself has become the biggest swindler and crook. A robbers' state! . . . If the horrified people notice that they can starve on billions, they must arrive at this conclusion: we shall no longer submit to a state which is based on the fraudulent idea of a majority and demand a dictatorship.[9]

Time would tell if these 'starving billionaires' could be mobilised to sweep the Nazis into power before the democratic government got the inflation under control. As yet, there was little sign of that.

20

'It Is Too Much'

In the late summer of 1922, the twenty-three-year-old soon-to-be-famous novelist Ernest Hemingway was still living in relative poverty among the American expatriate community in Paris. Because he wasn't making a living from fiction, Hemingway was forced to earn his crust as a correspondent for the *Toronto Star*. On the paper's behalf in mid-August he travelled with his wife to the eastern borders of France. They made the trip by the increasingly fashionable means of an aeroplane, half price for journalists.

He got an article for the *Star* out of that. He also got one out of a visit to the German border town of Kehl, just a walk across the bridge from the ancient city of Strasbourg, until recently German but now once more French. His task? To investigate for his paper's readers back in Canada the bizarre phenomenon that was German inflation:

> There were no marks to be had in Strasburg, the mounting exchange has cleaned the bankers out days ago, so we changed some French money in the railway station at Kehl. For 10 francs I received 670 marks. Ten francs amounted to about 90 cents in Canadian money. That 90 cents lasted Mrs Hemingway and me for a day of heavy spending and at the end of the day we had 120 marks left![1]

They bought some apples from a fruit stand, where 'a very nice looking, white-bearded old gentleman' watched them, then shyly asked how much their purchase had cost. When told, twelve marks, he smiled. 'It is too much.'

> He went up the street, walking very much as white-bearded old gentlemen of the old regime walk in all countries, but he had looked very longingly at the apples. I wish I had offered him some. Twelve marks, on that day, amounted to a little under 2 cents. The old man, whose savings were probably, as most of the non-profiteer classes are, invested in German pre-war and war bonds, could not afford the 12 mark expenditure. He is a type of the people whose income does not increase with the falling purchasing value of the mark . . .

Lunch at the town's best hotel cost the equivalent of fifteen Canadian cents. And the French invaded the place every afternoon to gorge themselves on the excellent German cream cakes. 'The proprietor and his helper were surly and didn't seem particularly happy when all the cakes were sold,' Hemingway commented. 'The mark was falling faster than they could bake.'

By January 1923, even the bare minimum of tolerance between French and Germans that Hemingway had witnessed in Kehl was a thing of the past. The Ruhr invasion had wrenched relations back to a level of bitterness as bad as, in some ways perhaps even worse than, the two nations had experienced between 1914 and 1918. And the mark, which in September been 800 to the Canadian dollar (valued at slightly less than the American) was now worth roughly one-fiftieth of that miserable sum. The old gentleman who had looked so longingly at the apples at the fruit stall in Kehl would have found a kilo of them, and by now much more besides, as far beyond any prospect of purchase as a kilo of Beluga caviar.

Hemingway could live decently in Paris because, for someone paid in dollars, it was cheap. Two and a half to three dollars a day, he said, would keep the visitor in comfort. 'At the present rate of exchange,' he wrote for the *Toronto Star* earlier in 1922, 'a Canadian with an income of one thousand dollars a year can live comfortably and enjoyably in Paris. If exchange were normal the same Canadian would starve to death. Exchange is a wonderful thing.'[2]

The cheapness of living in France – and the franc continued to decline, steadily though at a more modest rate than the mark, throughout this period – was a great lure to the 'lost generation', as were Paris's cultural riches, although escaping Prohibition was another one. Some other American expatriates went the whole hog and moved to Berlin, where in these years the economic power that their currency provided was, literally, fantastic. Matthew Josephson, the American writer and critic, moved to Germany in the early 1920s and ran a literary magazine from his apartment. A visitor from New York reported:

> For a salary of a hundred dollars a month in American currency, Josephson lived in a duplex apartment with two maids, riding lessons for his wife, dinners only in the most expensive restaurants, tips to the orchestra, pictures collected, charities to struggling German writers – it was an insane life for foreigners in Berlin . . .[3]

In November 1922, the London *Observer* reported on the 'very strong anti-foreigner movement which is growing among the population of Berlin'. It had begun, the report said, with resentment against the poor Jews who had arrived during and after the war from Galicia, the formerly Austrian part of Poland. Then, as it became clear that foreigners with 'hard currency' could live as they wanted, a wave of anger against them followed:

> There are whole neighbourhoods consisting of big blocks of buildings – 'mansions', containing from ten to fifty flats have been bought up by those who speculated in marks soon after the Armistice was signed, and who have viewed with ever-increasing dismay the depreciation of the paper they held. To buy anything that stood in brick or stone meant that some solid value might yet be obtained for the outlay. The German house owner was obliged to sell owing to the rental restrictions imposed by the government, which have reduced

landlords to beggary, and to sell quickly for the fear of 'socialisation'.

Half the professional classes owned some such house representing the family fortune, and the plight of the intellectuals is as inextricably bound up with their property as is their profession. The Spaniard, Dutchman, and, of late, the Czech, have bought whole streets, and refuse any more repairs than the law imposes on the unfortunate German landlord. One such house owner can incur the undying hatred of as many people as his property will hold. It is now being realised that when the mark is stabilised the actual ruin of the former possessing classes will be complete. A very great deal of the sudden proletarian 'hatred' [of foreigners] can be explained this way, and peculiar treatment in train, tram, and public places may be laid at its door.[4]

In January 1923, State Secretary Eduard Hamm of the Reich Chancellery wrote a report in which he called for strict immigration controls, not just on Jews coming in from the east (or not explicitly – he used the code word *Ostwanderer*, or 'east migrants'), but on all foreigners seeking to do business and to find (and especially buy) housing in Germany. He was an enthusiastic supporter of charging higher prices to foreigners in hotels, theatres, restaurants and other places of entertainment, and also of introducing special taxes and fees that would apply to foreigners, both on entry to the country and while living there. All this was clearly related to popular resentment, an all-too-understandable feeling that foreigners were exploiting Germany's time of weakness for their own pleasure and profit.

This idea was not new. Nor was the general, unofficial idea of squeezing the foreigner who, in the *Manchester Guardian*'s phrase, had a yen for exploiting the favourable exchange rate to enjoy 'that cheap holiday in Germany'.[5] The *Manchester Guardian* reported that the Prussian government was proposing a tax of four gold marks (no paper marks for the wise tax collector), then worth about five shillings sterling, for every day the foreigner spent in Germany.

The Times picked up the same story, running an even less forgiving headline: 'Fleecing the Foreigner. Germans Ready for the Tourist'. It continued: 'As the tourist season approaches in Germany the problem of exploiting the foreign visitor is eagerly discussed.' Noting the five shillings a day tourist tax, and frequent 'surcharging' techniques used against foreigners in shops, hotels and restaurants, it went on into a broader rant which perhaps owed something to the virulently anti-German views of its very hands-on proprietor, Lord Northcliffe, who had recently visited the Rhineland:

> In Germany the foreigner is swindled – it is well to call the thing by its real name – wherever the salesman sees a chance. There is not in the average intercourse in hotels and shops the vaguest glimmer of ordinary commercial morality. The surcharge can occasionally be easily defeated by employing a German acquaintance or even a German on commission; it can more easily be avoided by not completing the transaction when the price is manifestly excessive.
>
> One cannot altogether blame the German tradesman for wanting a share in the swindle when Governments set him the example. Bavaria, for instance, has announced that for admission to performances at any of the State theatres or opera houses British subjects are to be charged five times the prices charged to Germans; the inquisition is to be controlled by inspectors authorised to demand passports with all the attendant chicanery. The result is that the merry game of 'swindling the foreigner' has taken a firm hold in the Munich hotels and shops, on the assumption that what is right in the State cannot be wrong in the subject.[6]

Northcliffe would be dead three months later at the age of fifty-seven, suddenly taken ill at the French spa resort of Evian. There were contemporary rumours that the press magnate died from the effects of tertiary syphilis. The usually accepted explanation is that he succumbed to septic endocarditis, a bacterial infection of the heart valves, which might account for the fevered quality of his last weeks and days. Clearly unhinged at the time of his death, the never exactly temperate press magnate wrote numerous telegrams that, on medical advice, were never sent by his staff. One, to the editor of *The Times*, Wickham Steed, said: 'POISONED BY GERMANS BY ICE CREAM'.[7]

As the mark depreciated at an ever more precipitous rate during the early weeks of 1923, the currency situation became bewildering for the average foreigner. On a day when the mark was running at 22,800 to the dollar, or around 107,000 to the pound sterling,[8] a correspondent for the *Manchester Guardian* reported: 'There is a current story in Berlin of a woman who went shopping with a basket to carry her paper money. She put it down for a minute, and on looking round found that the basket had been stolen – but the paper money left behind!'

One puzzling thing for the inexperienced visitor was that officially set prices such as those of tram or railway tickets, or tickets for state-run theatres and opera houses, remained relatively low, since, unlike the manufacturer or the shopkeeper, the state or municipality employee was in no position to raise or lower public tariffs on some kind of daily indexed basis. The *Manchester Guardian*'s correspondent continued:

> For instance, in buying . . . a ticket for the opera, or in taking a tram ride, you remain among the hundreds [of marks]. That is why the high cost of living, while making it impossible for a German intellectual to carry on research or buy books, does not deprive the people of all intelligent enjoyment. 'I am hungry anyhow, so why not be a little hungrier and go to the opera!' said one young girl, philosophically, when asked for the reason of the packed opera-houses one found everywhere in Germany, even during the present crisis. 'The price of the ticket would not in any case buy a loaf of bread.'
>
> Such, however, is the anomaly of prices in German today, that directly you get away from theatres and trams and begin to buy

unrationed bread, on which most people subsist, or margarine, or Ersatz-Kaffee (coffee substitute), or, of course, sausage and meat and butter, you soon jump into the thousands.[9]

. . . So, it was possible to travel by train from Berlin to Dresden (200 kilometres) for the price of a pound of margarine. But how much to tip the porter at the station? And what about having the temerity to call a taxi when you get to your destination station? Then you find it costs more than the train trip for a three-minute ride.

Finally, when you have mastered, roughly, the incongruities of these different tariffs, there is always the chance that you may mix them all up again and offer somebody tens of thousands instead of thousands. Fortunately, in the case I have in mind, the kind waiter (a prisoner-of-war in England), who for three days concealed the fact that he spoke perfect English lest it should be thought a reflection on his client's German, gently returned them and saved her from paying 50,000 instead of 5,000 marks for an evening meal – an economy of about half-a-crown* at the rate of exchange then obtaining.

No German would, or for the sake of their survival could, make such a mistake. One of the many anomalies was, in fact, the situation of performers in Germany's theatres and opera houses. The relatively cheap theatre tickets celebrated by both foreigners and culture-hungry locals naturally left the managements of these places, unless they enjoyed state subsidies that were constantly adjusted to allow for inflation, hard pressed to pay their performers decently, or provide them with some job security, and still make a profit. Extra resentment was caused by the fact that the craftsmen and technicians, such as scene carpenters or electricians, being unionised, generally remained further ahead of the inflationary game than the 'creatives'. There was also resentment against the supposed vulgarisation of the theatres'

* 12½ pence.

programmes to suit the tastes of the inflation profiteers. By this, critics meant plays by Frank Wedekind (*Pandora's Box* – famous in the English-speaking world as the main component of the drama *Lulu*) and Arthur Schnitzler (*Der Reige*, known outside Germany as *La Ronde*). Such dramas were alleged to suit the new, nouveau riche theatre-goers who, due to the impoverishment of the educated classes, now made up the audiences and even, in some cases, controlled the boards of the commercial theatres. All this led at the end of November 1922 to an actors' strike in Berlin's privately owned theatres.[10]

The 'star' actors were better off than the mass, especially as they could also command high (and often, by negotiation, inflation-adjusted) salaries in the booming German film industry. All the same, outside the immediate realm of the day-to-day theatre, there was limited public sympathy for the strike. And, as things turned out, though begun in great passion, it was fairly short-lived, ending in some disarray just before Christmas.

Siegfried Jacobsohn, who had started out as a drama critic and had originally called his magazine *Die Schaubühne* ('The Stage') before broadening its content to include politics, economics and world affairs and changing its name to *Die Weltbühne* ('The World Stage'), criticised the actors for failing to see that their fate was similar to that of many thousands of other intellectual workers. He presented his argument playfully as an imaginary conversation between an actor, a theatre director and a drama critic, with the critic pointing out coolly:

What will become of the countless journalists, painters, lecturers, doctors? If 682 of the 2300 lawyers in Berlin do not have an income of more than 18,000 marks, then they have the choice of starving or changing their hopeless professions, and when they are forced to, they make their choice one by one. They, and whatever no longer has a function, cannot expect to be kept going by a pathetically impoverished people for their own sake, for the sake of their beautiful eyes, beautiful voices, beautiful legs.[11]

Jacobsohn also pointed out that, with less than a third of Berlin's theatres still open, because of the strike, the city was witnessing ten full theatres instead of thirty-five half-full ones as hitherto. Elementary, and pretty ominous, economics for actors, directors and theatre owners alike.

Writers, composers and painters were also presented with serious problems by the inflation. Even before the inflation, in fact before the war, the argument between creative producers of various descriptions and the publishers or purchasers of their works had been a passionate one, in Germany as elsewhere, as it naturally still is. Authors producing literary and scholarly works had always found themselves at a disadvantage when pitted against the economic power of the publisher, and without the popular writer's ability to use his or her high sales as a bargaining chip.

Even at a relatively early stage in the currency's decay, this situation got appreciably worse. Publishers, themselves struggling to adjust to a time of uncertain costs and even more uncertain profits, and with the educated class that represented a large chunk of their market in desperate financial straits, began driving a very hard bargain and demanding subsidies for scholarly books, with the possible exception of textbooks and reference works.[12] When in 1921 writers' and artists' organisations managed to get some political support for the idea of a 5 or 10 per cent tax on books, sheet music and concert performances – to be used to support distressed artists, composers and writers – the publishers struck back without mercy:

> The entire nation is in distress. We find ourselves in a 'shrinking economic basis for a highly cultured people.' No one has enough any more. Certainly one cannot disregard the fact that the material compensation for intellectual work has remained behind that of manual labour during and after the Revolution . . . But whoever places himself and his fate upon so uncertain a foundation cannot complain if the ground gives way when his creative powers fail or because he lives in a time of crisis.[13]

A bitter exchange followed over the next two years in the pages of *Die Weltbühne*. Low fees apart, with the depreciation of the mark accelerating, what had appeared to be a reasonable schedule of payments at time of contract might, months or even years later when the work was delivered, be more or less worthless. Publishers would insist on a 'mark-for-mark' policy (which was, in fact, official Reichsbank policy), making no allowance for changes in the purchasing power of the sum agreed and therefore allowing no inflationary indexing of payments. A writer might accept an advance payment involving a royalty based on a percentage fixed cover price for a print run of his/her book, only to find, every time he or she went past a bookshop where the work was displayed, the price ticket inexorably rising. Any author with the temerity to demand recompense for increasing bookshop prices did not get far. All the same, the publisher Kurt Wolff admitted to the author Herbert Eulenberg, with whom he and other publishers were involved in this fierce, continuing battle in the columns of *Die Weltbühne*:

> In the end the author in general stands at the coffin of the paper mark in a more weakened state than an economic enterprise such as a publishing house, for the publisher has had the possibility of using certain business techniques to create equivalents which, if they did not fully compensate for the mark depreciation, at least prevented the complete ruin of his operation. I am thinking of the inflation profits made through the possibility of being sometimes able to pay with bills of acceptance for new stocks of paper and printing and binding bills and then paying off the commercial bills of acceptance with currency that was worth less than on the day the bills were issued. Without such crutches the German publishing business would have shut down long ago.[14]

In effect, the publisher was the mini-Stinnes, producing print and paper rather than coal and steel, and able to pay off their bills and loans with devalued marks.

Elsewhere, the flight into 'material assets' continued.

* * *

The importation of food to Germany had always placed a burden on the country's balance of payments. This was so even before the war, and the surrender of around 15 per cent of German agricultural land to Poland and France in 1919 had made the situation worse.[15] Moreover, due to territorial losses in both east and west, a great many raw materials needed for German industry (especially coal and zinc from Upper Silesia, now Polish, and iron ore from Lorraine, now returned to France) had to be imported. The German government could therefore rightly complain in the postwar period that gold and foreign currency required for the importing of foodstuffs was either being diverted to other imports that before the war had been sourced within German territory, or was being demanded by the Allies as reparations, leaving the German people to go hungry.

The time of relative stabilisation in 1920–21, combined with the industrial recovery that followed the end of the blockade, had enabled Germany to import more food. The 'Goldilocks' policy of the government – the mark weak enough to subsidise exports, but strong enough to enable vital imports – had led to an improvement in the availability of food and, as a consequence, in the general level of public health (though not to the levels enjoyed before 1914).

The renewed depreciation of the mark after June 1921, accelerating through 1922 to hyperinflation, once more led to enormous problems with the importation of food. Foreign currency had to be released by the Reichsbank, which in turn, during the weeks following the Ruhr occupation, was forced to devote large proportions of its valuta reserves to supporting the mark as best it could. Shipments of food from abroad could get stuck in consignment at their German ports of arrival, waiting for the necessary foreign exchange to make its way through the system.[16]

German farmers were in no better position to make up this shortfall than they had been during the latter part of the war. Even allowing for the areas lost to Poland, the productivity of German agriculture had still not recovered to anything like the level reached before the war. Shortages of fertilisers, both natural and artificial, many of which had to be imported, remained serious. Nitrates had been systematically diverted from use as fertilisers to their other function, in explosives production, during the war. The neglected land had still not recovered. In any case, the authorities were having serious problems making the nation's farmers supply food to the population – particularly the urban population – at reasonable prices in exchange for paper money. In 1922–3, the agricultural interest was able, if it was not too finicky – which it mostly wasn't – to name its price when it came to selling either to individuals or to the wholesale merchants, honest or otherwise, who flocked from the urban areas to knock on its collective door seeking to buy up its produce.

A Bavarian official of the nationwide 'Price Examination Agency', whose job was to investigate, and if necessary prosecute, cases of blatant profiteering, wrote shortly before the hyperinflation took hold:

The concern about one's daily bread is increasing not only among the workers, employees and civil servants, but also among a large number of those who are self-employed, not to speak of the military and social pensioners and the small *rentiers*. In the cities and in the better-off agricultural districts, the antagonisms are particularly pronounced. On the one side are the various wholesale and other merchants and the better-off farmers, on the other side there are the consumers who are struggling with necessity. It is obvious that under such circumstances the political antagonisms should also become more severe. The discontent of the labouring people is directed chiefly against the Jews and the peasants, as one can hear daily in the conversations which are conducted in the railway trains. The National Socialists appear to find increasing membership. If they do not always show the necessary self-restraint, on the other hand they form a not to be underestimated check for the left radicals for whom the creation of a dictatorship of the proletariat appears as the ideal.[17]

Clearly, Berlin was (and, for that matter, is) not Germany. The exotic tales of decadence and high living on the one hand, tuberculoid poverty on the other, that are told about life in the capital, do not reflect life elsewhere in Germany at the height of the inflation. In rural areas, there was some always food of some sort, either to be bought, especially if one had 'contacts', to be bartered, or to be grown.

In the early 1920s, farmers or peasants of various sorts still made up a considerable proportion of the nation. More than 2 million individuals (not counting their families) earned a living exclusively from farming, a figure not much reduced over the past fifteen or twenty years.[18] Added to that, there were more than 3 million *Parzellisten*, owners of small plots of less than two hectares (approximately five acres). To make ends meet, many of these also worked in industry, or mines, or in a variety of other rural jobs. A third of all economically active Germans, making about thirteen million at this time, were dependent on the land in some way for their existence. The country dweller, even if he or she were not a proper farmer, usually had a garden, where vegetables could be grown, or a pig or some chickens kept. Even the least well-landed *Parzellist* might have to do without everyday luxuries, but he or she would not starve, no matter what happened to the paper mark or the mainstream economy.

August Heinrich von der Ohe, an assistant school headmaster and choirmaster in his fifties, was one of those Germans fortunate enough to live in a rural area, near Lüneburg on the north German plain. With some land to grow vegetables and keep animals, as well as possibly running a tavern or inn on the side, perhaps staffed by members of his family,* Herr von der Ohe seems to have struggled at times, but got by and, reading between the lines, even experienced a modest prosperity, certainly compared with millions of other Germans. He kept a diary which contained mostly lists of prices of food, clothing, livestock – we know that he had been born the son of a farmer, and as the inflation crisis went on, clearly depended more and more

* Herr von der Ohe refers to the *Wirtschaft* which provides extra income. This can mean a tavern or inn, or more generally just a 'business'.

on what he could grow or rear. He also included occasional comments
on his income from teaching duties. His salary was increased from
time to time, but for the most part not nearly enough to cope with
the rise in prices:

1 November 1921:
(Conversation with a music teacher) He was of the opinion that if we
now went bankrupt, we could start from the beginning again. But if
that were to be so, one would not know what one ought to do. If he
had some money, he would buy pictures or some such. I advised him
to buy stocks. He was of the opinion that this was also insecure.

10 November 1921:
At the mill no more coarse rye to be had. Only exchangeable for
unprocessed rye, but the farmers are not selling any unprocessed rye.
Maize costs 300 marks, potatoes cost 105, the dollar costs 300 marks.

5/6 December 1921:
A pound of butter costs 44 marks. A litre of milk in Lüneburg 5
marks, here 3 marks, a hundredweight of potatoes 100 marks, a
hundredweight of rye 300 marks; buckwheat, because not well grown,
500 marks; coarse maize at 160 marks, one egg 4 marks. We have got
a new salary law. According to this I receive a basic salary of 2600
marks; local and inflation supplement 8400 marks, child supplement
5600 marks, and nevertheless one cannot get by on this. If we did
not have our tavern, things would go badly for us.[19]

There was a massive increase during the war and into the period of
inflation in the number of Germans owning or renting small garden
plots, including those in, and on the edge of, cities. The figure for
those belonging to registered gardening clubs almost tripled between
1913 and 1919 from 37,000 to 91,000, and the actual number of
amateur gardeners could be expected to have reached several times
this figure. A national organisation for small gardeners was founded

in 1921 and rapidly reached a total membership of 400,000.[20] In Vienna, where inflation was raging in similar conditions, the number of eggs for sale from large-scale commercial production in 1918 was 13.7 million against 2 million from hens kept on small plots or allotments. By 1922 the figures were drastically changed: only 9.5 million came from commercial production while quantities originating from privately kept hens had increased almost tenfold to 19.2 million.[21] Despite the growth in the popularity of big-city allotments, for many town dwellers at this point the crucial factor was whether they had family in the country. Again and again, in personal accounts, the story of a schoolteacher's family in Silesia stands for the rest:

> Of course, a family with four children at this time could hardly live from the purchasing power of the 1920s. Here the farming background of both my father and my mother came to our aid. Whether it was from my mother's family in Himmelwitz, seven kilometres distant, or from Hohndorf, fifty kilometres away, as in my father's case, we received from those farms enough bread, smoked meat, ham, eggs and butter so that the teacher's children did not need to go hungry.[22]

For many in the early 1920s, faced with food shortages and employment difficulties in the towns and cities, a solution lay in choosing to contribute to a short-lived but in its way spectacular reversal of what had been a long-established and seemingly inevitable demographic trend: the steady urbanisation of the Reich. During the early post-war years, including the time of the hyperinflation, 2 million Germans emigrated from the urban areas back to the countryside.[23]

The city dweller who stayed put, who had no rural relations, who worked in a factory or mine or office or shop and lived in an apartment block with no garden, was faced with severe shortages or, as the inflation soared out of control, with unaffordable black market prices. In February, a little less than a month after the Ruhr invasion had sparked another dramatic fall in the mark, the London *Sunday Times* reported from Berlin:

. . . the general effect of the slump has been the rapid increase in the price of food. Meat, for instance, has gone up about 250 per cent in the last fortnight, and there have been food riots in several of the poorer districts in Berlin. The public takes it out on the retail dealer, for whom there also exists a special profiteers' court. But it is now generally admitted that the farmer is mainly responsible. He snaps his fingers at the Government orders, and quotes his prices only in the equivalent of dollars. He knows full well that any interference with him would bring the Agrarian party buzzing about the ears of Dr Cuno's administration.[24]

The answer to the shortages for many was expressed in the German verb *hamstern*, to forage. The needy townie would head out into the nearby countryside and try to buy, beg or barter food from the local farmers. Many a farmstead would suddenly acquire a store of someone else's heirlooms, many a farmer's wife or daughter would sport fine jewellery or clothing of recent provenance.

Not all of the urban population were prepared to go to the countryside to do deals with farmers for food. Some sought other, more drastic solutions to their plight. In Saxony, Germany's oldest, now somewhat rundown, industrial area, and the other major central German state, Thuringia, the left remained strong. In April 1923, following elections, the Social Democratic Party had taken power in Saxony with the support of the Communist Party, which had made strong gains at the local polls following its absorption of the left-wing members of the now defunct Independent Social Democratic Party. Later in the year, the local Social Democrat Premier in Thuringia would also go into a formal coalition with the Communist Party. This meant social as well as political polarisation.

Neither the middle classes in either of these states, nor the farming population, were prepared to cooperate with these left-wing governments. In response, socialist and Communist worker groups fanned out into the countryside, not to offer heirlooms for turnips, but to take what they felt the farmers were withholding from the working class.

Cases of workers leaving the towns and plundering farmers' fields for food were common, here as elsewhere in Germany during this time. In Saxony it was more organised, in fact semi-official. For instance, 500 workers from a porcelain factory at Radeberg, near Dresden, marched out to a nearby agricultural village, where they discovered and confiscated large quantities of dairy products. Admittedly, the farmers were issued with receipts for the produce, in exchange for a promise to supply the townspeople in future, but this was quasi-official expropriation on the Soviet model by any other name. Butchers arrived at the village a few days later, to slaughter livestock to feed the town.[25]

Even in the countryside, the battle for existence was taking on ugly forms. The war of all against all that became the most recognisable human symptom of the hyperinflation had begun.

Having decided to bet all the chips it held on 'passive resistance' in the Ruhr, Chancellor Cuno's government now decided to exploit the rare, and temporary, mood of unity in the Reich to try to regain some kind of stability in the economy and in the political life of the country. In February and March there was, despite everything, a short breathing space, where if things did not get better, they at least did not get much worse.

The question was whether this so-called 'government of experts' was capable of the task that had defeated every previous Weimar government. The omens were not good.

21

The Starving Billionaires

Faced with the inevitability of an enormous increase in his government's already huge budget deficit due to support measures for the 'passive resistance', the man who, before he became Chancellor, had been the country's most popular politician, put together a multi-faceted financial and diplomatic package. This, Cuno and his other 'technical experts' hoped, would enable Germany to weather the crisis, get the French out of the Ruhr, and come through on the other side with some kind of game-changing revision of the reparations terms.

In the excitement of the post-Ruhr invasion period, on 23 February 1923 the Reichstag, including the Social Democrats, passed an 'emergency law'. This allowed the Cuno government to introduce, without recourse to legislation, changes in welfare, financial, economic and judicial regulations that would normally require the Reichstag's approval.

Within the framework of these new government powers, stricter penalties for profiteering, unjustified raising of prices, the black market and transgressions against import and export restrictions were immediately announced. Finally, the government hoped, this would enable them to get a grip on prices, which were blamed precisely on profiteering by retailers.

There were two other prongs to the government's anti-inflation attack. The government also began to publicise an internal dollar (that is, gold-backed) loan that would pay 120 per cent in 1926 (in gold, not paper marks), and which would thereby raise, it was proposed, $200 million to bolster the financial exertions needed to support passive resistance in the Ruhr. The aim was to soak up some of the massive quantities of gold and foreign exchange held by German corporations and individuals. The appeal was to patriotism, as it had been in 1914. And, secondly, the Reichsbank was prevailed upon (initially unwillingly, it must be said), to use its already existing, and surprisingly well-stocked, gold and foreign exchange reserves to support the mark, which had tumbled in value to around 40,000 to the dollar at the end of January.[1]

The government's fear was that if the mark fell any further, the essential imports of food and coal from abroad necessary to survive the ever-tightening French stranglehold on the Ruhr would become unaffordable. Astonishingly, though the jury remained out on the success of the internal dollar loan (to which Stinnes, ominously, refused to contribute a single dollar, guilder, pound or Swiss franc), the mark did come down in February 1923, and as a result of system-atic and complex selling action by the bank, stayed down. For a while, British coal remained affordable and could replace the German coal impounded by the French in the Ruhr. Again, for a while.

Astonishingly, with the mark hovering at around 21,000 to the dollar, the new 'Goldilocks level', there were still those heavy indus-trialists who felt that it was too high for their export purposes. They pressured Havenstein of the Reichsbank to nudge the rate down to between 23,000 and 25,000.

Inflation had become an addiction. And, like all addictions, the stronger its hold, the more damage it inflicts on the body of the addict. Until, sooner or later, it reaches the point where it is a question of detox or die.

The domestic wholesale prices that dictated what ordinary people paid for the necessities of life had risen with the fall in the mark's value to 40,000 to the dollar in the weeks immediately following the occupation of the Ruhr. However, when the Reichsbank's support effort managed to all but halve that rate later in the month, there was no corresponding fall. True, prices by and large stabilised, but the consumer got almost no relief. Clearly producers, manufacturers and retailers did not sufficiently trust the turnaround on the exchanges to actually reduce their prices to ordinary customers as a result of the improvement in the currency.[2] If that was so, then they were right. The holding of the mark in the low 20,000s lasted longer than many observers expected – eleven weeks – but, finally, in the third week of April 1923, the dam broke.

There were any number of reasons. The dollar loan was drastically undersubscribed, proving that not enough of the real holders of wealth in Germany were prepared to underwrite the Ruhr passive resistance. It also became clear that the French were not going to give up. The mines were starting to produce again – not at the pre-occupation levels, but enough to show that the passive resistance was not having the hoped-for effect. Above all, Cuno's government faced the crippling expense of the Ruhr passive resistance. Berlin had promised compensation for the Ruhr industrialists who continued the policy of non-cooperation, who shut down their mills and blast furnaces, plus support for workers rendered unemployed by the non-cooperation policy. Moreover, there were the wages due to the tens of thousands of railway officials and civil servants who had been expelled by the French and decanted into Germany proper, where they were being paid by their employer, the government, to do nothing.

Germany was now producing and exporting drastically less than before the occupation. All the costs of passive resistance could be covered only by the printing of German currency on a massive scale. Apart from the main State Printing Office in Berlin, 130 other print works were involved in satisfying the near-infinite demand for paper currency. The situation was such that even the most energetic activities of the Reichsbank's currency exchange department could not keep the mark to dollar rate within bounds. By April, it was calculated that if the run on the mark continued, exacerbated by demands for foreign exchange from German businesses, the bank would be able to hold out for only another ten days before its reserves were exhausted.

In short, the support for the mark might have worked over a longer period, but only if Cuno had managed to pull off a diplomatic coup, or if the French had failed to make their occupation work. Neither of these had occurred. Neither the British nor the Americans, though they expressed disapproval of the Ruhr occupation, were prepared to put real pressure on the French to desist. And whatever the faults of the notoriously fractious French polity, in the matter of the Ruhr occupation, for the moment, it stood firm almost to a man. If the point of Cuno's administration had been some kind of ordering of the country's finances, his 'business' chancellorship might have made sense. In fact, the point was facing down the French, for which a tough and cunning diplomat was required.[3]

On 18 April, the mark, which had stood at 21,100 to the dollar four days earlier, had fallen in value to 25,000. It hit 29,900 a week later, in another week 34,275, next 42,300, and by the end of May 54,300. A month later, a greenback got its lucky owner 114,250 German marks. These were fantastic seeming figures, but in July they got even worse. The world had given up on the German currency. *The Times* wrote on 20 July that 'the Berlin Foreign Exchange Market has become a farce',[4] while the *Manchester Guardian*'s financial editor commented on 24 July, 'it seems almost idle to go on chronicling the complete disintegration of Germany's financial system'.[5] The paper's correspondent in Berlin went even further a few days later. 'The mark,' he reported, 'is becoming impracticable as a medium of exchange.'[6]

At the end of that month, the mark was exchangeable against the dollar for a seven-figure sum: 1,100,000. A week later, on 7 August, the rate was 3,300,000. In the course of sixteen weeks, the value of the mark had deteriorated to 1/130 of its already miserable equivalence in April, and around 1/700,000 of its long-forgotten pre-war value.

The German currency was now not just catastrophically diminished, but near enough worthless.

While the politicians, bankers and business leaders feared for the country and agonised over how to keep the economy halfway viable in the face of the Ruhr catastrophe, for ordinary Germans life in the summer of 1923 turned into a desperate game of pass-the-parcel. The problem was that you had to have a parcel to pass. If all you had was paper money, you were doomed. The social consequences of the inflation that had until now been only partly visible, or visible only to those with a critical eye, became impossible to ignore.

People with average incomes, and no access to agricultural produce or foreign exchange, were forced to hunt and queue for food – both because their incomes more often than not did not stretch to buying what they wanted on a particular day but also because there was, as the hyperinflation tightened its grip, a genuine shortage of food. With foreign exchange for importing food running short, and German farmers ever less willing to part with their produce for increasingly worthless paper money, the promise was of starvation amidst plenty.

In the diary of August Heinrich von der Ohe, the schoolteacher-cum-farmer on the north German plain, the entries between October 1922 and February 1923 are overwhelmingly about buying and selling. The route to survival in this crisis was clearly not through an academic salary:

30 October 1922:
Prices have undergone a huge increase. Rye 14,000 marks, coarse barley 9000 marks, a hundredweight of straw 2000 marks. Bought a farm cart from Schied for 125,000 marks. You have to pay 9000 marks for a ham.

2 December 1922:
In Celle I bought a pair of boots for 7980 marks. Straw costs 500 marks a hundredweight.

14 December 1922:
I bought a steer for 215,000 marks. The year and our money is at an end.

Today begins the year 1923:
What else will this year bring to us all?

6 January 1923:
Bought a second cow from Imker Rabe [probably a farmer neighbour] for 400,000 marks.

8 January 1923:
Salary from 1 January with supplement for December amounts to 310,000 marks.

18 January 1923:
The dollar has risen to 25,000 marks.

26 January 1923:
Sold a pig weighing 226 pounds, at 1300 marks per pound; next week it will be 1500.

3 February 1923:
The dollar stood at almost 50,000 marks. Rye costs 60,000 marks per hundredweight; pork 3000 marks per pound. I want to sell our cow. 1¼ million has been offered, but I want 1½. Sold our old cart for 200,000 marks. Sold a used plough for 35,000 marks. A pound of unrationed bread cost 900 marks. I was in money difficulties on many occasions, but successfully found my way out of them.

Recently bought: 1 cart for 125,000 marks, a steer for 215,000 marks, a cow for 400,000 marks, 3 piglets for 90,000 marks. For this I borrowed 425,000 marks; from my salary came a further 440,000 marks.[7]

For many Germans, especially after the French occupation of the Ruhr, conditions had returned to something like those they had experienced during the Allied blockade between 1914 and 1919 and had fervently hoped never to experience again. In what was rapidly becoming a barter economy, the agile and the cunning, not to mention dishonest, citizen was top of the Darwinian heap.

Earlier in the year, a Barcelona newspaper, *La Veu de Catalunya*, sent a journalist to report on the situation in Berlin. Even as the Reichsbank struggled to keep the mark from total collapse, Eugeni Xammar wondered at the chaotic conditions that pertained in the third largest city in the Western world.

The price of tram rides and beef, theatre tickets and school, news-papers and haircuts, sugar and bacon, is going up every week. As a result, no one knows how long their money will last, and people are living in constant fear, thinking of nothing but eating and drink-ing, buying and selling. There is only one topic on everyone's lips in Berlin: the dollar, the mark, and prices . . . Have you seen this? For heaven's sake, stop! I've just bought a six-week supply of sausages, ham and cheese.[8]

Almost everyone in a position to do so demanded to be paid on moveable values, or in food. Doctors and dentists had for some time since demanded cash rather than cheques or payment on account, and now in rural areas demanded payment in food from farmers who came to them for treatment.[9]

Painters and other artists, like writers, also suffered from large depreciations in sums contracted, the gap between invoice and payment alone involving a ruinous loss for the artist, particularly after the autumn of 1922. Even before that, in May 1922, there had been a case where a sculptor offered a piece for 20,000 marks and found himself, in September of that same year, when it went on the market, required to keep to the price, so taking a 100,000 mark loss on the cost of materials alone. In the mean time, the dealer or gallery might well have set a new, inflation-adjusted selling price, which they received from the buyer and from which they alone benefited.[10] This was the brutal equation of the inflation.

Even quite well known artists of the avant-garde, such as George

Grosz, young master of the grotesque, saw their fortunes take a downturn when the mark began to suffer its definitive breakdown. A Communist during the early years after the German revolution (though he left the party in late 1922 after witnessing the Soviet regime's oppressive authoritarianism during an extended trip to Russia, summarising its brand of 'Superman politics' as 'not for the likes of me'[11]) and an inveterate traducer of the old elite, Grosz was nonetheless supported by progressive establishment figures such as Harry Kessler. The resolutely liberal, trend-aware Count regularly visited Grosz's studio in Berlin-Wilmersdorf, and put together a small collection of his work, clearly accepting Grosz's own self-estimate as 'the German Hogarth'.[12]

All the same, Grosz and his friends seem to have found themselves in deep trouble as the inflation began to soar out of control. In his autobiography he describes their being condemned to a diet involving the likes of turnip coffee and muscle pudding. A brief upturn came about only when Grosz was befriended by a chef at a Berlin restaurant. The man had exploited his connections to build up a hoard of fine foods, which gave him a lucrative sideline as a black marketeer. One night, after midnight and more than one double Kirsch, they left the restaurant and got into a taxi, hailed by a uniformed doorman in exchange for a million-mark tip.

Grosz recalled the scene after the cab dropped them at a 'faceless house in Berlin's new west'. On the top floor, behind steel-reinforced and triple-bolted doors, was a wonderland:

We picked our way through the Berlin room. On either side there were crates, pots of jam, huge jars of tomatoes, gherkins and various delicacies, blue tins of Russian caviar, all piled as high as the ceiling – that is, as much as one could see of the ceiling, because from it dangled all kinds of wurst . . . spiced Italian salamis, tongue bolognas . . . countless slabs of bacon, lean and fat . . .

Then there was every type of ham, from smooth rolled *Lachsschinken* [smoked salmon] to oversized smoked Westphalian. A sight for sore eyes and grumbling bellies, and I had to pinch my nose, to see if I was dreaming.[13]

'I simply don't know where to put it all,' the chef confessed cheerfully. 'Money isn't worth a damn these days, so even the passage is bursting with the stuff . . .' He sat the incredulous Grosz down with a ham sandwich and a tumbler of gin – fabulous luxuries – and toasted the inflation: 'Cheers, my dear fellow. Long live this fool's paradise!'

Unlike George Grosz, most Germans, in Berlin or elsewhere, had no access to black-marketeer arts groupies. Chroniclers since have written gloatingly, and so far as it goes accurately, of the availability of bought flesh to those who possessed foreign exchange or other forms of 'material assets' in the Germany of the hyperinflation. The collapse of money and the collapse of morals become identical. At times, such description has come close to turning the history of hope, despair and humiliation that was the early Weimar Republic into a form of pornography. In the case of Berlin, in particular, accounts relentlessly reference the colourful world of the (1960s) musical *Cabaret* in their view of a world where all manner of nudity was constantly on display, and where both the traditional prostitute class (which had long been an infamous feature of the city) and the newly dispossessed daughters (and sons) of the educated middle class, who had now also taken to the sex trade, were endlessly available at a price – preferably in cigarettes, precious metals or hard currency rather than paper marks.

Berlin in the 1920s was not only, or mainly, a nest of vice but also an earnest, workaday town. What truth was contained in the popular image had more to do with desperation than a desire to titillate. The Russian writer Ilya Ehrenburg, who lived in Berlin between 1921 and 1923, described one particular night out in inflationary Berlin in the company of friends from Berlin's foreign colony. It started at the Café Josty on the Potsdamer Platz and got wilder as the night went on:

We . . . ended up in a thoroughly respectable bourgeois apartment. The walls were hung with portraits of the male family members in officers' uniforms, and there was a picture of a sunset. We were handed champagne, that is: Lemonade with a little alcohol in it. Then the two daughters of the house entered, in an unclothed state, and began to dance. The mother looked hopefully at the foreign guests: Perhaps her daughters would please them and would pay well, in dollars, of course. 'And this is what we call life,' the mother sighed. 'Actually it's purely and simply the end of the world.'[14]

A young journalist reporting the proceedings of the Reichstag later recalled walking home at night to the insalubrious area near the Alexanderplatz where he had taken lodgings:

My nightly walks home from the Reichstag to my working-class district were bad, the half-dark streets lined with women, many of whom were certainly offering themselves only out of sheer necessity, and with red-lit bars for foreigners with hard currency.[15]

In fact, the wave of nudity and free expression in the sexual arena that followed the abolition of the old Prussian and Imperial censorship laws after 1918 was already somewhat on the ebb by 1923. The most notorious and profitable of the nude and near-nude shows, starring 'Celly de Rheidt' (born Cäcily Funk, wife of a demobilised first lieutenant, Alfred Seweloh, who functioned as the act's manager and *conferencier*), was brought to court early in 1922. Despite protesting the 'artistic' nature of the undertaking (by this time expanded to include profitable sidelines in postcards and short films), Seweloh was fined and 'Celly de Rheidt' and her fellow performers forced to 'cover up'. Needless to say, thereafter the 'ballet's' public popularity underwent a steep, not to say terminal, decline.[16]

In 1923, after the French occupation of the Ruhr, the Prussian authorities used the situation as a pretext to take on emergency powers and as a consequence to ban any public entertainments, in Berlin and elsewhere in the state, that gave rise to 'concern' (*Bedenken*). Just as dancing and similar amusements had been forbidden during the world war, so now cabarets and shows were severely restricted. One of the reasons why the authorities took this step, moral considerations apart, may have been that the nude cabarets were popular among foreign, and especially American, tourists. It was felt that such displays of extravagance and licence would encourage, or for some observers confirm, the belief that Germany's public declarations of poverty (and therefore inability to pay reparations) concealed a world of private luxury.[17]

What was certainly true, by 1923, was that the whole of Germany had become a marketplace. In this world, for those who had neither the resources nor the nerve nor the skills to participate successfully in the great sell-off, there seemed no place any more. In Berlin and other major cities, members of the newly impoverished middle classes brought heirlooms and precious belongings to impromptu salerooms, where whoever had the money could bid for them. The sell-offs, often sponsored by middle-class housewives' associations, tended to be held in rooms provided by banks. The organisers made efforts to fix as fair a price as possible under the circumstances, but these were desperate times.

A walk through the small salesroom with its tables and glass cases is heart-rending. There lie spread out so many lovely things so pleasing to the eye . . . wonderful Turkish and embroidered silk shawls, finely carved figurines, old porcelain, clocks, inlaid pearl, embroidered linens, silver utensils – everything in short that once decorated a house is assembled here . . . There is some old piece, a picture, a porcelain cast, which appears to the loving but unskilled eye of the owner as a true rarity and who, if she must part with it, wants to receive as much as possible. One now has to tell her that it has neither material nor artistic value, and the sick, embittered souls are always inclined to take this as a personal affront and bad will . . . A look out the window – there slides by the restless life of the metropolis, the fine silk stockings and expensive furs, there sit autos with the fat figures of *Schieber* [profiteers] inside, and here inside, in the quiet room, an impoverished Germany quietly and painfully weeps in its silent misery.[18]

What perhaps contributed to the alleged decline of traditional morality, among young women especially, was the fact that in Germany after the First World War, despite the deaths of around 2 million males of military age, among the higher middle class especially, the old dowry system still helped to dictate which young woman could marry which young man. So, if the money were not forthcoming, the young woman stayed unmarried. A woman who had been young at the time recalled many years later:

> The inflation wiped out the savings of the entire middle class, but those are just words. You have to realise what that meant. There was not a single girl in the entire German middle class who could get married without her father paying a dowry. Even the maids – they never spent a penny of their wages. They saved and saved so that they could get married. When the money became worthless, it destroyed the whole system for getting married, and so it destroyed the whole idea of remaining chaste until marriage.
>
> The rich had never lived up to their own standards, of course, and the poor had different standards anyway, but the middle class, by and large, obeyed the rules. Not every girl was a virgin when she was married, but it was generally accepted that one should be. But what happened from the inflation was that the girls learned that virginity didn't matter any more. The women were liberated.[19]

Erich Maria Remarque (born Erich Paul Remark in the Westphalian town of Osnabrück), became an international literary celebrity with his war novel, *All Quiet on the Western Front*. In a later piece of fiction, *The Black Obelisk*, he writes of a young woman, engaged to her sweetheart during the inflation period, whose father invests the money intended for her dowry unwisely and loses it all. When the dowry is not forthcoming, the fiancé breaks off the engagement.

She is heartbroken, and the father commits suicide out of shame for his error.

Even if the money was safely delivered, it could go astray. When the great Weimar politician Gustav Stresemann got married, he received a dowry from his wife's wealthy family. The sum was invested by being lent out as mortgages. These were wiped out by the inflation, which meant the debts could be repaid at far less than their actual value. As his son Wolfgang reported many years later, Stresemann had to live from his salary as a Reichstag Deputy and, until he became a minister, some company board memberships. Ironically, especially after Stresemann got into government and could no longer take on directorships, the family was a lot less rich than it looked. After Wolfgang Stresemann completed his first year at Heidelberg University in August 1923, having been forced to call on his father for constant increases in his allowance because of the inflation, there was even some doubt that the family would be able to continue to fund his studies.[20]

Frau Stresemann's dowry had dwindled to nothing due to the currency's dizzying descent. Her and her family's loss was, of course, someone else's, perhaps another family's, gain.

People grabbed what advantage they could among the ever more bewildering financial chaos. Like the Pörtners in Bad Oeynhausen, who in 1922, confident in the steadiness of their father's job in a cigar factory, had signed up to buy a house that was being built on the western side of town. The price ran to 800,000 marks (the mark was still at around 2,000 to the dollar). Not so the following spring, when the account became due. 'When we moved in on 1 April 1923,' the son of the family wrote more than half a century later, 'this was a sum of money that even the most sensitive soul would not have managed to worry about. A single dip into one's wallet was sufficient to dispose of all liabilities, including the mortgage payments.'

Even the Pörtners' apparent stroke of luck was, however, double-edged:

Unfortunately the house was only half-finished when we took possession: half-finished, wretchedly built from old materials that had been
botched together. In the meantime the craftsmen would only work
in exchange for payment in kind. We could not do this, and the
money that father was paid, towards the end twice a day, was only
just sufficient for bare survival. Even in old age, he would still tell
stories about the defective stove pipe in the kitchen (our living room),
and the holes and cracks from which a foul and poisonous smoke
would billow. There was nothing we could do to correct this awful
situation. The pipe joint we needed was nowhere to be found, and
even if it had been, not for the ridiculous million-mark notes that a
week after they had been issued were no longer worth the paper they
were printed on.[21]

This is, in microcosm, an indication of an economy breaking down.
The mark was plunging like a stone. However, unlike in 1921–2,
neither the economy nor employment were growing as a result. After
some improvements in the early spring before the currency 'dam'
broke, both indicators were now beginning to go into decline. By the
autumn unemployment would reach catastrophic levels in many parts
of the country. In Prussia the numbers of supported unemployed and
dependants grew from 2.7 per cent in January 1923 to 24 per cent in
October; in Saxony from 8.4 per cent in January to 61 per cent in
October; in Hessen from a remarkably low 0.7 per cent to a dramatic
37.4 per cent; and in Hamburg, laid low by the steep fall in trading
activity as the exchange situation became more chaotic, from 11 per
cent in January to 64.8 per cent in October. At least 2 million workers
are thought to have become unemployed in the Ruhr by the autumn,
with half the entire population of Europe's greatest industrial area on
welfare.[22]

There were wry stories of the man who went into a café, ordered
a coffee for 1,000 marks, then settled in for a leisurely read of the
newspaper. Comfortably ensconced, he after a while requested a
second cup. When he got the bill, it was not for 2,000 but for 2,500.

Apologies, the waiter explained ruefully, but in between the first and second cup the price had gone up by 50 per cent . . .

Harsh everyday reality was less amusing. More than an extra cup of coffee was at stake. This was the time when employees in factories, offices and businesses, who had once been paid monthly or weekly, started to be paid, first twice or three times a week, and then daily – or even twice daily, like Herr Pörtner.

The pattern was quickly established and became a routine through Germany's year of currency insanity. Wages would arrive from the bank – there are photographs of the large carts and hampers used to transport them – and would be doled out to the employees, each receiving, as the year progressed, ever larger bundles in ever larger denominations. Then, with the employers' permission, the worker would hurry off – often joined by the spouse, who had been waiting outside for this moment – to spend the money on whatever provisions could be found. And then, once the money had been handed over to the retailer, it was up to the latter to haul it back to the bank, where – if humanly possible – he or she would change the mass of paper into dollars, pounds, Swiss francs or whatever 'hard' currency could be had.

The speed with which money could be paid into or taken out of the bank was vital. To handle the vast increase in the sheer quantity and complexity of financial transactions necessitated by inflationary distortions, the number of banks rose, as did the numbers of branches. The Deutsche Bank, which had a mere 15 branches in 1923, ten years later had 242. The Commerz- und Privatbank's network grew from 8 to 246 in the same period.[23] The number of staff employed in the sector almost quadrupled compared with pre-war levels, from 100,000 in 1913 to 375,000 in 1923, with the number of bank accounts serviced leaping from 552,599 in 1913 to an estimated 2.5 million in 1923. Sixty-seven new banks had been founded in 1921, and ninety-two in 1922. In 1923–4 the total was 401.[24]

The increase in banking business was not the consequence of a more intense economic activity. The work was increased because the banks were overloaded with orders for buying and selling shares and foreign exchange, proceeding from the public which, in increasing numbers, took part in speculations on the Bourse. The banks did not help in the production of new wealth; they merely managed the same claims to wealth, continually passed from hand to hand.[25]

Job advertisements in newspapers such as the *Vossische Zeitung* included those for bank workers, but also for retail clerks, where banking experience was specifically indicated. Such was the complexity of the financial transactions required to keep even a relatively straightforward buying and selling operation going in the conditions of the hyperinflation. Meanwhile, by August 1923 the *Vossische Zeitung* was down to one edition a day, often of just five or six pages. The perfect example of what was happening in the media and entertainment industries as a result of the hyperinflation was the fact that Kurt Tucholsky, the era's most amazingly prolific writer of poems, articles, songs, skits and sketches for magazines, newspapers and cabarets, found himself so financially straitened in the middle months of 1923 that he was forced to take work as a clerk . . . in a bank.[26]

Almost everything, even when transactions were conducted purely in German paper marks, depended on the exchange rate. The crucial time of day was three o'clock in the afternoon, when the dollar/mark rate was published. This was the signal, if – as was most often the case during the summer of 1923 – there had been a further overnight fall in the value of the mark against the greenback, for prices to go up in the wholesale and retail sectors. So, at the Junkers aircraft plant in Dessau, the company would give each worker a paper-mark sum equivalent to the price of three and a half loaves of bread. The men's wives, waiting outside the factory gates, would then rush off to the food shops, anxious to get there before the new dollar rate became known, since after that, in all likelihood, the money would no longer buy the bread ration it was supposed to cover.[27]

Above all, in that summer of 1923 in Germany, the only certain way to enjoy a decent standard of living was to have foreign currency.

Acquiring it, by any means possible, became a national obsession. A postal inspector who raided the mail stole $1,717, plus 1,102 Swiss francs, and 114 French francs – sufficient to buy two houses, set up his mistress in a flat (with a piano!), and make a substantial, conscience-easing donation to his church.[28] Meanwhile, as the inflation rocketed, Curt Riess, student son of the tailor who now accepted only dollars, was sent on a rest cure by his father:

I can still remember how grotesque conditions had become, because I got to experience it all on my own person. I had fallen ill, and I was sent off to convalesce on the 'Weißer Hirsch', the still-feudal spa resort in the hills above Dresden. For the fourteen days of the cure, my father had given me fourteen dollars, in bills that could be changed into marks. He had drilled it into me to wait every day until the new dollar exchange rate was announced. That would be around three p.m.

So, at three o'clock I changed a dollar and for it I got a corresponding sum in marks. With this I could pay the daily bill at the boarding house where I was staying, as well as the tram ride into Dresden, a ticket for the opera or the theatre, and the return trip. And all that for one dollar – if, in fact, I could manage to spend the whole dollar, or rather the vast sums of marks it bought, within the twenty-four hours.

And then I waited again until three o'clock in the afternoon, changed another dollar bill, and received a pile of money. Of course, the boarding house regularly raised its charges, and the tram company its fares, and of course over the period of two weeks one had to pay more and more for a seat at the opera house. But the authorities couldn't raise their prices fast enough to keep up with the plunging value of the mark.

Admittedly, I was in a privileged position. How many others could live off dollar bills?

Only the most privileged, of course. This class did not include an elderly Berlin literary man, Maximilian Bern, who in that year withdrew all his savings – 100,000 marks, formerly sufficient to support a modestly comfortable retirement – and purchased all it would buy by that time: a subway ticket. The old gentleman took a last ride around his city, then went back to his apartment and locked himself in. There he died of hunger.[29]

This could not go on. By August 1923, it was clear that Chancellor Cuno had, in fact, no solutions to the problems that his brilliant business brain had supposedly been perfectly attuned to master. A wave of Communist-influenced strikes in protest at the rapid depreciation in workers' standards of living and food shortages was spreading through the industrial areas of the economy, and the Social Democratic trade unions, keen to keep control, were forced to participate. The Communists are thought to have been responsible for the one-day strike that hit the Reich Printing Office on 10 August, despite the efforts of the moderate Social Democrats in the printers' union, halting production of currency for twenty-four hours. Even such a short pause in the manufacture of Germany's most vital product of the time – paper money – caused a discernible hiccup in the economy.[30] After suffering a no-confidence vote in the Reichstag, Cuno resigned on 12 August 1923.

President Ebert's choice for the new Chancellor was the German People's Party leader, Dr Gustav Stresemann. He headed a so-called 'Grand Coalition' of all the democratic parties, including the Social Democrats. There was no way of knowing it at the time, but with the appointment of this man, whose journey from extreme nationalist to apostle of European cooperation would mark him as one of the great German politicians of the twentieth century, President Ebert had opened up the possibility, at last, that the inflation could be confronted and defeated.

At a price, of course. After all, on 13 August 1923, when Gustav Stresemann took office as Chancellor and Foreign Minister of Germany, the mark stood at 3,700,000 to the dollar.

The German state was still haemorrhaging paper money on an unimaginable scale to keep the 'passive resistance' in the Ruhr going, though this was clearly long since a lost cause. The raptors of the right and left were gathering around the stricken form of the young German Republic. Communists were mobilising in central Germany, where their leaders had acquired a share of power, and the Nazis and their ultra-nationalist allies were raising citizen armies in the south, turning Bavaria into an armed camp. Adolf Hitler had great hopes of his 'starving billionaires', who would rise and sweep him to the position of absolute power that he craved.

The next three months – Stresemann's first months as Weimar Germany's most powerful and ultimately most respected leader – were going to be a roller-coaster ride, and everyone in the crisis-ridden country knew it.

22

Desperate Measures

Gustav Stresemann took power as the only chancellor the mainstream Weimar parties could agree to support in this latest, possibly fatal, time of crisis. A founder member of the German People's Party, he was the most right wing of the possible candidates.

It was on the face of things surprising that the Social Democrats, in particular, were prepared to hand the supreme power in the land to Stresemann. Earlier in his political career, he had been a fervent nationalist and a strong monarchist, while during the war he had favoured annexing large parts of the surrounding countries. Perhaps worst of all, from the left's point of view, for more than twenty years Stresemann had worked as a professional representative of big industry.

Since the left was not prepared to take on the responsibility of the chancellorship, however, the new leader had to come from one of the 'bourgeois' parties, and Stresemann was recognised as highly competent, a skilled political negotiator and a convincing, even inspiring, orator. And, after all, other powerful and capable figures on the business-orientated nationalist centre-right had veered towards an extreme, sometimes violently, anti-republican position during the post-war years (Karl Helfferich being perhaps the most spectacular example), but Stresemann had gone in the other direction. When forced to choose, the tavern-keeper's son from Berlin had moved steadily in the direction of acceptance of the Republic as an accomplished fact and of the parliamentary system as the one most capable of uniting the majority of Germans.

The fact that Stresemann's wife, Käthe (née Kleefeld), was the daughter of a Jewish industrialist who had, along with his wife, converted to Protestant Christianity, may also have formed part of the reason why the new Chancellor could never again feel comfortable with the nationalist right. After 1918, racial anti-Semitism (as opposed to the old-fashioned religiously based kind) had spread like a virus through its ranks. In his address to the Reichstag, on the day after his appointment to the chancellorship, Stresemann declared that, as befitted the seriousness of the situation, his government amounted to a 'coalition of all forces that support the constitutional idea of the state'.[1]

Both the nationalists and Communists, who for their different reasons blamed the inflation as well as the political chaos on the mainstream parties, now sharpened their attacks. Cuno, whose government had been supposedly 'above parties', had represented, for the nationalists, the hope that things might be moving back in the direction of an authoritarian state of the old pre-war style. The new administration, which included Social Democrats, resembled earlier Weimar governments and to that extent, for the far right, was a retrograde step. On the other hand, a big advantage for the nationalists was that if Stresemann and his fellow ministers were forced to call off the passive resistance in the Ruhr, they could be accused of 'betrayal' and lumped together with the so-called 'November criminals', who had, so far as the right was concerned, sold out Germany in November 1918. The fact that the crucial post of Finance Minister in the Stresemann cabinet had been awarded to the Social Democrat Rudolf Hilferding, an Austrian-born Jew, added further fuel to the right's propaganda fire.

That the plight of Germany had become desperate was clear to everyone. Drastic action to save the mark was clearly inevitable. In earlier years, though constantly wringing their hands and affirming the need to balance the budget, ministers had failed to take the difficult and predictably unpopular measures required. Given the underlying weakness of the Weimar political system during the immediate post-war period, this was to some extent understandable. Now, however, there was no choice but to act. For almost five years, inflation had severely affected some, but by no means all, Germans. On balance, given the alternatives, it had arguably acted to the advantage of stability. By the summer of 1923, however, the spiralling devaluation of the mark was killing the economy, threatening to cause food shortages and mass distress of the most extreme kind, and bringing the Reich itself to the brink of disintegration.

It was a measure of the anxiety felt by ministers that on 18 August, four days after the government had been officially formed, the socialist Hilferding invited no less a figure than the arch-conservative and sworn enemy of the Republic, Karl Helfferich, to address the cabinet. Helfferich duly presented his suggested solution to the collapse of the mark.

The former Imperial Secretary of the Treasury, who had done so much to promote the war loans that had helped feed the initial stages of the inflation, proposed that instead of gold being re-established as the new standard, the backing for the reform would be the country's reserves of rye. Helfferich's idea for a so-called 'Rye Bank', bizarre as it sounds to our current thinking, represented an attempt to do something that had become vitally necessary, at least at this stage in Germany's crisis: to decouple the worth of the mark from the credibility of the Reich government. The state's deficit was now so enormous and, particularly so long as the Ruhr crisis continued, so intractable, that no one had any faith in any fiat currency over which the government – or, for that matter, the Reichsbank, which was widely seen as its instrument – presided.

The idea for a rye-backed currency, based on a compulsory mortgage of the assets of German agriculture and industry, was something that, apparently, Helfferich had hit upon while on his regular summer break in the Swiss mountains.[2] He had already suggested it to the Cuno cabinet, with whom he and most other nationalists stood on good terms.

Although the idea survived the change in chancellor, as his presentation to the new cabinet showed, Helfferich was now faced with a socialist finance minister whose own ideas for a reformed and solid future currency were based, surprisingly, for a Marxist, on a fairly conventional scheme. This involved, at base, a swift return to the gold standard. To Finance Minister Hilferding, in any case, placing the fate of the German currency in the hands of a bank financed by industrial and agricultural interests gave off an unpleasant (to a socialist) whiff of the old collaboration between the Prussian landowning aristocracy and the iron and steel barons. This was the alliance which had excluded the workers from power in the Kaiser's time, and been derided by the left as the dominance of 'rye and iron'.

Weeks of argument, compromise and counter-compromise, proposal and counter-proposal, followed. The problem with Minister Hilferding's idea of an immediate return to a gold backing was, however, twofold: first, the Reichsbank didn't have nearly enough gold to provide the support that would give the precious-metal-backed scheme credibility; second, the attempt to get industry and private wealth to put up for a domestic gold loan under Cuno had already been a miserable failure.

As August turned to September and the arguments went on, it was starting to become clear that Helfferich's rye-based proposal would have to be adopted, probably in some dressed-up form to keep the gold enthusiasts happy. Meanwhile, however, away from the hothouse atmosphere of Berlin politics, the country was making its own arrangements with the crisis.

Although the 1923 harvest was proving to be a good one, Germany's landowners and farmers were clearly holding back the release of much produce on to the market in anticipation of receiving payment in hard currency once the reform of the mark finally came to pass. Throughout the country, barter had become the habitual mode of trade for millions of ordinary Germans who had no access to foreign currency. Because the amount of paper money now issued by the Reich in such huge six- and seven-figure denominations was still insufficient to meet all the public's needs, and in any case became all but valueless within days or even hours of coming into individuals' possession, states, municipalities, and even private companies had started printing their own promissory notes, based on whatever resources they controlled. These notes would be issued as currency, usually (but not always) valid only in a specific locality. Some indulged themselves in a little dark humour. One industrial firm printed a 500,000-mark note which was festooned with the larky motto: 'If a briquette of coal costs more than my face, feel free to stick me in the stove in its place'.

Until 1 January 1876 – easily within living memory, therefore, in the Germany of Stresemann and Helfferich – individual German states had enjoyed the right to issue their own currencies. Thalers, Gulden, Kreuzers and so on, plus their smaller denomination coins, had circulated throughout pre-unification Germany. In particular, the small-change coins of the various currencies were exchangeable in everyday use at rates known to ordinary Germans. More than most European countries, therefore, Germany had something of a tradition of localised currencies.

The practice of issuing 'emergency money' (*Notgeld*) had been going on since the war years, when local communities had been permitted to cover temporary shortages in low-value coins by issuing paper substitutes. By 1922–3 this had developed into a whole alternative monetary system. Until then, the Reichsbank had ensured that these notes, though subjected to a slightly larger discount than government-issued money, were nonetheless backed by securities deposited with the Reich Credit Corporation or the Reichsbank. By the summer of 1923, however, Finance Minister Hilferding estimated that between 60 and 70 trillion of the paper marks in circulation actually originated from unbacked sources of money. These were, strictly speaking, illegal. They might have been acceptable to many traders and customers but were actually issues of paper over which the government had no control and for which it provided no guarantee, adding further to inflation and to the generally chaotic currency situation.[3]

Total catastrophe was clearly on the cards. In Hamburg, a rich merchant city-state where long-established foreign trade and ready availability of foreign currencies conditioned the outlook, as early as mid-September there were plans in quite respectable political circles, including among members of Stresemann's own party, for introducing a hard, foreign exchange-backed currency for use within the city jurisdiction. This would become operative in the case, as seemed increasingly likely, that the German mark simply became worthless as a medium of exchange.[4] In areas occupied by the French and Belgians, farmers were demanding payment in francs, and the occupiers were encouraging this kind of desertion of the mark at every turn, as well as supporting small but active separatist movements in the occupied parts of the Rhineland and the Palatinate with money and official favour.

The message was stark: if the Reich government could not provide its people with a stable and reliable store of value and means of exchange, then the people, taken individually or communally, would have to do it for themselves. This was potentially disastrous for the continued stability and integrity of the fifty-year-old German state.

All the same, when it came to money, the real problem was the cost of the campaign of resistance against the French and their Belgian confederates in the Ruhr. When Hilferding took office on 14 August 1923 and cast an eye over the books, he was horrified at the disastrous state of the Reich's finances. During the next four weeks Germany faced an expenditure of 405 trillion paper marks, with 240 trillion going directly into the Ruhr struggle. Against this, the revenues of the government were 169 trillion, of which tax receipts, drastically shrunk by the inflation, represented a purely 'incidental' element.[5] In short, the Ruhr struggle was becoming unsupportable. It either had to be abandoned or a diplomatic solution had to be found, leading to a French withdrawal. Hilferding had spent the past few years criticising other politicians for blaming all Germany's economic ills on foreign policy, and especially Versailles and its attendant problems. Now, however, in the situation caused by the Ruhr occupation, he announced ruefully at a meeting of the Reichstag's Budget Committee on 23 August: 'A good foreign policy is the best financial policy!'[6]

The trouble was, the French had no intention of withdrawing from the Ruhr. The reason for this was quite simple. They were winning there. The German resistance was on the brink of collapse.

* * *

On 23 August, the same day that his Finance Minister wryly expressed the connection between German foreign policy and her financial state of health, Chancellor Stresemann admitted to a cabinet meeting that morale among the population in the occupied Ruhr, apparently fiercely strong back in January when the area had first been occupied, was now crumbling. It would not, he told his colleagues, survive the onset of winter.

No one present when Stresemann shared his pessimistic opinions saw fit to gainsay him. In fact, the Social Democratic Interior Minister of Prussia, Carl Severing, who was also at the meeting in an advisory capacity, took an even more pessimistic view. He thought that the resistance was basically over. The local police, Severing said, were now cooperating with the occupation forces, the Ruhr industrialists were in the process of making an accommodation with the French, and the morale of the workers, the backbone of the resistance, had now fallen so low that the once-vaunted discipline of the trade union movement in Germany's largest industrial region was shattered beyond short-term repair.[7]

When it came to the financial crisis, nothing, not even the government's plans for indexed tax collection, or the new decrees aimed at restricting and taxing private acquisition of foreign exchange in Germany, was working. On 1 September 1923, the mark stood at 10.5 million to the dollar, as opposed to 3.7 million a little more than two weeks earlier when the new government took office. Another two weeks, and the exchange rate had toppled to 109 million to the dollar.

One last hope of the German government and people had been a conference between Stanley Baldwin, the new British Prime Minister, and his French counterpart, Poincaré, in Paris in the third week of September. However, when the results of the discussions were announced on 19 September, it was grimly apparent that the British had failed to put any pressure on the French. The communiqué issued by the British embassy in Paris stated that there were no major differences of opinion between the two countries. The next day, the German cabinet met and agreed that a capitulation in the

Ruhr had become inevitable. Support for passive resistance there would have to be abandoned. The leaders of the resistance in the Ruhr, the premiers of the German states and leading politicians of the democratic parties would have to be prepared for the fact.[8] On 26 September, a joint announcement by Reich President and government, though still protesting the illegality of the French occupation of the Ruhr, nonetheless confirmed the end of Berlin's support for passive resistance.

The Social Democrats, in particular, had been nervous that abandonment of resistance in the Ruhr would lead to yet more accusations of a 'stab in the back'. Sure enough, the nationalist right, seeing its opportunity, launched into a torrent of accusations along those lines, even making the ludicrous claim that resistance had been on the brink of victory (just as the German army had supposedly been in November 1918). The German National People's Party called on the government to declare the Versailles Treaty null and void.

The nationalist-conservative government in Bavaria went even further. The state had been becoming ever more 'semi-detached' from Berlin since 1920, and now full separation seemed on the cards. On the same day that President Ebert and Stresemann's government jointly announced the end of support for the resistance struggle in the Ruhr, the Bavarian government responded to the new emergency by transferring presidential powers within the state away from Ebert in Berlin to Gustav von Kahr, currently District President of Upper Bavaria (which included Munich), former Premier of the state (1920–21), and champion of anti-Communist order. Under paragraph 48 of the Weimar constitution, the President in Berlin could assume semi-dictatorial powers. Now, according to the Bavarians' peculiar interpretation of their own legal rights, Kahr as 'General State Commissioner' superseded the national President and could exercise these powers in his place without consulting anyone. Sure enough, Kahr proclaimed martial law in Bavaria immediately on taking office.

Once again, the Reich government was faced with the fact that it could not prevent the Bavarians from doing what they were doing, unless it was prepared to use force. Moreover, even if it was theoretically prepared to do so, the Reichswehr had made it clear that it would not take action against a right-wing government of 'order'. A left-wing state government was another matter, as would soon become clear.

Further grist to the ever-sharpening tensions between the Berlin government and its supposed junior partner in Munich arose almost immediately, when the Reich ordered the banning of the official Nazi newspaper, the *Völkischer Beobachter*, which was published in Munich. The Nazi Party was already illegal in most German states, and on 27 September it pushed its luck even further by displaying a viciously anti-Semitic article entitled 'The Dictators Stresemann and Seeckt', attacking the Chancellor and the Reichswehr Minister, the first for being married to a Jewish woman, the second to a woman who was half-Jewish. On 1 October, the Reichswehr's commander in Bavaria, General von Lossow, refused a direct order from Seeckt to close down the offices of the *Völkischer Beobachter*. From now on, the power of the Reichswehr Minister – actually, of any Berlin minister – in Bavaria existed only on paper.[9]

The Nazi Party represented just one part of the reactionary forces in Bavaria in the late summer of 1923, but an exceptionally noisy and comparatively united one. Adolf Hitler's eloquence and energy had fuelled an extraordinary rise from poverty and obscurity that had turned him, at barely thirty-four, into a national figure. In the columns of the fashionable Berlin *Weltbühne*, the Nazis' self-proclaimed Führer appeared not at all in the first half of 1922, then three times in the second half. When initially mentioned, towards the end of November, Hitler is loftily dismissed as a 'demagogue of middling calibre', part of the entourage of General Ludendorff.[10] Suddenly, in the first half of 1923, a trawl through the index finds Hitler present twenty-six times; in the second half, forty-five!

By the latter part of the year of hyperinflation, Hitler is a name. An idea. What later generations would call a 'brand'.

It was not that the authorities in Berlin failed to realise the danger

presented by the rise of a figure like Hitler, or by the new kind of
paramilitary party organisation he had shaped and already come
close to perfecting. The problem was that, as things stood in the
autumn of 1923, they could do nothing about him. The writ of the
Reich simply did not run within Bavaria. So long as Kahr and his
Reichswehr chief, Lossow, now supposedly subordinate to the State
Commissioner rather than the Reich Minister, refused to take action
against Adolf Hitler's violent rhetoric and even more violent political
plans, then the Nazis would continue to flourish in Germany's south-
ernmost state.

The apparent powerlessness of the central government did not just
bear on the situation in the traditionally separatist south. Saxony and
Thuringia had always been strongholds of the socialist left – so much so
that even under the monarchy, Saxony had been known as 'the red
kingdom'. By 1923, while Bavaria and many rural areas of eastern Germany
had long since become reactionary strongholds, the populous and indus-
trialised central German states had moved to the other extreme. They
had started to create their own revolutionary institutions, including armed
socialist militias known as the 'proletarian hundreds' (*proletarische
Hundertschaften*). Similar workers' militias had been founded elsewhere,
including the Ruhr and other parts of Prussia, but had been suppressed.
Only in socialist-ruled Saxony and Thuringia, due to a more left-wing
Social Democratic leadership than in Prussia, and the involvement of a
rapidly growing Communist movement in the state government, did
they continue to develop and expand. By September, they were rumoured
to number 50,000–60,000, and to be engaged in military-style training
exercises in both the cities and the countryside.

With paramilitary organisations of the right, such as Hitler's
National Socialists, openly mobilising for a 'march on Berlin', it was
not hard to argue that the hundreds would be needed to defend
German democracy against its armed enemies.[11] Although by no
means all the socialist militia were Communists, there were also stories
of Moscow's involvement in financing and arming the hundreds. And
they seem to have been true.[12]

In Moscow, Lenin was suddenly no longer in charge. On 25 May 1922, a matter of months after the Bolsheviks had finally confirmed their hold on power, their leader had suffered the first of a series of strokes. A second in December and a third, wholly debilitating, stroke in March 1923 removed Lenin from politics altogether. He would live on, in a mute and paralysed condition, until the beginning of 1924, but meanwhile the Bolshevik regime was entering a long period of collective leadership, riven by rivalries and disagreements, which would end only with Stalin's assumption of unchallenged leadership half a decade later. With Germany – for many in Moscow always the next great revolutionary hope – in political and economic chaos and the entire capitalist system, at least to Communist eyes, imploding, it seemed an ideal time for a workers' uprising there.

Particularly among the group allied to the brilliant civil war general and intellectual firebrand Leon Trotsky, who believed in 'permanent revolution', this seemed the moment to strike. At a secret meeting of the Politburo on 23 August 1923, the green light was given for a Communist revolution in Germany, to be spearheaded by the 'proletarian hundreds'. A successful uprising in the world's second largest industrial country would bolster the Trotskyite cause within the Bolshevik leadership. It would also, incidentally, ensure that the new 'bourgeois' Stresemann government, which was clearly attempting to find a *modus vivendi* with the arch-capitalist British, would not abandon the Rapallo Treaty and become part of a possible anti-Communist block. Hence the Moscow leadership's authorisation of a secret fund, to be controlled by the Soviet ambassador in Berlin, for the promotion of the so-called 'German October' – or, rather, in Trotsky's case, a 'German November', for he argued that the Communist coup should take place on the ninth of that month, the fifth anniversary of the revolution that overthrew the Kaiser in 1918.

It is one of the special curiosities of this most strange of German autumns that Adolf Hitler had the very same fateful date in mind – 9 November 1923 – for his planned 'march on Berlin'.

* * *

As the crisis approached, not everyone in Germany perceived themselves to be in a hopeless position. Despite the tragic absurdity of the price rises, there were those who had found a way to live with it.

In July 1923, for instance, after a series of strikes and numerous demonstrations by members of the public service unions, the mass of German civil servants had become the first major income group in the country to have their earnings inflation-proofed – or, more precisely, subjected to an elaborate and ingenious indexing system that awarded civil servants constant updating and pre-payment in their wage payment arrangements. Moreover, these adjustments were based not on accomplished facts but on a formula for anticipating rises in prices. Although they were already privileged by the fact that their salaries were in many cases paid quarterly, or if not then monthly in advance, under this new agreement their adjusted inflation supplements – which by this time, with the currency falling so quickly, could amount to huge cash sums – would also be paid in advance, before the actual anticipated inflation had, in fact, occurred. The effect on the government budget of such huge (and nonsensical) payments was clearly highly inflationary. In fact, higher civil servants were accused of exploiting their possession of large quantities of cash to indulge in substantial foreign-currency speculation.[13]

All this did not, in the end, wholly protect civil servants from their share of the general suffering. By the late autumn of the year no one, no matter how often they were paid or their salary recalculated, could be protected from the total collapse of mark-denominated financial transactions that engulfed Germany and made her currency essentially worthless.

The respite awarded to civil servants during much of the hyperinflationary period did, however, make them even more unpopular with their fellow citizens than they had previously been (and they had not been much loved). It soon became apparent, moreover, that one of the chief aims of Stresemann's government was to begin the stabilisation of the government finances preparatory to rescuing the mark. To this end, it planned to use the bureaucracy's unpopularity among the general public as a weapon. The civil service, the lower ranks of which, particularly, had improved their position since 1918, was going to be subjected to a drastic, even brutal, programme of cuts.

Quarterly pay was unilaterally abandoned by the new government towards the end of August, to be replaced by weekly salaries, and the civil service unions' protests ignored. During September–October 1923, plans for sweeping redundancies in the numbers of bureaucrats were developed, and again conveyed without room for negotiation to their representatives. On 27 October, a 'Decree for the Reduction of Public Personnel' (*Personalabbauverordnung*) was issued. This allowed for a quarter of the entire public service, from blue-collar staff to white-collar bureaucrats – from school janitors to government councillors – to be dismissed over the next couple of years. Fifteen per cent would be gone by 31 March 1924, and the final 10 per cent at a point still to be determined. The leaders of the various public service unions complained, and there were even wild accusations of a 'pogrom' against civil servants being waged by an unholy alliance of government and big industry, but ultimately nothing was done.[14] In dealing with the bloated public-service sector, the Stresemann government had successfully shown it meant business.

Vigorous debates over the basis for the inevitable new currency – gold, or rye, or some hybrid – continued in the government committees and the public press. Meanwhile, there were other areas in which a foundation was also being laid for the inevitable end to inflation. The currency had to be rescued if Germany was not to be doomed to political and economic disintegration.

Erzberger's tax reforms had offered a brief window of opportunity during which solvency had become a realistic possibility, before the reparations crisis of summer 1921 had refuelled the inflation and rapidly wiped out most of the government's real income from the new charges. Succeeding governments had tried to close loopholes, keep pace with inflation and put a stop to late payment and capital flight, but without success. Tax avoidance had become not just easy, but socially respectable. Towards the end of September 1923, the

Reichstag passed a government bill raising taxes, introducing some new ones and also drastically increasing the 'multiplier' used, and providing for regular updating of this inflation-adjusting mechanism. The government also provided for steep increases in penalties for late payment. Only a reform of the financial system and the currency would fully solve the government's problem, but at least, for the first time since the inflation began, paying taxes was no longer 'optional' and delay no longer completely painless.[15]

There were indications that Stresemann's advent to power at the head of the 'Grand Coalition' had begun to turn the vessel of the German state around. In general, however, that was not how it looked to many of the Reich's citizens in those crucial weeks. The apparent inability of the supposed 'stabilisation administration' to carry out much in the way of visible stabilisation, and the ever-increasing political disorder in different parts of the Reich, gave an impression, in these early weeks, of weakness. Assistant headmaster Herr von der Ohe remarked in his diary on 10 October 1923:

> Siegfried [presumably Herr von der Ohe's son] was at the circus. The ticket cost ten million marks. A fellow student treated him to this. Think of it: children handing each other gifts of ten million. The dollar is said to be worth three billion. This will probably mean the end of the Stresemann ministry.[16]

Herr von der Ohe had the good fortune to run a small agricultural operation on the side, of course, and thus was granted extra protection from the breakdown of the money economy. He was wrong about the future of the government, however. Although that government had undergone a serious crisis just before Herr von der Ohe's diary entry, despite the multiple problems it still faced, and its serious divisions, it would see the stabilisation programme through.

However, the first step needed to save democracy was its suspension.

23

Everyone Wants a Dictator

It was astonishing that a government apparently constantly under threat of disintegration could have done what Gustav Stresemann's administration – or, rather, technically, two administrations – did in the 109 days between 13 August and the last day of November 1923.

The first cabinet of the 'Grand Coalition' lasted until 3 October. It fell because of disagreements, not over the necessity for emergency powers to solve the political and economic crisis, but over their extent.

Stresemann's ministry was subjected to intrigues from the right, including industrial interests inside the German People's Party around Hugo Stinnes, who were looking to completely reverse the worker-friendly laws that had been adopted in 1918, which they blamed for the country's economic plight. These included the eight-hour working day (Monday to Saturday, representing a forty-eight-hour week) and workers' representation on factory committees. In turning back the clock, this powerful group favoured not just temporary emergency powers but something close to a permanent dictatorship, similar to the regime in Bavaria. Clearly, they wanted the socialists out of the government and Stresemann, whom many even in his own party considered a dangerous moderate, out of power altogether.

The coalition also, however, suffered from rigidity on the part of the Social Democratic Party. Although the socialist ministers, realising that lagging productivity was a contributory factor in Germany's current travails, had agreed in cabinet to a compromise ruling on working time reforms, their own party refused to give an inch. The party also insisted that the Berlin government should take steps to force the defiant Bavarian reactionaries into line. This view, though legally and morally correct, was – given the Reichswehr's complete unwillingness to take up arms against Kahr and his paramilitary friends in Munich – almost comically impractical.

The crisis lasted for three days. The government fell on the evening of 3 October, when the Social Democrats refused to support the extension of emergency powers to the economy, which would have allowed the government to make changes to working conditions without consulting the Reichstag. Then, on 6 October, it rose again. In the interim, with President Ebert refusing to replace Stresemann as Chancellor, and no other possible political constellation in sight, someone found a form of words – involving 'fundamental recognition of the eight-hour day . . . but also the possibility of a contractually agreed exceeding of the current working time' that enabled the Social Democrats to vote for reform of the eight-hour day after all.[1]

The major personnel change in the new cabinet, however, was that the keen (but in many ways conventionally minded) socialist Hilferding was replaced as Finance Minister by a supposedly non-party figure. In fact, the new man, Hans Luther, was a moderate conservative expert who had already served as Food and Agriculture Minister and, as a former mayor of Essen, the home of Krupp, also stood close to the industrial interest. At the very least, he represented a more reassuring, or at least less controversial, figure than Hilferding. The socialist representation in the cabinet was reduced from four to three, and, with a man of Luther's background at Finance, the balance had tipped decisively towards the kind of base for the urgent currency reorganisation – drawing on national reserves of agricultural and industrial wealth – that had been put forward by the nationalist Helfferich earlier in the summer.

The way lay open for what would be known as the Rentenbank (literally 'annuity bank') and for a new system of money for Germany.

This was, essentially, the idea that Helfferich had first put forward under the title of 'Rye Bank'. It came not a moment too soon.

In July 1923, unemployment among the unionised workforce had stood at 3.5 per cent. By October it was heading quickly for the next month's total of a terrifying 23.4 per cent. The situation was disastrous, and it seemed out of control.

'There have been bread riots and plundering with collisions with the police all through the week,' wrote the London *Sunday Times's* correspondent in Berlin in October 1923. He continued:

> The whole trouble in Berlin was one of prices. The advocates of infla-
> tion at home should come to Berlin and see what happens when the
> debt falls due. There had been ominous clamourings for a fortnight
> past against the rising prices. It took a whole series of riots and an
> ultimatum of the trade unions leaders that if there was not an issue
> of new money in three days there would be a general strike to wake
> up the Government to a sense of the seriousness of the situation.
> Academic discussion had to be abandoned and somebody had to get
> busy.[2]

In an unnamed provincial town, another journalist, writing for the London *Observer*, described skilled men, 'aristocrats of labour', earning the equivalent, in British currency, of 'three-halfpence' an hour, making a shilling a day. 'But after all,' the man told the reporter, 'we have work, and ours is still an eight-hour day.' His brother, an unskilled labourer, married with three children, earned, so it was said, the price of three loaves of bread in a week. The sympathetic corres-pondent did some calculations for the paper's British readers, and worked out that the 'stupendous figure in marks' that it would cost to supply a thousand men, women and children with a nourishing meal in fact amounted to one guinea, or one farthing per head:

It is the lack of complaint that becomes so significant, in a way so depressing. Beggars are few and the most of these are blind or maimed; children, dogs and horses appear to be kindly treated; the queues that wait for bread or potatoes are patient almost to the point of apathy. In the grocer shops people come in, ask prices and go out again; shopkeepers, warned by telephone every hour of the latest movement in the valuta market, anxious to sell and yet afraid to part with their stock, are civil, even sympathetic. An old man had come in to ask the price of some tinned soup, and gone out again. 'He was among my best customers before the war,' said the grocer. 'Now he lives in one room with his wife, who is older than he is, and very ill. One of his friends told me to let him have a little parcel of grocery every month. He sent it back. He says that neither he nor his wife can accept charity, but I doubt if they get one meal a day.' I said nothing, for the professor seemed to typify the German spirit in adversity, and I remember the equally thin and threadbare scholar of another town who said that what he missed most was neither food nor sound footwear, but books.[3]

Of course, there were the usual crass contrasts, even as the crisis reached its grim apogee:

The winter season, such as it is, has begun. It has opened with the closing of one of the smartest restaurants for dinner in Unter den Linden, and another has shut a large part of its accommodation, because there are not enough dinner customers. Lunch has become the great meal.

At the same time there is a revival of dinner dancing. M. Marek Weber has moved with his band from the Hotel Esplanade to the Hotel Adlon, and on certain days a week when the Berliner is allowed by his paternal government to dance, things are quite gay again.

There were, of course, far too many people in Berlin and the rest of Germany for whom any meal at all would have been a great meal. Somewhere, however, there were those who could afford £8. 2s. 6d.

to fly from London to Berlin. The service had been running since the beginning of the year, landing and taking off from the airfield attached to the former Zeppelin airship works at Berlin-Staaken. It was now, at the beginning of November, due for expansion.

> The new route will connect London, Rotterdam, Hanover, and Berlin, Berlin being brought within eight hours of London. Napier D.H. 34 air limousines are to be used on the service, every comfort having been installed for passengers during the long journey. Air cushions are provided in the armchair seats, silk curtains are hung at the windows, and the cabin is heated by a circulation of warm air.
>
> Leaving London at 8 a.m. the limousines will descend at Hanover at 2 p.m. and at Berlin at 3.50 p.m., while on the return journey, starting at 8 a.m. from Berlin and 10 a.m. from Hanover, London is reached at 2.30 p.m. . . .
>
> Each passenger will be provided with a free luncheon basket, containing, in addition to food for the journey, a bottle of wine for the women passengers and a small bottle of whisky for the men.[4]

The London–Berlin flights would soon transfer to Tempelhof, the former parade ground of the Kaiser's army to the south of the city centre, where work had been under way for some months on constructing an airfield even at the height of the inflation. After being delayed by a combination of capital shortages (due to the economic situation) and bureaucratic obstruction (the original plan of the Berlin city fathers had been to construct an exhibition space for trade fairs), Tempelhof had been granted official airport status in October 1923. The Junkers Aircraft Company and Aero-Lloyd had already built wooden hangars-cum-terminals on the site.

Weimar Germany, for all her problems and struggles, despite her poisonous political divisions, the horrors and absurdities of the hyper-inflation, and the continuing, near-medieval suffering of wide swathes of her population, was ripe for the modernist revolution that was under way all over the developed world, especially in the real winner of the First World War, America.

That same hyperinflationary autumn also witnessed the first public radio broadcasts in Germany. At 8 p.m. on 29 October 1923, with a dollar worth 65 billion marks, at the Vox-Haus in the Potsdamer Strasse, seat of the eponymous record company, the slightly crackly tones of Germany's first radio presenter travelled over the air waves: 'Attention! Here is the Vox-Haus broadcasting station, on the 400 m frequency. We make the brief announcement that the Vox-Haus broadcasting station is commencing entertainment radio.'

The first music to be played – live – on German radio was a piece for solo cello and piano accompaniment, 'Andantino' by Kreisler. Eleven other pieces followed over the course of the next hour, the last of them a recorded version of the national anthem, played by a military band. Then the announcer's voice returned to urge the listeners: 'We wish you a good night. Please do not forget to earth your antennae!'[5] Two months later, the total number of officially licensed listeners (who paid a steep annual fee of sixty gold marks or 780 billion paper marks to the German post office[6]) had reached around 1,000. By the middle of the next year, 1924, the licence fee would have been reduced to a third of its initial level, there would be 100,000 legitimate listeners (illegal listening remained widespread), and by December more than half a million, clearly undeterred by the fact that this early public radio required the use of earphones.[7]

Beneath the chaotic surface, Germany was changing, waiting to fulfil her post-war promise. Inflation might have helped soften many of the blows inflicted by defeat in war, but now it was holding the country back. The question was whether during the past five years Germany had slipped too far away from a viable model of capitalism to be able to recover. On the far left, the Communists, and on the far right, the paramilitary nationalist groups for which Hitler was becoming a unifying figure, both sensed their moment.

Towards the end of October 1923, it seemed, to the extremists and the disillusioned, possible that violent change could be brought about.

The 'Grand Coalition', despite its lofty name, appeared too riven to summon the forceful and potentially unpopular response needed finally to push post-war German society through the door into modernism, welfare and democracy that had stood open ever since 9 November 1918. If Stresemann and his ministers did not do this, there were plenty of Germans prepared to push the country through another door entirely.

The enabling law requested by the Stresemann cabinet finally received President Ebert's signature on Saturday, 13 October 1923. It put the government in a position of temporary and carefully delineated dictatorship, whose powers were valid only so long as the current coalition remained in government, and even then would expire on 31 March 1924. The government was from this day empowered to take an extremely wide range of decisions that would usually require the Reichstag's approval.

Stresemann's ministry immediately used the opportunity to order reforms to unemployment benefit, to give the state a new and decisive role in the management of labour disputes and to dismiss large numbers (up to 25 per cent) of the Reich's civil servants. As agreed with the Social Democrats, the eight-hour day remained standard, but could be extended now to ten if a case could be made by the employer. The liberal *Vossische Zeitung* in its report of the vote called this a 'Restoration of Productivity'.[8] A cabinet discussion on the currency question was, the paper further informed its readers, set for the following Monday, 15 October. Things were starting to move.

Meanwhile, the stubborn attachment of Germany's industrial workers to their eight-hour day was a source of great resentment among the other classes. In all the great German cities, especially Berlin, what leisure the people had – and since the eight-hour day it was more than before – they devoted to loading themselves up with sacks and bags and embarking on trips into the countryside to hunt for food. The London *Observer* wrote:

But the only part of the weary journey worth recording is the tramp, from one farm to another along the Spree, the Havel, even the Elbe, on its long way through the flat fields to Hamburg. Most of the country dwellers are willing to part with their potatoes early in the morning at yesterday's prices; towards mid-day they are restive. 'The night watchman hasn't been round yet,' is the cryptic reply. It appears on inquiry that the night watchman's new function is to report the state of the dollar exchange on the Berlin Bourse from house to house and farm to farm, and that the hundredweight of the morning may cost another milliard [modern billion] in the afternoon. This is of interest to all and sundry, but the moot point comes when the man is a Berlin working-man, who complains not only of the price, but of the plenty which he sees around him. 'Work ten hours and more a day, the same as we do,' is the answer.[9]

In Saxony, with the Communists joining the Social Democrats in power, the situation was different. A journalist reported from Dresden:

There is a kind of rough-and-ready 'people's justice'. It is sometimes very rough. It is not only Communists who break into the market halls and compel the stall keepers to sell at prices the working-folk can pay, prices that often mean a heavy loss. The movement is a general mass movement, and Socialists, as well as Communists, sit on the 'control committees' that settle disputes between buyers and sellers, usually in a rather summary fashion.

There have been times when no fruit and vegetables or dairy produce have arrived from the country districts because the farmers have been loth to sell against depreciating paper marks. The urban masses have organised raids, have dug up the potatoes themselves, have cut down corn with shears (causing great waste and damage), or have forced the farmers to sell cheaply.[10]

Unemployment in Saxony was also rising fast, as elsewhere in Germany, more than quadrupling from 25,000 in August to a little over 112,000 at the beginning of October 1923. No fewer than 350,000 were on short-time, up from 41,000. Hundreds of factories were being closed down. The difference between this part of Germany and the others was that the leftist government in Saxony 'solved' the problem by simply making factory closures illegal.

Things could indeed get 'rough and ready' in beautiful Dresden, the 'Florence of the Elbe'. In the spring of 1919, a few months after the revolution, the then Saxon Minister of War, Gustav Neuring (a Social Democrat), had refused to personally receive a deputation of disabled war veterans. As a consequence, his ministry was invaded, he was seized and thrown into the River Elbe. Moreover, when the minister tried to swim back to shore, he came under fire from armed demonstrators lining the riverbank, and was killed.[11] Four years later, with inflation raging, 60 per cent unemployment in Dresden,[12] and the so-called 'proletarian hundreds' flexing their muscles, largely under Communist command, it looked as if the stage was set for more violence against the status quo.

The tens of thousands of uniformed members of the 'proletarian hundreds' in Saxony, who existed, technically, in order to support the forces of law and order, pointed to the threat of anti-republican forces in Bavaria as a justification for their military preparations.

Clandestinely supported by elements of the Reichswehr, armed units of the nationalist right, including the successors of the Erhardt Brigade and also Hitler's storm troopers, had begun massing on the northern border of Bavaria. The nationalist forces stood especially thick on the ground around the border city of Coburg, where 11,000 paramilitaries were commanded by none other than the founder of Organisation Consul, Naval Captain Erhardt. They seem to have been supplied with weapons mainly from the stores of the Bavarian police.[13] Here they faced into the state of Thuringia, which by the second half of October 1923 was likewise run by a socialist–Communist coalition. Further to the east, a short stretch of border also led from Bavaria into Saxony. The implications were all too clear.

The trouble was that the existence of the 'proletarian hundreds' undoubtedly raised the threat of a Communist coup in Saxony and Thuringia, which might then lead on to a Communist takeover in Berlin and other major cities, and eventually even to a Soviet Germany. This was precisely the justification that the far right in Bavaria needed in order to arm its own supporters to the teeth, and to threaten a 'march on Berlin' via Saxony and Thuringia. In other words, the far left and far right fed off each other's activities. Each group blamed its worryingly eager preparations for civil war on the other side.

Meanwhile, the government in Berlin, for a while, seemed helpless to intervene in either of these places. But if the Berlin government did finally summon the will to intervene in these parts of Germany where its writ had become all but ineffectual, where and how would this happen?

The situation in central Germany was coming to a head, in its different way, but absolutely of a pace with that in Bavaria. On 10 October, the Communists, who had hitherto merely provided parliamentary support for the Social Democratic Premier in Saxony, joined his government, as instructed by Moscow.[14] The Communists took over the finance and economy ministries in Dresden, and the party's leader became head of the cabinet office. A few days later, the Thuringian Communists were also given government posts, in the economy and justice ministries.

In fact, when steps were taken by the Berlin government, they were directed only at Saxony and its junior partner in leftism, Thuringia. On 15 October, the day the cabinet was due to make a final decision on the setting up of a new currency bank that would end the inflation, the commander of the Reichswehr's troops in Saxony, General Müller, issued a reprimand to the new socialist–Communist government. Its officials had put up posters explaining its programme in public places without the General's permission, which was required under the recent emergency laws. Socialists all over Germany protested at this, including the Social Democrat cabinet ministers in Berlin. Stresemann pointed out to his colleagues that this action had been agreed with President Ebert and that furthermore, as the cabinet record had it, 'if the government took no action in Saxony, the danger existed that those circles in Saxony who were threatened [i.e. business and farming interests] would turn to Bavaria for help. He did not need to go into details about how this would mean civil war and the disintegration of the Reich.'[15]

Not the best of days to decree the creation of the new currency bank, but then the government had no choice but to press on.

Everyone wanted a dictatorship. The Communists wanted one, of the proletarian kind. The conservative nationalists wanted one that bore some resemblance to the old monarchy. Hitler's Nazis thought of nothing else, and their obvious model was Mussolini, who had seized power in Italy in October 1922. Even the democratic 'Weimar' parties had decided, rather gloomily, that the country needed a strong hand, albeit on a temporary basis. Lastly, the man so many in Germany considered the country's secret ruler had also made a decision along these lines. Hugo Stinnes wanted a dictatorship, too.

So strongly did Stinnes feel on this issue, and had felt for some time, that he even approached the American ambassador, Alanson B. Houghton, in mid-September, seeking his support or at least tolerance for such a solution to Germany's problems. Stinnes told the American that he expected 3 to 4 million unemployed in Germany by the next month and that the Communists would exploit this situation to launch a general strike, followed by a nation-wide uprising. In response – and Stinnes thought it was important not to strike the first blow, for fear of losing international sympathy – parliamentary democracy would have to be suspended and a Bavarian-style authoritarian regime introduced that would use ruth-less force to defeat the Communists. A dictator would have to be found, Stinnes insisted, according to Houghton's subsequent dispatch to Washington:

> . . . equipped with the power to do everything necessary. Such a man
> must speak the language of the people and be himself of bourgeois

origins, and such a man stood ready. A great movement, originating from Bavaria, determined to restore the monarchy, was near.[16]

So, who was this unnamed man of destiny who would come out of Bavaria and clean up Germany? Was Stinnes referring to Hitler? It has often been claimed that Stinnes was among the supporters of Hitler in these critical days.[17] Stinnes's daughter, Clärenore, thought that he had met Hitler through General Ludendorff, whom Stinnes knew well (and admired) from his wartime relations with the High Command. Stinnes's sons Edmund and Hugo Jr, however, both stated later in life that their father had turned down a meeting with the Führer. What both Clärenore and Hugo Jr both definitely recalled (using exactly the same phrase) was that the hard-headed inflation king had dismissed Hitler privately as a 'fantasist' (*Fantast*), and for all his faults Stinnes did not waste time with fantasists. It seems more likely that the Bavarian 'messiah' Stinnes alluded to as one possible leader for Germany was, in fact, the wartime strongman, Ludendorff. The restless General had settled in Munich and had for some time been plotting, with Hitler and others, to set up exactly the dictatorship that the right and many of the major industrialists longed for.[18]

Key to Stinnes's thoughts in September was the prospect of a Communist uprising, which would give a decent pretext for a right-wing dictatorship. A month later, it seemed that this moment might have come.

Trotsky, with an eye for drama, had initially proposed 9 November, the fifth anniversary of the proclamation of the German Republic, for the date of the Communist revolution, the so-called 'German October'. However, the local leadership had other plans. General Müller, the commander of the Reichswehr troops in Saxony, had been granted full executive powers in the state by the Berlin government, and after the Communists joined the government he lost no time in putting a formal ban on the 'proletarian hundreds' in Saxony. When the units failed to disband, a confrontation was clearly on the cards, and if the Communists were, in fact, to mount a coup, it had to be soon.

Chemnitz, an important industrial city between Dresden and Leipzig, with a population of around 320,000, had become a Communist stronghold. It was here that the Communists summoned a conference of factory councils for 21 October 1923. Heinrich Brandler, chair of the Communist Party, and for a week since also head of the Cabinet Office in Dresden, travelled there to address the delegates. His speech was supposed to inspire the workers to declare a general strike against the tyranny of the Reichswehr, thus providing the trigger for nationwide armed revolution.

The Chemnitz conference turned into a fiasco, at least for Brandler and his comrades. His clarion call met with an almost complete lack of response from the workers' representatives. Despite the rocketing unemployment, the food shortages and the threat from the Reichswehr, the conference refused to vote for a general strike. Humiliating defeat in communism's Saxon stronghold could mean only one thing: the German working class was not interested in violent change. For Brandler and his hopes of revolution, it amounted – as one of his colleagues drily remarked – to a 'third-class funeral'.[19]

The plans for revolution were duly abandoned in Saxony and Thuringia. Only in that other great radical heartland (and unemployment black spot), Hamburg, did some hotheads around Ernst Thälman dare to hope that they could succeed where Brandler had failed. Between 23 and 25 October, after armed militants had seized public buildings, including police stations, there followed street fighting that left twenty-four Communists and seventeen police dead. However, in Hamburg, too, the mass of the workers refused to answer the activists' call. Again, the German Communist Party revealed itself to be isolated.

In the meantime, the Berlin government had moved against the Communist–socialist coalition in Saxony. The Reichswehr in Saxony was reinforced from outside the state, including troops from Berlin, and quickly occupied most major towns. Berlin then demanded that Erich Zeigner, the left-socialist Premier of Saxony, dissolve the coalition with the Communists. On 28 October, Zeigner issued a formal refusal. Within less than twenty-four hours, Stresemann invoked a further set of emergency powers, allowing his government to remove from office any ministers or officials deemed to be acting illegally. A Reich Commissioner was given full authority until a new government could be formed. Finally, the Reichswehr, in full military order, complete with a marching band, occupied the ministries in Dresden and forcibly removed the ministers and officials, including the Premier. Though technically compliant with orders from the democratic government in Berlin, the action was a pretty brutal display of old-fashioned militaristic arrogance.[20]

The affair was not quite bloodless. There was shooting in Chemnitz. In the mining town of Freiberg the troops fired on a crowd that refused to disperse, killing twenty-three and injuring thirty-one civilians. All the same, in the end the so-called 'Reich Enforcement' (*Reichsexekution*) action in Saxony was a much less drastic operation than had been feared. This was partly because Stresemann had refused to allow his Defence Minister to appoint a Reich Commissioner with indefinite powers for an indefinite period, as the minister had suggested. The man sent to Dresden from Berlin had executive powers, but for a specific mission that would end when its goal was achieved: to enable the formation of new government that did not include Communists. He achieved this within two days, after which executive power was handed back to the Social Democratic politician, Alfred Fellisch, who had been elected by his party to take the post.

There can be no question that the fall of the radical left coalition in Dresden came as a great relief to many, both inside and outside Saxony. As the US consul in Dresden, Louis Dreyfus, reported after the 'Reich Enforcement' operation:

The Saxon bourgeois population greeted this development. The entire life in the towns suddenly took on another aspect. The shops which had previously closed their show-windows throughout the day, opening, if at all, merely the entrance door in order to be able to shut down at once in case of a repetition of the daily riots of the unemployed, again displayed their goods. The cafés and restaurants in the cities whose guests had repeatedly been forced to leave were again opened. In Dresden . . . the public spirit seemed entirely changed. Instead of the dead impression, which the closed shops had given the city, the streets once more became full of life, more cheerful and crowded, quite in contrast with the situation where everyone hurried away from the centre of town in order not to be molested by occasional riots.[21]

The threat of a Communist uprising removed, the question remained: what would the Berlin government do about the Bavarians? After all, the Saxon and Thuringian governments, even at their most defiant, had not been guilty of the kind of extreme disobedience that had become routine for the Munich government, especially since Kahr had taken power. On 20 October, for instance, Seeckt had formally sacked the disobedient Reichswehr commander in Munich, General Lossow. The Bavarian government promptly declared the Reichswehr in Bavaria directly subordinate to its orders and reinstated Lossow as commander of what was now essentially a separate Bavarian army. Repeated appeals to dissolve paramilitary nationalist units were ignored. During the second half of October, the Bavarian government began to carry out openly anti-Semitic policies, expelling Jews of Polish origin whom it accused of profiteering and currency offences. These actions were obviously intended to garner support among the restive battalions of the far right, many of whom, including the Nazis, were demanding nothing less than the death penalty for such offenders. It turned out that many of these alleged criminals were in fact Munich residents of long standing and apparent respectability. It was a fateful precedent, a pre-echo of much worse horrors to come in following decades.[22]

The Berlin government's troubles were not by any means over. On 20 October, government aid for the Ruhr had ceased. There were food riots in the larger towns. Local political leaders in the Rhine and Ruhr, including the Mayor of Cologne, Konrad Adenauer, demanded the right to conduct independent negotiations with the French, raising the spectre of separatism in the west as well as the south of Germany. Stresemann, struggling to deal with several different crises at once, persuaded the Finance Minister, Luther, to maintain a slightly more favourable dole for the unemployed in the Ruhr, as a lingering recognition of their special sacrifice, but this could only be a temporary measure. It was only possible while the Reich continued to print paper money. Once the reform of the mark (and the reform of the Reich's finances required to make it stick) was completed, such payouts would have to be discontinued. Leaders in the occupied west were, of course, also perfectly aware of this fact, which again led to fears that they would make an agreement, any agreement at all, with the French – even involving a separate currency for the west – in order to survive. The new currency was not necessarily good news for everyone.[23]

On 2 November, subjected to huge pressure from their party's grass roots, which were outraged by the differences between the forceful suppression of the 'left-unity' governments in Saxony and Thuringia and the continuing failure to dare a similar confrontation with the far right in Bavaria, the Social Democratic ministers resigned from the cabinet. Stresemann was now Chancellor of a minority administration, and with the Social Democrats' exit from the government had automatically lost his special powers under the enabling act of 13 October.

Moreover, easily forgotten among the drama of the confrontations with far left and far right, the central issue of the currency remained as yet unresolved. Until the mark could be stabilised, almost anything the government in Berlin might do offered little prospect of restoring a real measure of order to the country.

24

Breaking the Fever

Stresemann had accepted the post of Chancellor on 13 August 1923, and he had also, following a habit of overwork that was probably to shorten his life, simultaneously become Foreign Minister. Hilferding's jest that the best financial policy was a good foreign policy had been even more pointed than it seemed.

Two months after gaining office, Stresemann found himself in a distinctly improving international situation. On 12 October, the British decided to take up the ten-month-old offer by Hughes, the American Secretary of State, to convene a new conference, which would re-examine the reparations problem within an economic context. Two weeks later, Poincaré, though still holding on tight to the Ruhr and Rhine, agreed, under certain conditions and subject to a thorough investigation of Germany's actual foreign exchange and investment holdings, to a reassessment of the Reich's treaty liabilities. The fact that Poincaré was losing political clout at home – the Ruhr occupation was not universally popular, and becoming less so – was an important factor. However, so was the Americans' promise to link the reparations question with the still-stalemated problem of repayment of inter-Allied loans. For the last five years, Washington had stubbornly insisted on full repayment of the billions she was owed by her erstwhile allies. Now, for the first time, the implication from Washington to Paris was: if you go easier on the Germans, maybe we'll go easy on you.[1]

The Rentenbank had finally been established on 17 October 1923, though the formal document recording this was dated the fifteenth of the month. The head of its administrative council was a deputy of the nationalist German National People's Party and former Prussian Finance Minister, August Lentze. Other members were also representative of the conservative elements in society, from landowners to industrialists and bankers. As one Finance Ministry official said at the time, 'they belong to that class whom the policy of inflation has enriched and whom the ineptitude of Division III of the Treasury (Tax Revenue) has allowed to escape the payment of their just dues to the state'.[2]

Nonetheless, since the world was being asked to accept that the holders of Germany's true national wealth were behind the scheme, it was understandable that the Rentenbank's upper echelons were stuffed with such worthies. The existence of the Rentenbank, and its ability to issue currency notes, was then approved by the Reichstag on 27 October.

The currency would be issued on 15 November in strictly limited quantities. The limited amount of the money to be put into circulation was to act as a straitjacket on inflation. Where for five years the Reichsbank had been printing money as needed for industry, the central government, states and municipalities, thus increasing the amount in circulation to a dizzying degree, all these bodies would now have to cut their cloth according to the amount of money available, which would not be much. In effect, it was also a tool in the process of reducing government spending.

The plan was that, beginning in November, a good proportion of the salaries of state and municipal employees would be paid in Rentenmarks. On the other hand, half of the pool of Rentenmarks would be going automatically to industry and commerce. With the printing of the old paper marks ceasing on 15 November at the same time as the new currency was introduced, the states and municipalities were going to have to cut their expenditure and their payrolls in order to ensure they could cover salaries with the limited amounts of Rentenmarks available.[3]

By the beginning of November, the issuing of the new currency was just over two weeks away. On the second day of the month, the Reichsbank issued a 100-trillion mark note. Everyone round the cabinet table agreed that after fifteen years at the helm it was time for Reichsbank Director Havenstein, now sixty-six, to go. Havenstein refused, pointing to the bank autonomy law. The Chancellor and his Finance Minister, Hans Luther, began casting around for someone they planned to call a 'Currency Commissioner', with ministerial rank, who, given the stand-off with Havenstein, could run the reform process and also, incidentally, be used to bypass the Reichsbank where necessary during the transition period. A youngish banker of some brilliance, Director of the Darmstädter and National Bank, with good relations to the British and the Americans, came under consideration. He did not think much of Helfferich's suggested solution to the currency crisis, but was ambitious and patriotic, and a member of the German Democratic Party. That ambition would take him a long way, in some cases to places he would regret having gone, but for now it seemed a wholly positive influence. His name was Horace Greeley Hjalmar Schacht.

In everyday dealings, preference was meanwhile being given, every-where, to those with foreign currency, or face-value certificates based on the domestic dollar loan. Yet another exchange law, passed on 23 October, firmly stated that foreign currency was to be exchanged only at the officially published rate, on pain of up to three years' imprison-ment and a fine up to ten times the value of the sum involved.[4]

Industry was vocal in its protests at the new fixed-exchange-rate law, which in practice deliberately overvalued the paper mark. It was claimed that this would seriously affect the cost of doing business, and would also – because in recent weeks almost all everyday transac-tions were conducted in gold values translated according to a daily rate into paper marks – raise prices for consumers. In practice, the millions of ordinary people who had become used to these calcula-tions simply ignored the new law.

How much (or, rather, how little) attention ordinary Germans paid to such government regulations was clear to all but the blindest bureaucrat. An Englishwoman long resident in Germany, and married into a German family, described shopping in an unnamed provincial city in November 1923 for a basic piece of household equipment (a smoothing iron). Having been lent a dollar note by her nephew, and bearing a bundle of high-denomination paper marks on her own account, she described visiting an ironmonger whose 'windows are covered with a stout iron grating as a protection against a possible rush of Communists attracted by aluminium saucepans in the window':

> I have a friend at the ironmonger's to whom I was very kind during the war. What ages ago! I brought her pears and tomatoes from my garden. Once I gave her a fresh egg. She is the head shop assistant. It is quite early and she is at liberty. She says she ought not to do it, but she will chance it and let me have the iron at yesterday's price. It is really 150 billions.* Because of the pears and the tomatoes I am to have it at 80. Discreetly, in a corner behind the counter, I produce the dollar bill, and mention with an air of finality that it is worth 55 billions today. Bank rate. She replies without a moment's hesitation that dollars are only to be accepted as representing 40 billions today . . . I make up the 80 billions and flee away with my iron. But I feel convinced that the dollar note will be changed for at least 75 billions tomorrow.[5]

In this no-man's-land between the extreme hyperinflation and the currency reform, 'articles in shops are now often ticketed with "gold prices" . . . [which] require fresh calculation every day'. The English-woman described another occasion when she bought a small packet of black dye:

---

* 'Milliards' in the original. German (long-scale) milliards are changed to Anglo-American (short-scale) billions and German billions to Anglo-American trillions throughout the text.

The youth at the *Drogerie* . . . says it costs 15 pfennig. I stare at him, and he stares back abstractedly. He makes calculations on a paper bag. They seem to worry him. He begins them all over again on the other side of the paper bag. There are several weary customers in the shop. (Shopping takes time nowadays.) At last he looks up and says, '375 millions'. I recover my breath and turn out my market basket, in which million mark scheins [notes]are done up in bales.

At home, she pays a seamstress for some repair work on the family's clothes. The bill is 24 billion marks. Her payment method is typically shrewd:

I offered her lard at 12 billion to the pound, and she jumped at it. I found out afterwards that lard had gone up that afternoon from 12 to 16½ billions. But I had bought a quantity of lard at 8 billions some time ago. That is my latest 'device'. When I have marks that I want to dispose of quickly, I invest them in edibles of a durable nature. This is the most stable form of circulating medium. I can pay my library subscriptions in rice or dried plums, and my dentist's bill in condensed milk. Eggs, too, are greedily accepted. But for ordinary shopping this kind of specie has its drawbacks, even when you take the perambulator with you as your purse.

It all seems light-hearted enough, even absurdly comical in its way. But our lady reporter from 1923 has a garden with pears and tomatoes, and by the sound of it, hens that lay eggs. She is not about to take part in a food riot, of the kind that is becoming increasingly common in German towns and cities. Nor would she, a correspondent of the *Manchester Guardian*, have had anything to do with other, even uglier disturbances that were taking place, in the first week of November 1923, in Berlin.

In the Scheunenviertel, the slum area in east-central Berlin, near the Alexanderplatz, significant numbers of Polish Jews had settled in recent years. Many scratched a living as pedlars and traders. On

Monday, 5 November, these immigrants, predominantly Orthodox and therefore easily identifiable, dubbed by the often hostile natives *Galizier*, were subjected to an attack by a mob. The attackers, however, were not Nazis but unemployed working-class Berliners, of the type who probably mostly voted Social Democrat or Communist.

As in Paris at the time of the French Revolution, the trouble started with the price of bread. On that Monday in the first week of November, it was announced by the local price authorities in Berlin that a loaf would henceforth cost 140 billion marks. Crowds began besieging bakeries and haranguing the store owners. The increase in the cost of their families' staple food caused thousands of angry unemployed men to gather in protest around the Alexanderplatz, the heart of working-class eastern Berlin. They called for an increase in their doles, which were paid out in the form of emergency money printed by the municipality. This was not forthcoming and, in any case, they were told that the authorities had run out of money with which to pay them. The crowd started to turn ugly.

All it needed was rumours – fed, so the press at the time asserted, by professional anti-Semitic agitators – that shady unofficial money changers among the *Galizier* had been trading gold loan certificates for this dole money. The activities of these Jews, the story went, had led to the shortage of money, leaving the needy working men of eastern Berlin destitute. A tide of violence, destruction and plunder, directed at businesses and homes identified as belonging to Jews, spread throughout the quarter.

One of the most sinister aspects of the violence was that, according to the *Vossische Zeitung*, the Berlin police initially chose not to intervene, but then, when forced to do so, actually beat up and then arrested, not the attackers but the Jews who were being assaulted. These were scenes which, as the paper pointed out, it would have been impossible to imagine before the war. During the night of 5 November, the attacks continued and spread throughout the working-class parts of the city, including the north and parts of Charlottenburg as well as the east, concentrating on bakeries, grocery stores, tobacco and cigar shops.[6] They did not diminish the next day, when it was announced that the bread price would not be rising so steeply after all. Only when Reichswehr units joined the hard-pressed Berlin police did the crowds finally begin to disperse.[7]

As the rioting subsided and order was restored in Berlin, the Social Democratic Trade Unions and their allied white-collar organisations issued a statement. They blamed the violence on nationalist agitators, pointing out that it was in the interests of such people to encourage this kind of disorder, not just to whip up hatred of the Jews, but to fuel the calls for a dictatorship of the right as the only solution to the country's problems.[8] Whether this was true or not, certainly the Scheunenviertel pogrom found an immediate echo elsewhere in Germany at the end of the first week in November 1923. Anti-Semitic violence followed in Erfurt, Nuremberg, Coburg, Bremen and Oldenburg. Even the banker Max Warburg left his native Hamburg for twenty-four hours when he heard that prominent Jews, himself among them, were being singled out by agitators.[9]

The 'red menace' in Saxony and Thuringia may have been dealt with, and the end of the hyperinflation may have been in sight, but the far right had not given up its ambition to destroy the Republic. If anything, for the real fanatics, the Berlin government's successes made action more urgent than ever.

Hitler, once the darling of the Bavarian regime, had become somewhat isolated during the past weeks. Kahr and Lossow had protected his party and his newspaper, the *Völkischer Beobachter*, from the legal restrictions that had made it hard for the Nazis to operate elsewhere in Germany. After the 'Reich Enforcement' against Saxony, however, the situation had changed.

With Communism suddenly no longer an immediate threat, the right-wing paramilitaries were robbed of their main rationale. Kahr and Lossow, and even Erhardt, spread along the northern border of Bavaria with his mix of old Freikorps hands and nationalist volunteers, now seemed to hesitate. The anti-Berlin rhetoric did not change, but the 'march on Berlin' no longer seemed an urgent prospect, especially as General Seeckt had finally made it clear that he would not support the planned imposition by force of an extra-parliamentary dictatorship.[10]

For Kahr and Lossow and the rest of the right-wing clique in charge in Munich, a violent strike against the Republic, while still desirable, was not, for the moment, an urgent political priority. It was time to rethink and regroup. Hitler, on the other hand, had spent the past four years building an attack animal of a political movement, specifically designed for the violent seizure of power. Quite rightly, from his point of view, he understood that without action, his political base, and with it his extremely promising career, would collapse.

On Thursday, 8 November 1923, Hitler made his move. Kahr was due to address his supporters that evening at the vast Bürgerbräukeller beer hall on the Rosenheimer Strasse, in the centre of Munich. Alongside him on the platform would be Lossow, the Reichswehr commander, and the third member of the triumvirate that ruled Bavaria, the state police chief, Colonel Hans von Seisser. The next day would bring the fifth anniversary of the declaration of the hated Republic – perfect timing for the 'march on Berlin' that would, so the nationalists hoped, destroy it.

So it was that, at around 8:30 p.m., Hitler stomped into the Bürgerbräukeller at the head of a group of armed followers. Kahr, flanked by Lossow and Seisser, was in the midst of delivering a blistering attack on the central government to a packed crowd of some 3,000 nationalists. He stopped in mid-flow, forced to watch as steel-helmeted Hitler supporters dragged a machine gun into position at the back of the hall. Pushing on into the cavernous, smoke-filled room, waving a Browning pistol and followed by his SA chief, Hermann Goering, and a gang of storm troopers, Hitler stood on a chair to address the crowd. Unable to make himself heard, he fired his pistol at the ceiling and, when the noise level dropped, explained that the building was surrounded by armed men. He then declared that the Bavarian government was deposed. The 'national revolution' had begun.[11]

Leaving Goering and the storm troopers to manage the crowd ('You've got your beer!' the future Reich Marshal assured them), Hitler and his acolytes herded Kahr and the other two at pistol point into a back room. There they were joined by General Ludendorff, who had arrived in full Imperial Army uniform. Once they had set up a new regime in Berlin, Hitler assured his captives, Ludendorff would be the new Commander-in-Chief with dictatorial powers, while Lossow was promised the post of Reichswehr Minister and Seisser Police Minister. Kahr would be appointed *Landesverweser* (Regent) of Bavaria. All they had to do was to promise their support for the 'national revolution'. After some further discussion, they agreed. Then, at Ludendorff's insistence, after giving more or less convincing speeches in Hitler's favour, Kahr and co. were released, on their word of honour that they would do nothing to oppose the Nazi takeover. These officials were, after all, 'honourable' men, were they not? Hitler then addressed the crowd himself and was received rapturously by the same huge audience that had applauded Kahr just a few hours earlier. The putsch seemed to have got off to a fine start. Hitler had found his hour.

Setting Kahr, Lossow and Seisser free proved, in fact, the conspirators' greatest mistake. The triumvirate promptly welshed on their promise – which had, after all, been extracted under duress – and spent the night hours energetically organising resistance to Hitler and Ludendorff. By the time dawn broke on 9 November, it was clear that, outside the Bürgerbräukeller, things had started to go wrong.

Hitler declared his determination to carry on to the death – never a good sign, as the future would prove – and urged his storm troopers likewise, although he apparently also sent a party out to seize bundles of 50-billion mark notes straight off the presses of the Bavarian State Printers, just to make sure they all had something to show for their trouble.[12] The Führer's paramilitaries also carried out some arrests of political opponents, including Social Democratic city councillors.[13]

The crunch came when, late the next morning, the Nazis' now

somewhat shaky putsch plan moved on to what they had hastily agreed would be stage two – a march on the Bavarian Defence Ministry. There the rebels found themselves opposed by troops and police.

Although Hitler's supporters and allies totalled around 2,000, the less numerous opposing forces held firm. When some hotheads on the Nazi side started shooting, a short but sharp gun battle followed. Within about half a minute, dead and wounded Hitlerites littered the street. General Ludendorff, however, unflinchingly continued to advance through the police ranks and into the ministry square. By then, most of his co-rebels, including Hitler, had already fled. The old soldier calmly gave himself up.

Other Nazis were arrested at the scene, though many fled over the border into Austria, including future leaders of the Third Reich such as Rudolf Hess and Hermann Goering. Hitler himself was taken into custody at the country house of a sympathiser outside Munich two days later.

Sixteen Nazi 'martyrs' had lost their lives, including Max von Scheubner-Richter, another nationalist writer who had joined forces with the Führer. He had been standing next to Hitler, arm in arm, when the shooting started. As the historian Ian Kershaw has averred, had the bullet been directed a foot to the right, the world's history might have taken a different course.

So, shortly after noon on 9 November 1923, the last great political threat to the young German democracy was dealt with – at least for now. Six days later, it was the turn of the economic enemy.

The irony was that, although Gustav Stresemann still occupied the Chancellor's residence, Germany did indeed have a dictator by the end of the night of 8/9 November 1923. After attending an emergency meeting of the cabinet late on the evening of 8 November, President Ebert delegated absolute command of the German armed forces, and also executive power in the Reich, to General Seeckt. It was a bold, or perhaps desperate move, for Seeckt was no friend of democracy and, as we now know, had indeed indulged in discussions with its enemies about establishing a dictatorial regime.[14] Fortunately, the same fastidious legalism that had, in the end, kept Seeckt from joining up with Kahr and friends guided him during the period to come. The Republic survived the time of Seeckt's supremacy, which would last into the new year.

On 11 November, Dr Schacht accepted the post of Currency Commissioner. Production of the new Rentenmark had already begun. Germans would once more have to deal with small-denomination coins as well as paper money. There were one- and two-pfennig coins minted of copper with a small amount of tin, and five-, ten- and fifty-pfennig pieces out of bronzed aluminium. These were to be produced at the Prussian mint. The notes, to be produced at the Reich Printing House and a selection of other trusted printing works, would run in eight denominations, from one to a thousand Rentenmarks. They would be printed on both sides (at the height of the hyperinflation, they had often, for ease and cheapness, been printed on just one), on high-quality paper, with designs redolent of virtuous agricultural productivity, appropriate to the currency's backing. Everything was calculated to inspire confidence.

By 10 November, only a little over 78,000,000 gold marks' worth of the new currency had been produced. This was slow going. The Rentenmark was supposed to be in restricted supply, but not this restricted. And then, not for the first time, the workers at the Reich Printing House went on strike.

According to Finance Minister Luther, the stoppage was motivated by a new fear for German printers – the fear that, because less money would now be produced and therefore many presses closed down, they would lose their jobs. The next day, Seeckt, entering into the spirit of his new responsibilities, issued an order banning all strikes in plants producing banknotes, and also took the precaution of having the strike leaders taken into protective custody. This, combined with the preparedness of white-collar and other workers at the printing offices to take on tasks usually done by the strikers, and the drafting in of volunteers from the *Technische Nothilfe*

(Technical Emergency Aid),* meant that the hiccup in production was not too severe.

By 15 November, some 200 million gold marks' worth were ready for distribution. It was still not really enough – one important factor seems to have been a shortage of the high-grade paper that the notes were printed on[15] – and there had been a brief hesitation before the decision was made to go ahead. The benefits to morale of having the new currency in circulation, even if in inadequate quantities, were thought so important (and a postponement correspondingly disastrous), that a delay was felt to be impossible. In any case, instructions had already been issued for 30 per cent of the next month's salary for government officials to be paid in Rentenmarks, and the order could not be rescinded.[16]

The issue of Rentenmarks went ahead, the printing of Rentenmarks continued, while at the same time the printing presses for the inflationary paper marks were stopped. It was the moment, or, rather the day, of truth for Germany.

The first Rentenmarks went out in the form of credits to banks and companies in agreed quantities. On 17 November, the *Vossische Zeitung* told its readers that, given the shortage of notes, it would be a few days before Rentenmarks were available over bank counters as cash:

First we should keep in mind that we have deceived ourselves, because of the illusion of huge numbers, about the amount of work that has to be accomplished if the task is to produce, for example, a hundred million Rentenmarks in one mark notes. That corresponds to a sum of a hundred quintillion paper marks, i.e. a great part of our entire circulation, represented in trillion notes.[17]

* An organisation set up in 1919 by former military engineers to help overcome post-war disruptions. Having become closely associated with the Nazi regime, especially during the war years, it was abolished in 1945 by the victorious Allies. It was, however, re-founded in West Germany in 1950 as the *Technisches Hilfswerk*, under which name it continues its work today.

Getting the German public, after years of big numbers, to think small, was obviously going to be one of the chief problems. Another problem was that for some days after the new currency was launched on 15 November, it was still not clear exactly what its exchange rate against the dollar would be, and therefore exactly its relationship to the old pre-war gold mark. On the actual date of the launch, the official rate of the paper mark was doubled to 2.2520 trillion to the dollar, or 600 billion to the gold mark. The rate remained unchanged for five days. There followed a behind-the-scenes struggle between conservative gentlemen of the Rentenbank (who were allowed to, and were keen to, make a profit) and the Reich and the Reichsbank. The Reich, which was allotted 300 million Rentenmarks as an interest-free loan from the Rentenbank, with another 900 million to be made available on a discretionary basis on the Rentenbank's part, was supposed to use this money to buy up the Reich Treasury notes in circulation (valued in inflationary paper marks), thus eliminating that debt. The more the paper mark depreciated, the cheaper the Reich could buy up the debt. It worked the other way round for the Rentenbank, which wanted to sell Rentenmarks for as many paper marks as possible, and for those paper marks to keep as much value as possible.

Not until 20 November 1923 was a fixed exchange rate announced, and this was conditioned largely by arithmetical convenience. Since the pre-war gold mark had for a long time bought 10/42 of a dollar, it was finally agreed that the exchange rate for paper marks would be set at 4.2 trillion to the dollar. The same applied to other foreign currencies, such as the pound, where the rate was fixed at 18 trillion paper marks, or 18 marks in the new currency. It followed that, since the value of the Rentenmark was fixed at one per 1 trillion paper marks, by lopping off twelve zeros this would automatically restore the old pre-war exchange rate.

And one more thing. With the establishment of a 1-trillion paper mark to one Rentenmark value, Germany's post-war domestic debt – founded overwhelmingly on all those virtuous citizens who had bought war bonds in the hope of a small regular reward for their patriotism – was reduced from 154 billion marks in November 1918 to exactly 15.4 pfennigs in November 1923.

Whatever its continuing wrangles over reparations, the government stood in the unique position internationally of owing virtually nothing internally. Correspondingly, of course, millions of Germans had seen government-fostered inflation finally and definitively rob them of their apparently blue-chip, government-backed investments.

By a bizarre coincidence, in the small hours of the same day, 20 November, when the value of the paper mark would be stabilised at such a surreal-seeming level, Reichsbank President Rudolf Havenstein, the man who to a great degree must be held responsible for bringing the currency and the economy to this pass, suddenly died of a heart attack at his official residence, aged sixty-six.

As late as 19 November, Havenstein had written a lengthy and passionate letter to Reich President Ebert, yet again refusing to resign, and bitterly protesting that he and other executives of the Reichsbank could not be dismissed under the Decree for Public Personnel Reduction without endangering the institution's precious independence.[18]

Havenstein's deputy, Glasenapp, immediately took over. An expert in currency and coinage, he stood firmly behind the currency reform. And unlike Havenstein, he supported the new policy of severely restricting credit, no matter how much both business and government complained about being short of money. Within two weeks the Reichsbank, under its acting president, would issue an order stipulating that all new credit must be taken out in 'valorised' (i.e. fixed rate) money, and repaid in it, too, at full value.[19] No more borrowing money and repaying it in worthless currency.

As for Schacht, in his capacity of Currency Commissioner the true master of Germany's money at this juncture, he moved very quickly. Within two days of the Rentenmark's appearance, he took action against the 'wild', unbacked issues of emergency money that had helped drive the hyperinflation into its terminal paroxysm. None would be accepted after 24 November, although there was a special exemption until the end of the month for the occupied territories in the west, which had problems of their own, and where the currency reform would not be introduced until the next year.

With Schacht cracking the whip, the Reichsbank also ended up refusing to accept the vast amount – 114.7 quintillion paper marks – of self-printed currency issued by the German Railways. Glasenapp, warming (now that his boss was dead) to his new role as assistant master of the nation's financial straitjacket, announced at the end of November 1923 that Germany had to learn discipline, however hard the experience. 'Impoverishment and shortage of capital,' he said, 'cannot be eliminated through artificial capital, the granting of credits and inflation.'

The new disciplinarianism was part of a chill wind from the right in German politics that gathered force as the inflation came to an end and Chancellor Stresemann's government entered its final, somewhat desperate phase. Though the immediate threat of a violent right-wing putsch was past, it became clear in the last two months of 1923 that the creation of the Rentenbank amounted to a kind of seizure of power by the old elite.

The Rentenbank's composition and structure, and its crucial role in the desperately hoped-for currency reform, placed representatives of industrial and agricultural interests in a position of extraordinary power over the government and the Reichstag. Government records show that, on 15 November, the administrative committee of the Rentenbank paid a visit to the Chancellor. The official reason was the inauguration of the Rentenmark. However, actually, it seems, the committee's members used the occasion to deliver a collective tirade calling for the abolition of the eight-hour day, the end of compulsory collective bargaining, reform of the unemployment relief system and a host of other pro-business reforms.

The Rentenbank could threaten to – and frequently actually did – withhold credit from the government, and from any organisations it considered, from its highly conservative point of view, unworthy. The realisation of this led the Social Democratic deputy, Otto Wels, to declare in an angry speech to the Reichstag that the budgetary power of that body had seemingly been transferred to the Agrarian League and the Reich Association of German industry. The liberal *Frankfurter Zeitung* agreed about the power of the Rentenbank, complaining that 'there are today in Germany astonishing notions of dictatorship: the exclusion of the parliament and the introjection of the chief powers of the private economy appears to be the ideal for many people today'.[20]

The interests represented by the Rentenbank would get a lot of what they wanted, but they would not get them from Chancellor Stresemann and his administration. In any case, General Seeckt now ran many aspects of the country's affairs that would formerly have been the responsibility of ministers. The Reichstag did not meet at all between 13 October, when the enabling law was passed, and 20 November. Stresemann's government had actually achieved an astonishing amount in a little more than three months, for the final three weeks of which it was reduced to a rump of its former power by the withdrawal of the Social Democrats. And it was the Social Democrats who now sealed its doom.

The vote of no confidence in the government which the Social Democrats tabled on 22 November 1923 was founded in the old accusation that Stresemann had sent the Reichswehr into action against socialist Saxony and Thuringia, but not against nationalist Bavaria. It never came to a vote, because Stresemann decided that, rather than cling to power, weakened by parliamentary attacks, he would preferred to propose a motion of his own, one of confidence, and so make an end to it one way or the other. Such a motion, asking the Reichstag to support him, failed, and he resigned.

President Ebert, knowing how destructive the Social Democrats' action would be, had tried two days earlier to persuade them to withdraw their motion of no confidence and thus allow Stresemann to remain in power until the crisis was finally past. When it became clear that they would not retreat, he chided his old socialist comrades with the bitterly prophetic remark: 'The thing that prompts you to bring down the chancellor will be forgotten in six weeks, but you will feel the consequences of your stupidity for ten years to come.'[21]

For good or ill, the fate of the German currency and economy was, for now, out of the hands of the politicians. If that left the formidable Dr Schacht, and the almost offensively rigorous administrative committee of the Rentenbank, largely in charge of the economy, this was perhaps not such a bad thing, from the point of view of impressing both the German public and the foreigners who would decide the currency's future. As the London *Times* commented, beneath the sceptical headline, 'Rentenmarks Issue: Risk of Failure':

> With the introduction of the Rentenmark the process of borrowing by way of discounted Treasury bills and thereby increasing the note circulation is to cease. For this cessation, Herr Schacht is to be responsible, and it is understood that he has every intention of keeping strictly to it. Whether the Rentenmark is to escape the fate of the paper mark will depend upon this factor . . . It is obvious that unless the budget is balanced by combining economy with taxation the Rentenmark is foredoomed to the same fate as the paper mark.[22]

It was all to do with trust, as was obvious from the start. That trust did not immediately appear. Schacht himself, the Currency Commissioner, in his authority's cramped, makeshift offices in part of the Finance Ministry building, famously did not go out much or process a lot of paperwork (although it is true he did go to the Ruhr in the last week of November to check up on the – predictably miserable – situation). According to his secretary of many years' standing, Fräulein Steffeck, his office was a storage closet, until recently used by the office cleaner. Asked about what his duties involved, she replied:

> What did he do? He sat on his chair and smoked in his little dark room which still smelled of old floor cloths. Did he read letters? No, he read no letters. Did he write letters? No, he wrote no letters. He telephoned a great deal – he telephoned in every direction and to

every German or foreign place that had anything to do with money and foreign exchange as well as with the Reichsbank and the Finance Minister. And he smoked. We did not eat much during that time. We usually went home late, often by the last suburban train, travelling third class. Apart from that he did nothing.[23]

Dr Schacht was busy creating trust, in other words.

The official rate quoted for paper marks remained at 4.2 trillion to the dollar in the days following 20 November – by law, since earlier that autumn, it was illegal to trade the currency within Germany at any other value. Abroad, however, its value continued to deteriorate. At one point the paper mark reached 6.7 trillion to the dollar in New York, but on 3 December it did, in fact, settle at the official rate. A triumph for Schacht and the Rentenbank.

The legend of the overnight success of the Rentenmark was nevertheless just that, a legend. A success it undoubtedly was, but it took time. A month after the Rentenmark's introduction, *The Times* was referring once again to 'German Financial Chaos' and claiming that the government was running out of money. Its correspondent claimed that the Rentenmark was being used only for hoarding, and that he personally had never actually seen one of the new currency notes.[24] Not until a few days before Christmas did the paper grudgingly admit:

The Rentenmark and the gold loan have brought a certain temporary stability. Prices, after soaring wildly, have begun to fall again, and the nerves of the population have been calmed by the substitution of something like steady values for the incalculably shifting millions.[25]

The *Manchester Guardian*, on the other hand, as early as 13 December enthusiastically wrote of 'New Confidence in Germany. A Stable Currency':

There is no doubt that the mood of the German people has changed profoundly during the last fortnight . . . despondency has given way to confidence, not very exuberant perhaps, but unmistakable. What are the causes? And is the outlook really as bright now as it was gloomy a month ago?

The predominating cause is the stabilising of the mark. The nightmare of astronomic figures and of brain-wearying calculations in millions, milliards and billions over every petty transaction has vanished. The purchasing power of paper money no longer dwindles to nothing overnight. The incalculable and shifting uncertainties caused by a depreciating currency are gone . . .

. . . Now that the currency is stable, the mistrust of the farmers has diminished, and the country is in fuller measure supplying the towns with food. The shortage of flour, potatoes, meat, and dairy produce, at one time almost desperate, has been relieved; not that there is plenty or even enough, but nevertheless there is an improvement.[26]

Hjalmar Schacht was finally appointed to the post of Reichsbank President on 22 December 1923, beating off a challenge from the inventor of the Rentenmark, Karl Helfferich, who in the end was considered too likely to alienate the Allied reparations and loans negotiators. Immediately after his appointment, Schacht was invited to London by the Governor of the Bank of England, Montagu Norman, who further made his positive feelings clear by meeting his new German colleague personally on arrival at Liverpool Street Station.[27] Schacht's move to the far grander surroundings of the Jägerstrasse undoubtedly helped confidence.

All the same, it would be well into the new year, by general agreement, before the new currency could truly be regarded as stable. The main reason was, as of old, doubt among the financial experts, especially internationally, about the ability of the German government, now – as *The Times* pointed out – chronically short of funds, to resist the temptation to surreptitiously start the printing presses turning again.

So far as most Germans were concerned, however, the *feeling* of change and hope was almost immediate. A million small incidents meant that, although weeks passed until the Rentenmark went into wide circulation, it quickly established a presence in the national psyche.

Not everyone had believed that the new currency would work, of course. A Munich lawyer, Karl Lowenstein, arrived by train at the German border after 20 November 1923, having been on a trip to Italy. He was surprised to find that the booking office at the station inside Germany demanded a valorised fare that amounted to much more money than he had on him. When Herr Lowenstein asked how, if this was so, he could get home to Munich, the ticket clerk gestured behind him. There were dozens of watches hanging from the wall of his booth. Like these travellers before him, Lowenstein would have to pawn his watch to pay his fare.[28] Welcome to the beginning of post-inflation Germany!

With less government money (and a tougher attitude towards spending it), this was going to be a hard winter for many. Unemployment was going to stay high for a while, made worse by mass sackings from the civil service and the railways, before it began to fall. In December, the new minority, non-socialist government, which after almost a week's hiatus succeeded Stresemann's, all but abandoned the eight-hour day and other revolutionary achievements that had benefited the workers (though not necessarily the wider economy). Adolf Hitler went on trial for his rebellion, though he was not, since the Weimar justice remained 'blind in the right eye', severely punished. Gustav Stresemann remained Foreign Minister, and would continue to do so for almost six years. And by early in 1924 Germany was finally discussing revisions to the Versailles reparations clauses, and a generous American loan. Of the new Chancellor, the somewhat bloodless Catholic lawyer, Wilhelm Marx, the *Manchester Guardian* wrote:

Herr Marx is a non-committal person who excites neither animosity nor devotion. Nobody wants to assassinate him, and nobody longs to die for him. A kind of twilight calm has set in; home politics lies dormant, so to speak.

After the terrible excitements of the previous five years, this almost
sounded like progress.

The end of inflation brought the German people down to earth
with a bump, and, although bruised by the fall, at least they finally
knew where they were and could make plans. As Herr von der Ohe,
the rural teacher and farmer who had coped better during the inflation period than many other Germans, would comment when he had
spent some months getting paid once again in marks that kept their
value: 'On 1 October I got 319 marks after deductions. In spite of
personal financial losses, we are happy to be able to lead a normal life
once more. We all hope that things will get better with the economy
as well.'[29] And for a while, the economy improved. Some even called
the next few years in Weimar Germany the 'Golden Twenties'.

But, of course, no one who had lost their money got it back. Not
the war bond holders, nor the savers, nor the professors and civil
servants and small business people who had seen their earnings
dwindle to nothing, and who had been forced to sell their 'things
of material value' to survive. When trouble came again, a little more
than half a decade later, they had nothing to fall back on. Moreover,
the government that faced the new economic crisis was too terrified
of renewed inflation to use the full array of financial options open
to it.

These factors, caused by the downfall of money, would in the fullness of time play a fatal role in the downfall of the first German
Democracy.

25

Bail-out

The Weimar hyperinflation – that dark, febrile carnival of the German mark – ended, not immediately but surprisingly quickly, with the introduction of the Rentenmark in November 1923. The Rentenmark was the construct upon which the German government and people, and also the international financial community, based their hopes for political and economic stability in the world's second most important industrial nation.

And, in fact, by the end of August 1924 Germany had a stable currency again. The Reichsmark put the country technically back on the gold standard – although direct convertibility, as it had existed before 1914, was never restored. It was equal with the Rentenmark, which remained in circulation. The inflation-era paper marks, initially still in circulation at an official fixed rate of 1 trillion to the new currency, disappeared from everyday use as the year went on.

The political fallout was not so quickly dealt with. Although Hitler had been arrested after the failed Munich putsch, and formally arraigned for high treason in February 1924, he had used the trial – aided by a cooperative nationalist judge – to successfully grandstand against the Republic and the 'November criminals'. Because Bavaria had 'opted out' of the 'Court for the Protection of the Republic' established after the assassination of Rathenau to punish such major political crimes, the proceedings took place, not in Leipzig, but in Munich. Justice all over Germany tended to go soft on right-wing crimes, but here in the counter-revolutionary south it all but bent over backwards to avoid real punishment.

For a bare-faced act of high treason, involving two dozen or so deaths, including that of police officers, the Führer was sentenced at the beginning of April 1924 to a mere five years' imprisonment. Moreover, time already served on remand was deducted. Parole would be possible after a mere six months, conditional on 'good behaviour'. Others received similar sentences. Ludendorff was acquitted altogether. High treason carried a maximum sentence of life in peacetime, in war one of death. After the 'Beer Hall Putsch', had the Bavarian courts possessed the will – or for that matter the desire – it would have been within their power to remove Hitler and the other violent enemies of democracy from the scene for many years to come. The courts did not choose to do so.

With the inflation stopped in its tracks, unemployment rose sharply, as the government had feared it would. The government parties were punished in the first of two nationwide elections held in 1924, losing more seats to the far right and the left. Despite the fact that its leader was in jail, Hitler's Nazi Party and its 'Folkish' allies won thirty-two seats in the Reichstag. The Communist Party's representation shot up to sixty-two.

Fortunately, that was not the end of the story. When another election was called in December 1924, in an attempt to break the political deadlock, the economy had started to expand once more and the job market to improve. The extremist tide proved to have ebbed. The Communists lost seventeen seats. The ultra-nationalist grouping's representation dropped even more dramatically by more than 50 per cent, back to fourteen. Although the extreme right's main leader, Hitler, was released from his comfortable imprisonment at Schloss Landsberg in that same month, relatively little would be heard of him for the next five years.

During the year or so following the end of the inflation, however, nature punished an astonishing number of the other main protagonists of the inflation saga by removing them from this world altogether, in the prime of their lives. Reichsbank Governor Havenstein had died suddenly in November 1923 in his mid-sixties. Then Hugo Stinnes, long a martyr to gall bladder problems, finally consented to surgical intervention in the spring of 1924. The richest man in Germany died on 10 April, a few days after the botched operation, at the age of fifty-four. Almost immediately, his business empire began a rapid disintegration. Stinnes was followed to the grave less than two weeks later by Karl Helfferich, who had promised the nation that the Allies would 'carry the weight' of financing the First World War. During his career, he had been Imperial Treasury Secretary, Vice-Chancellor of the Empire, passionate hater of the Republic, but nevertheless co-creator of the Rentenmark. Aged only fifty-one, Helfferich was killed in a railway accident while on holiday in Switzerland, where, so he said, he often got his best ideas, such as the 'Rye Bank' that had formed the basis of the currency reform. Suddenly, at the end of February 1925, President Ebert succumbed to 'septic shock' after an emergency operation for appendicitis, and thus the Republic lost its first leader and its most dependable political fixer. He was barely fifty-four.

Germany, with its currency and politics more settled, was neverthe-less now considered a better risk – even by the same foreigners who had lost a great deal of money betting on the mark in the early years of the inflation. She finally completed arrangements to borrow a great deal of money – to pay the reparations still owed to the Allies. This was the longed-for 'bail-out'. America was booming again, with capital to burn, and keen to put it to use in Europe, especially Germany. Over the next five years, 21 *billion* marks – 5 billion dollars at 1920s prices, probably between 60 and 70 billion dollars in today's values – flowed into the German economy, most of it from eager American investors.

In 1928, the standard of living of working Germans reached a level comfortably above that which they had enjoyed before the First World War. However, the country was not the same place it had been a decade and a half earlier. It had been transformed by war, and by the death and resurrection of its financial system. The inflation, horrendous as it was for many individuals, had made the country more equal in many ways, more like other advanced industrial societies.

One figure crucial to understanding the depth and social significance of the change in 1913 has already been mentioned. The proportion of Germany's national income going to *rentiers* – people living from the proceeds of their investments – had been 15 per cent. By 1925–6, it had fallen drastically to around 3 per cent. These so-called 'passive' capitalists (who included wide swathes of the educated middle class) became a far less important factor in German society. The 'active' capitalists – industrialists, bankers and traders – and the producers – manual workers – now prospered.

Meanwhile, the federal states and cities used their plentiful borrowed money and invested in modern housing for ordinary Germans, who for so long had suffered from terrible living conditions. Around 2.5 million new dwellings, housing some 9 million people, were built during the Weimar era. The new principle was one of 'light, air, sun'. They attracted architects of national and international reputation to design idealistic modern developments in all the major cities.

After the currency had stabilised, the 'passive' capitalists tried to get back what they had lost in the inflation – their mortgages, their investments, the interest on their war bonds. By and large, they failed to get compensation. The class that had suffered drastic downward mobility during these years did not, for the most part, regain anything close to its former prosperity.

Every commentator of the time, left or right, agrees that a major and lasting effect of the hyperinflation was to encourage cynicism and selfishness. Life in early Weimar Germany felt, for most Germans alive at the time, like a zero-sum game, in which the main object was to avoid being left holding worthless paper money. And where the race for survival belonged to the swift, the cunning and the ruthless. This was the shape-shifting, unpredictable, pitilessly exploitative world of Fritz Lang's famous film, *Dr Mabuse the Gambler*.

Another figure tells us why this may have been allowed to happen, and why the cynicism penetrated deep into the roots of the German psyche after the First World War. In 1918, the German government owed 154 billion gold marks in domestic war debt. When the twelve noughts were wiped off the mark at the end of the inflation to give values in the new Rentenmark, that debt amounted to a sum total of 15.4 new pfennigs.[1] Whatever the republican government's intentions – some scholars feel the inflation was a conspiracy, some not – it had, in practical terms, *confiscated* the money its most loyal citizens had lent it to fight the First World War.

All the same, the economy of the Weimar Republic seemed to have stabilised, and with it the political situation.

But by the end of the decade, behind the façade of the so-called 'Golden Twenties', which had turned Berlin, especially, into such a symbolic city of enjoyment and experiment, Weimar Germany was once more in trouble. Farming, which had booked such spectacular gains during the inflation, pretty much went bust. The unemployment rate remained, though not catastrophic in its extent, stubbornly high. There were banking crises, as the huge overseas debt proved near impossible to service. This was even before the Wall Street crash of 1929 brought the long boom in America to a disastrous halt. Weimar Germany had become, as later historians would describe it, a 'mortgaged democracy'.

And so it came about, that when the American bankers wanted their money back from their German creditors, the latter could not pay. A slump, 6 million unemployed and a return to extremism and fighting on the streets of Berlin and other German cities was the result.

October 1929 had also removed from the equation the one politician who, of all his peers, might have played a crucial role in holding German democracy together during the coming storm. On the morning of 3 October 1929, Gustav Stresemann rose early, ready to begin another day's work as Germany's Foreign Minister and key member of the governing coalition, positions he had held now continuously for more than six years. He died in the bathroom of his villa at 5.30 a.m., having suffered a stroke while shaving. His wisdom, intelligence and network of political influence could be replicated by no other political figure in the country. Neither could his relationships with foreign statesmen, which had facilitated Germany's efforts to reintegrate itself into the international system as a full and peaceful participant over the past half-decade. Like so many other prominent Weimar figures, he was only in his early fifties when he died.

Following the collapse of the last 'Weimar Coalition' in 1930, torn apart by disagreements about the response to the new economic crisis and the resignation of Hermann Müller, its Social Democratic Chancellor, Germany was governed by presidential decree. Three more chancellors, none with a Reichstag majority, struggled to put the crisis-ridden country back on her feet. Meanwhile, the real power in the land had become the octogenarian President von Hindenburg, populariser of the 'stab in the back' myth of defeat, symbol of the alleged Prussian virtues, elected by a national vote after Ebert's sudden death as what more than one commentator has called Germany's 'substitute Kaiser'.

Heinrich Brüning, Franz von Papen and General Kurt von Schleicher followed each other over the next three years, each with less of a base in the Reichstag and each lasting appreciably less long than his predecessor. Anxious not to repeat the disastrous mistakes of the inflation period, they all – especially Brüning, the only financial expert among them – pursued grimly orthodox, deflationary economic and financial policies. Whatever these measures may have done for the nation's balance sheet, they caused great suffering and resentment, arguably artificially prolonging the crisis and promoting ever-increasing levels of mass unemployment that proved politically catastrophic. So the hyperinflation cast its deadly shadow over the new German crisis.

Many of the masses lost what trust they had left in the Republic. Democracy withered. And then Hitler, the troublemaker from Munich, did finally conquer Berlin.

Afterword

Why a German Trauma?

Of course, it was economic depression, not inflation, that finally brought Hitler to the Reich Chancellery, on 30 January 1933. But then he did not care which horse of the apocalypse he rode to power. Hyperinflation in the early 1920s had nurtured the seed of Nazism. A decade later, depression – accompanied by what might be called hyperausterity – brought the toxic plant into fruit.

Specifically a *German* trauma, though? Why is this? After all, the German inflation of 1914 to 1923 – it was a much slower, and more toxic, process than most people think – was not the only example of this phenomenon. For instance, after the First World War, Austria, Hungary, Russia and Poland suffered from hyperinflation. In fact, Hungary underwent the experience once more after the Second World War, on an even worse scale. As did Greece. France and Italy at various points suffered from severe to hyperinflation, too, but none of these countries seems to have been permanently scarred by the experience in the same way.

Almost every German after 1918 experienced the humiliation of defeat. Most suffered in some way, often severely, from the results of that defeat – shortages, political instability, rises in prices. A great country fell from a great height, and it is to that extent hardly surprising that the pain was all the more severe. But does this explain the lasting, almost obsessive memory of ruin that has persisted there ever since?

It was peculiar to Germany that the country's extensive and exceptionally privileged educated middle class, the *Bildungsbürgertum* – higher civil servants, academics and teachers, Protestant clergy, lawyers, doctors – suffered, arguably, most comprehensively. This was a class that had bought large numbers of war bonds, whose value had started to fall even before the end of the war. In the years following 1918 the return from these would dwindle to nothing. Professional salaries and fees had also started a steep decline during the war, a fact that had caused bitter complaint even while the Kaiser was still on the throne.

With socialists in power after 1918, the wages and welfare of ordinary workers, manual and junior white-collar alike, were far more important to the republican government. The incomes of the pre-war elite, which had already declined relative to that of the average German worker, did not increase sufficiently to keep up the standard of living such men and their families had been used to. The private wealth, based on property, savings and fixed-income investments, which had cascaded down the generations, suddenly all but evaporated. Their sons could not afford to study as their fathers and grandfathers had.

Crucially, it was not just a question of money. The prestige of the class to which most of these students belonged, since the eighteenth century closely associated with its services to the German monarchical states, also took a tumble. After 1918, with the glamour and power of monarchy no longer a decisive factor in Germany, even the social status of this class seemed doomed.

The *Bildungsbürgertum* felt humiliation arising from defeat in the war – it had always been keenly patriotic – political alienation from a republican system that seemed bent on denying its values and handing the country over to the ignorant proletariat – and, to cap it all, it was experiencing financial ruin, which it could blame on the inflationary financial policies of the republican government. No wonder the educated middle class decamped, in its overwhelming majority, to the nationalist right.

A cartoon in the satirical magazine *Simplicissimus* showed a threadbare member of the educated middle class begging a little soup from a gang of well-fed workers. It was a shameless exaggeration – many workers were also suffering from the ills of the country after 1918, and had less to fall back on than the *Bildungsbürgertum* – but there was enough truth in it to help explain the terrible divide that opened up in Germany during the early years of the Weimar Republic. The Herr Professor forced to beg. The self-description of the educated class as the 'new proletariat' or the 'new poor' became widespread at this time.

So, who did well out of the inflation in Germany? Creditors lost almost everything. By contrast, everyone, broadly speaking, who owed money, had their debt liquidated by inflation. And there were the profiteers and speculators, obviously. People who worked in banks – an area of business that mushroomed during the inflation. Investors in stocks and shares – unlike fixed investments, these increased in price along with inflation and over the years in many cases provided an excellent return. Farmers, who could pay off their mortgages and other debts, and who – especially if they were prepared to sell on the black market to middlemen and desperate town-dwellers – could charge high prices for their produce. And the industrialists such as Hugo Stinnes, who could borrow money from the Reichsbank at low interest, and pay it back in depreciated marks. They could also sell in export markets and use the foreign exchange from the sales to buy up businesses, properties and other material assets inside Germany. This is how Stinnes, by the time of his death, came to own or part-own a large shipping line, many hotels, newspapers, engineering, timber and pulp, and other enterprises, reckoned to have reached about 4,500 in total, as well as the mining and steel businesses where he had first made his fortune before the First World War. He was not alone in this, merely the best-known of the 'robber barons' of the inflation.

Even the workers did not, in most cases, suffer a steep fall in their standard of living until the runaway hyperinflation brought complete economic chaos from the spring of 1923 onwards, ended only by the currency reform in November 1923.

The hyperinflation ended in the winter of 1923–4 because the situation became so destructive and chaotic that even those (quite large) sections of the population that had coped with and even done well out of inflation almost until its end realised that things had gone too far. Even if the end of the inflation brought slump and unemployment – which it did for a while – by the autumn of 1923 its end was a national necessity.

As John Maynard Keynes had warned three years earlier, inflation was a means for governments to 'confiscate . . . an important part of the wealth of their citizens'.

The German educated middle classes certainly thought so, and with good reason. And what the *Bildungsbürgertum* felt and thought was, above all, extremely important in the formation of public opinion. It taught, it wrote, and even in the changed circumstances after 1918 it knew how to publicise its grievances. The collective memory of this group within German society was – perhaps remains, nine decades later – suffused not just with a sense of economic loss but also of stark social decline. Add into this mix a profound, almost existential bitterness, arising not just out of military defeat and revolution, but of being made to pay the price of a war for which they and most Germans – with some reason – never acknowledged sole responsibility. The resulting historical echo resonates beyond mere economics or even politics. As already noted, other countries have suffered from inflation, some equal to Germany's and some even worse, but it does not seem to have affected their national psyches to the same extent.

It seems, in the case of Germany, that this is in good part because a relatively small but once extraordinarily privileged social group, the *Bildungsbürgertum*, lost more than anyone else, as a result both of inflation and the lost war. This group also suffered from the demise of the elaborate network of monarchical privilege, spread over many localised power centres, that had been a particular feature of pre-1914 Germany, and in which the *Bildungsbürgertum*, as a kind of intellectual seneschal class, had played a key supporting role. Its children (and grandchildren) might not have matched the previous generations' exalted status and financial security, but because of their continuing inheritance of education, of pride and self-confidence, they turned out to be a great opinion-forming force during the next three-quarters of a century. Every educated family in Germany seemed (and even now seems still) to have a story of how the inflation had caused drastic forfeiture of status and wealth.

The fall of the *Bildungsbürgertum*, when it occurred, took place from a great height. It went from a position of unchallenged privilege within continental Europe's most powerful country to become, in practical terms, just one group competing in a modern political and economic marketplace for which it felt little else but contempt and loathing.

It was, of course, the sons of this class who provided the shock troops of the anti-Republican movement, acting as assassins and terrorists for the far right and its shadowy armed wing, represented by groups such as Organisation Consul. The conspiracy to murder Weimar's brightest and finest, Walter Rathenau, exemplified this principle. Interestingly, Erich von Salomon, after serving his five-year sentence for involvement in the Rathenau plot, became a well-known writer. His novel-cum-memoir *Der Fragebogen* (The Questionnaire), written after the Second World War as a critical response to the Allied denazification campaign, included something of an apologia for why young men of his cultivated background and intelligence became enemies of German democracy. The inflation, Versailles, national humiliation. It was all in there. After its publication in 1951, the book became a major bestseller of its time, exercising a profound influence on opinion in the new Federal Republic of West Germany and elsewhere in the world.

Thus, the Weimar-era *Bildungsbürgertum* passed an understandable and seemingly indelible sense of loss, grievance and injustice on to new generations. This phenomenon played an important, perhaps crucial, part in transforming the experience of the inflation, which had been a harsh but more or less bearable experience for many, even most, Germans – one shared by the populations of many other countries during the twentieth century – into a unique consensus of universal national catastrophe. This consensus still haunts the nation's collective memory and constitutes a decisive influence on German government policy, even in the twenty-first century.

To drive home the point about the fragility of money as a store of value, Germany was forced, after the Second World War, to experience a second dose of drastic devaluation. This time, it was one administered from outside.

For four and a half years, following the horribly drawn-out defeat of Hitler's regime, the country had no central government of its own. During the period after the First World War, Germany, though vanquished, had kept its own sovereign central administration, exercising a freedom of choice, regarding her political and economic options, which was hindered only by the disarmament and reparations clauses of the Versailles Treaty. After 1945, by contrast, the Reich was divided into four zones, each under direct military rule of the victorious Allies. Initially only the tiniest administrative units remained in the hands of Germans. All of the other main state powers were reserved for the foreign soldiers and for administrators appointed by the occupying countries.

This second bout of devaluation, following the demise of the Third Reich, all but rendered the currency worthless. The prized 'material assets' that in this instance formed the basis of the post-war economy consisted of cigarettes, black-market agricultural produce and illegally traded ration items originating from the occupying forces. In the end, as in 1923, a new currency had to be introduced in order to re-establish some universally acceptable expression of value.

As was the case when the Rentenmark came into being, the birth of the Deutschmark in June 1948 (confined at the time to the western zones of occupied Germany) permitted the release of large amounts of produce of all kinds that had been hoarded in anticipation of a reliable means of exchange. The Reichsmark, successfully established in 1924, had later been subjected to secret debasement by the Nazis, especially during the Second World War, when its fate resembled that of the old goldmark between 1914 and 1918. By the final stage of the Hitler regime's death struggle, in 1944–5, it had been thoroughly devalued. Once Germany had been defeated, and her central government ceased to exist, the Reichsmark became all but worthless.

Weimar Finance Minister, and later Chancellor, Hans Luther had spoken at the height of the hyperinflation in 1923 of Germany 'starving with full barns' (*bei vollen Scheuern verhungern*), and the same was true in late spring of 1948, just before the new Deutschmark was launched. 'Material assets' – valuables, food, above all, cigarettes – were the key to survival, and the black market ruled. And as in 1923–4, during 1948–9, goods and services that had for years been impossible to purchase with money quickly became available once more upon presentation of the new, valorised currency.

Thus, those who had suffered in the 1920s inflation suffered again, and young Germans of the 1940s generation also gained a taste of what it meant for money to be worthless. The suffering of German civilians was, moreover, increased by the fact that drastic food shortages, exacerbated by punitive policies on the part of the victorious powers (especially the so-called 'Morgenthau Plan'), caused widespread malnutrition and even starvation. Added to this, whereas in 1918 Germany's towns had remained undamaged, by 1945 massive Anglo-American air raids had destroyed vast swathes of housing, industrial plant and infrastructure of all kinds, as well as laying waste on a horrendous scale the country's rich architectural and cultural heritage. It was widely perceived that national reconstruction would take decades to achieve.

Nevertheless, although in many ways the plight of the German people in the years after 1945 would have appeared much worse than that of the previous generation, this proved not to be the case. Five years after the Second World War, in 1950, Germans found themselves in a far more stable, improving and generally hopeful situation than they had at the equivalent stage following the First War. In precisely that year, 1923, the Ruhr had been occupied, the hyperinflation had just reached its height, unemployment was rocketing, the economy trembled on the point of collapse and coups and uprisings were still part of the everyday political picture.

Nothing of that sort applied to Germany a few years after the end of Hitler's war. The country was divided by the Iron Curtain, and there was much political pain. All the same, during the 1950s, with a stable West German currency, and a world market rapidly recovering from war, the international demand for the high-quality capital goods, machinery and machine tools and consumer electricals – the German specialities – seemed inexhaustible. The export-led West German 'economic miracle', which lasted with only minor hiccups well into the 1990s, led to something like permanent full employment. Remarkably, capitalist economic vigour was combined with a welfare system and a social safety net that became the envy of the world, and certainly far beyond the dreams of even the most optimistic German politician during the 1920s.

Moreover, none of this was achieved on the back of inflation, let alone hyperinflation. In fact, the German government, under the watchful eye of the all-powerful Bundesbank (Federal Bank) – part of whose formal remit became precisely the prevention of inflation – pursued, and continues to pursue, strict deflationary policies. An industrious, skilled workforce has been prepared to make sacrifices where necessary to ensure that Germany remained 'export world champion', as the saying went, and that relatively low unemployment continued to be the modern German norm. Even the vast expense of absorbing and modernising the decrepit Communist German Democratic Republic, following the collapse of the Iron Curtain, appeared manageable. Germany from the 1950s onwards came to be seen as the 'gentle giant' of Europe, eager to prosper peacefully and to abjure any suspicion of domination. The country entered her seventh post-war decade solvent and quietly powerful.

What could possibly go wrong?

The First World War was, above all, a human tragedy. It cost many millions of dead, disabled, widowed and orphaned. Ancient monarchies were toppled, states that had existed for centuries were suddenly consigned to history. It was, however – and perhaps more lastingly – a socio-economic catastrophe, with the violent, unhappy Germany of the hyperinflationary years as its ominous exemplar.

The situation after 1918 was that almost all the major powers, hitherto (apart from Russia, the eternal exception) prosperous members of a global community based on free trading and free movement of human beings, owed money. Cripplingly enormous sums of money. France, Britain, Belgium and Italy's external debts were owed mainly to America, while Germany's were mainly the result of the punitive financial clauses of the Versailles Treaty (her huge domestic debt was, as we have witnessed, a different matter).

Looked at in this way – that is, without the moral question of whether reparations were right or wrong – the situation in the early 1920s was of a debt merry-go-round. America, playing the role of 'Uncle Shylock', refused to forgive the debts of its erstwhile allies, insisting that normal commercial terms, and the rigours of the financial market place, be applied. As we have seen, in good part because of this refusal, the other victorious countries – especially the French, who owed the most – were therefore unwilling to back down on the question of German reparations, no matter how harmful the international situation created by this stubborn insistence. The Americans insisted on their money. The French, their stance further stiffened by anxieties about a future German national resurgence, in turn insisted on theirs.

The Germans had signed the Versailles Treaty, admittedly under duress (as one side in a peace treaty generally does), but then, it might be said, resorted to systematic inflationary behaviour as the only way

of avoiding a commitment whose legitimacy, deep down, they could
not acknowledge. However, if the Germans were in many ways right
to hate Versailles, the French were also right to take the view that
Germany was deliberately making herself incapable of paying reparations. And so it went on, until the Ruhr invasion in January 1923
transported the whole situation into the realms of madness.

In the end, no one really got their money, not even the Americans.
Germany used the American loans it received under the 1924 Dawes
Plan to pay reparations to the French and the British, who in turn
used the money to service their own debts to the USA. Then, during
the Great Depression, all the major powers, including Germany,
France and Britain, effectively defaulted on what they owed to
America, and into the bargain the Germans defaulted on reparations.
In the meantime, of course, immeasurable political, social and
economic damage had been done, and a toxic inheritance stored up
for the brutal edification of the next generation.

When defeat was visited on Germany once more in 1945, initially
the victors' urge for revenge seemed even stronger than it had in 1919.
The miracle, however, was that, for both negative reasons (fear of
losing Germany to Communism) and of positive insight (the realisation that America could not pull out and leave Europe to its devices,
as it had after the First World War), America remained as guarantor
of stability and financier of European reconstruction – including
energetic support for the second German democracy, founded in the
three Western-occupied zones in 1949.

Though compensation was imposed, the new post-Hitler Germany
was not, in the final analysis, burdened with crippling reparations as
she had been a generation earlier. In fact, under the Marshall Plan
she received generous aid. Economic and political collaboration with
France, Italy and the Low Countries began as early as 1952 with the
European Iron and Steel Community, leading in 1957 to the establishment of the European Economic Community, which would later
become the European Union.

Germany actually still owed a considerable amount, including money from the First World War, in fact. Or, rather, she owed the debt to America that had been incurred under the Dawes Plan (1924) and later the Young Plan (1929), in order to pay off what was left of the reparations bill. However, under an international debt agreement signed in London in February 1953, following tortuous negotiations, Germany was forgiven half her pre-war and immediate post-war debts, while the rest was restructured to ensure that the recovering second German Republic would not suffer as her Weimar predecessor had done. The West needed a prosperous, peaceful Germany (though not so peaceful that she could not fulfil a useful industrial and military role in NATO). Much, including the arrears of interest on the money borrowed in the 1920s from America, would become payable only after German reunification, at that point a rather remote prospect.

So it was that over the next half-century, West Germany (as it was until formal reunification in 1990) punctiliously repaid up to $100 billion in total reparations and reparations-related debt (including many billions to Israel and to individual Jewish victims of the Holo-caust).[1] When the two post-war Germanys finally became one, the remaining arrears that thus became due under the London agreement were turned into bonds that matured on 3 October 2010, the twentieth anniversary (not coincidentally) of the country's formal reunification. Newspaper articles across the world celebrated the 'final end of German reparations'.

With the 2010 settlement, Germany finally repaid its obligations from more than ninety years earlier. The Cold War was over. Trade was booming. Having passed through the reunification crisis and reformed her labour market, she had retained her position as a peaceful, prosperous country in a peaceful Europe. A book written, say, five years ago, would have had only a happy ending to relate. Unfortunately, at the time of writing (April 2013), Germany finds itself widely hated and resented in the very Europe she played such a determined role in creating. At the root of the problem is, once more, a currency in difficulties.

Germany gave up her own currency on the first day of 1999, but not because it was unstable or unreliable. On the contrary. The Deutschmark was generally admired as among the very hardest of hard currencies. The transition from the mark, controlled by the monetary martinets of the Bundesbank, to the euro, was at base a result of increased national strength, not weakness. The project of a single European currency had been a French pet, and the story goes that President Mitterrand of France, made nervous by the prospect of an overmighty Germany, extracted as his price for approving German reunification in 1990 German commitment to a new level of economic and financial integration in Europe, including the adoption of a common currency – something which had been often discussed, but which would almost certainly never have occurred so quickly without the changes of attitude that followed reunification.[2]

In effect, the acceleration of monetary union was yet another stage in the apparently endless French struggle to limit, by force or persuasion, the ability of its powerful eastern neighbour to damage the interests of *la Grande Nation*. No war, no Ruhr occupation, no crippling reparations bill to keep Germany tame, but instead ever more internationalisation of the German state and economy within a European context. The common currency made obvious sense in terms of ease of trade and general convenience, but it was also a political construct. Many Germans saw membership of the euro (and the abandonment of their precious mark) as yet another sacrifice for the sake of a peaceful continent.

All nonetheless seemed to work fairly well, despite doubts about some of the other members of the monetary union, particularly those on the Mediterranean periphery. The European Central Bank looked much more like the Bundesbank than originally planned – the German Chancellor, Helmut Kohl, had managed to gain a few concessions on the way to the euro's launch – but the economies, and fiscal and financial arrangements, of the seventeen countries that eventually made up the euro bloc could not have been more different. In the case of Greece, especially, it was clear that the criteria for membership (a manageable national deficit, and a minimum level of financial probity) had been stretched to their limit and beyond, again for political reasons. Suddenly countries that had traditionally experienced problems borrowing on the international markets on affordable terms could borrow at much lower rates. Roughly the same rates, in fact, as if they were Germans. But without the discipline.

The banking crisis that first made itself felt in 2007 may have had its origins in runaway American debt, but in Europe, as the financial tide went out, the underpinnings of much of the continent's banking and investment system were shown to be equally, perhaps even more, unstable than those of Bear Sterns, Lehmann Brothers, Freddie Mac and Fanny Mae. German banks lost money as a result. Although restricted in their domestic market by laws designed to prevent the kind of 'casino banking' that had been the downfall of banks in America, Britain and elsewhere, German financial institutions had eagerly joined in the lending spree going on outside Germany's borders. Thus when the Spanish and Irish real estate booms, and the Greek government's heedless spending on an extraordinarily generous welfare system and a bloated public sector, hit the buffers, German bankers were threatened with huge losses in the same way as their French and Italian colleagues.

The so-called 'bail-outs' that followed were often described as 'saving' the countries involved. In reality, they mostly saved the foreign financial institutions that had lent the money, including German banks. This was a fact not lost on populations who were now expected to pay higher taxes, tolerate reduced welfare benefits and wages, and to suffer increased unemployment, in order to pay back the money their governments had unwisely borrowed. In Greece, it became a political cliché to show German Chancellor Angela Merkel as a Nazi oppressor, often kitted out in an SS uniform. There were mutterings about demanding proper reparations for the money and resources the Germans had stolen from Greece during the Second World War. In debtor countries, commentators darkly contrasted German rigour with the 'soft' treatment of Germany after the Second World War, which had made possible her dramatic recovery.

To most Germans, however, it was just a matter of hard-learned prudence. In the 1920s, Germany too had maintained a bloated public sector, partly as an employment-creation scheme (the German railways at that time, like the Greek railways in the twenty-first century, were a notorious money pit), had introduced the eight-hour day, thus undermining badly needed productivity, had failed to collect taxes fairly or efficiently, and had attempted to maintain a welfare system that she could not actually afford. The fate of the Weimar system had taught Germans many hard lessons, and a key one had been that financial stability was vitally important. From Heinrich Brüning at the beginning of the Great Depression to Angela Merkel eighty years later during what has been dubbed 'the Great Recession', Germany's politicians (with the great exception, in this and almost all else, of Hitler) had kept the purse strings tight, no matter the short-term political cost.

When the mighty cost of integrating the so-called 'new provinces' (*neue Bundesländer*) of East Germany after 1990 had threatened to destroy the post-war 'economic miracle', the country had reluctantly submitted to heavy extra taxes, plus extensive labour market and welfare reforms. The experience was painful. However, if practical results are any guide, these sacrifices successfully relaunched Germany as 'export world champion'. Those countries that had thrown away the genuine development opportunities presented by the euro system, and instead awarded themselves inflated welfare benefits and real estate profits, would now also have to suffer pain in order to achieve gain, as Germany had during the period around the turn of the millennium.

Systemic and ingrained social problems apart, the problem for the eurozone countries that have been forced to accept 'bail-out' loans on what seem like draconian terms is that, unlike Germany, they do not have broad-based economies. The latest, Cyprus, for instance, developed an identity, in the last decades of the twentieth century, as a tax haven, especially favoured by Russian businessmen. Like British author Somerset Maugham's pre-war French Riviera, Cyprus became a 'sunny place for shady people'.

Formerly a British colony, Cyprus had remained a British military base, with, back in the 1970s, agriculture and tourism as its other main earners. Now its burgeoning financial sector became the basis of the island's prosperity, leaving its economy increasingly dependent on a banking monoculture. This remained the case even after it joined the euro at the beginning of 2008. As a result, when it came to paying back the 2013 'bail-out' loan, Cyprus's creditors considered that only the island's banking sector could provide the funds. Hence the bail-out providers' imposition of a startlingly novel 'bank deposits tax' that, ominously, freezes and then guts bank accounts containing deposits of €100,000 or more. Capital and currency controls have been forced on Cyprus, completely against the spirit and letter of the EU's founding principles – as if such controls had suddenly popped up on the border between, say, Connecticut and the rest of the United States.

In this context, Germany, as the richest and most populous country in Europe and therefore the main paymaster, is seen – to return to the similarities with the Weimar era – as a kind of combination of merciless financial vigilante, like France bearing down on Germany after Versailles, and 'Uncle Shylock', like the American bankers who would not forgive the loans taken out by France, Britain and its other co-combatants in the First World War. Had not the combination of these two factors condemned post-First World War Europe to permanent austerity and a 'beggar-my-neighbour' struggle for survival?

The real problem, arguably, is that, because they (voluntarily) remain within the monetary straitjacket of the eurozone, the modern debtor countries must abide by its rules, of which Germany is the undoubted guardian. Specifically, as a result, they cannot devalue their national currencies. Unlike Germany in the 1920s, they cannot 'inflate their way out of trouble', thereby, first, making their economies more competitive and, second (less virtuously), in effect cheating their creditors by repaying them in debased money.

Of course, as this entire story shows, Weimar Germany may have 'inflated its way out of trouble' for a while. The eventual result, however, was to help create another, even worse, kind of trouble – one that manifested itself a decade down the line in the shape of the Nazi dictatorship. This is a fact of which modern Germans are well aware. The spectacle of the Anglo-Saxon countries 'solving' the recession by conjuring money up from nowhere to keep the economy going unsettles minds east of the Rhine. London and Washington may call it 'quantitative easing', but to those Germans with even the dimmest memory of the early 1920s, the story of the Reichsbank's printing presses clattering away around the clock to produce million, billion and trillion mark notes, and the chaos that resulted, is irresistibly brought to mind.

Germans' awareness of their own history, including the price they paid for the hyperinflation – financial aversion therapy of the most drastic sort – as well as the benefits of financial discipline, which transformed the country after the Second World War, makes it obvious to most Germans that a similar course of action must be pursued by their troubled eurozone friends if they are to lift themselves out of the mire. The problem is that while this attitude may appear to opinion formers in Berlin to reflect simple common sense, to those on the southern European periphery, where the suffering is not decades in the past but very much an urgent thing of the present, it feels much more like arrogant indifference to wasted lives and crushed hopes.

Meanwhile, the communal memory of the hyperinflation lingers in the subliminal regions of the German unconsciousness, occasionally rising into the national awareness at times of crisis. 'There is anecdotal evidence,' as the correspondent of the London *Observer* wrote at the end of March 2013, 'that some Germans have begun removing their savings from banks, and that others have opened new accounts to spread their savings around and avoid getting caught like Cypriot depositors with more than €100,000. The financial daily *Börsen-Zeitung* commented that while Germans – still collectively haunted by the currency collapses experienced by their forefathers – were not necessarily planning a run on the bank with their feet, "they are already doing it in their heads".[3]

Clearly, for all Germany's renewed prosperity, the ninety-year-old national sense of trauma has not yet been fully overcome. The problem for the world may be that Germany's instinct is correct.

Appendix

Timeline of Key Events

Date	Events	Rate of Mark to US Dollar (monthly av.)
1914		
August	Germany at War. Mark decoupled from Gold Standard.	4.19
December	First wartime Christmas.	4.50
1915		
December	Stalemate on the Western Front.	5.16
1916		
December	German advances on the Eastern Front.	5.72
1917		
March	First Russian (democratic) revolution.	5.82
October	Second (Bolshevik) Russian revolution.	7.29
December	Germany's war position strengthens.	5.67
1918		
March/April	Treaty of Brest-Litovsk. Massive German territorial and economic gains in the east. German breakthrough on the Western Front.	5.11

August	German advances on the Western Front halted. Retreat begins.	**6.10**
November	Revolution in Germany. Monarchy overthrown. Armistice signed.	**7.4**

1919

January	Bolshevik-style Spartacist uprising in Berlin suppressed. Rosa Luxemburg and Karl Liebknecht murdered.	**8.20**
April	Avant-garde 'Bauhaus' art institute founded in Weimar.	**12.61**
April/May	So-called 'Bavarian Soviet Republic' in Munich. After its violent suppression, Munich became a centre of militant right-wing reaction.	**12.85**
June	Versailles Treaty. Scheidemann resigns as first post-war chancellor and is succeeded by Gustav Bauer.	**14.01**

1920

March	Unsuccessful right-wing (Kapp) putsch in Berlin causes crisis. Gustav Bauer makes way for Hermann Müller.	**83.89**
June	Elections. Parties of the right resurgent. Müller resigns. Fehrenbach Chancellor. The mark temporarily stabilises. Foundation of the *Völkischer Beobachter*, newspaper of the Munich-based National Socialist German Workers Party (NSDAP = Nazi Party).	**39.13**

1921

May	Fehrenbach resigns. Parties divided over acceptance of Allied reparations ultimatum. Wirth becomes Chancellor.	**62.30**
July	32-year-old Adolf Hitler becomes leader of the Nazi Party, which claims 3,600 members.	**76.67**
August	Matthias Erzberger, reforming former Finance Minister and signatory of the 1918 armistice, assassinated by ultra-nationalists.	**84.31**
October	Germany loses most of the key industrial area of Upper Silesia to Poland.	**150.20**

1922

January/ February	Hard-line nationalist cabinet in France under Poincaré takes aggressive line on reparations.	**207.82**
March	Release of Friedrich Murnau's film *Nosferatu: A Symphony of Horror*, based on Bram Stoker's *Dracula*.	**284.19**
May	Fritz Lang's film *Dr Mabuse: The Gambler*, a paranoid moral fantasy portraying contemporary decadence, fraud and the abuse of money, opens in Berlin and is a huge hit.	**290.11**
June/July	Crisis follows the murder of Walther Rathenau, German Foreign Minister, by far-right assassins. Emergency Law passed by Reichstag. Germany demands moratorium on cash payments of reparations.	**493.22**
August	Poincaré demands 'productive guarantees' including surrender of state forests and	

	mines in Western Germany to the Allies, plus majority of shares in major German chemicals concerns.	**1,134**
October	Fall of Lloyd George in the UK. End of Greco-Turkish War. Mussolini seizes power in Italy.	
	The German government makes illegal the use of foreign currencies as payment within Germany. Inflation accelerates still further.	**3,180**
November	Growing crisis over German failure to meet reparations demands. Fall of Wirth government. New administration under a non-political businessman, Wilhelm Cuno. Reparations negotiations unsuccessful. Albert Einstein is awarded the Nobel Prize for Physics.	**7,183**
December	Berthold Brecht's first play, *Drums in the Night*, successfully premieres in Berlin.	
	Just before Christmas, Germany is declared in default of reparations.	**7,589**

1923

January	France and Belgium invade and occupy the Ruhr to enforce reparations. The German government proclaims a policy of 'passive resistance'. Railway workers refuse to handle coal shipments bound for France. In Munich, the Nazi Party holds its first national conference, causing the Bavarian government to declare a state of emergency.	**17,972**
February	Courtesy of a hard-currency donation	

from a foreign sympathizer, a huge sum
when translated into paper marks, the
Völkischer Beobachter becomes a daily paper.
The Reichstag passes a law (*Notgesetz*) against
profiteering and the black market.   **27,918**

March   Thirteen workers killed by French troops
suppressing a demonstration at the Krupp
plant in Essen.   **21,190**

April   Tempelhof Airfield, Berlin, officially opened.
Reichstag passes a supplementary finance
bill adding 4.5 billion marks to the budget
for that year, representing the cost of
supporting 'passive resistance' in the
Ruhr, buying imported coal to replace
stocks confiscated by the French, etc.
Freud's *Das Ich und das Es* (The Ego
and the Id) published.   **24,475**

May   Police in Munich prevent clashes
between leftist demonstrators and Nazis,
the latter 1,200 strong and armed with
weapons including machine guns.
In the Rhineland, Rhenish separatists,
supported by the French occupiers, carry
out the first of several unsuccessful coup
attempts.
The German saboteur Albert Schlageter is
executed by a French firing squad in the Ruhr
and becomes an instant national martyr.   **47,670**

June   Mass expulsions of resisting German railway
workers from the Ruhr reach 4,500 per month
(plus 11,000 dependents).
Anti-inflation riots in Leipzig end in 7 dead
and 100 serious injuries.
Danzig airport opened.

Inflation supplement for German civil
servants increased from 2,900 to 6,000
per cent.
The German government introduces
stricter laws against currency
speculation.   **109,966**
July   Postal, telegram and telephone charges
drastically raised. Rail tickets and
goods charges further increased.
The Government Printing Works delivers
the first 500,000-mark notes to the banks.
Inflation increases dramatically. Million-
mark notes soon follow.
According to a German government
report, 92 Germans have been killed
during the Ruhr occupation and 70,000
expelled from the occupied area. British
Prime Minister Stanley Baldwin
demands French withdrawal.
The fall in the mark becomes an
uncontrollable torrent.   **353,412**
August   Sudden death of American President
Warren G. Harding. Vice-President
Calvin Coolidge succeeds him.
Food riots in French-occupied Wiesbaden.
Grocers' and butchers' shops looted. The
French turn back all food shipments
from the Reich to the occupied area that do
not have customs duties paid on them,
causing widespread hunger. By presidential
decree, trading in German marks outside
the Reich is made illegal.
Cuno loses a vote of confidence in the
Reichstag. Centre-right politician Gustav

Stresemann becomes chancellor. Plans
made to abandon 'passive resistance' in the Ruhr.
One gold mark now equals 1,000,000
paper marks. In December 1922 it was 1,000.
The fall continues and accelerates.
On 20 August a loaf of bread in Berlin
costs 200,000 marks.
Unemployment in Germany almost doubles
in one month from 3.5 to 6.3 per cent. **4,620,455**

September   A massive earthquake in Japan kills
140,000 and makes half a million homeless.
100,000 supporters of the far right gather
at Nuremberg. Prominent among them
are members of the Nazi Party. Adolf
Hitler takes political leadership of the
unified 'German League of Struggle'
founded after this rally.
The inflation soars catastrophically out
of control. On 3 September the dollar is
worth 9.7 million marks, on 6 September
33.2 million, the next day, 7 September,
53 million, and on 13 September 92.4 million.
Rumours of a right-wing coup in Munich,
and fighting between communists and
police in Saxony. The Reich government
warns that it will not tolerate rebellion
in the provinces from either political extreme.
State and provincial leaders agree to the
abandonment of passive resistance in
the Ruhr and this becomes central
government policy.   **98,860,000**

October   On 1 October the mark trades at
242 million against the dollar.
On 8 October 838 million.

On 10 October a communist-socialist
coalition government is sworn in in
Saxony. The French reject German offers
to normalise the situation in the Ruhr.
By 10 October the mark's value has collapsed
dramatically to 2.9 billion (American =
1,000 million).
In Bavaria, the Munich government refuses
to sack its ultra-nationalist, anti-Semitic
army commander and calls the Reich
cabinet 'a Jew-government'.
In Saxony the communist Finance Minister
supports the arming of workers' militias.
The commander of the regular military
responds by banning the militias. The stage
is set for a violent confrontation.
An Enabling Law (*Ermächtigungsgesetz*)
is passed, empowering the Reich
government to assume dictatorial powers
in case of national emergency and overrule
local state governments.
Meanwhile, the stage is being set for financial
reform. Tax liabilities will be calculated in
gold marks. A 'rent' bank is set up based
on the 'real' worth of businesses,
agricultural assets, etc., preparatory to
reform of the currency. Holders of this
notional value will guarantee it with
6 per cent of their worth, entrusted to
the government as a kind of debt provision
deposit.
President Ebert voluntarily forfeits half of
his official allowance as an example of
austerity.

The mark reaches 41 billion against the dollar.
A communist uprising in Hamburg is
suppressed by government forces.
The Exorcism (*Die Austreibung*), a new
film by Friedrich Murnau, is released.
A Berlin station begins regular radio
broadcasts for the general public. 'Radio
mania' is unleashed.
Drastic cuts in the civil service planned,
totalling 1.5 million. Unemployment has
trebled in three months and now stands
at 19.1 per cent.
Using its new powers, the government
sends troops into Saxony, deposes the
socialist/communist coalition and installs
a 'Reich Commissar' in its place. **25,260,000,000**

November   On 12 November, President Ebert
appoints the banking expert Hjalmar
Schacht as Reich Currency Commissar,
with crucial powers to overrule any
ministerial decisions he considers harmful
to currency normalisation.
On 16 November, under Schacht's
direction, the government issues a new
currency, the Rentenmark – initially
confined to domestic use in the Reich
itself – each new Rentenmark worth
1 trillion paper marks. All printing of the
latter ceases. It is the beginning of
the end for hyperinflation.
Poincaré admits in a speech to the Chamber
of Deputies that financially, the occupation
of the Ruhr has cost France more than it
has brought in.

A Reparations Commission, including
for the first time German representatives,
begins new discussions about Germany's
ability to pay reparations.   **(Average estimate
impossible – 1 November
exchange rate 133 billion to
the dollar, 15 November on the
eve of currency reform,
approx. 2.5 trillion)**

December   The introduction of the fixed-value
Rentenmark causes severe but temporary
hardship for many Germans. Prices continue
to rise for a while, and the new money is
in short supply.
Because the Rentenmark is a purely domestic
currency – technically not even legal
tender – the paper mark continues to be
bought and sold in foreign exchanges. Its
value against the dollar rises to 6.7 trillion
marks on 1 December before stabilising at
4.2 trillion on 3 December.
The President approves emergency
legislation to ensure that all major taxes
and government obligations are carried
out in Rentenmarks.
On 22 December, some weeks after the
sudden death of Reichsbank President
Havenstein, Schacht is finally appointed
to his post, while also remaining Reich
Currency Commissar. There will be struggles
ahead, but the end of the hyperinflation
is now in sight.   **4,200,000,000,000**

NOTES

CHAPTER 1: FINDING THE MONEY FOR THE END OF THE WORLD

1 See Hew Strachan, *The First World War: A New Illustrated History*, vol. 1: '*To Arms*', Oxford, 2003, p. 833f.
2 Gerald D. Feldman, *The Great Disorder: Politics, Economics and Society in the German Inflation 1914–1924*, New York and Oxford, 1996, p. 32.
3 See Leonard Gomes, *German Reparations, 1919–1932: A Historical Survey*, Basingstoke and New York, 2010, p. 10f. And also Niall Ferguson, *The Pity of War 1914–1918*, London, 1999, p. 250f.
4 See Helen McPhail, *The Long Silence: Civilian Life under the German Occupation of Northern France, 1914–1918*, London, 2000, p. 36n.
5 Feldman, *The Great Disorder*, p. 34.
6 Ibid., p. 5f for the details and for the protests.

CHAPTER 2: LOSER PAYS ALL

1 Quoted in Ferguson, *The Pity of War*, p. 252.
2 For the declaration and its consequences see Alexander B. Downes, 'Desperate Times, Desperate Measures: The Causes of Civilian Victimization in War', in *International Security*, vol. 30, no. 4 (Spring 2006), pp. 185–8. He argues that the blockade was not actually caused by the German U-boat declaration, but that the latter provided a justification in the face of neutral opinion, which at that time included the USA, for the British and their allies to do something they had already been planning for some time.
3 Downes, ibid., p. 186.
4 Martin Gilbert, *First World War*, London, 1995, p. 256, cites the figures for 1915 and 1916, and on p. 256n the total for the entire war. As Prof. Gilbert points

out, this was roughly equal to the numbers of German civilians killed by the Allied bombing offensive in the Second World War – a campaign undertaken for very similar reasons to the blockade thirty years earlier, and with an equally dubious justification so far as the accepted laws of war were concerned.

5 Elizabeth H. Tobin, 'War and the Working Class: The Case of Düsseldorf 1914–1918', in *Central European History*, vol. 18, no. 3/4 (Sept.–Dec. 1985), p. 281.

6 Ibid., p. 283.

7 Ferguson, *The Pity of War*, p. 253.

8 Ibid., p. 253f. And for the sales of foreign securities.

9 See T. Balderston, 'War Finance and Inflation in Britain and Germany, 1914–1918', in *The Economic History Review*, New Series, vol. 42, no. 2 (May 1989), p. 240.

10 Helfferich's speech to the Reichstag on the Reich Budget, 20 August 1915, in *Verhandlungen des Deutschen Reichstages*, Stenographische Berichte XII. Legislaturperiode II. Sitzung Bd. 306, p. 224 (available online at http://www. reichstagsprotokolle.de).

11 Gomes, *German Reparations*, p. 11.

12 Ibid., p. 21.

13 For the full text see Fritz Fischer, *Germany's Aims in the First World War*, trans. Hajo Holborn, with an introduction by James Joll, New York, 1967, p. 105.

14 See Gilbert, *First World War*, p. 155, for the plans of the group led by the chair of the supervisory board of Krupp and Pan-German extremist Alfred Hugenberg (1865–1951). Hugenberg was, as we shall see, later a major press and media magnate, one of Hitler's chief helpers and in 1933 Economics Minister in the first Nazi-dominated cabinet.

15 Quoted in ibid., p. 309.

16 Gilbert, *First World War*, p. 398f.

17 Gerald D. Feldman, *Army, Industry and Labour in Germany 1914–1918*, Providence, RI, and Oxford, 1992, p. 457f.

18 See Strachan, *The First World War*, p. 281f.

CHAPTER 3: FROM TRIUMPH TO DISASTER

1 Gilbert, *First World War*, p. 399.

2 Quoted in chapter 18, Charles B. MacDonald, 'World War One: The U.S. Army Overseas' in *American Military History*, p. 392 (available online as http:// www.history.army.mil/books/AMH/amh-toc.htm).

3 Richard Bessel, *Germany After the First World War*, Oxford, 1993, p. 37.

4 See Feldman, *The Great Disorder*, p. 58.

5 See Feldman, *Army, Industry and Labour*, p. 459.

6   Sebastian Haffner, *Geschichte eines Deutschen: Die Erinnerungen 1914–1933*, Stuttgart and Munich, 2000, p. 20.

7   Gilbert, *First World War*, p. 407f.

8   Feldman, *Army, Industry and Labour*, p. 493f.

9   Strachan, *The First World War*, p. 289.

10 Feldman, *Army Industry and Labour*, p. 493.

11 See ibid., pp. 429ff.

12 See Heinz Hagenlücke, *Deutsche Vaterlandspartei: Die nationalen Rechte am Ende des Kaiserreiches*, Düsseldorf, 1997, p. 353f.

13 Figures for textiles and construction in Bessel, *Germany After the First World War*, p. 16.

14 Reproduced from Ferguson, *The Pity of War*, p. 250.

15 For the Hindenburg Programme see Bessel, *Germany After the First World War*, p. 13, and Feldman, *Army, Industry and Labour*, especially p. 154.

16 For figures on tobacco and wine, beer and general agricultural decline, see Ferguson, *The Pity of War*, p. 251.

17 Ibid., p. 254.

18 For these figures see Feldman, *Army, Industry and Labour*, p. 472.

19 Bessel, *Germany After the First World War*, p. 32, table 8.

20 Ibid., p. 33.

21 Ibid., p. 31.

22 Feldman, *Army, Industry and Labour*, p. 464f. And for the quote below.

23 Ibid., p. 506.

24 Sönke Neitzel, *Weltkrieg und Revolution, 1914–1918/19*, Berlin, 2008, p. 148.

25 Quoted in Otto Friedrich, *Before the Deluge: A Portrait of Berlin in the Twenties*, New York, 1995, p. 22.

26 Haffner, *Geschichte eines Deutschen*, p. 31.

27 Quoted in Hans-Ulrich Wehler, *Deutsche Gesellschaftsgeschichte*, Bd. 4: *Vom Beginn des Ersten Weltkriegs bis zur Gründung der beiden deutschen Staaten 1914–1949*, Munich, 2003, p. 193.

28 Sebastian Haffner, *Die deutsche Revolution 1918/19: Wie war es wirklich?*, Munich, 1979, p. 83.

29 See figures in Konrad Roessler, *Die Finanzpolitik des Deutschen Reiches im Ersten Weltkrieg*, Berlin, 1967, p. 79.

CHAPTER 4: 'I HATE THE SOCIAL REVOLUTION LIKE SIN'

1   Haffner, *Die deutsche Revolution 1918/19*, p. 87.

2   Ibid.

3   Neitzel, *Weltkrieg und Revolution*, p. 153.

4   Seaman Richard Stumpf's comment on 4 November 1918 in Peter Englund, *The Beauty and the Sorrow: An Intimate History of the First World War*, London, 2011, p. 491.

5   See an interview from 1958 with Karl Artelt, a torpedo technician and one of the leaders of the uprising, reproduced in http://www.kurkuhl.de/de/novrev/stadtrundgang_06.html.

6   See http://www.kurkuhl.de/de/novrev/artelt_bericht.html

7   Neitzel, *Weltkrieg und Revolution*, p. 156.

8   Heinrich Winkler, *Weimar 1918–1933*, Munich, 1993, p. 32.

9   Haffner, *Die deutsche Revolution 1918/19*, p. 70f. See also Winkler, *Weimar 1918–1933*, p. 29.

10 Text in Philipp Scheidemann, *Memoiren eines Sozialdemokraten* (reprint Severus, 2010), Bd. 2, p. 245f. Translation by the author. There is disagreement about whether this version was a result of some later 'tidying up', but the sentiments are unarguable.

11 See ibid., p. 246.

12 Liebknecht's proclamation at http://www.dhm.de/lemo/html/dokumente/liebknecht/index.html (in German).

13 Friedrich, *Before the Deluge*, p. 25.

14 LeMo Kollektives Gedächtnis, *Aufzeichnung aus dem Tagebuch des jüdischen Fabrikanten Oskar Münsterberg (1865–1920) aus Berlin* (DHM-Bestand), online at http://www.dhm.de/lemo/forum/kollektives_gedaechtnis/weimar.html.

15 Riess's account in Rudolf Pörtner (ed.), *Alltag in der Weimarer Republik: Kindheit und Jugend in unruhiger Zeit*, Munich, 1993, p. 31.

16 *Die Weltbühne* Jahrgang XIV Nr. 51, 19 Dezember 1918, p. 591.

CHAPTER 5: SALARIES ARE STILL BEING PAID

1   Trans. and ed. Charles Kessler, *Diaries of a Cosmopolitan: Count Harry Kessler 1918-1937*, London, 1971, p. 7f.

2   See Winkler, *Weimar 1918-1933*, p. 38f.

3   Ibid., p. 34.

4   Article 'Die Revolution in Berlin' reproduced in Ernst Troeltsch, *Die Fehlgeburt einer Republik: Spektator in Berlin 1918 bis 1922* (Zusammengestellt und mit einem Nachwort versehen von Johann Hinrich Claussen), Frankfurt-on-Main, 1944, p. 5.

5   Ebert's speech to the National Assembly in Weimar, 6 February 1919 in *Verhandlungen der verfassungsgebenden Deutschen Nationalversammlung*, Stenographische Berichte Bd. 326 pp. 2–3 (available online at http://www.reichstagsprotokolle.de).

CHAPTER 6: FOURTEEN POINTS

1 Text of Armistice reproduced in *Manchester Guardian*, 12 November 1918. Available online (slightly differing from the cited text) at http://www. firstworldwar.com/source/armisticeterms.htm.

2 For the announcement of this false dawn see *Manchester Guardian*, 16 December 1918, p. 4.

3 Feldman, *The Great Disorder*, p. 103.

4 Ibid., pp. 99ff. for this and the following.

5 Quoted in ibid., p. 101.

6 'Mangin at Mainz: Plight of Returning Prisoners', in *Manchester Guardian*, 8 January 1919, p. 6.

7 Quoted in Robert McCrum, 'French Economic Policy at the Paris Peace Conference, 1919', in *The Historical Journal*, vol. 21, no. 3 (Sept. 1978), p. 631.

8 'Hungry German Cities: The Internal Blockade', in *Manchester Guardian*, 22 January 1919, p. 6.

9 'Wiesbaden Still a Luxury Town', in *Manchester Guardian*, 28 January 1919, p. 4.

10 Feldman, *The Great Disorder*, p. 101.

11 Quoted in Monika Woitas, Annette Hartmann (eds), *Strawinskys, 'Motor Drive'*, Munich, 2009, p. 145.

12 Ernst Engelbrecht and Leo Heller, *Die Kinder der Nacht: Bilder aus dem Verbrecherleben*, Berlin-Neu-Finkenkrug, 1925, chapter 'Berliner Schwoof', p. 140f.

13 See Haffner, *Geschichte eines Deutschen*, p. 39f. and for a different point of view H. W. Koch, *Der deutsche Bürgerkrieg: Eine Geschichte der deutschen und österreichischen Freikorps 1918–1923*, Berlin and Frankfurt-on-Main, 1978, pp. 43ff.

CHAPTER 7: BLOODHOUNDS

1 For the development of early 'Free Corps' units in the autumn of 1918 see Koch, *Der deutsche Bürgerkrieg*, p. 45f.

2 Haffner, *Die deutsche Revolution 1918/19*, p. 134. Koch, *Der deutsche Bürgerkrieg*, p. 48, prefers the more nonchalant version of Ebert's response.

3 Winkler, *Weimar 1918–1933*, p. 54f.

4 Kessler, *Diaries of a Cosmopolitan*, p. 51.

5 Johannes Fischart, 'Politiker und Publizisten XLII: Karl Liebknecht', in *Die Weltbühne* Jahrgang XIV Nr. 51, 19 Dezember 1918, p. 573. Johannes Fischart was a pseudonym for the prolific journalist Erich Dombrowski (1889–1972).

6 Winkler, *Weimar 1918–1933*, p. 50.

7 For a particularly clear and concise account of the January uprising, see Hajo Holborn, *Deutsche Geschichte in der Neuzeit: Das Zeitalter des Imperialismus*

(1871–1945), Munich, 1971, Bd. 3, pp. 309ff. Sequence of events here based on Holborn except where otherwise indicated.

8 Kessler, *Diaries of a Cosmopolitan*, p. 55.

9 See Haffner, *Die deutsche Revolution 1918/19*, p. 139, and Winkler, *Weimar 1918–1933*, p. 56f.

10 Quoted in Haffner, *Die deutsche Revolution 1918/19*, p. 150.

11 See ibid., p. 158.

CHAPTER 8: DIKTAT

1 Morgan Philips Price, *Dispatches from the Weimar Republic: Versailles and German Fascism* (ed. Tania Rose), London and Sterling, VA, 1999, p. 31.

2 LeMo Kollektives Gedächtnis, 'Revolution und Wahl 1918/19', contribution from Henning Wenzel (b. 1910) at http://www.dhm.de/lemo/forum/kolle-ktives_gedaechtnis/weimar.html

3 See Rolf Hosfeld and Hermann Pölking, *Wir Deutschen: 1918 bis 1929, Vom Kriegsende bis zu den goldenen Zwanzigern*, Munich and Zürich, 2009, p. 67.

4 Ibid., p. 49f.

5 See Emil Julius Gumbel's list of political murders in Germany between 1918 and 1922, published in 1922 as *Vier Jahre politischer Mord* and available online at http://www.deutsche-revolution.de/revolution-1918-102.html. Gumbel (1891–1966) was a Bavarian statistician and political writer, himself subjected to death threats and forced to emigrate after the Nazi seizure of power to the USA.

6 From Josef Hofmiller, '*Revolutionstagebuch*', in *Josef Hofmillers Schriften*, Bd. 2, p. 226, available through the Bayerische Staatsbibliothek digital collection at http://daten.digitale-sammlungen.de/~db/0001/bsb00016411/images/index.html?id=00016411&fip=193.174.98.30&no=&seite=226. The man's name is misspelled as 'Reichardt' throughout, but has been corrected in the quoted text.

7 Kessler, *Diaries of a Cosmopolitan*, p. 85.

8 George Grosz, trans. Arnold J. Pomerans, *A Small Yes and a Big No!*, London and New York, 1982, p. 93.

9 'Revolution und Inflation: Hermann Zander geb. 1897 erzählt', at the website Kollektives Gedächtnis, http://www.kollektives-gedaechtnis.de/.

10 Margaret MacMillan, *Peacemakers: Six Months that Changed the World*, London, 2002, p. 471. For the 'life-raft' observation and for the following quote from Ellis Dresel.

11 See Marc Trachtenberg, 'Versailles after Sixty Years', in *Journal of Contemporary History*, vol. 17, no. 3 (July 1982) *passim* for the argument and p. 491 for the quotation.

12 Ibid., p. 474.

13 Ibid., pp. 474–6.

14 David Lloyd George, *The Truth about the Peace Treaties*, London, 1938, vol. 1, p. 684.

15 LeMo Kollektives Gedächtnis, *Aufzeichnung aus dem Tagebuch des jüdischen Fabrikanten Oskar Münsterberg (1865–1920) aus Berlin* (DHM-Bestand), online at http://www.dhm.de/lemo/forum/kollektives_gedaechtnis/weimar.html

16 Text of Versailles Treaty available at http://avalon.law.yale.edu/imt/partviii.asp.

17 Quoted in MacMillan, *Peacemakers*, p. 478.

18 Ibid., p. 479.

19 See Antony Lentin, 'Treaty of Versailles: Was Germany Guilty?', in *History Today*, vol. 62, issue 1, 2012.

20 Hosfeld and Pölking, *Wir Deutschen: 1918 bis 1929*, p. 71.

21 Quoted in H. A. Winkler, *Der Lange Weg Nach Westen: Deutsche Geschichte vom Ende des Alten Reiches bis zum Untergang der Weimarer Republik*, Munich, 2002, p. 399.

22 MacMillan, *Peacemakers*, p. 480.

23 Winkler, *Weimar 1918–1933*, p. 93.

24 Ibid., p. 95.

25 MacMillan, *Peacemakers*, pp. 484ff. And for the following.

26 Quoted from article 'Die Aufnahme der Friedensbedingungen', in Troeltsch, *Die Fehlgeburt einer Republik*, p. 44.

27 Kessler, *Diaries of a Cosmopolitan*, p. 103.

28 Feldman, *The Great Disorder*, p. 160. And for the following quote.

CHAPTER 9: SOCIAL PEACE AT ANY PRICE?

1 Details of Stinnes's biography available in an English translation of an article in the *Neue Zürcher Zeitung*, 22 November 1920, by Johannes Fischart (see n5, Chapter 7, for his comments about Liebknecht in *Die Weltbühne*), reproduced under the title 'Hugo Stinnes: An Industrial Ludendorff', in the American magazine *The Living Age*, 15 January 1921. Retrievable at http://www.unz.org/Pub/Living Age-1921jan15-00148. Also for this quotation and following biographical details.

2 See Feldman, *The Great Disorder*, p. 106f.

3 Quoted in Bessel, *Germany After the First World War*, p. 143.

4 See Winkler, *Weimar 1918–1933*, p. 45f.

5 Feldman, *The Great Disorder*, p. 109, quoting Fritz Tänzler, Director of the Federation of German Employer Organisations (*Vereinigung Deutscher Arbeitgeberverbände*), addressing his colleagues on 18 December 1918.

6 See Feldman, *The Great Disorder*, p. 107f for a summary of the discussion between Legien and Walther Rathenau of AEG, 11 November 1918, in which Rathenau, as an employer, questioned whether such an agreement was wise from the unions' point of view.

7   See Bessel, *Germany After the First World War*, pp. 144ff.
8   Feldman, *The Great Disorder*, p. 119.
9   Ibid., p. 117f.
10 Ibid., p. 121.
11 Text of Weimar Constitution available online (in German) at http://www.dhm. de/lemo/html/dokumente/verfassung/index.html. (Translation by the author.)
12 Ibid., p. 127.
13 Eric D. Weitz, *Weimar Germany: Promise and Tragedy*, Princeton, NJ, and Oxford, 2009, Paderborn, 1978, p. 21f.
14 See F.-W. Henning, *Das Industrialisierte Deutschland 1914 bis 1976*, p. 54.
15 Feldman, *The Great Disorder*, p. 129.
16 See Karl Hardach, *The Political Economy of Germany in the Twentieth Century*, Ewing, NJ, 1981, p. 19.
17 Quoted in Feldman, *The Great Disorder*, p. 131.
18 Quoted in ibid., p. 160.
19 Theo Balderston, *Economics and Politics in the Weimar Republic*, p. 25f.
20 Ibid., p. 163.
21 Quoted in ibid., p. 176.
22 See Winkler, *Weimar 1918–1933*, p. 110.

CHAPTER 10: CONSEQUENCES

1   See online entries in *Deutsche Biographie* at 'Achterberg, Erich, Havenstein, Rudolf Emil Albert', in *Neue Deutsche Biographie*, 8 (1969), S. 137 [Onlinefassung]; http://www.deutsche-biographie.de/pnd116550295.html (for Havenstein); and Götzky, Michael, 'Glasenapp, Otto Georg Bogislav von', in *Neue Deutsche Biographie*, 6 (1964), S. 428 [Onlinefassung]; http://www.deutsche-biographie. de/pnd116653124.html (for Glasenapp). Glasenapp's translations were published in 1925, after his retirement from the Reichsbank.
2   See Feldman, *The Great Disorder*, p. 203f.
3   Dollar rates are hard to source for this period. January 1919 and May 1919 rates from Henning, *Das Industrialisierte Deutschland*, p.64; rates for July and September from the *Vossische Zeitung*, 18 July 1919, p. 13, and 7 September 1919, p. 13, respectively (exchange rates for returning prisoners of war). Scans of original editions of *Vossische Zeitung* (1918–34) available online at http://zefys.staatsbibliothek-berlin. de. Later the rates were published daily as part of the business section.
4   For remarks on reasons for the mark's decline see Henning, *Das Industrialisierte Deutschland*, p.64. Mark/dollar rate at end of 1919 from *Vossische Zeitung* online, 31 December 1919, late Edition, p. 4.
5   Kessler, *Diaries of a Cosmopolitan*, p. 117.

6 See Winkler, *Weimar 1918–1933*, pp. 87ff.

7 Ibid., p. 95. And for the attitude of the DVP and DNVP.

8 MacMillan, *Peacemakers*, p. 485.

9 *Die wirtschaftlichen Folgen des Friedensvertrages*, Duncker & Humblot, Munich, 1920.

10 Feldman, *The Great Disorder*, p. 206f.

11 Ibid., pp. 204–7.

12 Mark/dollar rates from *Vossische Zeitung* online: 25 January 1920, p. 14; 22 February 1920, p. 14; 7 March 1920, p. 14 (rates quoted as on the Cologne Currency Exchange).

13 Feldman, *The Great Disorder*, p. 207.

14 Winkler, *Weimar 1918–1933*, p. 117. And see Robert Leicht, 'Patriot in der Gefahr', in *Die Zeit*, 18 August 2011, Nr 3, available at http://www.zeit.de/2011/34/Erzberger/komplettansicht. For Hirschfeld's sentence and parole see Burkhand Asrus *Republik Ohne Chance? Akzeptanz und Legitimation der Weimarer Republik in der deutschen Tagespresse zwischen 1918 und 1923* (Beitrage Zur Kommunikationsgeschichte, Bd. 3), p. 341.

CHAPTER 11: PUTSCH

1 See Winkler, *Weimar 1918–1933*, p. 119; Hosfeld and Pölking, *Wir Deutschen: 1918 bis 1929*, p. 75f.

2 See Hosfeld and Pölking, *Wir Deutschen: 1918 bis 1929*, p. 76f.

3 Quoted in Hosfeld and Pölking, *Wir Deutschen: 1918 bis 1929*, p. 77f. And for Reinhardt's response to Braun's question.

4 Winkler, *Weimar 1918–1933*, p.126. And for the fates of the rebels.

5 Haffner, *Geschichte eines Deutschen*, p. 45f. And for the following quotes.

6 Price, *Dispatches from the Weimar Republic*, p. 72.

7 LeMo Kollektives Gedächtnis, *Erinnerungen von Walter Koch (* 1870) aus Dresden, Gesandter von Sachsen in Berlin* (DHM-Bestand), online at http://www.dhm.de/lemo/forum/kollektives_gedaechtnis/weimar.html.

8 Winkler, *Weimar 1918–1933*, p. 127, for the Brandenburg Gate incident.

9 Ibid., p. 135.

10 *Vossische Zeitung*, 8 April 1920 (morning edition), p. 1: 'Blutiger Zwischenfall in Frankfurt a.M. Marokkanische Maschinengewehre gegen Ansammlungen'.

11 Report of Müller's speech in *Vossische Zeitung* (morning edition), 13 April 1920, p. 2.

12 Koch, *Der deutsche Bürgerkrieg*, p. 197.

13 See Hosfeld and Pölking, *Wir Deutschen: 1918 bis 1929*, p. 79f. Also Joachim C. Fest, *Hitler*, p. 133.

14 Quoted in Ian Kershaw, *Hitler 1889–1936: Hubris*, London, 2001, p. 154. Mayr

later abandoned the far-right movement in favour of the Social Democrats. He found refuge in France after 1933, was captured there by the Gestapo in 1940 and murdered in Buchenwald shortly before the end of the Second World War.

CHAPTER 12: THE RALLY

1 Kessler, *Diaries of a Cosmopolitan*, p. 128f.
2 Figures available online as above from: *Vossische Zeitung* (evening edition), 8 March 1920, p. 6; and ibid. (evening edition), 11 March 1920, p. 6.
3 *The Times*, 13 March 1920, p. 16: 'Exchange Rallying'.
4 *The Times*, 16 March 1920, p. 23.
5 Mark/dollar rates in all these cases, unless otherwise stated, from the *Berliner Devisen* list in *Finanz- und Handelsblatt der Vossische Zeitung* (evening edition) of the days concerned.
6 Article of 7 November 1919 printed in Price, *Dispatches from the Weimar Republic*, p. 49.
7 'Germany To-Day: Food and Money Problems' (by a Special Correspondent), *Observer*, 4 April 1920, p. 7. For this and the above remarks.
8 See Carl-Ludwig Holtfrerich, *The German Inflation 1914–1923: Causes and Effects in International Perspective*, Berlin and New York, 1986, p. 208.
9 See Ferguson, *The Pity of War*, p. 127.
10 See Strachan, *The First World War*, p. 975.
11 John Maynard Keynes, *The Economic Consequences of the Peace*, London, 1988, p. 285.
12 Gomes, *German Reparations*, p. 5.
13 Ibid., p. 21.
14 Ibid., p. 6.
15 See William C. McNeil, *American Money and the Weimar Republic: Economics and Politics on the Eve of the Great Depression*, New York, 1986, p. 40f.
16 See Feldman, *The Great Disorder*, p. 211f. As Professor Feldman points out, the title of 'Great Depression' was not held for long before being awarded ten years later to another, far more fearsome, slump.
17 Holtfrerich, *The German Inflation 1914–1923*, p. 209.

CHAPTER 13: GOLDILOCKS AND THE MARK

1 Feldman, *The Great Disorder*, p. 218.
2 Ibid.
3 Ibid., p. 219.
4 For Rathenau's remarks, see Holtfrerich, *The German Inflation 1914–1923*, p. 210f.
5 For a summary of this entire extraordinarily complex issue, see Gomes, *German Reparations*, pp. 65–71.

6   Feldman, *The Great Disorder*, p. 349.

7   Gomes, *German Reparations*, pp. 65–71.

8   Ibid., p. 69.

9   Becker-Arnsberg, 6 May 1921, quoted in Feldman, *The Great Disorder*, p. 339.

10 See Feldman, *The Great Disorder*, p. 346f.

11 See Winkler, *Weimar 1918–1933*, p. 117f.

12 See Robert Leicht, 'Patriot in der Gefahr', in *Die Zeit*, as above.

13 Hosfeld and Pölking, *Wir Deutschen: 1918 bis 1929*, p. 89.

14 See Robert Leicht, 'Patriot in der Gefahr', in *Die Zeit*, as above. Both men were tried for Erzberger's murder after the Second World War and sentenced to long jail sentences, although these were later reduced to parole. Tillessen was said to have become haunted by his role in the killing with time and to have expressed genuine remorse.

15 Quoted in Winkler, *Weimar 1918–1933*, p. 161.

16 Article of 12 September 1921 in *Der Kunstwart*, reproduced in Troeltsch, *Die Fehlgeburt einer Republik*, p. 218.

CHAPTER 14: BOOM

1   For estimated US unemployment see Christina Romer, 'Spurious Volatility in Historical Unemployment Data', in *Journal of Political Economy*, vol. 94, no. 1 (Feb. 1986), p. 31.

2   See Winkler, *Weimar 1918–1933*, p. 143.

3   'German Trade Boom and the Sinking mark' (from our Berlin Correspondent), in *Manchester Guardian*, 11 October 1921, p. 7.

4   Quoted in Niall Ferguson, 'The Balance of Payments Question', in Boemeke, Feldman and Glaser (eds), *The Treaty of Versailles: A Re-Assessment after 75 Years*, Washington, DC, and Cambridge, 1998, p. 406.

5   See Feldman, *The Great Disorder*, p. 284.

6   Niall Ferguson, 'Keynes and the German Inflation', *The English Historical Review*, vol. 110, no. 436 (Apr. 1995), p. 378.

7   Quoted in Feldman, *The Great Disorder*, p. 393.

8   Pörtner, *Alltag in der Weimarer Republik*, p. 32.

9   See Feldman, *The Great Disorder*, pp. 568ff.

10 Quoted in ibid., p. 288.

11 For the business card see ibid., p. 284.

12 Ferguson, 'Keynes and the German Inflation', p. 379.

13 Feldman, *The Great Disorder*, p. 257.

14 Ibid., p. 598.

15 See McNeil, *American Money and the Weimar Republic*, p. 47. And for the debate over government control of capital exports.

16 See the discussion of the contemporary and more recent estimates, including Carl-Ludwig Holtfrerich's, in Stephen A. Schuker, 'American "Reparations" to Germany', in Gerald D. Feldman (ed.), *Die Nachwirkungen der Inflation auf die deutsche Geschichte, 1924–1933*, Munich, 1985, p. 367.

17 Ferguson, 'Keynes and the German Inflation', p. 379f.

18 Quoted in Feldman, *The Great Disorder*, p. 598.

19 Editorial in *Vossische Zeitung*, 'Der Kampf ums Leben', Sunday, 1 January 1922, p. 1f.

CHAPTER 15: NO MORE HEROES

1 See Gomes, *German Reparations, 1919–1932*, p. 106f.

2 'Germany's Hopes from Genoa: A Remarkable Survey by Dr. Rathenau', in *Manchester Guardian*, 17 April 1922, p. 5. And for the following.

3 Gomes, *German Reparations, 1919–1932*, p. 107.

4 Winkler, *Weimar 1918–1933*, p. 169.

5 Both quotes ibid., p.171. Hirsch's remarked in German that the treaty meant sacrificing: '. . . für die russische Taube auf dem Dach der fette Reparationsspatz in der Hand'.

6 See table 'The Correlation Between the Dollar Exchange Rate of the Mark and Political News in 1922', in Feldman, *The Great Disorder*, p. 505.

7 'Der Dollar 318½', in *Finanz- und Handelsblatt der Vossischen Zeitung*, Monday 12 June 1922 (evening edition), online as above.

8 Quoted in Friedrich, *Before the Deluge*, p. 105.

9 Quoted in Winkler, *Weimar 1918–1933*, p. 173.

10 Song quoted (in German) in Volker Ulrich, *Fünf Schüsse auf Bismarck: Historische Reportagen*, p. 154. Free English translation by the author.

11 For an account of the attack see 'Fehlgeschlagenes Attentat auf Scheidemann', in *Vossische Zeitung*, 6 June 1922 (morning edition), p. 1. For a further explanation of the effects of the poison see 'Der Anschlag auf Scheidemann: Das Echo der Presse', in *Vossische Zeitung*, 7 June 1922 (morning edition), p. 3.

12 Friedrich, *Before the Deluge*, p. 104.

13 Gomes, *German Reparations, 1919–1932*, p. 109.

14 Feldman, *The Great Disorder*, p. 441.

15 Ibid., p. 446.

16 Ibid., p. 445.

17 For the quote and the comment on its significance see ibid., p. 439. See also Gerald D. Feldman, *Hugo Stinnes: Biographie eines Industriellen 1870–1924*, Munich, 1998, p. 757.

18 For this evening and the conversations at Ambassador Houghton's house,

including those mentioned in the following paragraph, see Edgar D'Abernon, *An Ambassador of Peace: Lord D'Abernon's Diary*, vol. II, *The Years of Crisis June 1922–December 1923*, London, 1929, 28 June 1922, p. 47f. The British ambassador's description of that evening is based on an account given to him by Houghton and also, regarding the supposed unity of mind between Stinnes and Rathenau, by Stinnes himself. Curiously, D'Abernon gives the wrong date, 28 June, as the day of Rathenau's assassination.

19 For an immediate account see 'Der Reichsminister Rathenau Ermordet', in *Vossische Zeitung*, 24 June 1922 (evening edition), p.1. The building worker's account is in 'Der Bericht eines Augenzeugen', in *Vossische Zeitung*, 25 June 1922 (Sunday), p. 6.

20 Kessler, *Diaries of a Cosmopolitan*, p. 185.

21 Price, *Dispatches from the Weimar Republic*, p. 126.

22 Figures in Peter Lempert in *Forum*, 24 June 2012, 'Die Ermordung Walther Rathenaus', online at http://www.magazin-forum.de/die-ermordung-walther-rathenaus.

23 Pörtner, *Alltag in der Weimarer Republik*, p. 301.

24 Haffner, *Geschichte eines Deutschen*, p. 53.

25 Friedrich, *Before the Deluge*, pp. 115–17.

26 See the memoirs of Walther Rathenau's niece, Ursula von Mangoldt, *Auf der Schwelle Zwischen Gestern und Morgen: Erlebnisse and Begegnungen*, Weilheim/Oberbayern, 1963, p. 43.

CHAPTER 16: FEAR

1 Feldman, *The Great Disorder*, p. 446.

2 Winkler, *Weimar 1918–1933*, p. 181.

3 Feldman, *The Great Disorder*, p. 450.

4 Ibid.

5 Ibid., p. 451.

6 See Winkler, *Weimar 1918–1933*, p. 181f.

7 Feldman, *The Great Disorder*, p. 451.

CHAPTER 17: LOSERS

1 Andrew MacDonald, 'The Geddes Committee and the Formulation of Public Expenditure Policy', in *The Historical Journal*, vol. 32, no. 3 (Sept. 1989), p. 649.

2 Dan P. Silverman, *Reconstructing Europe after the Great War*, Cambridge, MA, and London, 1982, p. 143f. And for the following.

3 Haffner, *Geschichte eines Deutschen*, p. 58.

4   'Hermann Zander geb. 1897 erzählt', at the website Kollektives Gedächtnis, http://www.kollektives-gedaechtnis.de, as above. And for the following quotation.

5   Haffner, Geschichte eines Deutschen, p. 59.

6   Wehler, Deutsche Gesellschaftsgeschichte, Bd. 4, p. 294. He estimates the strength of the Bildungsbürgertum in the strictest sense at some 135,00, and by adding family members arrives at a figure of between 540,000 and 680,00, or some 0.8 per cent of the population for this class as a whole.

7   See Holtfrerich, The German Inflation 1914–1923, p. 268.

8   For student incomes see Merith Niehuss, 'Lebensweise und Familie in der Inflation', in Carl-Ludwig Holtfrerich, Gerhard A. Ritter and Peter-Christian Witt (eds), Die Anpassung an die Inflation, Berlin, 1986, p. 259f.

9   Friedrich, Before the Deluge, p. 122.

10 Wehler, Deutsche Gesellschaftsgeschichte, Bd. 4, p. 298.

11 Haffner, Geschichte eines Deutschen, p. 60f.

12 Wehler, Deutsche Gesellschaftsgeschichte, Bd. 4, p. 298.

13 Niehuss, 'Lebensweise und Familie in der Inflation', in Die Anpassung an die Inflation, p. 245.

14 Pörtner, Alltag in der Weimarer Republik, p. 170.

15 Quotation from essay 'Die intimen Seiten der deutschen Lage', 4 March 1922, in Troeltsch, Die Fehlgeburt einer Republik, p. 255f.

16 See Deborah Cohen, The War Come Home: Disabled Veterans in Britain and Germany, 1914–1939, Berkeley, CA, 2001, p. 7.

17 See Gerald D. Feldman, 'The Fate of the Social Insurance System in the German Inflation, 1914 to 1923', in Die Anpassung an die Inflation, pp. 437ff.

18 Feldman, The Great Disorder, p. 563.

19 Notes to Price, Dispatches from the Weimar Republic, p. 129.

20 Ibid. article., p.130.

21 See Steven B. Webb, 'Fiscal News and Inflationary Expectations in Germany After World War I', in Journal of Economic History, vol. 46, no. 3 (Sept. 1986), p. 786.

22 Niehuss, 'Lebensweise und Familie in der Inflation', in Die Anpassung an die Inflation, p. 252.

23 Friedrich, Before the Deluge, p.126.

24 Ibid., p. 253f.

25 Ibid., p. 256f.

26 Pörtner, Alltag in der Weimarer Republik, p. 341.

27 Ibid., p. 254f.

28 'The New Berlin Crisis. Oscillations of the Mark', in Manchester Guardian, 26 March 1922, p. 8.

CHAPTER 18: KICKING GERMANY WHEN SHE'S DOWN

1 'Valuta und Fondsmarkt: Der Dollar 6300', in *Vossische Zeitung*, 22 November 1922 (Saturday edition), p. 9.
2 'Dr. Cuno To Be Chancellor: At Work on New Cabinet', in *The Times*, 17 November 1922, p. 9.
3 Kessler, *Diaries of a Cosmopolitan*, p. 197.
4 See Gomes, *German Reparations, 1919–1932*, p. 110.
5 Figures in Hosfeld and Pölking, *Wir Deutschen: 1918 bis 1929*, p. 106.
6 See Conan Fischer, *The Ruhr Crisis, 1923–1924*, Oxford, 2003, p. 40.
7 Feldman, *The Great Disorder*, p. 631f.
8 Fischer, *The Ruhr Crisis*, p. 35.
9 Account of Keynes's visit, with quote from his address, in Niall Ferguson, *Paper and Iron: Hamburg Business and German Politics in the Era of Inflation, 1897–1927*, Cambridge, 1995, p. 358f.
10 See the telegram containing these details sent by Foreign Minister Rosenberg to the German ambassador in Paris for his information, 12 January 1922, in Winfried Becker (ed.), *Frederic von Rosenberg: Korrespondenzen und Akten des deutschen Diplomaten und Außenministers 1913–1937*, Munich, 2011, p. 227.
11 Feldman, *The Great Disorder*, p. 635.
12 Fischer, *The Ruhr Crisis*, p. 86.
13 Ibid., p. 39.
14 Price, *Dispatches from the Weimar Republic*, p. 151.
15 See Koch, *der Deutsche Bürgerkrieg*, p. 334.
16 Price, *Dispatches from the Weimar Republic*, p. 159.
17 Pörtner, *Alltag in der Weimarer Republik*, p. 188.
18 See the article at the local railway website, http://www.eisenbahn-in-dalheim.de/historie.htm.
19 Gomes, *German Reparations, 1919–1932*, p. 120.
20 Fischer, *The Ruhr Crisis*, p. 208f.
21 Winkler, *Weimar 1918–1933*, p. 194. Krupp was released after seven months when the Berlin government finally abandoned passive resistance in the Ruhr.
22 Ibid.
23 Ibid. Also Fischer, *The Ruhr Crisis*, p. 169.
24 Koch, *Der deutsche Bürgerkrieg*, p. 339.

CHAPTER 19: FÜHRER

1 Winkler, *Weimar 1918–1933*, p. 81.
2 See Winkler, *Der Lange Weg Nach Westen*, p. 436.
3 Koch, *Der deutsche Bürgerkrieg*, p. 334f.

4 Kershaw, *Hitler 1889–1936: Hubris*, p. 192.

5 '"An Army of Revenge". Munich Fascist Threats', in *The Times*, 15 January 1923, p. 10.

6 'Militarism in Bavaria. Fascist Movement Spreading', in *The Times*, 22 May 1923, p. 11.

7 'Aggressive Bavarian Nationalists. Demonstration in Force', in *The Times*, 11 June 1923, p. 11.

8 Text of interview reproduced in Truman Smith and Robert Hessen, *Berlin Alert: The Memoirs and Reports of Truman Smith*, Stanford, CA, 1984, p. 61.

9 Quoted in William L. Shirer, *The Rise and Fall of the Third Reich*, London, 1973, p. 62.

CHAPTER 20: 'IT IS TOO MUCH'

1 See Ernest Hemingway, 'The German Inflation', in *Toronto Star*, 19 September 1922, reproduced in William White (ed.), *Dateline Toronto: The Complete Toronto Star Dispatches, 1920–1924*, New York, 1985, pp. 266–9. And for the following quotes.

2 See the article by Hemingway reproduced as part of 'The Hemingway Papers' at http://ehto.thestar.com/marks/a-canadian-with-1000-a-year-can-live-very-comfortably-and-enjoyably-in-paris.

3 Quoted in Friedrich, *Before the Deluge*, p. 125.

4 'Anti-Foreign Movement in Germany. Speculation in Houses', in *Observer*, 26 November 1922, p. 8.

5 'That Cheap Holiday in Germany. Berlin Planning a Tax for Foreigners', in *Manchester Guardian*, 2 May 1922, p. 10.

6 'Fleecing the Foreigner. Germans Ready for the Tourist', in *The Times*, 20 May 1922, p. 9.

7 Paul Ferris, *The House of Northcliffe: Biography of an Empire*, London, 1971, p. 265.

8 Rates as in *Finanz- und Handelsblatt der Vossischen Zeitung*, 1 March 1923 (evening edition), p. 4.

9 'Paper Money. The Foreigner in Germany', in *Manchester Guardian*, 1 March 1923, p. 4. And for the quote immediately below.

10 See Feldman, *The Great Disorder*, p. 534f.

11 'Der Schauspielerstreik (Gespräch zwischen Theaterdirektor, Schauspieler und Kritiker)', in *Die Weltbühne*, XVIII. Jahrgang, Nr 49, 7 December 1922, pp. 601–5.

12 See Feldman, *The Great Disorder*, p. 536.

13 Ibid., p. 537.

14 Kurt Wolff, 'Brief an Eulenberg', in *Die Weltbühne*, XX. Jahrgang, Nr 5, 31 January 1924, p. 136.

15 Wehler, *Deutsche Gesellschaftsgeschichte*, Bd. 4, p. 331.

16 Feldman, *The Great Disorder*, p. 707.

17 Ibid., p. 574.

18 See Wehler, *Deutsche Gesellschaftsgeschichte*, Bd. 4, p. 331f.

19 See 'Auszüge aus dem Tagebuch des Konrektors und Kantors August Heinrich von der Ohe aus den Jahren 1922/1923' at the website Kollektives Gedächtnis, http://www.kollektives-gedaechtnis.de/texte/weimar/ohe/inflation1923.htm.

20 See the website of the *Kleingartenverband München* at http://www.kleingartenverband-muenchen.de/fileadmin/Downloads/Chronik%20des%20%20Verbandes.pdf.

21 Figures on garden clubs and egg production in Niehuss, 'Lebensweise und Familie in der Inflation', in *Die Anpassung an die Inflation*, p. 252f.

22 Pörtner, *Alltag in der Weimarer Republik*, p. 404 (Erich Mende). See also ibid., p. 420 (Wilhelm Krelle): 'We did not need to go hungry. My father often travelled on a Sunday to Rietzel, where my grandfather's farm was, and then returned with a rucksack full of food.'

23 Wehler, *Deutsche Gesellschaftsgeschichte*, Bd. 4, p. 277. The process of urbanisation resumed during the 'golden' era between 1924 and 1929, only to undergo another reversal during the Great Depression. As the economy recovered after 1933, the exodus to the cities picked up once again, and, despite all the Nazi propaganda about 'blood and soil', increased during the Hitler dictatorship at a far faster rate than at any time since the beginning of the century.

24 'Life To-Day in Berlin', in *Sunday Times*, Sunday, 11 February 1923, p. 11.

25 Feldman, *The Great Disorder*, p. 701.

CHAPTER 21: THE STARVING BILLIONAIRES

1 See Feldman, *The Great Disorder*, p. 642f. A lot of experts, including most vociferously Hilferding and Bernhard, had for some time criticised the Reichsbank for refusing to intervene. No currency, they said, had ever collapsed to such an extent with as much gold available as was then contained in the vaults of the Reichsbank.

2 Feldman, *The Great Disorder*, p. 647.

3 Ibid., p. 657: 'Of all those who had ruled Germany since 1918 . . . Cuno was the least suitable person to guide his nation out of the morass. He profoundly misread the political situation and the way in which he could use his powers most effectively.'

4 'Mark Exchange Chaos', in *The Times*, 20 July 1923, p. 11.

5 'Money & Stocks', in *Manchester Guardian*, 24 July 1923, p. 11.

6 'The Death of the Mark', in *Manchester Guardian*, 27 July 1923, p. 9.

7 Heinrich von der Ohe, diary, Kollektives Gedächtnis website, as above.

8 Quoted in Alexander Jung, 'Nationales Trauma', in *Spiegel-Geschichte* 4/2009 available online at http://www.spiegel.de/spiegel/spiegelgeschichte/d-66214356. html and translated into English as 'Millions, Billions, Trillions: Germany in the Era of Hyperinflation', in *Spiegel-Online* (English language edition), 14 August 2009.

9 Feldman, *The Great Disorder*, p. 573.

10 Ibid., p. 542.

11 Grosz, *A Small Yes and a Big No!*, p. 142f.

12 Kessler, *The Diaries of a Cosmopolitan*, 5 February 1919, p. 64.

13 Grosz, *A Small Yes and a Big No!*, p. 101f.

14 Quoted in Hosfeld and Pölking, *Wir Deutschen: 1918 bis 1929*, p. 33.

15 Pörtner, *Alltag in der Weimarer Republik*, p. 74.

16 For the story of Celly de Rheidt's career, see Peter Jelavich, *Berlin Cabaret*, Cambridge, MA, 1996, pp. 155ff.

17 Ibid., p. 158.

18 Article from the *Niederdeutsche Zeitung*, November 1922, quoted in Feldman, *The Great Disorder*, p. 556.

19 Friedrich, *Before the Deluge*, p. 127.

20 Pörtner, *Alltag in der Weimarer Republik*, pp. 101ff.

21 Ibid., p. 302f.

22 Feldman, *The Great Disorder*, p. 766.

23 Ibid., p. 274.

24 All figures from Constantino Bresciani-Turroni, *The Economics of Inflation: A Study of Currency Depreciation in Post-War Germany, 1914–1923*, New York, 2006, p. 216.

25 Ibid.

26 Jelavich, *Berlin Cabaret*, p. 140.

27 Jung, 'Nationales Trauma' in *Spiegel-Geschichte* 4/2009, as above.

28 Weitz, *Weimar Germany: Promise and Tragedy*, p. 139.

29 Friedrich, *Before the Deluge*, p. 126.

30 Winkler, *Weimar 1918–1933*, p. 201.

CHAPTER 22: DESPERATE MEASURES

1 'Zusammenschluss aller den verfassungsmäßigen Staatsgedanken bejahenden Kräfte'. See 'Der Wortlaut der Regierungserklärung', in *Vossische Zeitung*, 15 August 1923 (morning edition), p. 3.

2 For the origins and most of the details of Helfferich's plan, see Feldman, *The Great Disorder*, pp. 708ff, and Winkler, *Weimar 1918–1933*, p. 208f.

3 Feldman, *The Great Disorder*, p. 711.

4 Ibid., p. 733.

5 Ibid., p. 711.

6 Ibid., p. 712.

7 Account of the cabinet meeting on 23 August 1923 in Winkler, *Weimar 1918–1933*, p. 209. For Stresemann's own confessions about business's readiness to negotiate with France, see Feldman, *The Great Disorder*, p. 720.

8 Winkler, *Weimar 1918–1933*, p. 209. And for the parties' reactions, including that of the right.

9 Ibid., p. 211.

10 Ernst Merkel, 23 November 1922, 'Rundschau: Hanover und Bayern', in *Die Weltbühne*, XVIII. Jahrgang, Nr 47, p. 558.

11 Winkler, *Weimar 1918–1933*, p. 213.

12 Ibid., p. 214f. For this and the material regarding Moscow's involvement that follows.

13 For the agreement, its complications and its consequences, see Andreas Kunz, *Civil Servants and the Politics of Inflation in Germany, 1914–1924*, Berlin and New York, 1986, pp. 363ff.

14 For the 'pogrom' accusation, see ibid., p. 369n.

15 Feldman, *The Great Disorder*, p. 700.

16 See Heinrich von der Ohe's diary, at Kollektives Gedächtnis website, as above.

CHAPTER 23: EVERYONE WANTS A DICTATOR

1 Winkler, *Weimar 1918–1933*, p. 221.

2 'Berlin To-Day' from Own Correspondent, in *Sunday Times*, 28 October 1923, p. 17.

3 S. L. Bensusan, 'Life in Germany To-Day: Notes from a Provincial City', in *Observer*, 11 November 1923, p. 9.

4 'Daily Air Service to Berlin. Daimler's New Scheme', in *Manchester Guardian*, 7 November 1923, p. 9.

5 Programme and details of the first broadcast from the Vox Haus at http://www.dra.de/rundfunkgeschichte/75jahreradio/anfaenge/voxhaus/index.html.

6 See 'Broadcasting in Germany', in *The Times*, 6 October 1927, p. 6.

7 Thilo Koch, *Die Goldenen Zwanziger Jahre*, Frankfurt-on-Main, 1970, p. 50.

8 'Zur Wiederherstellung der Produktivität', in *Vossische Zeitung*, 13 October 1923, p. 1 (Abendausgabe). For the new proposals on modifying the eight-hour day see 'Das neue Arbeitszeitgesetz', in *Vossiche Zeitung*, 14 October 1923 (Sunday), p. 4.

9 'Daily Life in Berlin. The Rural Hunt for Provisions', in *Observer*, 21 October 1923, p. 8.

10 'In "Red" Saxony. Unemployment and Food Raids. Tension with Bavaria', in *Manchester Guardian*, 23 October 1923, p. 10. And for the following figures on unemployment and remarks on factory closures.

11 Dresdner Geschichtsverein e.V., *Dresden: Die Geschichte der Stadt von den Anfängen bis zur Gegenwart*, Dresden, 2002, p. 200f.

12 Ibid., p. 207.

13 Koch, *Der deutsche Bürgerkrieg*, p. 369.

14 Winkler, *Weimar 1918–1933*, p. 224. And for the Thuringian developments.

15 Ibid., p. 225.

16 Houghton's account of his meeting with Stinnes on 15 September 1923 described in Feldman, *Hugo Stinnes*, p. 888.

17 See Jörg-R. Mettke, 'Das Grosse Schmieren', in *Korruption in Deutschland (III): Geld und Politik in der Weimarer Republik*, series in *Der Spiegel*, Nr. 49/1984, 3 December 1984, p. 185. Available from the *Spiegel* online archive at http://www.spiegel.de/spiegel/print/d-13510803.html.

18 Feldman, *Hugo Stinnes*, p. 888f.

19 Winkler, *Weimar 1918–1933*, p. 225.

20 Ibid., p. 227.

21 Feldman, *The Great Disorder*, p. 774f.

22 Ibid., p. 778.

23 Ibid., p. 770f.

CHAPTER 24: BREAKING THE FEVER

1 Winkler, *Weimar 1918–1933*, p. 232.

2 Feldman, *The Great Disorder*, p. 753.

3 See ibid., p. 790.

4 For the penalties see §7 in the full text of the new regulation as reproduced in 'Wirtschaftliche Notverordnungen der Reichsregierung', printed in *Vossische Zeitung*, 23 October 1923 (evening edition), p. 4.

5 An Englishwoman Living in Germany, 'Shopping in Germany: A Perambulator for a Purse', in *Manchester Guardian*, 27 November 1923, p. 6. And for the two other quotations from this article immediately following.

6 See 'Krawalle im Berliner Zentrum. Antisemitische Ausschreitungen', in *Vossische Zeitung*, 6 November 1923 (morning edition), p. 5.

7 'Die gestrigen Unruhen. Reichswehr wird Eingesetzt', in *Vossische Zeitung*, 7 November 1923 (morning edition), p. 5.

8 'Ruhe in Berlin. Wachsende Arbeitslosigkeit', in *Vossische Zeitung*, 7 November 1923 (evening edition), p. 4.

9 Feldman, *The Great Disorder*, p. 781.

10 For the change of heart by the Bavarian leadership, see Koch, *Der deutsche Bürgerkrieg*, p. 369, and Kershaw, *Hitler, 1889–1936: Hubris*, p. 204.

11 For the Beer Hall putsch, see Kershaw, *Hitler, 1889–1936: Hubris*, pp. 206ff.

12 Ibid., p. 209.
13 See photograph in Bundesarchiv-Bildarchiv, Bild 146-2007-0003.
14 Winkler, *Weimar 1918–1933*, p. 230.
15 See 'Unser neues Geld. Die Rentenmark', in *Vossische Zeitung*, 17 November 1923 (evening edition), p. 4.
16 Feldman, *The Great Disorder*, p. 793f.
17 'Unser neues Geld', in *Vossische Zeitung*, as above.
18 Feldman, *The Great Disorder*, p. 795.
19 Ibid., p. 795f. Also for Schacht's activities in attacking the problem of uncovered emergency money and Glasenapp's lecture to the nation on credits and inflation.
20 Ibid., p. 797, for the 'inaugural visit', Wels's speech, and the quote from the *Frankfurter Zeitung*.
21 Winkler, *Weimar 1918–1933*, p. 240.
22 'Rentenmarks Issue. Risk of Failure', in *The Times*, 16 November 1923, p. 13.
23 Quoted in Adam Fergusson, *When Money Dies*, London, 2010, p. 211.
24 'German Financial Chaos: Appeal to the Powers', in *The Times*, 13 December 1923, p. 12.
25 'A Little Leaven', in *The Times*, 22 December 1923, p. 9.
26 'New Confidence in Germany. A Stable Currency', in *Manchester Guardian*, 13 December 1923, p. 10.
27 Feldman, *The Great Disorder*, p. 826f.
28 Ibid., p. 803.
29 August Heinrich von Ohe, diary entry of 28 September 1924, on website, Kollektives Gedächtnis, as above.

CHAPTER 25: BAIL-OUT

1 See, significantly enough, the official website of the German Bundesbank, at http://www.bundesbank.de/Redaktion/DE/Standardartikel/Bundesbank/Wissenswert/historisches_inflation_lehren_aus_der_geschichte.htm

AFTERWORD: WHY A GERMAN TRAUMA?

1 Gomes, *German Reparations*, p. 220.
2 See David Marsh, *The Euro: the Politics of the New Global Currency*, New Haven, CT, and London, 2009, p. 133.
3 Kate Connolly, 'Germans greet Cyprus Deal with a mixture of relief and fear', in *Observer*, 31 March 2013 (online at http://www.guardian.co.uk/world/2013/mar/31/germans-greet-cyprus-deal-mixture-relief-fear?INTCMP=SRCH)

BIBLIOGRAPHY

Secondary Works

Asmuss, Burkhard, *Republik Ohne Chance? Akzeptanz und Legitimation der Weimarer Republik in der deutschen Tagespresse zwischen 1918 und 1923* (Beitrage Zur Kommunikationsgeschichte, Bd. 3), Berlin, 1994.

Balderston, Theo, *Economics and Politics in the Weimar Republic* (New Studies in Economic and Social History), Cambridge, 2002.

Becker, Winfried (ed.), *Frederic von Rosenberg: Korrespondenzen und Akten des deutschen Diplomaten und Außenministers 1913–1937*, Munich, 2011.

Bessel, Richard, *Germany After the First World War*, Oxford, 1993.

Boemeke, Manfred F., Gerald D. Feldman and Elisabeth Glaser (eds), *The Treaty of Versailles: A Re-Assessment after 75 Years*, Washington, DC, and Cambridge, 1998.

Bresciani-Turroni, Constantino, *The Economics of Inflation: A Study of Currency Depreciation in Post-War Germany, 1914–1923*, New York, 2006.

Cohen, Deborah, *The War Come Home: Disabled Veterans in Britain and Germany, 1914–1939*, Berkeley, CA, 2001.

Dresdner Geschichtsverein e.V., *Dresden: Die Geschichte der Stadt von den Anfängen bis zur Gegenwart*, Dresden, 2002.

Englund, Peter, *The Beauty and the Sorrow: An Intimate History of the First World War*, London, 2011.

Feldman, Gerald D. (ed.), *Die Nachwirkungen der Inflation auf die deutsche Geschichte, 1924–1933* (Schriften des Historischen Kollegs Band 6: Kolloquien), Munich, 1985.

— *Army, Industry and Labour in Germany 1914–1918*, Providence, RI, and Oxford, 1992.

— *The Great Disorder: Politics, Economics and Society in the German Inflation 1914–1924*, New York and Oxford, 1996 (pbk).

— *Hugo Stinnes: Biographie eines Industriellen 1870–1924*, Munich, 1998.

Feldman, Gerald D., Carl-Ludwig Holtfrerich, Gerhard A. Ritter and Peter-Christian Witt (eds), *Die Anpassung an die Inflation/The Adaptation to Inflation* (Veröffentlichungen der Historischen Kommission zu Berlin Band 67), Berlin, 1986.

Ferguson, Niall, *Paper and Iron: Hamburg Business and German Politics in the Era of Inflation, 1897–1927*, Cambridge, 1995.

— *The Pity of War 1914–1918*, London, 1999 (pbk).

Fergusson, Adam, *When Money Dies*, London, 2010 (pbk).

Ferris, Paul, *The House of Northcliffe: Biography of an Empire*, London, 1971.

Fest, Joachim C., *Hitler*, London, 1982.

Fischer, Conan, *The Ruhr Crisis, 1923–1924*, Oxford, 2003.

Fischer, Fritz, *Germany's Aims in the First World War*, trans. Hajo Holborn, with an introduction by James Joll, New York, 1967.

Friedrich, Otto, *Before the Deluge: A Portrait of Berlin in the Twenties*, New York, 1995 (pbk).

Gilbert, Martin, *First World War*, London, 1995 (pbk).

Gomes, Leonard, *German Reparations, 1919–1932: A Historical Survey*, Basingstoke and New York, 2010.

Haffner, Sebastian, *Die deutsche Revolution 1918/19: Wie war es wirklich?*, Munich, 1979.

Hagenlücke, Heinz, *Deutsche Vaterlandspartei: Die nationalen Rechte am Ende des Kaiserreiches*, Düsseldorf, 1997.

Hardach, Karl, *The Political Economy of Germany in the Twentieth Century*, Ewing, NJ, 1981.

Henning, F.-W., *Das Industrialisierte Deutschland 1914 bis 1976*, Paderborn, 1978 (pbk).

Holborn, Hajo, *Deutsche Geschichte in der Neuzeit: Das Zeitalter des Imperialismus (1871–1945)*, Bd. 3, Munich, 1971.

Holtfrerich, Carl-Ludwig, *The German Inflation 1914–1923: Causes and Effects in International Perspective*, Berlin and New York, 1986.

Hosfeld, Rolf, and Hermann Pölking, *Wir Deutschen: 1918 bis 1929, Vom Kriegsende bis zu den goldenen Zwanzigern*, Munich and Zürich, 2009.

Jelavich, Peter, *Berlin Cabaret*, Cambridge, MA, 1996.

Kershaw, Ian, *Hitler 1889–1936: Hubris*, London, 2001 (pbk).

Keynes, John Maynard, *The Economic Consequences of the Peace*, London, 1988 (pbk).

Koch, H. W., *Der deutsche Bürgerkrieg: Eine Geschichte der deutschen und österreichischen Freikorps 1918–1923*, Berlin and Frankfurt-on-Main, 1978.

Koch, Thilo, *Die Goldenen Zwanziger Jahre*, Frankfurt-on-Main, 1970.

Kunz, Andreas, *Civil Servants and the Politics of Inflation in Germany, 1914–1924*, Berlin and New York, 1986.

MacMillan, Margaret, *Peacemakers: Six Months that Changed the World*, London, 2002 (pbk).

McNeil, William C., *American Money and the Weimar Republic: Economics and Politics on the Eve of the Great Depression*, New York, 1986.

McPhail, Helen, *The Long Silence: Civilian Life under the German Occupation of Northern France, 1914–1918*, London, 2000.

Marsh, David, *The Euro: The Politics of the New Global Currency*, New Haven, CT, and London, 2009.

Neitzel, Sönke, *Weltkrieg und Revolution, 1914–1918/19*, Berlin, 2008.

Roessler, Konrad, *Die Finanzpolitik des Deutschen Reiches im Ersten Weltkrieg*, Berlin, 1967,

Shirer, William L., *The Rise and Fall of the Third Reich*, London, 1973 (pbk).

Silverman, Dan P., *Reconstructing Europe After the Great War*, Cambridge, MA, and London, 1982.

Strachan, Hew, *The First World War*, vol. 1, '*To Arms*', Oxford, 2003.

— *The First World War: A New Illustrated History*, London, 2006 (pbk).

Ulrich, Volker, *Fünf Schüsse auf Bismarck: Historische Reportagen*, Munich, 2002.

Wehler, Hans-Ulrich, *Deutsche Gesellschaftsgeschichte*, Bd. 4: *Vom Beginn des Ersten Weltkriegs bis zur Gründung der beiden deutschen Staaten 1914–1949*, Munich, 2003.

Weitz, Eric D., *Weimar Germany: Promise and Tragedy*, Princeton, NJ, and Oxford, 2009 (pbk).

Winkler, Heinrich August, *Weimar 1918–1933*, Munich, 1993.

— *Der Lange Weg Nach Westen, Erster Band: Deutsche Geschichte vom Ende des Alten Reiches bis zum Untergang der Weimarer Republik*, Munich, 2002.

Woitas, Monika, and Annette Hartmann (eds), *Strawinskys, 'Motor Drive'*, Munich, 2009.

Diaries, Autobiographical Writings and Contemporary Memoirs

D'Abernon, Edgar Vincent, *An Ambassador of Peace: Lord D'Abernon's Diary*, vol. II, *The Years of Crisis June 1922–December 1923*, London, 1929.

Engelbrecht, Ernst, and Leo Heller, *Die Kinder der Nacht: Bilder aus dem Verbrecherleben*, Berlin-Neu-Finkenkrug, 1925.

Grosz, George, trans. Arnold J. Pomerans, *A Small Yes and a Big No!*, London and New York, 1982.

Gumbel, Emil Julius, *Vier Jahre politischer Mord* (1922), available online at http://www.deutsche-revolution.de/revolution-1918-102.html.

Haffner, Sebastian, *Geschichte eines Deutschen: Die Erinnerungen 1914–1933*, Stuttgart and Munich, 2000.

Hofmiller, Josef, '*Revolutionstagebuch*', in *Josef Hofmillers Schriften*, Bd. 2, available through the Bayerische Staatsbibliothek digital collection at http://daten.

digitale-sammlungen.de/~db/0001/bsb00016411/images/index.html?id=00016
411&fip=193.174.98.30&no=&seite=226.

Kessler, Charles (trans. and ed.), *Diaries of a Cosmopolitan: Count Harry Kessler 1918–1937*, London, 1971.

Lloyd George, David, *The Truth about the Peace Treaties*, vol. 1, London, 1938.

Pörtner, Rudolf (ed.), *Alltag in der Weimarer Republik: Kindheit und Jugend in unruhiger Zeit*, Munich, 1993 (pbk).

Price, Morgan Philips, *Dispatches from the Weimar Republic: Versailles and German Fascism* (ed. Tania Rose), London and Sterling, VA, 1999.

Scheidemann, Philipp, *Memoiren eines Sozialdemokraten*, Bd. 2, Hamburg, 2010 (reprint from Severus-Verlag).

Smith, Truman, and Robert Hessen, *Berlin Alert: The Memoirs and Reports of Truman Smith*, Stanford, CA, 1984.

Troeltsch, Ernst, *Die Fehlgeburt einer Republik: Spektator in Berlin 1918 bis 1922* (Zusammengestellt und mit einem Nachwort versehen von Johann Hinrich Claussen), Frankfurt-on-Main, 1994.

Von Mangoldt, Ursula, *Auf der Schwelle Zwischen Gestern und Morgen: Erlebnisse and Begegnungen*, Weilheim/Oberbayern, 1963.

White, William (ed.), *Dateline Toronto: The Complete Toronto Star Dispatches, 1920–1924*, New York, 1985.

Parliamentary Records

Verhandlungen der verfassungsgebenden Deutschen Nationalversammlung (Procee-dings of the Constitutent German National Assembly, 1919-1920) and *Verhandlungen des Deutschen Reichstages* (Proceedings of the German Reichstag, to 1918 and after June 1920), both available at http://www.reichstagsprotokolle.de

Contemporary Newspapers and Periodicals

Die Weltbühne, searchable facsimiles of all issues available online at the Internet Archive, http://archive.org/search.php?query=die%20weltb%C3%BChne%20AND%20collection%3Aopensource

ProQuest Historical Newspapers, Archive of the *Manchester Guardian* and the *Observer*, accessed via the London Library website (subscription service).

Sunday Times Digital Archive 1822–2006, accessed via the London Library website (subscription service).

The Living Age, available online at http://www.unz.org/Pub/LivingAge

Times Digital Archive 1785–1985, accessed via the London Library website (subscription service).

Vossische Zeitung, searchable facsimiles of all issues available online at http://zefys.staatsbibliothek-berlin.de/list/title/zdb/25338766/1919/

Articles and Essays

Balderston, T., 'War Finance and Inflation in Britain and Germany, 1914–1918', in *The Economic History Review*, New Series, vol. 42, no. 2 (May 1989).

Connolly, Kate, 'Germans greet Cyprus Deal with a mixture of relief and fear', in *Observer*, 31 March 2013.

Downes, Alexander B., 'Desperate Times, Desperate Measures: The Causes of Civilian Victimization in War', in *International Security*, vol. 30, no. 4 (Spring 2006).

Ferguson, Niall, 'Keynes and the German Inflation', *The English Historical Review*, vol. 110, no. 436 (April 1995).

Jung, Alexander, 'Nationales Trauma', in *Spiegel-Geschichte* 4/2009 (also available online in English as 'Millions, Billions, Trillions: Germany in the Era of Hyper-inflation', in *Spiegel-Online* [English language edition], 14 August 2009).

Leicht, Robert, 'Patriot in der Gefahr', in *Die Zeit*, 18 August 2011, Nr 3.

Lempert, Peter, 'Die Ermordung Walther Rathenaus', in *Forum*, 24 June 2012.

Lentin, Antony, 'Treaty of Versailles: Was Germany Guilty?', in *History Today*, vol. 62, issue 1, 2012.

McCrum, Robert, 'French Economic Policy at the Paris Peace Conference, 1919', in *The Historical Journal*, vol. 21, no. 3 (September 1978).

MacDonald, Andrew, 'The Geddes Committee and the Formulation of Public Expenditure Policy', in *The Historical Journal*, vol. 32, no. 3 (September 1989).

Mettke, Jörg-R., 'Das Grosse Schmieren', in *Korruption in Deutschland (III): Geld und Politik in der Weimarer Republik*, series in *Der Spiegel*, Nr 49/1984, 3 December 1984.

Romer, Christina, 'Spurious Volatility in Historical Unemployment Data', in *Journal of Political Economy*, vol. 94, no. 1 (February 1986).

Tobin, Elizabeth H., 'War and the Working Class: The Case of Düsseldorf 1914–1918', in *Central European History*, vol. 18, no. 3/4 (September–December 1985).

Trachtenberg, Marc, 'Versailles after Sixty Years', in *Journal of Contemporary History*, vol. 17, no. 3 (July 1982).

Webb, Steven B., 'Fiscal News and Inflationary Expectations in Germany After World War I', in *Journal of Economic History*, vol. 46, no. 3 (September 1986).

Other online sources

www.kurkuhl.de/de/novrev (material for Kiel November Revolution).

www.dhm.de/lemo/forum/kollektives_gedaechtnis/weimar.html (website of German Historical Museum, Berlin).

www.deutsche-revolution.de/revolution-1918 (German Revolution website).

www.kollektives-gedaechtnis.de (website for local historical material based around Hamburg).

www.deutsche-biographie.de (online version of *Deutsche Biographie* and *Neue Deutsche Biographie*).

ehto.thestar.com (*Toronto Star* website with reprints of historical articles by Ernest Hemingway).

www.dra.de/rundfunkgeschichte/75jahreradio (website of the German Radio Archive/*Deutsches Rundfunkarchiv*).

www.spiegel.de (website and archive of *Der Spiegel* magazine).

www.eisenbahn-in-dalheim.de/historie.htm. (Dalheim local railway society website).

Acknowledgements

Anyone casting an eye over the sources I have used for this book will notice that, more than ever, digitally stored and organised information has come to play an important role. As a writer who matured professionally in the company of the printed word, and who once viewed digital sources with some reservation, I initially had to force myself to embrace the internet. Now, however, I have arrived at a point where I find it hard to conceive of a working life that does not rely heavily on the treasures to be found (along with the dross, of course) within the ever-expanding online universe.

In researching *The Downfall of Money*, a book dealing with a historical period outside the scope of most living human memory, I have not been able to conduct interviews, as I have for my other work. However, I have been able to access newspapers of that time through an internet connection. Where, even at the beginning of this century, one still had to trek to libraries and archives, and spend days or even weeks trawling through thousands of pages of newsprint, it is now possible to read the thoughts, words and observations of men and women, recorded in print ninety or more years ago, through the medium of a home computer connection – and with searchable databases enabling huge savings in time and energy. To be able to check the value of the mark against the dollar or other foreign currencies, for every day between 1919 and 1924, through the financial pages of a Berlin newspaper of the time – and by referring to other press sources to compare the quotidian financial reality with the often tragic fates of the human beings affected by it – has been a terrific gift. We may worry about the future of the printed word, and the viability of the traditional book, but for research purposes ours is in many ways a new golden age. To those who have digitised millions of such precious pages and made them available online, profound thanks.

Thanks are due especially to the London Library, another of the world's great literary resources. I have used its extensive electronic library, and also its book borrowing facilities, to their utmost. The staff, ever patient and helpful, have ensured that any book ordered online one day usually arrived at my door, three hundred miles from London, no more than forty-eight hours later.

Among all the books I read for this project, it would be criminal not mention those written, over a period of many years, by the late Professor Gerald Feldman of UC Berkeley. I was already acquainted, from my postgraduate days in the 1970s, with his ground-breaking book, *Army, Industry and Labour in Germany, 1914–1918*, but like anyone attempting to write sensibly about the early Weimar years, I have leaned heavily on his huge master work, *The Great Disorder*, as well as his biography of Hugo Stinnes and his many articles. I could not but express my profound thanks for and debt to this fine historian's lifetime achievement.

Once again, Bill Swainson, my editor at Bloomsbury in London, has facilitated this project from the outset with his usual quiet determination, aided by Peter Ginna and the team at Bloomsbury in New York. At Siedler-Verlag in Germany, Tobias Winstel and Karen Guddas have also provided sterling support. And to Jane Turnbull, my agent, who is, as always, there for the troughs as well as the peaks, my most heartfelt gratitude.

The motivation for this book came in good part from Brian Perman, who has also read and commented on the writing as it has gone forward. Since I embarked on the project, a European credit crisis has become a European money crisis, with the whole question of currency viability at its heart and Germany, with its historical anxieties on this score, ever more involved in (and blamed for) the problems of the euro. Brian always thought this might be so, and so far he has been proved right.

My brother-in-law and sister-in-law, Ed and Peggy Kavounas, have made finishing this book immeasurably easier through their generosity and hospitality. Lastly, my thanks to my wife, Alice, who put up with my working absences, and a hard writing winter, without a single complaint. This book is, as ever, for her.

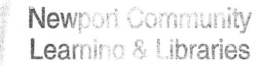

INDEX

A Note on the Author

Frederick Taylor was educated at Aylesbury Grammar School, read History and Modern Languages at Oxford and did postgraduate work at Sussex University. He edited and translated *The Goebbels Diaries 1939–41* and is the author of three acclaimed books of narrative history, *Dresden*, *The Berlin Wall* and *Exorcising Hitler*. He is a fellow of the Royal Historical Society and lives in Cornwall.

A Note on the Type

The text of this book is set Adobe Garamond. It is one of several versions of Garamond based on the designs of Claude Garamond. It is thought that Garamond based his font on Bembo, cut in 1495 by Francesco Griffo in collaboration with the Italian printer Aldus Manutius. Garamond types were first used in books printed in Paris around 1532. Many of the present-day versions of this type are based on the *Typi Academiae* of Jean Jannon cut in Sedan in 1615.

Claude Garamond was born in Paris in 1480. He learned how to cut type from his father and by the age of fifteen he was able to fashion steel punches the size of a pica with great precision. At the age of sixty he was commissioned by King Francis I to design a Greek alphabet, for this he was given the honourable title of royal type founder. He died in 1561.